THE POWER
OF
LEGAL PROJECT
MANAGEMENT

A PRACTICAL HANDBOOK

Susan Raridon Lambreth | David A. Rueff Jr.

THE POWER
OF
LEGAL PROJECT
MANAGEMENT

A PRACTICAL HANDBOOK

Defending Liberty
Pursuing Justice

Cover design by Andrew Alcala/ABA Publishing.

Interior art direction by Anthony Nuccio/ABA Publishing

The materials contained herein represent the opinions of the authors and/or the editors, and should not be construed to be the views or opinions of the law firms or companies with whom such persons are in partnership with, associated with, or employed by, nor of the American Bar Association or the unless adopted pursuant to the bylaws of the Association.

Nothing contained in this book is to be considered as the rendering of legal advice for specific cases, and readers are responsible for obtaining such advice from their own legal counsel. This book is intended for educational and informational purposes only.

Printed in the United States of America.

18 17 16 15 14   5 4 3 2 1

Library of Congress Cataloging-in-Publication Data

Lambreth, Susan Raridon, author.
  The power of legal project management : a practical handbook / by Susan Raridon Lambreth and David A. Rueff, Jr.
     pages cm
  Includes bibliographical references and index.
  ISBN 978-1-62722-462-8 (alk. paper)
1. Project management--United States. 2. Law offices--United States. 3. Practice of law--Economic aspects--United States. 4. Lawyers--Fees--United States. 5. Attorney and client--United States. I. Rueff, David A., Jr. author. II. Title.
  KF318.L255 2014
  340.068'4--dc23

                         2014003411

Contents

About the Authors

Susan Raridon Lambreth
    Principal, LawVision Group
Founder and Chair, Legal Project Management Institute
(615) 377-3128 – office
(615) 545-5530 – mobile
slambreth@lawvisiongroup.com
slambreth@lpminstitute.com

Susan Raridon Lambreth has over 25 years of experience as a consultant to the legal profession. She is nationally recognized as one of the top leadership and practice management consultants for law firms. She has given hundreds of speeches and written dozens of articles on topics ranging from trends, leadership and practice management issues to process improvement and project management. Ms. Lambreth has helped law firms of all sizes improve their profitability and enhance their lawyers' leadership and management skills.

Susan is the Chair and Founder of the Legal Project Management Institute. She chairs the annual Practising Law Institute program, Project Management for Lawyers, typically attended by over 300 lawyers from law firms and legal departments and the West LegalEdcenter program, Managing Litigation, for in-house counsel. She has worked with dozens of firms on their legal project management initiatives or training. She has trained over 3,000 lawyers and other legal professionals in the skills of legal project management.

Ms. Lambreth is author of two books on practice group management. Ms. Lambreth has helped over 40% of the AmLaw 200 implement or improve their practice management structure. Over the past 20 years, she has trained over 5,000 lawyers, who hold firm or practice management roles, how to lead and manage more effectively.

Susan has been a leader in many organizations shaping the legal profession. She is a Fellow of the College of Law Practice Management and previously served on its Board. She was active in leadership roles in the ABA for 25 years including serving in the House of Delegates for six years. She was also an officer in the Pennsylvania Bar Association for more than 10 years, including serving on the PBA Board of Governors for three years and as the Chair of the PBA Young Lawyers Division. She was on the board of NALFMA (now the Legal Marketing Association (LMA)).

Prior to helping to found LawVision Group, she was a partner with Hildebrandt International (or its successor, Hildebrandt Baker Robbins) for almost 20 years and with Altman & Weil for almost seven years. She received her JD from University of Pennsylvania Law School and her MBA, from Villanova University.

David A. Rueff, Jr.
Shareholder and Legal Project Management Officer
Baker Donelson Bearman Caldwell & Berkowitz, PC
(601) 351-2469 – office
(601) 454-3349 – mobile
drueff@bakerdonelson.com
http://www.bakerdonelson.com/david-a-rueff-jr/

David Rueff is a shareholder in the Jackson office of Baker, Donelson, Bearman, Caldwell & Berkowitz, PC and has been a practicing attorney for over 15 years with experience in both litigation and transactional practices. He has been listed in *The Best Lawyers in America*® since 2010, in *Chambers U.S.A: America's Leading Business Lawyers* since 2008 and is currently listed in *Martindale-Hubbell* with a rating of BV® Distinguished™. Mr. Rueff's practice also includes unique experience working with a State Project Management Office on the administration of disaster recovery grants in the wake of Hurricane Katrina. He served as Senior Legal Counsel for the State's Community Development Block Grant (CDBG) program where his responsibilities included design and administration of a project management information system, management of a legal team of 11 attorneys and 20 paralegals and oversight of the legal components of grant processing for thousands of applications for assistance.

In addition to being a practicing attorney, Mr. Rueff is a certified Project Management Professional (PMP™) through the Project Management Institute and serves as Baker Donelson's Legal Project Management Officer. He was the first attorney at Baker Donelson to implement legal project management in his practice, and through Baker Donelson's LPMO has implemented legal project management in litigation and transactional matters, in both single matters and portfolios of litigation. As LPM Officer, he is responsible for the development and implementation of the Baker Donelson's award winning legal project management system, *BakerManage*™, and management of a team of project managers and attorneys who provide training and implementation of legal project management, litigation support, eDiscovery solutions and contract counsel review teams. Also in his role as LPM Officer, he works regularly with Baker Donelson's Pricing Team to evaluate responses to request for proposals, prepare budgets and design alternative fee proposals.

Mr. Rueff is a regular speaker and writer on the topic of legal project management and has conducted seminars for the American Bar Association (ABA), the National Bar Association, the Atlanta Bar Association, the Project Management Institute, the International Legal Technology Association (ILTA), the Legal Marketing Association (LMA), West, Thomson Reuters and the Practising Law Institute (PLI). He is also an adjunct law professor and teaches one of the first law school courses on legal project management.

About the Contributors

Joseph B. Altonji
   Principal
LawVision Group
   Joseph Altonji, a Co-Founder of LawVision Group, has spent nearly three decades consulting to law firms and their leaders, in the U.S. and internationally. Prior to launching the LawVision Group, he spent 22 years with Hildebrandt Baker Robbins, and its predecessor firm, Hildebrandt International, as a strategist and a senior Managing Director. Mr. Altonji has been a leader in advancing law firm strategic and management development, and a strong advocate of fundamental business model change in response to significant change in the economic conditions of the industry. He has consulted with hundreds of law firms on improving their strategic focus and business management on both a firm and practice level. He is a frequent author and speaker on topics related to law firm strategy, governance, compensation and economic performance.

Wendy L. Bernero
   Chief of Strategic Initiatives
Proskauer LLP
   Wendy Bernero has more than 20 years of experience as a law firm business development and marketing professional and currently serves as Chief of Strategic Initiatives at Proskauer Rose LLP. She previously served as Chief Marketing Officer of Fried Frank and Paul, Weiss, and as a partner in Hildebrandt International (now LawVision Group), where she consulted on law firm strategy, practice management and business development issues. In recognition of her contributions to the legal profession, the New York Chapter of LMA honored Wendy with its 2013 Thought Leader of the Year award. Her experience also includes serving as director of marketing for

Washington Bancorporation, press and legislative aide to a U.S. Congressman, and chief of staff for a Florida State Senator.

Eva E. Booth
Roundtable and Program Director
LawVision Group LLC

Eva Booth has been the Roundtable and Program Director with LawVision Group LLC for the last two and a half years. Prior to joining LawVision Group, she worked as a consultant with Hildebrandt International and Altman Weil. She has over 15 years experience consulting in the legal industry. In addition, Eva has her JD and MBA, and is licensed to practice law in Pennsylvania and New Jersey. Eva contributed to the editing of the book.

Sally Gonzalez
Independent Consultant

Sally Gonzalez is an independent consultant who is recognized as a leading expert in knowledge management, strategic technology planning, and process improvement for the legal services industry.

Sally has over 30 years of experience in strategic planning and implementation of complex, knowledge and information-intensive solutions that require tight integration of policy, process, people and technology. She brings her clients strong leadership, facilitation, analytical and advisory skills combined with innovative thinking and practical implementation experience with top-tier law firms based in the U.S., UK, and Canada.

During her career, Sally has provided consulting services to the UK's "Magic Circle," Toronto's "Seven-Sisters" and AmLaw 100 law firms as well as the legal departments of global Fortune 100 companies. She has also held top KM and IT leadership positions in top-tier U.S. law firms.

Sally is on the Editorial Advisory Board of Law Technology News, is a sought-after speaker for industry and educational conferences, and has numerous articles published in the legal trade press. She has served on the judging panels for several legal industry awards, including the Managing Partner Forum's Practice Management Awards and the Legal IT Awards.

Colin Jasper

Director

Jasper Consulting

Colin Jasper has consulted to over 200 professional services firms during the past 15 years. In this time he has had the opportunity to work with leading law firms in the U.S., the UK and throughout Asia. As the Director of Jasper Consulting, Colin's focus is on assisting professional service firms to create greater value for their clients and to capture a fair share of that value for themselves. His articles have been published in a range of journals and magazines including Professional Service Firms Journal and the Journal of the Professional Pricing Society. Colin has developed and led numerous in-house training programs.

Niki Kuckes

Professor of Law

Roger Williams University of Law

Niki Kuckes is a professor of Law at Roger Williams University School of Law, where she focuses on teaching professional responsibility and civil procedure. Prior to teaching law, Professor Kuckes practiced law as a partner in two Washington, D.C. law firms, handling complex civil and criminal litigation. She also served as a federal law clerk for the U.S. Court of Appeals for the District of Columbia Circuit, where she clerked for then-Judge, now Supreme Court Justice, Antonin Scalia. Professor Kuckes has written for a wide variety of publications, both popular and academic, from the Georgetown Journal of Legal Ethics, to the Rhode Island Bar Journal, to the magazine Legal Affairs. She also lectures regularly on ethical issues for legal audiences. Her recent presentations address such issues as billing ethics and the ethical dimensions of using digital communications in law practice, including cloud storage, metadata, e-mail, and social media

Carla Landry

Senior Consultant

LawVision Group LLC

Carla Landry is a Senior Consultant with LawVision Group LLC. She has worked in the legal industry, both in-house and as a consultant, for more than 20 years. Carla is a certified Yellow Belt in Lean Sigma/Process Improvement for Law Firms and works with firms to identify cost savings opportunities through resourcing legal services and improving existing legal processes. She also coaches legal teams on implementing legal project management techniques into their matters. Together with Susan Lambreth, Carla created the first project management certification program designed specifically for the legal profession nearly four years ago. They subsequently launched the first online e-learning courses in LPM.

Carla has her MBA and also frequently works with firms to evaluate their economic performance, identify issues or opportunities, and develop means to enhance performance. She is an adjunct faculty member at George Washington University, teaching Economics and Profitability of Law Firms as part of a Master's Program in Law Firm Management. Carla's earlier consulting experience included working as a manager in PricewaterhouseCoopers LLP's Legal Systems group. In that capacity, she served as a project manager leading an international, multi-disciplinary team responsible for the analytical and diagnostic processes related to an investigative database.

Aileen Leventon
President and Founder
QLex Consulting Inc.

Aileen Leventon is a business counselor to the legal industry and a practicing lawyer with over 30 years of experience. Through QLex Consulting Inc., which she founded in 2006, Aileen and her team provide customized coaching, training and consulting services to enable lawyers to integrate business practices with their work. Her clients include some of the most well-respected companies as well as prestigious and profitable law firms in the AmLaw 100 and 200. She also has been trained by the National Institute of Trial Advocacy to deliver training on business skills relevant to lawyers.

Aileen began her legal career at Proskauer Rose LLP in New York, followed by an equal period as a lawyer at Equitable Life/AXA specializing in M&A, new product development and corporate compliance programs. After receiving her MBA in 1994 from Columbia Business School, Aileen served as a partner in the global legal management consulting practice at PricewaterhouseCoopers LLP followed by two years as a partner at the

U.S. office of Blaqwell Inc. She has also held positions with entrepreneurial organizations in the legal and non-profit sectors.

Aileen graduated Cornell Law School in 1977, where she was Managing Editor of the CORNELL LAW REVIEW, and from Stony Brook University (State University of New York) in 1974, where she was elected to Phi Beta Kappa.

In addition to her consulting practice, she contributes to the legal profession by providing pro bono training for lawyers through NYC Bar Association, serving as project manager for the Legal Project Management Task Force of the American Bar Association Committee on Mergers & Acquisitions and designing the pilot program for the Association of Corporate Counsel's Legal Services Management curriculum.

Megan McGrew

Legal Project Management Business Support Project Manager
Baker, Donelson, Bearman, Caldwell and Berkowitz, PC

Megan McGrew is the Legal Project Management Business Support Project Manager at Baker, Donelson, Bearman, Caldwell and Berkowitz, PC in the Firm's Jackson, MS office. Prior to this, she worked primarily in the political sector in both administrative and campaign management positions for local, statewide and national campaigns. Upon licensure, Megan began working in the disaster recovery efforts to assist the Mississippi Gulf Coast repair and rebuild after Hurricane Katrina. During this time, she served in both project management and legal capacities. Megan has her JD and is licensed to practice law in Mississippi. She is a certified project management professional (PMP™) through the Project Management Institute. Megan contributed as an editor of the book.

Larry Richard, J.D., Ph.D.

Founder and Principal Consultant
LawyerBrain LLC

Dr. Larry Richard is recognized as the leading expert on the psychology of lawyer behavior. He has advised a large proportion of the AmLaw 200 law firms on leadership, change management, building resilience, assessment, and other aspects of strategic talent management. Widely known as an expert on the lawyer personality, he has tested thousands of lawyers and has over 42,000 lawyer personality scores.

A graduate of the University of Pennsylvania Law School, Dr. Richard practiced law for ten years. He then earned a Ph.D. in Psychology from Temple University. For more than 25 years, he has provided consulting services exclusively to the legal profession. He was formerly a partner with Altman Weil, and more recently chaired the Leadership & Organization Development practice at Hildebrandt International. In 2011, he launched his own consulting firm, LawyerBrain LLC, which focuses on improving lawyer performance through personality science.

He is a frequent author and speaker on the use of positive psychology and applied behavioral science in helping law firms to succeed.

Joseph Spratt
Communications Director
Seyfarth Shaw LLP

Joseph Spratt from Seyfarth Shaw LLP. As communications director, Joe leads a number of strategic programs designed to strengthen attorney engagement and accelerate culture change within the law firm. Joe has an extensive background in executive communications, organizational change and reputation management. He has worked extensively with the Association of Corporate Counsel on its Value Challenge efforts and has helped develop curriculum for the ACC's Legal Services Management programs for in-house and outside counsel. Joe is a certified Lean Six Sigma Green Belt and serves as a member of the firm's SeyfarthLean Steering Committee.

Andrew Terrett
Co-Leader, BLG Adroit: Lean Project Management and Director of Knowledge Management Borden Ladner Gervais LLP, Toronto.

Andrew Terrett originally qualified as a solicitor in the UK in the early 1990's. He has spent much of his career focused on technology for enhancing legal practice from various different perspectives: as a consultant with Baker Robbins (London), as an in-house project manager with Masons, now Pinsent Masons (London), as a Project Manager with Hummingbird, Computer Associates and with BLG (Toronto) as both Project Manager and Director of KM. He is also a certified project manager and is in the final stages of acquiring his Black belt in Lean Six Sigma through Six Sigma Academy (SSA).

Foreword and Acknowledgments

The idea for this book grew out of the experiences of the authors conducting training sessions for lawyers in the U.S. and internationally, conducting one of the first law school courses on LPM, implementing legal project management in litigation and transactional matters, through numerous speaking and writing engagements and importantly through the shared experiences of early adopters who participated in the LawVision Group Legal Project Management Roundtable, led by author Lambreth. Through all of these experiences, the authors identified that the concepts of legal project management were dramatically evolving and that a new guide needed to be developed to capture what were fast becoming best practices.

The authors would like to especially acknowledge the participants of the Legal Project Management Roundtable who have contributed to this book. Over three years ago, in the fall of 2010, author Lambreth hosted the first meeting of the Legal Project Management Roundtable. The intent was to pull together representatives from a cross section of the legal marketplace to share techniques, experiences and innovations in legal project management. The group continues to meet twice a year. With each meeting, the group has grown in size to include representatives from several dozen law firms and corporations. Author Rueff has been an active participant.

After the third meeting in September 2011, the group began to form more of a common bond - a passionate belief that the principles of legal project management were good for the legal profession and their clients. This bond was also cemented by the challenges each roundtable member experienced in their own efforts to facilitate change with the lawyers in their organizations. With each meeting, roundtable members began to experience something very unique - concerns for competitive advantage were pushed aside and members shared openly to help each other make progress in implementing LPM approaches in their respective organizations. The result was a group of professionals who willingly shared their experiences in the hope that collectively, greater innovations could be realized by all.

For this reason, members of the Roundtable have been consulted on some of the content in this book, along with other legal organizations who have been leaders in implementing LPM. The authors acknowledge that portions of this book would not have been possible without these invaluable contributions. The authors are grateful to these contributors for their willingness to share their own experiences and make this book a more comprehensive and practical guide.

Introduction

Welcome to The Power of Legal Project Management: A Practical Handbook. To begin, there are several important points to explain about the book: the objectives, the audience, its format and the context. Each will be described below.

First, there are multiple objectives of the book, as follows:

- To provide an individual lawyer – whether in small or large firm practice, in-house or outside counsel – a simple, easy-to-use framework that can be applied from start to finish in a matter or with just some elements of it applied here and there to bring a bit more structure to it;
- To provide the first comprehensive review and discussion of legal project management – the business case, the definitions and application, the ethical considerations and the issues and constraints in implementation at the organizational level; and
- To provide a desk reference for anyone implementing LPM to find helpful examples, case studies, tools and methodologies.

Some readers may be focused on all of these objectives; others may simply have one. The book is designed to be used in various ways. The reader might read cover to cover to get the full picture for how legal project management is applied in legal organizations. On the other hand, a lawyer wanting to apply LPM in his or her personal practice might just read Sections 1, 2 and 3, as they may not need information about applying it in a larger organization. Finally, it might be used as a reference book simply to pull out useful tips to improve one's practice and client relationships or to implement a particular part of LPM such as planning or budgeting or to review the ethical limitations.

Second, this book has different audiences. It is designed to help lawyers in all types of practices and practice settings to implement the basic concepts of project management, in an ever changing legal marketplace. There will be numerous examples from medium and large firms because these organizations have been the first to explore and implement these concepts in the legal profession – not because these approaches only apply to those firms. Solo practitioners and small firms will find the LPM approaches and methodologies equally applicable to their practices – though they may not have experienced elements of the business case described in the first section and may not have need for the fourth section of the book on organizational approaches and issues. LPM provides a framework to improve a lawyer's relationship with their client regardless of the size of the firm.

This book also incorporates insights from current and former corporate counsel who have also been some of the first legal professionals to implement project management concepts, applying them to the work of legal departments. We have included their commentary on the differences for in-house counsel. Again, the concepts, approaches and methodologies in this book apply to in-house lawyers but where there are differences from the approach for lawyers in private practice, Law Department Notes, provide additional information, examples and contrasts.

Third, the context for the book is important. Throughout the book, the reader will see examples of three different, but consistent, approaches. First, the framework developed by author Lambreth will be used to teach the core principles and methodologies of LPM in Section 2 of the book. Second, the BakerManage™ framework and system developed author Rueff and others in his firm will be used to show an example of these principles as applied in a major law firm that has been a leader in implementing LPM. There are many other ways to implement LPM but the authors used these two methods to illustrate the points made in Section 2 of the book. Third, to ensure application to in-house lawyers as well as private practice lawyers, Aileen Leventon of QLex Consulting has provided examples and background information in the Law Department Notes and throughout the book. Finally, the authors gathered contributions from almost 30 different law firms and legal departments, consultants and LPM software vendors to cover this topic from a wide range of viewpoints. In Section 3 and 4, the reader will see some chapters that were prepared by or with input from other consultants.

Last, the book is organized into four sections: The Business Case for LPM/ Need for a Solution, Implementing Legal Project Management, Considerations for Lawyers Implementing LPM and Considerations for the Organizations in Implementing LPM. The "roadmap" for the book is shown below.

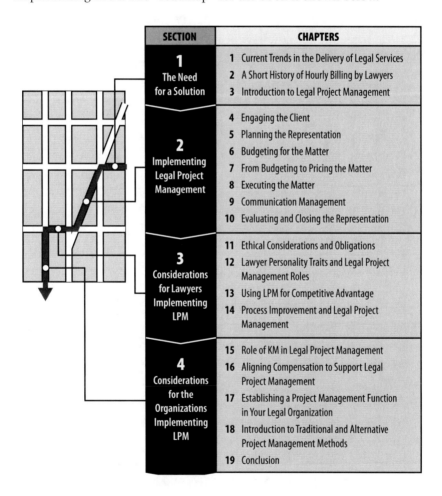

SECTION	CHAPTERS
1 The Need for a Solution	1 Current Trends in the Delivery of Legal Services 2 A Short History of Hourly Billing by Lawyers 3 Introduction to Legal Project Management
2 Implementing Legal Project Management	4 Engaging the Client 5 Planning the Representation 6 Budgeting for the Matter 7 From Budgeting to Pricing the Matter 8 Executing the Matter 9 Communication Management 10 Evaluating and Closing the Representation

3
Considerations
for Lawyers
Implementing
LPM
	11 Ethical Considerations and Obligations
	12 Lawyer Personality Traits and Legal Project
	    Management Roles
	13 Using LPM for Competitive Advantage
	14 Process Improvement and Legal Project
	    Management

4
Considerations
for the
Organizations
Implementing
LPM
	15 Role of KM in Legal Project Management
	16 Aligning Compensation to Support Legal
	    Project Management
	17 Establishing a Project Management Function
	    in Your Legal Organization
	18 Introduction to Traditional and Alternative
	    Project Management Methods
	19 Conclusion

A brief description of each chapter follows:

- Chapter 1: Current Trends Driving Legal Project Management - This chapter identifies the market trends which have caused lawyers to investigate the efficiencies that project management can bring to the practice of law.
- Chapter 2: A Short History of Billable Hours – This chapter provides background about how law firms began to bill by the hour, which over time arguably led to the frustrations for clients and their drive for greater efficiency from law firms.
- Chapter 3: Introduction to Legal Project Management - This chapter provides an overview of how lawyers have drawn from traditional project management techniques implemented by other industries such as manufacturing and construction to improve service delivery for clients. It also introduces a framework for legal project management which will form the structure for the section on implementing LPM.
- Chapter 4: Engaging with the Client - This chapter covers the first phase of LPM, including how lawyers can clarify client expectations, understand stakeholders and develop a detailed scope document. Doing this at the outset of a matter by gathering more information from the client helps ensure that both the client and the lawyer clearly understand the objectives and goals of the representation.
- Chapter 5: Planning the Matter - This chapter describes the core elements of a project plan which, if properly created, provides the basis for active management of the matter throughout its life.
- Chapter 6: Budgeting for the Matter - This chapter provides a simple technique for creating a reliable budget for the engagement and the framework for utilizing that budget to manage the engagement.
- Chapter 7: From Budgeting to Pricing the Matter - This chapter takes budgeting a step further and identifies the variables that should always be considered when converting a project budget to pricing and, where appropriate, developing value based fees.
- Chapter 8: Executing the Matter - This chapter discusses how the project plan and budget can be used to actively manage the matter to the

client's expectations and to a successful engagement which meets all of the client's goals and expectations.

- Chapter 9: Communication Management - This chapter addresses an issue that is commonly overlooked by lawyers - best practices to continually communicate with clients regarding the performance against the project plan, changes in the engagement and metrics of progress and success.

- Chapter 10: Evaluating and Closing the Matter - The conclusion of the engagement offers significant opportunities for improvement. This chapter identifies methods to conduct matter debriefs and close matters to ensure that necessary improvements are identified and incorporated into processes and forms.

- Chapter 11: Satisfying Ethical Considerations and Obligations Through Legal Project Management - Many of the LPM approaches that have been developed over the past three years do not identify the close relationship between LPM and a lawyer's ethical responsibilities. This chapter provides an overview of the ABA Model Rules of Professional Conduct which have a direct correlation to project planning and implementation.

- Chapter 12: Lawyer Personality Traits and Legal Project Management Roles - This chapter addresses the issues which must be considered when implementing a change from current legal practice techniques to those incorporating project management concepts. This chapter will discuss how different lawyer personalities will have an impact on their willingness and ability to use LPM approaches.

- Chapter 13: Using LPM for Competitive Advantage - Legal project management techniques offer a significant opportunity for early adopters. This chapter will discuss how lawyers can use improved management techniques to differentiate themselves from the competition.

- Chapter 14: The Relationship Between Process Improvement and Legal Project Management - Although used interchangeably, the concepts of "process improvement" and "project management" are significantly different. This chapter will provide some clarity as to how these concepts work in tandem, provide background on methodology and share examples of how key process improvements have been implemented through these techniques.

- Chapter 15: Role of KM in Legal Project Management - This chapter will discuss how LPM and KM can provide a powerful solution to improve the ability of lawyers to more actively manage their matters and to provide more regular information to clients regarding matter progress.
- Chapter 16: Aligning Compensation to Support Legal Project Management - For those organizations seeking to energize improved matter management practices, this chapter will identify strategies for aligning incentives to support LPM, which can speed the process of adoption.
- Chapter 17: Establishing a Project Management Function in Your Legal Organization - There are many ways to approach staffing the LPM function in a legal organization. This chapter will describe the various roles that can support the LPM function, how a well-staffed LPMO can help drive and sustain change within your organization or firm and considerations in implementing these roles.
- Chapter 18: Introduction to Traditional and Alternative Project Management Methods - The LPM approaches outlined in this book draw from traditional project management principals, but are designed for implementation by lawyers. This chapter will explain traditional project management and alternative approaches that are used in industry and in some law firms and the authors' views on the pros and cons of some of the approaches as they are applied in legal organizations.
- Appendix 1: Case studies in implementing LPM - Legal training teaches lawyers to rely primarily on statutes, regulations or legal precedence. Therefore, many lawyers are resistant to change unless there is proof of success. This Appendix provides 17 case studies from legal departments and firms to arm the reader with evidence of how LPM can improve the delivery of legal services.
- Appendix 2: Project Management Information System Tools for LPM - Many software companies that serve the legal profession have recognized the value that project management techniques can add to the management of legal practices and are investing heavily in research and development of software tools. This Appendix provides a survey of some of these software programs based upon interview questions prepared by the authors.

- Appendix 3: Legal project management templates - Some of the early books on LPM provided paper templates and forms which were drawn from implementation in other industries. Forms are not useful unless they are designed for use by lawyers and are based upon actual experiences implementing LPM. Appendix 3 provides templates used by the authors and contributors in their own legal project management implementations.
- Appendix 4: Job descriptions for legal project management positions - This Appendix is a supplement to chapter 17 which discusses establishing a legal project management roles. If your organization has made the decision to dedicate resources to its LPM initiative, the materials in this Appendix will provide you with a head start on identifying who will be best suited to lead and support LPM.
- Appendix 5: Summary of PMBOK project management processes - This Appendix is a supplement to chapter 18 which provides an overview of traditional project management. This Appendix provides more detail on the 42 plus processes within the traditional framework.

We hope this book is helpful and takes the discipline of legal project management to new levels in our profession. We welcome input on the ideas and opinions expressed here as well as for future writings on this subject.

Glossary of Legal Project Management Terms

ABA task codes	See UTBMS
ABA Model Rules of Professional Conduct 1.0 (e) - Informed Consent	"Informed consent" denotes the agreement by a person to a proposed course of conduct after the lawyer has communicated adequate information and explanation about the material risks of and reasonably available alternatives to the proposed course of conduct.
ABA Model Rules of Professional Conduct 1.0 (n) - Writing	"Writing" or "written" denotes a tangible or electronic record of a communication or representation, including handwriting, typewriting, printing, photostating, photography, audio or videorecording, and electronic communications. A "signed" writing includes an electronic sound, symbol or process attached to or logically associated with a writing and executed or adopted by a person with the intent to sign the writing.
ABA Model Rules of Professional Conduct 1.1 - Competence	A lawyer shall provide competent representation to a client. Competent representation requires the legal knowledge, skill, thoroughness and preparation reasonably necessary for the representation.
ABA Model Rules of Professional Conduct 1.2 (c) - Scope of Representation and Allocation of Authority Between Client and Lawyer	A lawyer may limit the scope of the representation if the limitation is "reasonable" under the circumstances and the client gives informed consent.

ABA Model Rules of Professional Conduct 1.4 - Communications	(a) A lawyer shall: (1) promptly inform the client of any decision or circumstance with respect to which the client's informed consent, as defined in Rule 1.0(e), is required by these Rules; (2) reasonably consult with the client about the means by which the client's objectives are to be accomplished; (3) keep the client reasonably informed about the status of the matter; (4) promptly comply with reasonable requests for information; and (5) consult with the client about any relevant limitation on the lawyer's conduct when the lawyer knows that the client expects assistance not permitted by the Rules of Professional Conduct or other law. (b) A lawyer shall explain a matter to the extent reasonably necessary to permit the client to make informed decisions regarding the representation.
ABA Model Rules of Professional Conduct 1.5 (a) - Fee Arrangements	A lawyer shall not make an agreement for, charge, or collect an unreasonable fee or an unreasonable amount for expenses. The factors to be considered in determining the reasonableness of a fee include the following: (1) the time and labor required, the novelty and difficulty of the questions involved, and the skill requisite to perform the legal service properly; (2) the likelihood, if apparent to the client, that the acceptance of the particular employment will preclude other employment by the lawyer; (3) the fee customarily charged in the locality for similar legal services; (4) the amount involved and the results obtained; (5) the time limitations imposed by the client or by the circumstances; (6) the nature and length of the professional relationship with the client; (7) the experience, reputation, and ability of the lawyer or lawyers performing the services; and (8) whether the fee is fixed or contingent.
ABA Model Rules of Professional Conduct 1.5 (b) - Basis for the Fee Arrangement	The scope of the representation and the basis or rate of the fee and expenses for which the client will be responsible shall be communicated to the client, preferably in writing, before or within a reasonable time after commencing the representation . . . Any changes in the basis or rate of the fee or expenses shall also be communicated to the client.
ABA Model Rules of Professional Conduct 1.6 - Confidentiality of Information	(a) A lawyer shall not reveal information relating to the representation of a client unless the client gives informed consent, the disclosure is impliedly authorized in order to carry out the representation or the disclosure is permitted by paragraph (b) . . . (c) A lawyer shall make reasonable efforts to prevent the inadvertent or unauthorized disclosure of, or unauthorized access to, information relating to the representation of a client.

ABA Model Rules of Professional Conduct 5.1 - Responsibilities of Partners, Managers, And Supervisory Lawyers	(a) A partner in a law firm, and a lawyer who individually or together with other lawyers possesses comparable managerial authority in a law firm, shall make reasonable efforts to ensure that the firm has in effect measures giving reasonable assurance that all lawyers in the firm conform to the Rules of Professional Conduct.
ABA Model Rules of Professional Conduct 5.3 - Responsibilities Regarding Nonlawyer Assistance	With respect to a nonlawyer employed or retained by or associated with a lawyer: (a) a partner, and a lawyer who individually or together with other lawyers possesses comparable managerial authority in a law firm shall make reasonable efforts to ensure that the firm has in effect measures giving reasonable assurance that the person's conduct is compatible with the professional obligations of the lawyer; (b) a lawyer having direct supervisory authority over the nonlawyer shall make reasonable efforts to ensure that the person's conduct is compatible with the professional obligations of the lawyer . . .
ABA Model Rules of Professional Conduct 7.1 - Communications Concerning a Lawyer's Services	A lawyer shall not make a false or misleading communication about the lawyer or the lawyer's services. A communication is false or misleading if it contains a material misrepresentation of fact or law, or omits a fact necessary to make the statement considered as a whole not materially misleading.
Agile	A project management technique which emerged to address the challenges with software development which is based on the premise that a project manager or team should spend less time at the outset trying to develop the entire universe of specifications and, instead, acknowledges that the project is an iterative process. Agile techniques allow the product to evolve over time based on information that emerges during the course of the project. Planning is not diminished, but the plan, its assumptions, the work breakdown structure, and the definition of a successful result are regularly reevaluated and tested and frequently reconsidered. See also Scrum.
Agile Certified Practitioner (PMI-ACP)	A PMI credential that recognizes demonstrated knowledge and skill in Agile project management techniques.
Alternative fee model	See value based pricing
assumptions	Factors assumed to be true at project initiation that must be validated throughout the life of the engagement. These include factual assumptions that, if proved untrue, could result in expansion of the scope and additional tasks to be performed, and procedural or strategic assumptions. For examle, the opposing parties' litigation or negotiation tactics maybe factored into the tasks to be performed and time estimates.

bottom-up estimating	A budgeting technique which starts at the most granular level of the budget and identifies the resources to be assigned, the amount of time required for the subtasks or activities and the fee for the subtask or activity. These figures are then consolidated for all subtasks / activities and rolled up into a total budget for tasks, and then rolled up for a total estimate for phases, and ultimately the matter. This method of estimation is generally the most reliable but is also the most time-consuming, because it requires budget estimators to consider the appropriate resource and appropriate time necessary for the completion of all assignments.
budget	A document that identifies the project pricing or fee for a matter and can include the phases, tasks, activities, deliverables, proposed staffing, rates for staffing and estimated time for completion. This is distinguishable from the "cost" of the matter, that is the firm's investment necessary to perform the work, versus the price or fee charged to the client. Budgeting techniques can include top-down or bottom-up estimating.
change impact table	A table used to identify changes that are likely to occur, the possible impact on the project if the change occurs and the matter team's approach if the change occurs. This tool is used in conjunction with the change management plan.
change management plan	A document which identifies the matter team's process for communicating and confirming scope, resource or timing changes with the client and which may be a policy statement or involve processes to obtain client approval. A tool used for the development of the plan is the change impact table.
client	The term "client" refers to the traditional client of a law firm, but also describes the internal clients within an organization who utilize the services of an in house legal department. The client may refer to one person who is the lawyer's main or primary contact, or may simply be the person through which the lawyer will interact with all the other stakeholders within the client organization. In some cases, the "client" may actually be a board or committee, not an individual.
communication plan	A document which identifies all the key stakeholders with whom the matter team needs to communicate, what type of communication is preferred, who is responsible for the actual communication, and how it will occur.

constraints	Limitations that affect the project parameters or the matter team's ability to complete the project and meet the client objectives or expectations for budget or other outcomes.
cost-plus pricing	A pricing approach that evaluates the costs involved in producing a product or service and adds an appropriate profit margin to create a price. Provided a cost is estimated accurately, one will make money on every "sale" or in the case of lawyers, a matter.
dashboard	Visualization tool developed and utilized by legal organizations and software vendors for internal or external use to manage legal projects. The tools may be designed to provide up-to-date intelligence and drive decision-making. It may include financial management data such as budget-to-actual and profitability measures such as leverage, effective rate, realization, work in process etc. See also project management information system.
disaggregation	A technique for creating a work breakdown structure which disaggregates a process into its component parts and subsidiary pieces to identify the staffing and time necessary to accomplish the work.
DMAIC	Process improvement technique that incorporates the following steps: (1) Define the problem and why it needs to be solved. (2) Measure the current performance of the process. (3) Analyze the opportunities to reduce waste or variation. (4) Improve the process by piloting, implementing, and validating process changes. (5) Control the process to ensure improvements will be sustainable.
Lean	A process improvement methodology which focuses on the identification and elimination of waste and "non-value-added" activities to promote a process that provides what is needed, when it is needed, and in the amount needed, with the minimum materials, equipment, labor, and space.
Lean Six Sigma	Lean increases speed and Six Sigma increases accuracy. Lean Six Sigma methodology incorporates a methodology which utilizes the best techniques of each of this approaches and uses a set of five principles as a framework for process improvement: define, measure, analyze, improve, control (DMAIC).
LEDES™	The Legal Electronic Data Exchange Standard is a file format used by the legal industry for exchanging electronic billing and matter information.

legal process improvement	The evaluation of the practice of law and development of a repeatable model of execution. This includes enhancing or reengineering work processes by analyzing its existing state, identifying areas for increased efficiencies, and eliminating waste or rework to deliver desired business outcomes. See also Lean, Six Sigma, Lean Six Sigma, voice of the client and processing mapping.
legal project management	A proactive, disciplined approach to managing legal work that involves defining, planning, budgeting, executing, and evaluating a legal matter; the application of specific knowledge, skills, tools, and techniques to achieve project objectives (the client's legal organization's); and the use of effective communication to set and meet objectives and expectations.
legal project management office	The centralized team of professionals within a legal organization responsible for developing LPM resources and tools, implementing LPM with matter teams, providing training and technical marketing for the organization on the benefits of LPM, providing support for the evaluation of budgets and pricing arrangements and/or promoting change to more efficient processes within the legal organization.
legal project manager	The individual on a matter team who typically facilitates development of the scope of work and project plan components and monitors the budget performance. The LPM may also resolve issues and manage conflicts within the project team and stakeholders, manage stakeholder perceptions and expectations, distribute performance information and handle any change requests regarding staffing, scope, resources, deliverables and timing.
lessons learned	Identification of improvements to work processes or form documents which can be implemented in the current matter or future matters to achieve an improved level of service for the client. See also matter debrief.
market-based pricing	A pricing approach which takes the view that, in a competitive market, it does not matter how much it costs to produce the service, rather what is important is the price it will take to win the work by evaluation of competitors and what they are charging.

matter debrief	A meeting performed at the end of a matter and attended by the key members of the matter team to gather data about how the matter was handled. Topics include the cost of the matter, changes that occurred which affected project outcomes, issues that affected stakeholder expectations or relationships, and an evaluation of lessons learned. It can be done internally with just the legal team or done in conjunction with the client contact or team. See also Plus-Delta Analysis
organizational process assets	Documents, forms or reusable assets that capture the intellectual property and best practices of the legal organization.
Plus-Delta Analysis	A technique for matter debriefs which facilitates an evaluation of the performance of the matter team. The "plus" (+) stands for "what worked well" during the matter, and the "delta" (Δ) stands for change or "what could be changed for the next similar matter."
PMBOK Guide	A Guide to the Project Management Body of Knowledge is a management guide and international standard that identifies and defines the fundamental techniques, tools, inputs and outputs of traditional project management processes and knowledge areas. The fourth edition of the PMBOK is used as a reference for this book; however a fifth edition of the book is available from PMI.
Probability / Impact Matrix	A matrix used to evaluate all risks identified by the matter team during the planning phase and which analyzes each risk in terms of probability of occurrence and potential impact. The matrix is used to create a risk register which ranks each risk, identifies those risks that will be assumed and absorbed by the firm if they occur (i.e. no budget or fee increases will be incurred by the client if the risk occurs), and identifies those risks that will not be assumed or absorbed by the firm. The matrix is an important tool for communicating with clients about the types and levels of risk, making determinations of who assumes the risk and determining if there are any mitigation or other strategies to deal with the risk.
process mapping	A diagram, roadmap or playbook of a matter which is developed by the matter team to identify all the steps that must be undertaken in the matter, including the administrative and the legal processes. See also value stream mapping.
progressive decomposition	A technique for creating a work breakdown structure that takes a requirement (in this case, a matter) and segregates it into the steps, checklist items, or work that will be necessary to accomplish the requirement.
project charter	See scope of work

project management information systems (PMIS)	A technological system used to collect and capture information related to a project that is accessible by the entire project team and is used to plan, execute, and close project management goals. These systems can either be developed by the legal organization or third- party software and are typically connected to financial, time entry, and resource databases in order to provide the matter team with real time information regarding the status of the matter. See also dashboard.
Project Management Institute (PMI)	A non-profit, international organization that sets standards for project management in order to allow professionals to speak with common language, no matter the industry or their geographic location.
Project Management Professional (PMP)	A PMI credential that recognizes demonstrated knowledge and skill in leading and directing project teams and in delivering project results within the constraints of time, cost, and scope (the triple constraint). Eligibility requirements include a four-year degree, three years of project management experience with 4,500 hours leading and directing project tasks, and 35 hours project management education.
project plan	A document which forms the basis for the active management of the matter throughout its life cycle in order to ensure that client and key stakeholder expectations are achieved. The project plan should include a schedule, resource/staffing plan, communication plan, risk management plan, change management plan and budget.
RACI chart	A matrix that matches major project activities or workstreams with relevant stakeholders and defines responsibilities and assignments. "R" is for who is responsible for working on the activity and can be more than one person. "A" 'is for who is accountable for the work to be accomplished and is typically one person. "C" is for who is consulted or has input on the performance of the work. "I" is form who is informed or copied about the progress of the work.
request for proposal (RFP)	Request by a client to law firms to provide a fee proposal for a pre-defined scope of work which requires the law firm to identify and evaluate scope, work breakdown structures, assumptions, risks, schedules, staffing, estimate or budget for the work and potential alternative models for compensation such as fixed fees, blended rates, etc.

resource / staffing plan	A component of a project management plan which identifies who will perform each of the items on the schedule and when, and can include both professionals and staff within the legal organization and outside the legal organization who are necessary to complete tasks such as experts, vendors, e-discovery professionals, etc.
resource assignment matrix	See RACI chart
risk	Any factor that could affect the matter team's ability to have the project meet the expectations or objectives of key stakeholders including the budget, timing, or the schedule for the matter. Risks can include not only legal risks, but also broader risks such as an aggressive opposing counsel, a difficult judge, failure to obtain necessary financing or regulatory approvals, "bad facts" uncovered in discovery, etc.
risk analysis matrix	See Probability / Impact Matrix
risk management plan	A document which identifies project risks, the probability of the risk, the potential impact of the risk and the strategies for addressing each risk.
risk register	A listing of each project risk identified by the matter team which can include an estimate of the probability of occurrence, an estimate of the impact (in terms of a potential budget increase), an identification of the phases or tasks which will be impacted by the risks occurrence and, based upon an evaluation of these factors, a ranking of the risk. The risk register is used in conjunction with the Probability/Impact Matrix.
root cause analysis	A process improvement technique that identifies the cause of a repetitive problem in a process. One root cause technique is the fishbone (or Ishikawa) diagram. The fishbone analysis is a graphical illustration used to identify defects, potential causes, contributing factors, and identify those factors and causes that should be prioritized to remove or minimize the defect.
schedule	A listing of a project's milestones, activities and deliverables, usually with intended start and finish dates. Scheduled items are often estimated in terms of resource allocation, budget, and duration and linked by dependencies and other scheduled events.
scope creep	After the scope of the project is identified, uncontrolled changes or continuous growth in a project's scope that is outside the original budget prepared by the matter team and communicated to a client.

scope of work	A written statement (also called a project charter) prepared at the outset of an engagement which provides more detail than the standard engagement letter and which clearly defines what is in and out of the scope of responsibilities for the matter team, identifies key metrics of success and required deliverables, provides an initial assessment of assumptions and risks that could affect the ability of the matter team to meet the client's objectives with regard to strategy and budget, and confirms all of the client's expectations with regard to the work to be performed by the matter team.
Scrum	The Scrum process is a method of Agile project management techniques that was developed in the early 1990s by Ken Schwaber and Jeff Sutherland to aid with the management of product requirements that are constantly changing. The hallmark of the technique is performing work in uninterrupted iterations or sprints that limit the work in progress and permits the project team to focus on functionality that is immediately necessary. Periodic "scrums" are used to identify the work completed since the last iteration, ask questions necessary for continued work, and to set priorities for the next iteration.
ScrumMaster® (CSM)	A Scrum Alliance credential that recognizes knowledge and skill in Scrum techniques.
Six Sigma	Six Sigma is a statistical term that refers to quality or effectiveness of a process such that at Sigma One there are 690,000 defects per one million opportunities in a process, while at Sigma Six, the process is greatly improved such that number drops to 3.4 defects per one million. The theory of Six Sigma is that 99.9 percent is good enough.
stakeholder	Anyone who is affected by or who can affect the outcome of a legal matter (negatively or positively). Examples include various individuals within the client organization, business unit, company executives, client counsel, opposing counsel, judges, plaintiffs in an adversarial proceeding, contacts at regulatory agencies, shareholders of the company being acquired or employees of a client or a company affected by the transaction/litigation.
stakeholder analysis	Evaluation of the key influencers of a matter in order to identify each individual's objectives or expectations for the matter, interest in the outcome, ability to exert power or influence over the matter and communication requirements.

top-down estimating	A budgeting technique that identifies a fixed price for the engagement and distributes that amount across the phases, tasks to be completed and to the resource assignments. The technique starts with an overall budget number and allocates portions of that budget number to phases, tasks, subtasks and resources. Budget allocations by resource are then used to estimate the amount of time required or allowed to perform the task. These time estimates are not as reliable as bottom-up estimating.
traditional project management	Project management technique described by the PMBOK Guide. See also waterfall project management.
triple constraint	Term used in traditional project management to identify the three primary variables that must be controlled in a project which are scope (tasks to be performed), time (deadlines imposed on the matter) and cost (resources performing the work and size of the team). Changes in one of these variables will impact and may require adjustments in the other variables.
Uniform Task Based Management System (UTBMS)	A unified and standard billing format developed by the ABA, Association of Corporate Counsel and PriceWaterhouseCoopers (now administered by the LEDES™ Oversight Committee) which uses task-based billing codes to provide a more detailed classification of services performed by law firms and includes templates for litigation, project (transactions), counseling, bankruptcy, patent, trademark, eDiscovery and expenses. The templates are also referred to as "ABA Codes".
value stream mapping	A process mapping technique that uses a graphical depiction of work processes to analyze the flow of information required to deliver a service to the client. The method identifies both value-adding steps and non-value-adding steps to locate potential waste.
value-based pricing	A pricing approach which involves evaluating how much the product or service is worth to a client and then setting the price accordingly.
voice of the client	Process improvement technique that takes into consideration the client's specific needs, objectives and requirements by asking a set of predefined questions to ensure that the process will result in success.

waterfall project management	Project management technique that involves a large investment in upfront planning to develop a plan that can be used to manage the engagement to completion. The scope is controlled, and changes or dramatic deviations from the plan are not encouraged, and is based on the theory that significant changes in direction should be resisted since they have a high likelihood of requiring modification of the plan that all the parties have embraced. The term "waterfall" refers to the steps for implementation that are sequential and flow downward from a higher level of specification (project identification) to a more detailed level (project definition and execution).
work breakdown structure (WBS)	The progressive decomposition or disaggregation of the work required to be undertaken in a matter into work packages of varying detail (i.e. phases, tasks, subtasks, activities or deliverables) that must be executed by the matter team to accomplish the project/matter objectives. The lowest level of the WBS is used by the matter team to create the task lists to be performed by each team member, the estimate of time to complete each task and the estimated fee to perform each task.

Section 1

The Need for a Solution

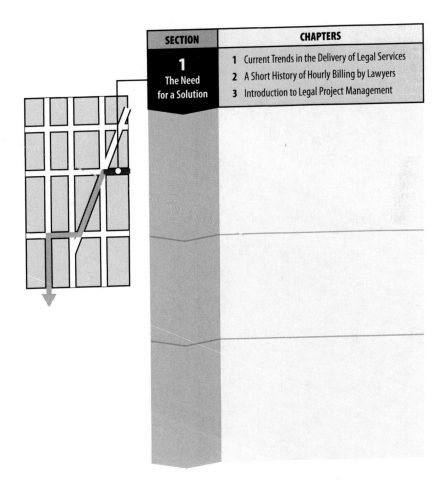

SECTION	CHAPTERS
1 The Need for a Solution	1 Current Trends in the Delivery of Legal Services 2 A Short History of Hourly Billing by Lawyers 3 Introduction to Legal Project Management

Chapter 1

Current Trends Driving Project Management

Changing Market for Legal Services Places New Focus on Project Management

Not that many years ago, clients would characterize a matter as successful if their lawyer was able to obtain a satisfactory result in litigation or close a deal upon favorable terms. The legal fees or the hours a lawyer spent were less important and rarely scrutinized unless the client considered them to be egregiously high. Today, clients are redefining what a successful legal engagement means. Clients now equate success to not only meeting their objectives, but to also providing predictable and fair pricing. Inside the law firm, success is also based upon whether the matter was profitable for the law firm, regardless of the outcome.

So what are the hurdles to meeting this new definition of success? Many lawyers have a general idea of what it costs to manage their cases and may well communicate those general initial estimates to the client. The reasons this approach may be unsuccessful today are: (1) the lawyer may fail to clarify the client's expectations with regard what is included in the fee; (2) the lawyer's team may never know that there is a budget or that they are expected by the client to operate within that budget; (3) new issues arise which may increase the fee estimate and the lawyer may not communicate these issues to the client before work begins which can result in surprises on the bill for the client; (4) a lack of active management against

3

the fee estimate, rather than only monthly monitoring; and (5) all of the above can lead to requests by the client to write down or write off time on the bill which can make the matter and the client relationship unprofitable.

Is there a solution? Other industries have implemented project management practices for decades to more accurately predict costs and to gain more control over their projects. In a similar way, the legal project management (LPM) can be an effective approach to enhance planning, budgeting and more efficient delivery of an organization's legal services.

LPM is important for many reasons in today's legal organizations. One is that it is part of the next evolution of management as law firms and legal departments grow and expand in terms of size, practice mix and geography. As has been well documented over the past 50 years, the management of legal organizations evolves as the organization grows and as the market changes. The management approaches that worked when a law firm had 150 lawyers in one office no longer works with 750 lawyers in eight offices. Law firms have recognized this as they evolved over the past 30 years from partner-run democracies to centralized firm management. Then, over the past two decades, most small to large law firms evolved to practice management (which for many large firms includes departments, practice groups, and industry and client teams).

Client demands, competition, and economic pressures now combine to drive the next evolution in law firms from managing at the practice level down to also managing at the matter or "project" level. As a result, improved project management is fast becoming a key component for law firm profitability and growth in client relationships. Similarly, in-house legal departments, like all other functions and business units in the company, are expected to reduce legal spending both within the department (to minimize corporate overhead) as well as when using third-party vendors and outside counsel. In striving to demonstrate the value they provide for their company, general counsel have turned to—and even embraced—the process improvement initiatives and project management techniques that their business counterparts have been using for many years. Today's challenge is to appropriately apply these concepts and tools to the practice of law.

Law Department Notes

Over the past 30 years, corporate legal departments have likewise evolved. What began as a fairly limited role within companies has now become a full-fledged staff function, and which can be a cost-effective substitute to law firms. Moreover, the general counsel has emerged as a trusted advisor to senior management, with the ability to command the resources to support that role. In today's world, legal departments provide critical long-term institutional knowledge and a broad perspective of business and legal consequences; in-house counsel is the custodian of the corporate risk profile. Because in-house departments do not produce revenue, they are regarded as overhead and are under pressure to simultaneously deliver value and manage the cost of law firms. Due to in-house counsel's unique position; however, they are able to identify opportunities and reconcile competing interests that the internal client may not see.

There are four main trends in the delivery of legal services that are driving the implementation of project management across the legal profession: (1) increased pressure on legal departments and purchasers of legal services, (2) changing demands and expectations for outside counsel, (3) increasing competition for legal work, and (4) changing profit equation for law firms. Another related issue is the recognition of the problems with the billable hour as a measure of value, which will be covered at the end of this chapter. Together, these trends indicate a radically changed market for legal services now and in the foreseeable future.

Increased Pressure on Legal Departments and Purchasers of Legal Services

Even prior to the 2008 recession or the global financial crisis (GFC) as it is called outside the U.S., the Association of Corporate Counsel (ACC) had worked on an initiative called the ACC Value Challenge.[1] This initiative called for a change in the nature of the relationships between inside and outside counsel and an increase in the correlation between the value provided by outside law firms and the way their services were priced and delivered. The impetus for the Value Challenge revolved around the increasing frustration experienced by in-house counsel and other organizations hiring outside counsel. It focused on the disconnect between the value of the services provided by law firms and the pricing of those services—which was primarily the billable hour (the history of which will be described in chapter 2). Law firm approaches and processes, or lack thereof, became the target of corporate counsel efforts to bring about change in the law firm—client relationship. The Value Challenge was just beginning to be discussed in law firms and taken seriously when the recession began in fall of 2008.

Then, as the recession began and the U.S. economy struggled, companies looked for ways to cut costs. Legal fees became a target for reduction—especially in instances where in-house lawyers could not explain the value provided by some of the service providers. Like every other part of the corporation, legal departments were being required to operate in a more structured, predictable manner with the goal of reducing costs each year, rather than increasing them (as had been typical for the legal budget). Legal departments became a target for review by their company's finance and procurement professionals, who were less concerned about the caliber of lawyers hired for a given matter and more concerned about efficiency and return on investment for the legal fees spent. In a growing number of companies, when the corporate entities, including senior management, found in-house counsel had failed to keep outside counsel costs sufficiently

---

1. The ACC Value Challenge was an initiative begun by the Association of Corporate Counsel that resulted in numerous programs, white papers, and other resources. The ACC Value Challenge is an initiative to reconnect the value and the cost of legal services. Believing that solutions must come from dialogue and a mutual willingness to change, the ACC Value Challenge is based on the concept that law departments can use management practices that enhance the value of legal service spending, and that law firms can reduce their costs to corporate clients and still maintain strong profitability. The ACC Value Challenge promotes the adoption of management practices that allow all participants to achieve their key objectives. See http://www.acc.com/valuechallenge/index.cfm, *ACC Value Challenge*, ASS'N OF CORPORATE COUNSEL (last visited Nov. 2, 2013) and http://www.acc.com/valuechallenge/about/index.cfm, *About: ACC Value Challenge*, ASS'N OF CORPORATE COUNSEL (last visited Sept. 16, 2013).

under control, the procurement departments became increasingly involved in the selection and management of outside counsel—frequently focused on the cost of legal services as a prime factor in the hiring process for outside counsel.

As stated in the *Guide to ACC Value Challenge Project Management*, "the overarching challenge is the need to define and articulate the [legal] department's value in business terms, to the CEO, CFO, and other executive management."[2] This concept of viewing in-house legal departments in business terms has become commonplace. In many legal departments, in-house counsel are now measured and compensated by how well they are managing legal costs (inside and outside). In fact, their very jobs can even depend upon their management of legal costs as their key performance indicators (KPIs) often include how well they manage their total legal expenses or what their outside counsel spend. Some lawyers in private practice have expressed outrage that in-house counsel would be measured by (and compensated on the basis of) such factors (which essentially bring down a company's legal costs and make the company more profitable) but they fail to see that it is no different than law firm partners being compensated for high billable hours that are designed to make their firm more profitable.

Changing Demands and Expectations for Outside Counsel

The second trend driving legal organizations toward better project management is the changing (and increasing) client demands and expectations for outside counsel. These are primarily a function of the pressure on the in-house counsel and the fact that there is an oversupply of legal service providers. Beginning in the fall of 2008, the demand for legal services dropped precipitously, and clients of law firms realized they were in the driver's seat and had a buyer's market for legal services (see figure 1–1).[3] The pressures

---

2. ASS'N OF CORPORATE COUNSEL, GUIDE TO ACC VALUE PROJECT MANAGEMENT 2 (2011).

3. The charts showing economic data for law firms are provided by Thomson Reuters Peer Monitor. Peer Monitor is a dynamic live benchmarking program that provides real-time economic data that allows a firm to compare itself against chosen peers, with details for

on in-house counsel and executives in companies large and small to cut costs and to remain successful accelerated their requests for reduced legal costs from their providers, for greater efficiency in the delivery of legal services and for greater predictability in costs from outside counsel. As part of this, requests also increased for alternative fee arrangements (AFAs) or

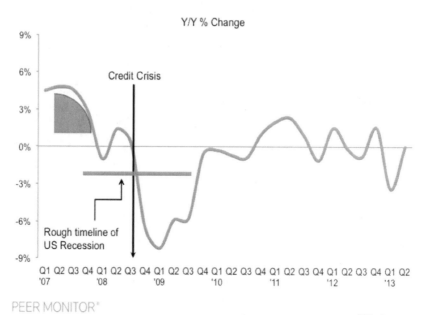

Figure 1-1
Six-Year Pattern for Demand Growth

value-based fees (VBFs), which are typically non-hourly pricing.

With tremendous cost pressures on in-house counsel, they began to expect law firms to stick to the budgets they had provided for the client's matters. Previously, a budget or fee estimate was provided to a client but it was rarely seen as a firm commitment. If the matter changed in any way, there was an expectation the client would pay the law firm whatever the "necessary"

---

practice performance, in-depth metrics critical to firm assessment including demand, rates, productivity, and expenses.

costs were to handle the matter. Then, almost overnight, this changed and it was such a dramatic change that many lawyers were unprepared for managing matters to the budget. As a result of a lack of experience with managing matters to a set budget and the client expecting the lawyer to write off any overage on the original budget, many law firms saw significant increases in write-offs and write-downs. At a conference for U.S. managing partners sponsored by the legal consulting firm, Hildebrandt Baker Robbins, in February 2010, the managing partner of one Am Law 50 firm reported that the firm had studied all of its 2009 litigation matters and found that over 50 percent of the matters were over budget and had write-offs. Their findings are just one example of the overarching reality that lawyers simply did not have the tools or disciplines to adjust to the clients' shift from 2008, in which clients asked for budgets to "check off the box" for their bosses and file it away, to 2009 and after where clients then expected that budget to be essentially a "cap" on the legal fees.

While clients still expect to receive "A+" level legal services, they do not want to pay for any inefficiencies and often expect economies-of-scale savings from the firms to whom they give significant volumes of work. When they do not feel their company needs an "A+" job, or the "scorched earth" approach to a particular legal matter, they expect the law firm to be able to provide what some call the "80 percent solution" to fit their budget—even on highly sophisticated matters. While they do not want errors on their work, sophisticated clients believe that many matters are relatively routine and can be driven by better processes and management and do not need to be over-lawyered to be handled well.

Another indication of today's client expectations is reflected in the fact that virtually every request for proposal (RFP) requests information regarding the law firm's approach to increasing efficiency in client matters—through questions about project management or process improvement specifically or through more general language proving they are more efficient than their competitors.

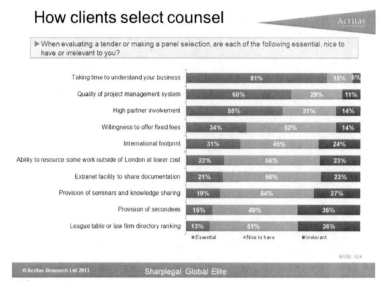

Figure 1-2
Acritas Research from Sharplegal Global Elite Survey

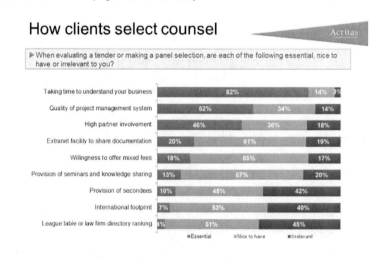

Figure 1-3
Acritas Research from Sharplegal U.S. Survey

As evidence of this, figures 1-2 and 1-3 represent information gathered by leading market research firm Acritas in its annual Global Elite and U.S. surveys, and indicate the importance many companies place on the project management and other efficiency efforts by law firms.

Other evidence of changing client demands is the excerpt below from a recent RFP sent to over 500 major law firms by a major financial institution:

1. Indicate the number of dedicated legal project managers employed by your firm.
2. Indicate the number of dedicated legal project managers that your firm will commit to providing on our matters.
3. Describe the key tasks performed by your firm's legal project managers.
4. What were the quantifiable benefits achieved by utilizing legal project managers on these matters?

Another U.S. corporation's RFP included the following:

For legal projects, whether transactional or litigation, strategic plans and budgets are the primary mechanisms by which we collaborate with outside counsel to promote the best legal/business result possible. This enables us most effectively to manage and monitor a project, to control costs and plan internal department budgets, and to mobilize needed in-house resources. In litigation matters, it permits us to evaluate potential exposure, to analyze settlement values and approaches and to develop the most effective strategies for successful dispute resolution.

Requests for more efficiency are also finding their way into many corporate guidelines for outside counsel, such as the example below from a major U.S. corporation:

[Company Y] seeks to engage and develop relationships with firms which not only deliver the highest quality advice and outcomes, but in a manner that achieves those ends in a cost disciplined and efficient manner. We increasingly place a premium on firms that have or are prepared to fundamentally reassess their own processes to find more cost-efficient ways of yielding equally high quality services. Given the cost pressures that we are asked to manage, a desirable outcome at a cost that exceeds expectations is not a success . . . In our assessment of firms, we are increasingly focused on internal incentives a firm creates and devices it employs to drive efficient, strategic choices and time utilization, while still delivering high-quality work and results. Among approaches that we have found valuable is . . . project management. We value firms that have implemented (or are prepared to adopt) project management principles and methods. We have found that the adoption of these principles to the administration, valuation, and pricing of matters can significantly help achieve the efficiencies we seek.

These three examples from RFPs or outside counsel guidelines all show that clients now expect their outside counsel to manage their matters differently from the past—with more structure, systems, and approaches that will result in greater efficiency and lower legal costs.

Increasing Competition for Legal Work

The third major trend driving project management is increasing competition for legal work stemming from new forms and types of competitors, as well as more aggressive competition by traditional law firms. Some of these new competitors are using different business models from traditional law firms and, as a result, have lowered the cost of providing certain types of legal work. This is putting additional pressure on traditional firms to find ways to lower their costs and/or be more efficient. The new competitors include legal process outsourcers who handle significant volumes of e-discovery, diligence, contract reviews, research, and other relatively routine (though often expensive) work. Other new forms of competitors include virtual law firms and legal service providers that are, essentially, aggregators of contract lawyers who are seconded to clients.

At the same time there are new types of competitors, demand for the type of legal services provided by most medium and large law firms is also flat or declining. As a result, some law firms have resorted to very aggressive price competition—even for what has historically been considered high-end work. The legal press has referred to this as "suicide" pricing. For example, in recent years, numerous midsize law firms have been underbid for work by major New York–based firms or other international/U.S.-based firms offering the same work at a cost 40 to 60 percent lower and even in the midsize firms' "home" markets. These larger and very prestigious firms underbid local firms for specific client work by 40 percent on product liability litigation, 60 percent on IP litigation, and 60 percent on renewable-energy projects, just to name a few examples.

This underbidding has been a particular shock to many midsize firms that historically competed with larger firms by pitching the angle that they were "just as good but less expensive" due to lower costs in the locations where they had most of their lawyers. What this approach by the midsize firms neglects to consider is that the larger firms have historically had greater volume of work in any given area. So, if Megafirm A covers 20 matters of a particular type in a year and Midsize Firm B does only three, Megafirm A has some economies of scale and could pass a portion of those savings/efficiencies on to its clients. Prior to the recession, Megafirm A had no incentive to do so, as there was plenty of demand for its high rate work. However, now, with demand much lower, they can selectively price work to win new business, even beating smaller firms on a price point.

The larger firms' ability to underbid the midsize firms also revolves around the fact that more large firms have embarked upon process improvement or project management than have smaller firms. As a result, some large firms have actually been able to reduce their costs of doing certain types of work, not just through the economy of higher volume. National and global firms, like Seyfarth Shaw LLP and Eversheds LLP, have invested heavily in process improvement, project management, or both to be able to reduce their costs for certain kinds of work and enhance client relationships.[4]

A third factor helping large law firms compete against smaller ones is their "outsourcing" of back-office and staff lawyer operations to less expensive

---

4. Tyco has reported client satisfaction ratings for their use of Eversheds increased after implementation of LPM. The case study submitted by Seyfarth demonstrates the quantifiable results they have observed from their LPM and Legal Process Improvement ("LPI") program.

locations in the United States. Orrick LLP was the first major firm to move its back office operations and, later, staff lawyers to lower-cost markets (i.e., Wheeling, West Virginia). Since then, a growing number of firms have continued this trend in outsourcing, including WilmerHale LLP outsourcing to Dayton, Ohio, and Pillsbury LLP to Nashville, Tennessee, among others.

The culmination of these three factors allows larger firms to reduce their overhead costs and, ultimately, either pass cost savings on to the clients or to increase their profit margins, thus reducing the historical cost advantage for many smaller or midsize firms versus larger firms. The dramatically increased competition for work outlined above has caused a growing number of firms to embark upon LPM initiatives as both a defensive measure to deal with the market trends and an offensive one to differentiate themselves from others in the competition for legal work.

Changing Profit Equation for Law Firms

The fourth trend is the changing profit equation for law firms. From 2000 to 2007, law firms primarily increased their profits per partner (PPP) by increasing billing rates. Every other factor that drives law firm profitability was trending negatively during that same time period (at least on average for law firms). Specifically, productivity (hours per lawyer) were trending down from the high in the late 1990s, realization rates were dropping (though not as much as they did after the fall of 2008; see figure 1–4 below), overhead costs were going up at rates exceeding 10 percent a year in many firms, and leverage was declining. On the other hand, today, opportunities for billing rate increases are limited. While many firms have some opportunity to raise rates in selective practices, across the board rate increases of 5 to 10 percent seen in the first part of the last decade are almost unheard of.

Clients expect law firms to find ways to decrease, not increase, their cost of doing business and, therefore, their legal fees. And, while many lawyers get incensed over their inability to increase rates, lamenting that clients should not expect them to provide the same level of services for lower costs than the year before, most clients of law firms are in industries where reducing product costs year after year is the norm and necessary for market competition. Finally, when clients know roughly the compensation levels of partners in major law firms and they compare that to their organizations—particularly the increases in PPP of the Am Law 200 firms even during the recession—they are not particularly sympathetic to law firm statements that they cannot cut rates without cutting quality of legal services. Clients believe there are many excellent firms to choose from for most areas of work and, if one firm will not cut costs or start to change the way it does its work to be able to do so, other fine firms will.

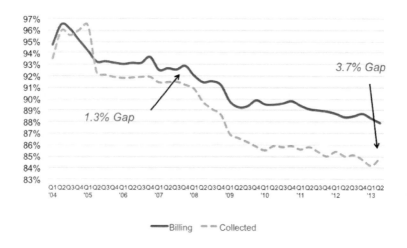

Note: collected rate growth 1H'13 v 1H'12 was 3%.

PEER MONITOR®

Lawyers only

Figure 1-4
All Segments: Realization Against Standard

Coincidentally, as law firms are feeling the profitability pressures from many directions, in-house law departments are experiencing their own economic pressures as described earlier. In some organizations, legal departments are the only departments where costs have increased—which makes them a target for increased attention from company management and their procurement professionals. In response to this scrutiny, law departments are now enforcing budgets on or applying a limit on legal spend by outside counsel. Law departments are not pressuring outside counsel for lower legal bills just because they can; they are doing so because it is a business imperative for their organization to continue to succeed. They must find ways to reduce the costs of legal services, even if it means not undertaking certain projects that would have historically been pursued, finding lower-cost providers (including nontraditional providers of legal services) or by bringing more work in-house. This only puts more pressure on the historic law firm profit levers.

Recognition of the Problems with the Billable Hour

While not a trend per se, for the past decade, there has been growing recognition of the issues associated with charging clients fees based on the time expended, in many cases without regard to the value the client received. In August of 2002, the ABA Commission on Billable Hours published a report that outlined the challenges of the legal industry's most common fee arrangement—the billable hour. Though the commission's purpose was to evaluate alternative fee models, the research also identified professional practices that had evolved after decades of the use of the billable hour by lawyers and firms.

The practices identified in the report included:

- client solutions lacking sufficient planning and rewarding inefficiency and lack of productivity;
- case/matter management practices resulting in rework, duplication of effort, and flawed staffing;
- legal costs not reflective of value and that could not be determined until matter closure; and
- rate differentials failing to account for actual experience and productivity.

Each of these practices can be reduced or eliminated through use of effective project management. In fact, even back in 2002 when the report was published, the report identified that the billable hour perpetuated the lack of an emphasis on project management in law firms.[5] During this time period, it was reported that though the cost of most professional services rose 20 percent, the cost of legal services rose 75 percent. The inefficiencies in the delivery of legal services by outside counsel identified in the report were considered a significant part of the increase in the cost of legal services. And, importantly, in the clients' view, the emphasis on billable hours in law firms' incentive systems contributed to these increases. For those interested in learning more, an interesting history of billing by the hour in the legal profession is covered in chapter 2.

In summary, one or more of these four primary trends are what make up the "business case" for LPM in many legal organizations. In some law firms, it is the business imperative to reduce write-offs that are in the tens of millions. In others, it is to differentiate from their competitors. In some legal departments, it is the need to show their business counterparts the strong control they have over legal expenses. In others, it is to show their regulators the level of quality control and assurance they have over the handling of legal matters. Overall, these trends are causing firms and law departments to realize they need to implement a different business model in order to be successful. Legal project management is a critical part of this new model. The following chapters will explain LPM and how to apply it in a legal organization large or small and for inside or outside counsel.

---

5. ABA COMMISSION ON BILLABLE HOURS REPORT 10 (2001–2002).

Chapter 2

A Short History of Hourly Billing by Lawyers

As was discussed in chapter 1, hourly billing and the pressures in law firms to increase the billable hours of each fee earner is frustrating to many clients – so much so that these were major drivers of the ACC Value Challenge. But how did the legal profession get to this point? What caused the shift from lawyers actually billing for value many years ago to the situation today with an emphasis on time recorded more than value provided – at least as viewed by many clients of law firms? This chapter provides a historical perspective that is interesting background to the evolution now underway with legal project management, process improvement and the movement away from primarily hourly billing.

Why the Billable Hour?

Charging by the hour is not a self-evident choice for pricing legal services. After all, what lawyers sell is not hours but legal services. What the client wants is not the lawyer's time, but a court matter handled to conclusion, a

This chapter was contributed by Niki Kuckes. Ms. Kuckes is Professor of Law at Roger Williams University School of Law, where she focuses on teaching professional responsibility and civil procedure. Prior to teaching law, Professor Kuckes practiced law as a partner in two Washington, D.C. law firms, handling complex civil and criminal litigation. She also served as a federal law clerk for the U.S. Court of Appeals for the District of Columbia Circuit, where she clerked for then-Judge, now Supreme Court Justice, Antonin Scalia.

contract negotiated, a corporation formed, and so on. Even in other fields where hourly billing is common, such as for painters, repairmen, and house cleaners, such laborers generally offer a choice of hourly billing or a total cost for the job. The same is true of contractors and architects, who typically provide a project price, even on highly complicated construction matters.[1] Yet billing by the hour has, over the last 50 years, been far and away the dominant method lawyers use to charge their clients for legal services in most segments of the market. Despite periodic criticisms, this practice has remained surprisingly entrenched.

On the clients' side, hourly billing has clear downsides. Hourly billing creates a lack of certainty as to the overall cost of legal matters, and makes it difficult to budget legal costs. Lack of shared risk as to the time required for a project discourages lawyers from using efficient means, and encourages wasteful procedures. At the margins (if not more often), billing by the hour can lead to billing fraud—especially in an environment in which lawyers feel pressured to increase the hours they bill.[2]

The "billable hour" has also made many lawyers' lives miserable. If a law firm's income depends on the hours billed by lawyers, there are only two ways to generate more income for the firm: increase hourly billing rates or have lawyers work more hours. Both have been growing trends in the legal market, to the detriment of the legal profession. Lawyers must often put in grueling hours, making it hard to find the time to do pro bono work and have a healthy home life.[3] Meanwhile, increasing costs mean that ordinary citizens often cannot afford legal services.

How did the practice of hourly billing come to so dominate the legal market? A little history is both interesting and eye-opening.

---

1. *See, e.g.*, Jeffrey Liss, *Against the Clock*, LEGAL WK. GLOBAL (Feb. 11, 2003).
2. *See generally* ABA COMMISSION ON BILLABLE HOURS REPORT 5–7 (2001–2002) [hereinafter BILLABLE HOURS REPORT].
3. *Id.*

Historic Billing Traditions in the Legal Market

Law firms' reliance on the hour as their primary billing currency did not emerge until the 1950s. In the country's early history, state law strictly limited charging clients for legal fees.[4] Instead, fees were generally paid by the losing side in a case, a practice carried over from England (this early presumption of fee-shifting contrasts with the modern "American rule," which assumes that each side will pay its own lawyers).[5] Historically, lawyers supplemented their income with bonuses from satisfied clients—like tips for a waiter—or with annual retainers.[6]

As economic regulation fell out of political favor in the 19th century, however, such maximum-fee laws were repealed.[7] By the early 20th century, lawyers used a combination of billing methods: fee schedules for particular tasks, annual retainers, and a discretionary "eyeball" method.[8] After 1908, when the ABA changed course and approved contingency fees as an ethical billing practice, lawyers also began to take cases on contingency, taking their payment from any funds generated by a case (if resolved successfully).[9] Lawyers rarely billed by the hour.[10]

In the late 1930s and 1940s, state bar associations that were interested in increasing legal fees started publishing minimum-fee schedules that set standard prices for different services.[11] The schedules would "suggest" one fee for handling a contested divorce, for example, and another for drafting a will. While nominally voluntary, schedules were enforced by the threat of disciplinary action against a lawyer whose fees were regarded as too low. The Virginia State Bar, for example, warned that lawyers who "habitually" charged less than the suggested fees would be presumed guilty of

---

4. *See* William G. Ross, The Honest Hour: The Ethics of Time-Based Billing by Attorneys 10–12 (Carolina Academic Press 1996) [hereinafter The Honest Hour].

5. John Leubsdorf, *Toward a History of the American Rule on Attorney Fee Recovery*, 47 Law & Contemp. Probs. 9, 10–11 (1984).

6. *See* The Honest Hour, *supra* note 4, at 11.

7. *Id.* at 13.

8. *Id.* at 13–14.

9. *See* Lester Brickman, *Contingent Fees Without Contingencies: Hamlet Without the Prince of Denmark?*, 37 UCLA L. Rev. 29, 37 (1989).

10. *See* The Honest Hour, *supra* note 4, at 16.

11. *Id.* at 14.

misconduct.[12] The ABA's model ethical code, which was in effect until 1970, said that it was unethical for a lawyer to "undervalue" his legal services.[13]

As time passed and the practice of law became more complex, fee schedules and other flat-fee arrangements, like retainers, proved increasingly unworkable. The reform of the Federal Rules of Civil Procedure in 1938, which were later copied in large part by the states, dramatically expanded lawyers' workloads before civil trials by extensively reworking the pre-trial discovery rules.[14] These changes have been credited with transforming "trial lawyers" into "litigators," who spend more time preparing cases and exchanging motions with the other side than appearing in court.[15] As the work involved in any given case became unpredictable—and subject to vagaries beyond the lawyer's control—it became difficult to set a reasonable flat fee in advance. Over the next few decades, regulation of business activities increased dramatically, which meant that transactional work also increased in complexity and became harder to price.[16]

The Supreme Court eliminated set-fee schedules entirely in 1975, declaring in *Goldfarb v. Virginia State Bar* that they were a "classic illustration of price fixing" that violated federal antitrust laws.[17] Meanwhile, clients had grown impatient with "eyeball" techniques of legal billing, which left them unsure how a lawyer arrived at his gross fee.

Emergence of the "Billable Hour" as the Dominant Billing Method

Against this backdrop, hourly billing appealed to clients and lawyers as a more transparent way to value legal services. It did not take the profession long to figure out that the billable hour could be used to turn the practice of law into a more profitable business.

---

12. *See* Goldfarb v. Va. State Bar, 421 U.S. 773, 777 (1975).
13. *See* Canons of Prof'l Ethics Canon 12 (1908) (in effect until 1970).
14. *See, e.g.*, George B. Shepherd & Morgan Cloud, *Time and Money: Discovery Leads to Hourly Billing*, 1999 U. Ill. L. Rev. 91, 94.
15. *Id.*
16. *Id.* at 97–98.
17. *Goldfarb*, 421 U.S. at 783.

In the late 1950s, an ABA committee put out a pamphlet called *The 1958 Lawyer and His 1938 Dollar.* The pamphlet lamented the "economic plight" of lawyers and their failure to keep pace with the earnings of other professions, particularly the income of doctors and dentists.[18] By devoting themselves unduly to the high ideal of "devotion to public interest," the committee concluded, lawyers were flopping as businessmen. The ABA urged them to take a businesslike look at their work habits—beginning with time records, the lawyer's "sole expendable asset."[19]

For the next decade, the bar mounted a nationwide campaign to "preach the gospel that the lawyer who keeps time records makes more money," as one ABA speaker put it.[20] Initially, hourly fees were used as a baseline, and adjusted to account for other factors, like a project's success. By the late 1970s, however, pure hourly billing came to prevail.[21] Eventually, it became the standard for nearly every variety of legal work.[22]

Hourly billing allowed clients to "correlate the 'product' that they were buying to the products that they themselves produced and sold," one commentator observed, and fit in well with the move toward business accounting methods.[23] In the process, notes Geoffrey Hazard, a professor of legal ethics at the University of Pennsylvania, "a subtle transformation occurred: The time sheet—created as a control on 'inventory'—now became the 'inventory' itself."[24]

"Commoditizing" Law Practice

What seemed like a simple enough change—altering the method of charging clients for legal services—proved to be a major force contributing to a

---

18. *See* SPECIAL COMM. ON ECON. OF LAW PRACTICE FOR THE ABA, THE 1958 LAWYER AND HIS 1938 DOLLAR 3 [hereinafter THE 1958 LAWYER AND HIS 1938 DOLLAR].

19. *Id.* at 7.

20. *See* Shepherd & Cloud, *supra* note 14, at 149.

21. *Id.* at 155.

22. *Id.*

23. Mary Ann Altman, *A Perspective—From Value Billing to Time Billing and Back to Value Billing, in* BEYOND THE BILLABLE HOUR: AN ANTHOLOGY OF ALTERNATIVE BILLING METHODS 11, 13 (Richard C. Reed ed., 1989).

24. Geoffrey C. Hazard, *Ethics,* NAT'L L.J., Feb. 17, 1992, at 19.

seismic and, in the view of many, fundamentally damaging shift in the legal market. By thinking of the lawyer as selling a "product"—and identifying that "product" as the hours billed—legal services were in effect commoditized. This was a stark departure from the thinking about law practice as a service profession in earlier decades.

Compare influential bar leaders from an earlier era, like Roscoe Pound, who in 1953 defined law practice as a group of people "pursuing a learned art as a common calling in the spirit of public service."[25] Today, this definition would seem a romanticized and outdated view of law practice—though one that many would like to return to.

Less than 25 years later, Chief Justice William H. Rehnquist decried the trend toward maximizing law firm profit. He observed in a 1987 speech that law firms with a focus on increasing profitability treat associates "very much as a manufacturer would treat a purchaser of one hundred tons of scrap metal." He further explained the firms' attitude by saying: "If you use anything less than the one hundred tons you paid for, you are simply not running an efficient business."[26]

Chief Justice Rehnquist understood that the modern law firm, once revered for its collegiality, had become in many ways indistinguishable from the corporate clients such firms served. By the late 20th century, financial reports, profit targets, billable hour tallies, and the like had become the fodder of partnership meetings at most large firms. Cadres of consultants began to advise law firms about ways to increase their "productivity"— defined as increasing the work "product" or billable hours (like increasing the production of widgets to improve performance of a corporation).

During the years leading up to the 21st century, there were sporadic efforts to encourage the use of alternative methods such as "value" billing (focusing on the value of work performed rather than time spent) or fixed fees.[27] However, the billable hour proved surprisingly resistant to reform, for a number of reasons, including one important one: the concept had

25. ROSCOE POUND, THE LAWYER FROM ANTIQUITY TO MODERN TIMES 5 (1953).

26. William H. Rehnquist, *Dedicatory Address: The Legal Profession Today*, 62 IND. L.J. 151, 153 (1987).

27. *See generally* Altman, *supra* note 23.

become not simply a billing method, but also an important law firm management tool.

The Emergence of Law Firm Billable Hour Targets

One critical, if underappreciated, factor leading to the dominance of hourly billing involves law firm management. In particular, law firms realized that hourly billing targets could be used as a tool for assessing performance of the firm itself—and that of individual lawyers.

In recent years, particularly at the top end of the legal market, law firms have merged, grown in size, and become increasingly "corporatized."[28] While many large firms are still nominally partnerships, in many cases, firm management essentially run them like companies.[29] As law firms expand or merge, they must search for measures to predict income, expenses, and budget. Billable hours have presented a ready standard because they can easily be measured, compared, and reduced to "realization rates" (which compare hours worked with the fees collected on those hours). They can be translated into precise expectations that can be used to guide lawyers' performance.[30]

Over recent decades, to improve "productivity," law firms have adopted policies requiring lawyers to bill a certain number of minimum hours each year.[31] Initially, this seemed like a harmless enough step—until the number of those hours began to rise steadily beginning in the 1980s.[32] Firms raised their hour requirements to maximize the profits of partners and, subsequently, to pay for a dramatic increase in associate salaries fueled by the fear of losing young lawyers to the dot-com boom.[33] By 2001, large Washington, D.C.,

---

28. *See, e.g.*, Bruce E. Aronson, *Elite Law Firm Mergers and Reputational Competition: Is Bigger Really Better?*, 40 Vand. J. Transnat'l L. 763, 765 (2007).

29. *See* Milton C. Regan, Jr., *Corporate Norms and Contemporary Law Firm Practice*, 70 Geo. Wash. L. Rev. 931, 934 (2002).

30. *See* Billable Hours Report, *supra* note 2, at 7–11.

31. *See id.* at 3.

32. *Id.*

33. *See, e.g.*, Susan Zentay, *Firms and Associates Have Adjusted Expectations Since the Salary Boom*, Legal Times, Oct. 4, 2004; Susan Saab Fortney, *The Billable Hours Derby:*

law firms typically asked associates to bill 2,000 billable hours a year.[34] In other cities nationwide, most firms reported minimums of almost as many hours a year. Some firms required more.[35]

Billing 2,000 hours a year (still a standard billing expectation in many firms today) may not seem onerous. The total can be reached in just over eight hours billed a day, setting aside four weeks of the year for vacation and national holidays. But studies consistently show that a lawyer must spend a total of three hours in the office for every two hours of billable work.[36] Lawyers can't simply bill time. They have to read and respond to mail and firm memos, go to meetings, read legal publications, and eat lunch—not to mention touching base with colleagues, if not chatting with friends. To do all of this and make the 2,000-hour target, a lawyer must spend the equivalent of 12 hours in the office for each working day. The honest lawyer who commits to working "full-time"—to a schedule of 2,000 billable and thus 3,000 total hours—is giving his or her life to the firm. Former ABA president Robert E. Hirshon deemed this the "tyranny of the billable hour."[37]

Most firms break billable hours into pieces, typically charging clients for each six-minute increment expended by a lawyer or paralegal.[38] This method of billing requires a degree of precision that is virtually impossible to achieve. Still, the conscientious lawyer strives to record, in his or her daily diary, each telephone call, meeting, letter, memo, draft agreement, research project, and document review. The result is relentless timekeeping from arrival to departure each day, and often at home again at night. It's no wonder, then, that lawyers have increasingly complained of feeling like piecemeal workers in a factory.

Empirical Data on the Problems and Pressure Points, 33 Fordham Urb. L.J. 171, 172 (2005) [hereinafter *Billable Hours Derby*].

34. *See* Otis Bilodeau, *A Lawyer's Call to Arms,* Legal Times, June 25, 2001.

35. *See generally* Susan Saab Fortney, *Soul for Sale: An Empirical Study of Associate Satisfaction, Law Firm Culture, and the Effect of Billable Hour Requirements,* 69 UMKC L. Rev. 239, 250 (2000).

36. *See, e.g.,* William G. Ross, *The Ethics of Hourly Billing by Lawyers,* 44 Rutgers L. Rev. 1, 14 (1991).

37. Robert E. Hirshon, *Law and the Billable Hour,* A.B.A. J., Feb. 2002, at 10.

38. *See, e.g.,* Lawrence J. Fox, *End Billable Hours Goals . . . Now,* 17 A.B.A. Prof. Law. 1 (2006).

Critiques of the Billable Hour

The billable hour's appeal as a management tool is also its greatest threat. Treating legal services as a commodity that can be measured in units of time diminishes the importance of both the quality of the work produced and the results achieved. Hirshon put it aptly when he observed bluntly, in 2002, that the "billable hour is fundamentally about quantity over quality, repetition over creativity."[39]

Few other industries would thrive if they measured productivity by the time their workers spent without regard to what those workers created. The standard invites inefficiency, as well as fraud. The potential for conflicts of interest is obvious—it's in the firm's financial interest for lawyers to spend as many hours as possible on a particular matter, while the client's interest is best served by limiting the time spent.

Billable hour standards exert serious pressure on lawyers, whether they are openly described as "quotas" or are referred to as "targets." Often, such policies have been enforced with financial incentives or penalties.[40] In most law firms, the hours billed by an associate are routinely reviewed by higher-ups in the firm. Hours billed by an associate are often considered in setting bonuses and deciding on promotion to partner.[41] In some firms, associate bonuses have been tied expressly to billing a specific number of hours.[42] The effect of such principles is evident: if a bonus kicks in at 2,000 billable hours, few associates will end the year billing less.

Meanwhile, the benefits of seniority have rarely included the opportunity to work less—only the rarest of successful rainmakers have been exempt from the pressure to bill time. Both partners and associates have been routinely required to bill clients a high number of hours, though the targets for partners are sometimes slightly lower than those expected of associates (reflecting higher expectations for partners in terms of business generation

---

39. *See* Hirshon, *supra* note 37.
40. *See generally* Melissa Mortazavi, *Lawyers Not Widgets: Why Private-Sector Attorneys Must Unionize to Save the Legal Profession*, 96 Minn. L. Rev. 1482, 1492 (2012) [hereinafter *Lawyers Not Widgets*].
41. *See Billable Hours Derby*, *supra* note 33, at 176–77.
42. *Id.*

and supervisory duties).[43] Even when partners do not have an express billing target, a partner's hourly output still often matters for important firm
decisions like compensation, hiring needs, and practice group or office
profitability.[44] In the apt words of one law firm manager, associates have
come to feel that achieving the coveted promotion to partnership is "like a
pie-eating contest where first prize is all the pie you can eat."[45]

There is a striking contrast between a lawyer's reasonable workday in
1958 and modern professional expectations. In that year, the ABA announced
that unless a lawyer worked overtime, there were "only approximately
1,300 fee-earning hours per year."[46] This assumed a five-day workweek
plus half-days on Saturday. At that time, the ABA set a "realistic" goal of
five or six billable hours a day.[47] Today, a billable hour target of 1,300 billable hours a year would amount to a very civilized part-time schedule—the
equivalent of a three-day, part-time workweek in most large firms.

Lawyers who have left private practice speak of the relief and pleasure
of not having to record their time. The pressure is particularly acute when
a lawyer's case is in hiatus, or when a firm goes through a downturn in
business. However little work the lawyer may have to do, the billable hour
statistics continue to be compiled by the firm, day after day.

The loss of collegiality bemoaned by lawyers is not the only casualty
of the time pressure. The opportunity to do free work for poor clients or
chosen causes—for many lawyers, the most satisfying work of their legal
career—gets eaten away. Instead, tedious but hour-consuming tasks like
travel, document review, and proofreading corporate reports become valued
assignments.[48] An associate who wants to see his kids must pass on taking
a course in trial advocacy or running for a position on a bar committee. He
also can't find time to write articles or have lunch with business contacts
that could help him become a partner. Partners are similarly reluctant to
spend time working with associates to help them sharpen their skills, or

---

43. *See* THE HONEST HOUR, *supra* note 4, at 32.
44. *See, e.g., Lawyers Not Widgets, supra* note 40, at 1495.
45. Thomas Adcock, *Associates Are Giving Up on Becoming Partners*, N.Y. L.J., Oct.
3, 2003.
46. THE 1958 LAWYER AND HIS 1938 DOLLAR, *supra* note 18, at 10.
47. *Id.*
48. *See, e.g.,* BILLABLE HOURS REPORT, *supra* note 2, at ix.

taking on other non-billable tasks like serving on firm committees dealing with pro bono cases.

The need to bill 2,000 hours a year also means that "there are bound to be temptations to exaggerate the hours actually put in," as Chief Justice Rehnquist has said.[49] The possibilities for fraud abound, though fraud is often hard to detect. Lawyers can cheat by writing down hours they didn't work or by exaggerating the hours they did. They can credit themselves for hours worked by paralegals and secretaries. They can bill one client for work already paid for by another, or double-bill two clients for the same hours. The ABA materials in 1993 provided that it is unethical to bill one client for travel time and a second client for work performed en route, but surveys suggest that the practice has still not been entirely eliminated.[50]

Academics tend to see fraudulent billing as endemic; practitioners tend to see it as the exception rather than the rule. Anecdotal evidence suggests that most of the lawyers disciplined by the bar for questionable billing are solo or small-firm practitioners. In some notorious cases, however, senior partners in major law firms have padded their bills, forcing clients to pay them millions of unearned dollars. When Webster Hubbell, the former high-ranking Clinton Justice Department official, pled guilty to defrauding the Rose Law Firm and its clients of close to $500,000, the criminal charges against him included bill inflation.[51] Billing practices also led to the disbarment or resignation from the bar of partners at several nationally prominent firms.[52]

Some lawyers who have left private practice point to the billable hour as a central motivation for their departure. Patrick Schiltz left law practice to become a law professor (and subsequently was appointed to the federal bench). In leaving the firm, he gave up a stake in the very large fees earned by his firm from the Exxon Valdez oil-spill litigation. Schiltz would tell his students that they are entering a profession that is "one of the most unhappy and unhealthy on the face of the earth—and, in the view of many, one of

49. Rehnquist, *supra* note 26, at 155.
50. *See* Ronald D. Rotunda, *Why Lawyers Are Different and Why We Are the Same: Creating Structural Incentives in Large Law Firms to Promote Ethical Behavior*, 44 Akron L. Rev. 679, 722–23 (2011).
51. *See* Lisa G. Lerman, *Blue-Chip Bilking: Regulation of Billing and Expense Fraud by Lawyers*, 12 Geo. J. Legal Ethics 205, 245 (1999).
52. *Id.* at 214.

the most unethical."[53] Much of the blame, he would warn, lies with "the hours." "You should not underestimate the likelihood that you will practice law unethically," Schiltz advised new lawyers. The problem, he warned, will "begin with your time sheets."[54]

Billable Hour Reform and the ABA

The organized bar, which so enthusiastically urged the billable hour on the legal profession 50 years ago, has developed its own doubts in more recent years. In 2001, the ABA assembled the Commission on Billable Hours. Thereafter, the commission issued a report, conceding that "required hourly minimums . . . can lead to questionable billing practices ranging from logging hours for doing unnecessary research to outright padding of hours."[55]

The commission expressed concern that the billable hour "penalizes the efficient and productive lawyer" and causes a host of harms, including damage to firm culture, loss of time for pro bono work, duplication of effort, and a disconnect between the value of projects and the legal fees generated.[56]

The report reflected that the relentless pressure to turn time into money had robbed the legal practice of many of its joys and satisfactions—those that come from giving good advice, avoiding a lawsuit, preventing a corporate bankruptcy, sparing a client prison time, or negotiating a successful deal. These are the landmarks that lawyers recall when they review their careers, but their value isn't reflected in the way lawyers bill. With good reason, lawyers have increasingly come to feel that what matters isn't how they do their work but how much work they do.

Over a decade ago, the *ABA Commission's Report on the Billable Hour* bowed, in some respects, to pragmatism over idealism. While expressing concern about the weaknesses of reliance on billable hours, the commission bowed to the reality that "many, perhaps most, firms continue to believe

---

53. *See* Patrick J. Schiltz, *On Being a Happy, Healthy and Ethical Member of an Unhappy, Unhealthy, and Unethical Profession*, 52 VAND. L. REV. 871, 872 (1999).
54. *Id.* at 917.
55. BILLABLE HOURS REPORT, *supra* note 2, at 43.
56. *Id.* at 5–7.

in minimum hourly requirements."[57] In contrast to the ABA's 1958 conclu-sion that billing 1,300 hours a year is a reasonable full-time job, the report endorsed advising associates that 1,900 hours of billable client work is the amount "sufficient for evaluation and compensation purposes."[58] The commission also recommended making plain to associates that on top of those 1,900 hours, they should generally expect to put in 100 hours of firm service, 100 hours of pro bono work, 75 hours of client development, 75 hours of training and professional development, and 50 hours of service to the profession. That's 2,300 hours a year—many long days and weekends.

If the commission considered abandoning billable hour targets, it appar-ently concluded that scrapping the billable hour strayed too far (at that time, at least) from the realities of running a law firm as a business. While the report's model policy for firms ostensibly espoused "no set hard-and-fast minimum levels" of billing, it sent a somewhat mixed message, simultane-ously giving associates "guidance" about the typical level of effort that the firm "expects in order to meet its revenue and profitability goals."[59] While decrying practices that rigidly tie compensation to billable hours, the report also recognized the "imperative of rewarding productivity—often measured in billable hours."[60]

Ultimately, the commission's report recommended warning associates that deliberate inflation of time will not be tolerated—an important step, though one that puts the onus on associates to put in the time and to do so honestly.[61] The commission also encouraged the use and development of alternative billing methods, such as fixed fees, contingency fees, and bonus arrangements.[62]

For the decade that followed, it often seemed as if the "alternative billing method" movement was slow to pick up steam, despite the enthu-siasm expressed by leaders of the bar, and that billable hours were firmly entrenched, in spite of efforts to dislodge them. However, since the 2008 recession, the percentage of legal work using non-hourly billing has increased

---

57. *Id.* at 44.
58. *Id.* at 50.
59. *Id.*
60. *Id.* at 46.
61. *Id.* at 49.
62. *See generally id.* at 15–30.

significantly. While not enough in the opinion of some, it is strong evidence of movement in that direction. As discussed in the previous chapter on trends, client and competitive pressure on law firms has pushed them to change the traditional law firm business model in many ways. Finally, there is greater receptiveness to more meaningful change—to significantly more use of non-hourly billing and to the use of the legal project management ideas that are advanced in this book.

Chapter 3

Introduction to Legal Project Management

Deriving a Project Management Approach for the Practice of Law

The project management processes outlined in this book provide a foundation for lawyers to plan, execute, manage, and control a legal engagement in order to obtain an outcome for a client at a predictable cost. Lawyers customarily perform some of these processes when undertaking a legal engagement; however, the methods employed historically have been inconsistent and episodic and, except in repetitive engagements, do not always provide the client with a reliable expectation of service or cost from one similar engagement to the next.

With regard to the cost of legal services, lawyers historically held a unique position of trust with their clients. A client often came to a lawyer with a problem or project (either a lawsuit, transaction or other legal matter), and unless the client had prior experience, he most likely had little idea about what was a reasonable cost of representation. The client trusted that the lawyer would provide the service for a fair price.

At the same time, lawyers were trained that to provide excellent legal service they should evaluate every possible option and risk for a client, which would often require significant time to research and typically result in a higher cost. As billing rates rose dramatically over the past few decades, this could mean exorbitant legal fees for some matters. Also, the "leave no stone unturned" approach was not always necessary for a client's work and it became increasingly at odds with the client's interest in paying what was considered reasonable or as low as possible to achieve the desired result.

As a result, many clients felt they had little control over the cost of their legal matters, as if they were leaving an open checkbook lying on the lawyer's desk. As described in chapter 1, this has been the subject of many discussions by in-house counsel and, in fact, drove the development of the ACC Value Challenge to address this issue, among others.

The following table pairs a list of the common concerns expressed by in-house counsel about outside counsel (left column) against the possible benefits of the implementation of a project management approach to deal with each one (right column).

Inside Counsel Concerns	Project Management Solutions
Lack of internal law firm controls over the scope of the engagement	Process of determining the scope and communicating it to the client
Inability or unwillingness of lawyers to communicate about changes in scope on a timely basis	Formal change management/control process
Failure to communicate budget and schedule changes resulting from strategy changes in the middle of the engagement	Planning and collaboration on scope, assumptions, and risks at the outset of an engagement and with discussions throughout
Unpredictable opposing counsel, judges or regulatory agencies	Evaluation of matter risks and planning for risks/communication by the law firm about the risks
Immediacy of matter drives up costs	Early matter/project planning
The tendency of lawyers to leave every stone unturned	Collaboratively identifying what the client's objectives/expectations are, what is in and out of scope and clearly defining roles and responsibilities
Resource allocation to matter by law firm does not fit budget or client expectations	Control and monitoring by clients through the budget and identification of resources by the law firm

LPM provides methods and techniques to address the above concerns in a way that is time and resource efficient for today's lawyers. This approach provides an alternative to the approaches used in other industries that have many similarities, but also many differences from legal and other professional services.

No industry standard for LPM currently exists. As a result, some corporate legal departments and law firms, both international and within the U.S., have spent millions of dollars on the development of proprietary LPM processes and software systems to improve the delivery of legal services and to create better information for alternative pricing models. Some of these systems have been developed strictly or loosely using the traditional project management techniques described in chapter 18 and process improvement methodologies such as six sigma and lean described in chapter 14. Others are based on a flexible project management approach called Agile, which is covered in chapter 18.

This book primarily covers two approaches as models for LPM, used by the authors in their organizations or with their clients, as well as case studies from numerous law firms and legal departments that have implemented LPM, each in its own unique ways. We hope the information in this book will enable legal organizations to implement an approach to LPM that fits their culture, lawyers and the client's needs.

What Is Legal Project Management?

Currently, there are various definitions of project management in the legal industry, developed by legal commentators, corporate legal departments, law firms, and consultants. They all have recurring themes. The following is a definition of legal project management (LPM) that draws upon the best attributes of these definitions:

1. a proactive, disciplined approach to managing legal work that involves defining, planning, budgeting, executing, and evaluating a legal matter;
2. the application of specific knowledge, skills, tools, and techniques to achieve project objectives (the client's and law firm / legal department's); and
3. the use of effective communication to set and meet objectives and expectations.

Legal project management is not about dissecting a matter from beginning to end to identify efficiencies (that is legal process improvement, explained in chapter 14). Rather, it is fundamentally about using more structure, tools, and communication while actively managing the engagement to enhance the likelihood of meeting client and law firm / legal department expectations. While many lawyers have performed some aspects of project management in their work over the years, the current market for legal services demands a higher level of management and efficiency on legal matters.

As an overview, project management involves the following key areas:

1. Development of a more thorough understanding of the project/matter at the outset, especially as it relates to understanding the client's situation and expectations. This involves beginning each matter with an in-depth analysis of the key influencers affecting the matter (called "stakeholders"). The analysis evaluates the level of interest in and influence over a matter. This analysis drives the understanding of the client's expectations, individuals who will affect the direction or approach to the matter, the types of communications that will be needed during the matter, the budget, and more.

2. Enhanced communication with the key influencers in the client organization and with the project team inside the law firm throughout the matter but especially at the beginning to define criteria for success, limitations on the matter, budget/cost expectations, etc.

3. Development of a "scope of work" statement at the outset of the matter that defines what is "in" and "out" of scope for the particular matter. The scope of work, combined with an assessment of risks that can affect the ability to meet the client's objectives and the assumptions upon which the scope and budget are based, enables a matter team to ensure they are on the same page with clients and to manage the matter and budget accordingly.

4. Development of a template for how the work will be done (called a "work breakdown structure" by project managers) so a more accurate budget can be developed and the matter can be managed to that budget.

5. Ongoing monitoring throughout the life of the matter, including bud-get to actual, key milestones for progress with the client's objectives, changes in scope, risk, or influencers, and more.
6. Evaluating a matter at the end to identify "lessons learned" and how similar matters with the same or different clients can be improved in the future—resulting in future efficiencies and/or improved results for the client.

While both process improvement and project management offer great opportunity for legal organizations to improve their service delivery model, improve client retention, and win more new business, to date, more firms and legal departments are adopting project management approaches first because it requires less cultural change. They do not have to convince the lawyers to undertake an entire overhaul of a type of legal work through legal process improvement (LPI) in order to gain significant benefits. However, it is expected that, over the next few years, virtually all legal organizations will be using LPM and LPI approaches in at least some of their practices. While the focus of this book is on LPM, chapter 14 provides an overview of process improvement techniques.

Benefits of Legal Project Management

Project management is taking hold in the legal profession primarily because of the benefits achieved when organizations implement it. If the steps outlined above are integrated into legal matter management, many benefits accrue to both the client and the firm. Based on the experience of many law firms and legal departments, these benefits include:

Benefits to the lawyer/law firm:
- improved profitability of matters (law firm) / reduced cost (legal department)
- greater client satisfaction
- increased revenues from clients
- enhanced risk management

o greater differentiation from competitors
o greater consistency across offices
o enhanced morale and teamwork among project team members
o improved knowledge management/capturing of intellectual property

Benefits to client/legal department:
o greater predictability
o improved communication/"no surprises"
o a more managed approach to legal work
o on budget/on time
o greater efficiencies
o enhanced quality of the work/greater consistency
o improved experience working with outside counsel

Many law firms are implementing LPM because of the potential to improve profitability of matters, reduce write-offs, capture the best practices of lawyers, and/or use it to differentiate their firm from the competition and, thus, win work. However, one of the most important benefits of LPM is the creation of a collaborative environment among the legal team (whether inside a law firm, between a law firm and in-house counsel, or inside a legal department). This is realized in the form of the improved teamwork, enhanced lawyer training and development, and the resulting improvement in morale and engagement within the firm or legal department.

In the business world, company employees of very large companies demonstrate a high degree of employee loyalty and sense of belonging. Companies typically create this loyalty by organizing and managing with small groups and teams. Our research shows that lawyers in many law firms have lost much of the sense of personal "ownership" or engagement that they once had, even among those who still are technically "owners," or partners. Having well-functioning matter teams with strong leadership through LPM can be a key way for legal organizations to re-instill this sense of ownership and belonging. When lawyers have this sense of belonging, it results in less interest in leaving their organization.

The Legal Project Management Framework

There are many descriptions of LPM and many different frameworks being used in law firms or legal departments currently. Because there is not yet a "standard," this book will apply the Legal Project Management Institute's LPM framework developed by LawVision Group[1] to teach the critical LPM concepts and approaches, depicted in figure 3–1.

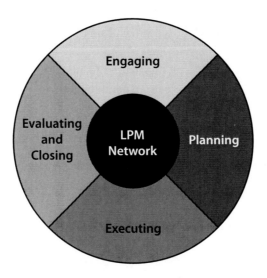

Figure 3-1
Legal Project Management Institute (LPMI) Framework

To provide another example from a law firm implementing LPM, this book will also describe the alternative method developed by Baker, Donelson, Bearman, Caldwell & Berkowitz PC called BakerManage,™[2], depicted

1. The LawVision/Legal Project Management Institute LPM Framework was developed by Susan Raridon Lambreth and Carla Landry, consultants with LawVision Group, along with the input of many certified Project Management Professionals, several of whom had worked extensively with law firms, and academic organizations known for their project management curriculum. Lambreth is the founder of the Legal Project Management Institute.

2. The BakerManage™ process model (figure 3-2) was developed by author David Rueff, who is a practicing lawyer and shareholder with Baker Donelson and a certified Project

in figure 3–2. In addition, examples will be included regarding how various law firms have implemented LPM in their firms—some of which resemble the Legal Project Management Institute 's framework and others that diverge from that particular model. Although there is a great deal of variance among the implementations, virtually all cover the same elements of LPM. Baker Donelson's BakerManage™ model identifies three phases with these "objectives": (1) Develop - identify client needs and develop project plan; (2) Execute - implement client goals and communicate; and (3) Closure - client solution and satisfaction.

Most LPM models have been developed using a combination of individuals trained in project management and those familiar with how legal services function and interact with clients to achieve the best of both worlds. Most LPM models incorporate three main themes:

1. better communication with the client upfront—to set expectations, clarify project details, and define parameters
2. development and use of detailed budgets and project plans, including detailed work schedules, a communication plan, and a risk management plan (covering both project and legal risk)
3. active management of the work throughout the matter, including regular and proactive communication.

Until recently, at best, most law firms developed a rough budget, approximate time lines, and resource allocations—and mostly then only if requested by a client. Today, whether because clients expect it or because the law firm has had serious issues with write-offs and write-downs on matters that got off track, many legal organizations are developing standard and customizable documents that detail the scope of the work, the budget, and a plan for getting the work done in a way that meets or exceeds client expectations.

Manager Professional (PMP), in consultation with William Painter, Baker Donelson's Chief Strategic Planning Officer. Rueff and Painter refined the process after evaluation of the firm's experience implementing traditional project management techniques in high-volume legal matters and a review of litigation and transactional best practices for matter management.

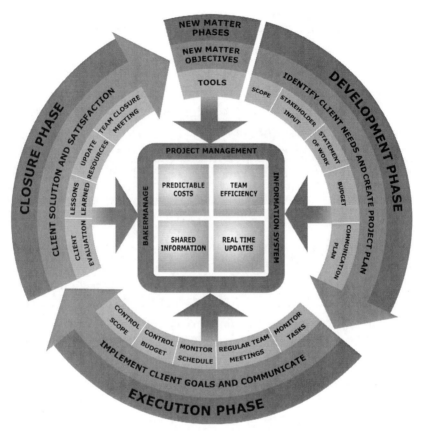

Figure 3-2
The BakerManage™ Model

The phases of LPM are not in a neat linear progression. They are itera-tive and have some overlap.[3] The subsequent chapters will provide detail about each phase and how one can use them despite the inherent level of uncertainty at the outset of a matter, as well as sample forms, templates, and tools to aid in the implementation of LPM phase and steps.

---

3. There are many LPM models currently being promoted within the legal industry that draw upon traditional waterfall project management, Six Sigma, Lean, Agile, or Scrum, and other techniques. The LawVision model and the BakerManage model discussed in this book are two different approaches to accomplish the same objectives. It is the intent of the authors to provide the reader with an overview of these two approaches, to contrast them where appropriate and to distinguish other techniques where applicable.

A Word of Caution to Law Firms:
Integrate LPM with Matter Intake

When beginning to implement a LPM approach in a law firm, it should be thoroughly integrated with matter intake procedures to avoid obtaining duplicate information. Lawyers will become immediately frustrated if they are required to provide information for purposes of complying with firm administrative systems to get the matter opened, and then are required to provide some of the same information again when initiating LPM for a particular matter.

Cases from a *new* client are typically initiated after a response to a request for proposal, several telephone conversations and/or in-person meetings (sometimes through a client interview process). On the other hand, cases from an *existing* client may be initiated by either a telephone conversation, in-person meetings, e-mails, or letters. Matter intake information may be in the form of handwritten notes by the lawyer taking the call or participating in the meeting. Notes from the call may be in no particular format and may be simply based upon the organized thoughts of the client regarding the case. Matter intake information received by written or e-mail correspondence may have more detail and include relevant documents or key facts related to the matter, or it may be more limited to information provided by the client and possible responses to ad hoc questions raised by the lawyer.

When a new matter is received by a lawyer, it kicks off a series of administrative steps internally within the law firm, typically non-billable to the client, to: (1) secure a standard engagement letter, (2) evaluate and resolve conflicts, (3) identify the individuals responsible for working, billing, and overseeing the engagement, and (3) set up any firm technology necessary to support the new matter. The firm must invest administrative resources in the above processes simply to determine if the matter can be handled by the firm prior to starting work. The information collected at this stage has historically been based on the technical information required to support the initial conflicts determination and required by law firm matter intake systems. However, some of this information may be duplicative of information necessary for the LPM evaluation process. Additionally, LPM methods can improve the information gathered at matter intake so that it automatically flows into the firm's LPM resources.

Another consideration is that for matters requiring urgent or immediate responses, the firm also bears the risk that the client has conducted a thorough early case assessment and obtained the information necessary to evaluate the cost and benefits of engaging counsel. While these risks may be reduced for sophisticated clients, such as those with in-house counsel, they can also be mitigated by the implementation of a more comprehensive intake and interview process that is tied to project management principles.

Some clients, especially those with an in-house legal function, have implemented systems for working with outside counsel and can be more organized than some outside law firms. Some law departments were implementing process improvement and project management long before most law firms. On the other hand, most outside lawyers have also had experience with clients who engage outside counsel prior to organizing the information related to their matter. For example, many clients will rely on their lawyer to identify and request key documents, organize the factual history of the matter, and identify individuals within the client organization with key information. If clients invest time to conduct their own internal assessment and collect key information related to the matter prior to engaging counsel, the client could realize a significant cost savings for the due diligence phases of an engagement.

On the other hand, in a transactional matter, if the client engages a lawyer after an agreement has been signed or the deal has been struck, there may be additional expense resulting from the failure of the agreement to address all necessary deal terms. The key is to engage counsel early enough in the process to identify a strategy and plan, and then to identify the points in the engagement where legal advice is needed and where clients can handle issues on their own.

Similarly, in litigation engagements, the lawyer is typically engaged either at the time the client desires to initiate an adversarial proceeding or is responding to one. In either case, planning should involve a clear discussion of the potential costs that can be incurred in various phases of the case. Too often, complaints and answers are filed on behalf of clients without providing them with a clear understanding of the life cycle of the case and the potential expenses that may be incurred to manage all aspects of the engagement. All of this can be improved with a more consistent and comprehensive matter intake process that is tied to LPM principles.

The key is to strike a balance at matter intake to collect enough information about the matter to perform the necessary conflicts and to assist the lawyer with initiating work on the matter consistent with the client's expectations. However, a thorough project plan assessment should not begin until conflicts have been cleared. The key is to obtain more information at matter intake than just the nature of the engagement and the identification of parties (represented, adverse, and related). The intake process could include a questionnaire (designed by each practice area or group) that captures any information that should be considered by the law firm prior to initiating work on the case, but may not include all the information that would typically be included in the Planning Phase discussed in chapter 5.

The following is a basic example of a series of questions and topics that could be addressed at matter intake to kick off both firm administrative processes and LPM and that could help to initially clarify the client's expectations regarding the representation:

- Provide a general description of the nature of the matter. Identify whether there is any specialized legal advice required in this matter.
- Identify the other parties involved in the matter.
- Is there any documentation or other material that you can provide related to this matter?
- Describe in detail the factual circumstances of your matter or project.
- Are you making any assumptions about the facts based upon third-party information or do you have firsthand knowledge of these facts?
- Who are the stakeholders or key personnel who can make decisions regarding this matter? Please identify them by name, contact information, role in the organization, area of expertise, and role in this matter.
- Is there urgency with this matter, such as any immediate deadlines or milestones that you are required to meet?
- Are there any aspects of this legal representation that you intend to handle within your organization?
- Have you worked with another lawyer or firm on this matter?

- If your organization has instructions or requirements for outside counsel, please also attach a copy of those instructions. Do you have any specifications or requirements regarding the following:
  o billing format (such as paper, e-billing, or other) or timing
  o exclusions from billings—i.e., matters that should not be billed
  o limitations on expense reimbursement
  o status reporting (other than standard billing)
  o communications (periodic meetings, blogs, extranets)?
- Do you have an expectation of the amount of legal fees that will be incurred in this engagement? Do you have an expectation of the amount of time necessary to undertake and complete this engagement?
- What is the basis for your estimate of legal fees (estimate from a firm lawyer, estimate from another lawyer, fees incurred in a similar matter with this firm, fees incurred in a similar matter with another firm, internal estimate prepared by your legal department or by your risk management department, etc.)?

The list of matter intake questions above is designed to capture more information than has typically been obtained during the initial call with the client. While not comprehensive of all the information that <u>can</u> be obtained, it should be stressed again that, for ethical reasons, there is a limit to the amount of information that <u>should</u> be obtained prior to conflicts clearance.

The remaining chapters of this book that address the LPM framework assume that conflicts have been cleared and that the firm or legal department is moving forward with the engagement of the client. The next seven chapters will cover all the elements of the Legal Project Management Institute framework in a way that enables a lawyer in any practice setting to use the methodologies and approaches. The next chapter will explain the first phase of LPM, the Engaging Phase.

Section 2

Implementing Legal Project Management

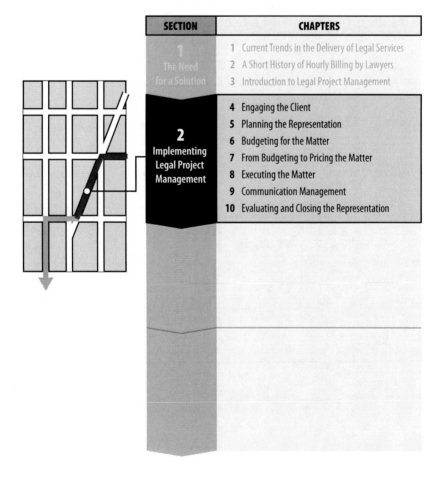

Chapter 4

Engaging with the Client

Activities & Processes
- Identify stakeholders
- Set matter expectations & parameters
- Establish initial objectives

Deliverables & Work Product
- Stakeholder analysis
- High-level matter timeline/schedule
- Scope of work agreement

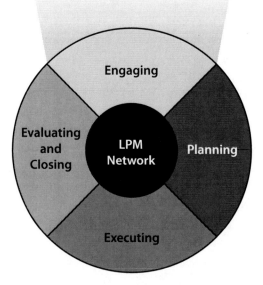

Figure 4-1
The Engaging Phase of LPM

Introduction to Engaging Phase

The Engaging Phase is the first stage of legal project management. This phase is also often called the Initiating Phase (or the Development Phase in BakerManage™) in organizations applying traditional project management because it is the beginning of the project or, in the case of a legal organization, an engagement or a matter. This phase involves identifying the steps to begin a new project and defining the parameters of that project once a law firm is hired or the legal department accepts a matter.[1]

The Engaging Phase has three primary goals:

1. to begin a communication process within the law firm or department and with the client that will form a foundation for a successful engagement/matter
2. to define the major elements of the engagement so all parties involved will "be on the same page" and can discuss early on if there is any disconnect or disagreement
3. to provide sufficient detail about the parameters of the engagement that at least a high-level budget can be prepared and provided to the client (whether internal for a legal department or external for a law firm)

In traditional project management, the Initiating Phase signifies the beginning of the project. However, at least in law firms today, this Engaging Phase may just be the beginning of a time-consuming and costly process of competing to be retained by a client. Many aspects of the Engaging Phase must be addressed in order to respond to a typical request for proposal (RFP) where sophisticated clients ask law firms to provide much of this detail, along with a fee quote or matter budget (detailed scope of work, assumptions, detailed or high-level budget, proposed staffing, etc.). Even if

---

1. In law firms, if this is a matter the firm has been hired for (and not one they are simply bidding for), it is assumed that the law firm has already completed initial matter intake and cleared conflicts prior to this phase. This would also require a preliminary engagement letter that may be supplemented later in the process. From an ethical standpoint, it is critical for law firm to confirm that there are no conflicts prior to obtaining detailed information regarding the matter from the client, which is necessary for the Engaging Phase of the process.

not requested under an RFP, a law firm bidding for work may go through these steps to ensure it understands the project at least at a high level to accurately provide the client with predictable pricing, a timeline, and other information the client needs to decide which firm to hire. This process of defining the details of a matter is also critical to determining whether some of the work is to be done in-house and if the in-house lawyers are subject to legal department or other budgetary constraints.

As will be discussed in chapter 12, according to personality research, lawyers exhibit high levels of a trait called "urgency,"[2] one manifestation of which is lawyers' distaste for taking time for up-front planning. When initially retained, most lawyers want to display their legal expertise as soon as possible. Therefore, many lawyers do not wish to take time at the outset of a matter to map out details for the Engaging Phase, despite the results or value that can come through planning. However, collaboratively developing a scope of work document with a client from the outset can enable lawyers to display their expertise best *and* demonstrate their efficient approaches to their work.

The Engaging Phase is primarily focused on ensuring that the lawyers and the client (external as with law firms or internal for in-house lawyers) are on the same page regarding the details of the matter as they are known at the outset. This phase involves discussions with the key contacts in the client to identify their expectations for outcome, the manner in which they want the matter handled, and the details of what is and is not included in the matter (also known as scope). It also involves discussions with many people within the law firm or legal department regarding previous experience with similar matters or clients, how the firm/legal department can and should handle the matter, at least a high-level understanding of what various parts of the matter will cost, and how it will impact available firm/legal department resources.

The three most critical activities in the Engaging Phase in the Legal Project Management Institute model 4–1 are:

---

2. This trait measures the tendency to take quick action in order to obtain immediate results. It is a measure of an individual's sense of immediacy and a need to get things done.

- identifying and analyzing stakeholders,
- defining client expectations, and
- preparing the "project charter" or scope of work document (including clarifying client objectives and success factors and a detailed scoping of the work).

Each will be described in detail below.

Law Firm Implementation Example

In the BakerManage™ Development Phase, the LawVision Engaging Phase and Planning Phase are combined, but capture similar information. At this stage, BakerManage™ provides attorneys with template forms to capture a clear statement of scope, gather stakeholder information and develop a statement of work (which includes assumptions, risks, budget and expense constraints and what is out of scope). This information is used by the lawyer to populate other BakerManage™ templates for budgeting and planning communications. BakerManage™ templates are included in Appendix 3.

Stakeholder Analysis

The first critical step in the Engaging Phase is the identification and analysis of stakeholders. A stakeholder is anyone who *is affected by* or *who can affect* that particular project. In a legal matter, this can include various individuals within the client organization, business unit, company executives, client counsel, opposing counsel, business unit executives in a company, judges, plaintiffs in an adversarial proceeding, contacts at regulatory agencies, shareholders of the company being acquired, employees of a client or a company affected by the transaction/litigation and many others. While lawyers often look to the negative side of issues, stakeholders can have a positive or negative effect on the project or be affected in positive or negative ways. Because a key to successful legal project management is meeting or exceeding expectations, it is critical to identify all the stakeholders so one can determine their expectations.

The first action in conducting a stakeholder analysis is to identify all the possible stakeholders in the matter/project. When starting a matter with a new client, or even a new type of matter with an existing client, it is especially important that the project team members discuss the possible stakeholders at the outset. This does not have to be time consuming, but it is critical to understand those individuals or groups who could have a significant impact, both positive and negative, on the matter. The identification of stakeholders also provides the members of the project team with a common understanding.

Business is dynamic and, as such, strategies, market conditions, and risk profiles are subject to change over the course of the matter. Keep in mind that the stakeholders initially identified may not continue in the same position as the matter evolves. Be sure to keep track of changes to the matter context, the business climate, and the players to ensure a current list of matter stakeholders. Some stakeholders are intrinsically tied to the working concept of success since they are integral to determining the definition of it. As stakeholders shift, so may goals. Since a law firm's ability to provide legal services is limited by knowledge of changing circumstances, this means in-house counsel need to communicate these shifts to outside counsel. Stakeholders also can affect project risk, which will be discussed later.

The identification of stakeholders can be initiated by the lead lawyer for the matter or the project manager and then run by the other members of the project team or it can be done as a group in an initial project team meeting. It can be performed using brainstorming techniques, which provides the group an opportunity to think more broadly about possible stakeholders, or it can be performed with a more focused list that may have been used in similar matters. For important and/or large matters, it is best if the identification is done in the team meeting so team brainstorming can ensure all possible stakeholders are identified and that all team members understand the stakeholders. The process can often be done for a small matter in 10 to 15 minutes or, even for a larger matter or with a larger team, in no more than an hour or even less.

Law Department Notes

To see the full extent of the gap in stakeholder consensus, this brain-storming exercise can be conducted blindly. Have each member of the project team produce an exhaustive list of stakeholders independently—then compare outputs. The amount of variance among the lists may be surprising. It is not sufficient to store information about stakeholders "in one's head." The strongest teams are those that are able to appreciate why making this type of information explicit empowers all stakeholders. This is particularly relevant for in-house counsel, as company employees often have dramatically different access or visibility into areas of their company.

It is important to keep in mind that although not all stakeholders have an obvious or immediate impact on a project at the outset, their roles and power/influence can change throughout a matter. There are many examples in which a lawyer failed to identify all stakeholders upfront and an unidentified stakeholder ends up influencing the outcome and derailing a project. The likelihood of such an outcome can be reduced when as many stakeholders as possible are named up front. For example, consider the situations in which an outside law firm assumes the main stakeholder in the matter for the client is the in-house lawyer, when in reality there is a business unit executive who has authority over settlement decisions (as his business unit's budget would be affected by the legal and settlement costs). The firm may spend significant time with the in-house lawyer and use the parameters as set forth by the in-house lawyer to obtain an "acceptable" settlement offer. If the business unit executive has to be significantly involved in the offer development, it is important for the outside lawyer to know this. Otherwise, there will likely be protracted and costly negotiations to achieve a new agreement. If the law firm handles the matter on a fixed-fee basis and does not anticipate this risk when developing its price quote, profitability can suffer. The matter can only be handled effectively when all the key stakeholders are identified, considered, and managed.

Some lawyers believe that the stakeholder analysis process is a waste of time because they "already do this in their heads" for their matters. One of the challenges with this rationale is that, if it is only "in their heads" and has not been discussed clearly with all the members of the project team, it is likely that everyone is not on the same page in understanding the needs and expectations of each stakeholder. This, in turn, can affect the legal work, client service, and internal efficiencies at a minimum.

Some outside, or firm, lawyers have stated that they do not feel it is their job to deal with or understand stakeholders inside the client organization, other than their primary contact. However, many in-house counsel have the same mind-set as James Buckley, former associate general counsel with Lockheed Martin Corporation, who describes the importance of understanding and managing stakeholders as follows:

> A critical skill for all lawyers is knowledge of the client's business—not just what it does but how it gets it done. That is through the complexities of the corporate organization: business units, the c-suite (including the CFO who is watching the costs of both the lawyers' fees and the revenue and expenses of the business), the Board of Directors, regulatory compliance, marketing and the in-house lawyers. There are lots of internal stakeholders that are implicated in the business and in the legal work. In order to be effective, the in-house lawyer has to address all of these. A law firm that knows the client's business has the 'back' of the in-house counsel. The firm makes sure that all of the interests of the internal stakeholders are out in the open and addressed in developing a legal strategy. And when that strategy is implemented, the lawyers—both outside and inside counsel squarely weigh how tactics affect the stakeholders. In-house counsel needs outside counsel to be on top of this because they are objective. In addition, in-house counsel are also stakeholders and need to be checked with in making sure they don't overweight their agenda in reconciling the interests of all the stakeholders.

In addition to the questions asked during intake (if the lawyer has been engaged already), these questions can assist in identifying possible stakeholders within the client organization:

- Who else in the organization has a budget affected by this matter?
- Who needs to be involved in discussions of matter strategy or budget?
- Who do you want to have copied on matter correspondence?
- Who would you like to have us meet with to gather the initial information and perspective about the matter?
- Are there varying views of what "success" looks like within your leadership team?

By seeking the answer to these questions, one can determine at the outset of the matter if there are individuals who affect the matter who are "behind the scenes" but who might play a role and affect the budget or outcomes later in the process.

Law Firm Implementation Example

BakerManage™ Development Phase is designed to capture this information for specific categories of stakeholders such as the Project Sponsor (the client lawyer or originating lawyer), the Project Manager (the lawyer who will be identified as responsible for the management of the matter), other internal stakeholders (such as legal team members), external stakeholders (within the client organization or related parties) and third party stakeholders (such as experts, consultants or vendors). BakerManage™ streamlines the stakeholder process by capturing the following information for each of these categories of stakeholder: position, contact information, classification, expertise, responsibility, decision making authority, expectations or goals and whether or not they are to receive updates regarding the matter. This information is captured in a document or website that is shared with the team and client. This is similar to a Communications Plan discussed in chapter 5. The BakerManage™ process captures the decision making authority of the stakeholder so that the legal team clearly understands who within the firm and the client organization has the ability to approve changes to the original project plan.

After as many stakeholders as possible are identified for a given matter, the project team must analyze the list of possible stakeholders to complete a stakeholder analysis. The stakeholder analysis is critical to many future steps in project management and, as a result, forms a foundation for an accurate budget or price and the project plan. The stakeholder analysis affects:

1. **expectations.** By identifying all the key stakeholders evident at the outset of a matter, one may begin the process of understanding expectations of stakeholders both within the client organization and firm/legal department. Because the project charter/scope of work document is based upon understanding the client's expectations and success factors, a lawyer cannot meet or exceed client expectations if the lawyer/

legal team does not know who all of the stakeholders are. Once initial expectations are identified, the lawyer can begin to identify the impact they may have on the budget, schedule, deliverables, desired outcomes, and other details of the matter. Expectations can change throughout a matter, and the lawyer needs to communicate regularly so he or she understands these changes (this is covered in more detail in chapters 9 and 10).

2. **risk/budget.** In identifying stakeholders, one is able to begin identifying potential project risks important for building a budget that is realistic and as accurate as possible. Project risks, if not understood up front, can derail the chances of staying on budget or meeting client objectives.

3. **communications.** When one develops a project plan for the matter during the Planning Phase, it is necessary to understand the key stakeholders to build an effective communication plan.

After identifying the possible stakeholders for a particular matter, the next step is to analyze them in terms of their power/influence versus their interest in the matter. This is a subjective analysis of each stakeholder identified for the matter. The power/influence of a stakeholder is determined by assessing many factors. These can include whether a stakeholder's input or decisions are required for action in the matter or whether they can affect issues such as staffing, legal strategy or budget approval. Interest in a matter can be limited to mere involvement in the matter even if not as decision makers. Examples can include firm/legal department staff, paralegals, or associates assigned to the matter, subject matter experts, plaintiffs in a class action who individually have little power, financial professionals of the law firm or department who might want to ensure the matter meets budget but who don't affect it directly, etc. Interestingly, and sadly—at least to the authors—most stakeholder analyses done for legal matters identify the judge as having high power/influence but low interest in the matters. Perhaps this is a function of the large docket of cases that judges are managing. Below in Figure 4–2, a Power/Interest Grid is shown which shows how stakeholders are evaluated based upon their power/influence vs. their interest.

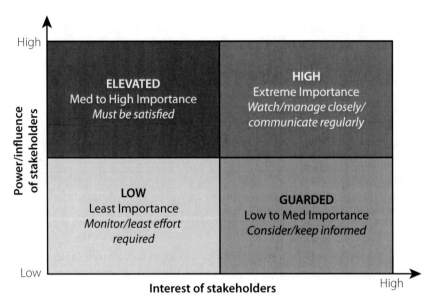

High

ELEVATED
Med to High Importance
Must be satisfied

HIGH
Extreme Importance
*Watch/manage closely/
communicate regularly*

LOW
Least Importance
*Monitor/least effort
required*

GUARDED
Low to Med Importance
Consider/keep informed

Power/influence
of stakeholders

Low

Interest of stakeholders

High

Figure 4-2
Power/Interest Grid

   In the process of analyzing the stakeholders and placing them on the Power/Interest Grid, stakeholders are prioritized in terms of importance to help one understand the impact they may have on the matter. Those who are high power/influence and high interest are called "high importance" stakeholders. Those who are high power/influence but low interest are called "elevated importance" stakeholders. Stakeholders who have high interest but low power/influence are called "guarded" stakeholders. The last category of stakeholders is called "low importance," which have low power/influence and low interest. The titles are often not important in a legal organization, particularly where lawyers resist jargon. But, the thought process for analyzing each and their impact on the matter is critical.

   It is imperative to monitor high-importance stakeholders (high power/ influence and high interest) carefully throughout a matter and to communicate regularly with them, unless it is not appropriate or legal to do so. For example, the plaintiff in a litigation matter would typically be a high importance stakeholder but the defense lawyer or firm is not allowed to communicate directly with the plaintiff, only through his or her lawyer.

Elevated stakeholders (high power/influence but low interest) are very important to monitor since they can often affect the direction or outcomes of the matter and, thus, it is important to meet their expectation. But, one must be careful in communicating with them because they are not that interested and are likely to either not pay attention to any attempts at communication or become bothered should they be inundated with unnecessary or lengthy communication. Examples of "elevated importance" stakeholders often include judges, regulatory agency contacts, law firm management, various business executives in the company who are not actively involved in the matter but who could exert influence if so desired, etc.

Guarded stakeholders (high interest but low power/influence) often want to stay actively involved, but since they do not have a lot of power or influence, communication with them must be efficient so as to avoid unnecessary bills or otherwise distract from doing the necessary legal or project work important to the high power/influence stakeholders. Examples of a guarded stakeholder include an associate, paralegal, or other staff member assigned to the matter or a partner in another practice group in a law firm that also works for the client but does not affect this particular matter.

The last category of stakeholders is called "low importance" (low power/influence and low interest). Examples might include support staff of the lawyers involved in the matter, employees in the company not actively involved in the matter, and even, in some cases, shareholders in a company involved in the matter (though they might be listed in another stakeholder category for other matters). This category typically does not affect the matter in terms of communication needs or decisions. But, because stakeholders can change their power/influence during the course of the matter, it is important to identify them and monitor them through the matter's ongoing project management efforts and meetings.

The mechanics of the process of mapping out stakeholders on the grid is often accomplished with a project team meeting where the stakeholders are first identified. After the stakeholders are identified, a two-by-two matrix can be drawn on a flip chart stand with paper. While the project manager or another person facilitates the discussion, each team member can write the names of possible stakeholders on sticky notes to be placed in the appropriate box on the grid (i.e., the stakeholders who have high power/influence and high interest in the upper right box for "high," etc.). It is important to "map" out as many of the identified stakeholders as possible; but it is important to note that the sticky notes do not have to be viewed as permanently placed. If this version of the stakeholder grid is not transferred to an electronic version, the paper version should be brought to each project team meeting to be amended and edited as more information is gained regarding the matter or if the matter evolves. This is an important part of each team meeting to ensure that the information each team member has gained as the matter progresses is discussed and the grid is revised. Some firms now use simple and inexpensive software tools to capture and update the stakeholder analysis for each matter.

A stakeholder analysis is a very valuable exercise which can help:

- provide understanding of the different influencers in the client organization
  - o Assure group understanding of the players and the hierarchy, not just the senior counsel in a legal department or the client relationship partner in a law firm.
- manage expectations—of each stakeholder/group
  - o Who must be pleased? What does that require?
- prioritize the issues in a matter and identify potential obstacles to achieving client's objectives
- identify the right people in the firm or outside who are needed for the project
- build a communications plan and manage it
- minimize/lessen project risk issues with more thorough analysis of stakeholders up front
- prevent dissatisfied clients through enhanced communication
- reduce write-offs for law firms/reduce legal costs for law departments

A template for the stakeholder analysis grid is attached as appendix 3–1.

Setting Key Stakeholder Expectations

After identifying stakeholders and those that are "key" (the high and elevated ones usually, and particularly the ones in the client organization), the next step is to determine stakeholder expectations and objectives for the matter. This can be done in a telephone call or meeting, and should not be done primarily with e-mail, as this is too fraught with potential for miscommunication.

Listed below are questions that can be used to interview stakeholders to gather information. Asking key stakeholders one or more of these questions can help determine the primary business purpose for the matter, what objectives they seek to achieve, how success will be measured, and other information that helps create the project charter/scope of work document. Developing a list of questions tailored to different types of matters, practices, or even specific clients can be extremely useful and can assist lawyers new to this type of matter or a particular client relationship to get up to speed more quickly and avoid pitfalls experienced by others on past similar matters.

- What are your goals (or objectives)?
- For your organization, what would be a successful outcome from this matter?
- What is a good result from your perspective?
- Are there varying views of what "success" looks like within your leadership team?
- What experience has your company had in similar matters in the past?
- What would be the impact of an adverse ruling on your business?
- Are there grounds for a counter claim?
- Are there any other open matters or legal issues pending that could affect this matter?
- Can you suggest ways for us to understand your business better?
- Is there anything else that we can do to make your efforts more successful?
- Are there parts of this matter that you want to handle within your organization?
- How do you want us to communicate with you and your team? How often?
- What types of communication do you prefer (or require)? With what frequency?
- Is this a standalone issue or does it have a broader impact in your organization?
- [If you have worked with them before] Is there anything that we should stop/start/continue doing?
- What level of understanding of your business do you expect from your outside counsel?
- Are there situations or experiences you want to avoid happening again?
- What have been some of the best practices you have seen with other firms with whom you have worked?
- Other than you, who else will be involved in the matter from your organization? What are their roles? Where are they based?
- What if any of these issues will you deal with internally or allocate to another firm?
- Is there urgency with this matter, such as any immediate deadlines or milestones that you are required to meet?
- Do you have an expectation of the cost of this matter?
- What is the basis for your estimate of cost - estimate from another lawyer, fees incurred in a similar matter, internal estimate prepared by your legal department or by your risk management department?

Figure 4-3
Questions to Understand or Clarify Expectations

Project Charter/Scope of Work Statement

The second activity in the Engaging Phase is the development of what clients call a project charter, which has become known as a scope of work document or statement of work in legal organizations. To formulate this document/information, the lead lawyer, project manager, and/or the project team develop a document covering all of the elements discussed below. This can be done in a single, multi-hour meeting of the team as a whole or among a few individuals. It can also be developed by dividing up the responsibilities among the team members, gathering all the information, and reviewing it as a whole document.

The nine main elements of the scope of work statement are

- **Project/Matter Title.** This is simply the matter name or title assigned to the project. Legal organizations often have a nickname for a matter that differs from the full legal title. For example, the matter of Elizabeth Jones v. Acme Corp. might simply be called the "Jones matter."
- **Matter Definition and Description.** This is a broad overview of the matter, but its main purpose is to define the client's expectations and criteria for success. The definition of client expectations and success criteria is best done by considering the following:
  - **Problem/Opportunity Statement.** What is the client trying to do? What is the business issue or problem the client is trying to solve? Lawyers do not always have sufficient conversations with the client stakeholders about what the client ultimately wants to do, what the impact on their business might or should be, etc. For example, lawyers often focus on the desired legal outcomes ("win" or settle a matter, close the deal, etc.) but not the client's business outcomes—such as speeding up the closing process so properties are operational more quickly, avoiding negative publicity, minimizing business interruption, acquiring the company at X price, etc.
  - **Objectives/Expectations.** What are the client's and the law firm's/legal department's objectives and expectations (both subjective and objective)? For example, common objectives include meeting the budget provided to the client, ensuring the client's and any

externally driven deadlines are met, minimizing the business interruption to the client's organization, and working collaboratively
with the client's stakeholders.

    o **Success Factors.** What are the criteria for determining matter success
from the client's and the firm's or legal department's perspective?
What does a "win" look like to a client? A "win," even in a litigation matter, does not always mean winning the lawsuit. It might
mean settling the case quickly and at a price the client considers
attractive. It might mean closing the deal quickly with minimum
business interruption. Other success factors can include that the
purchase price for an acquisition is within certain parameters or
that the total cost of the lawsuit and legal expenses are less than X.

- **Key Deliverables (both legal work and project deliverables).** A deliverable is a tangible or quantifiable item, document, product, or service
to be provided to meet the project stakeholders' expectations. What
are the key deliverables needed to meet client expectations? These can
include legal documents such as pleadings, early case assessment, a
complaint, a letter of intent, or "turns" of a deal document. They can
also be project-related documents such as a budget or status reports.
Other deliverables could be an extranet or shared workspace to share
information with the client's key stakeholders and the lawyers' team
or a project or communication plan.

- **In Scope and Out of Scope**—The "heart" of a project charter is the
clear definition of what is in and out of scope for the legal matter. This
is why many legal organizations call them "scope of work" documents
or a similar name. Project scope is defined by the Project Management
Institute (PMI) as "the work that needs to be accomplished to deliver
a product, service, or result with the specified features and functions."[3]
The process of scoping means providing a detailed description of the
services that are "in scope" for the particular matter. Adherence to
the scope of work is important, especially if there is an alternative fee
agreement (AFA) or a budget in place. If services that are "out of scope"

---

3. PROJECT MGMT. INST., A GUIDE TO THE PROJECT MANAGEMENT BODY OF KNOWLEDGE
(PMBOK GUIDE) (4th ed. 2008).

are performed under a budget or AFA, more time is amassed than was ascertained on the outset of the case, which, in turn, affects the profitability of that particular matter.

A relatively small percentage of legal work is priced on an alternative fee (non-hourly) basis in most law firms (under 20%). However, when the matters using AFAs are added with the total number of matters based upon a budget or estimate that is essentially a "not to exceed" (and therefore, much like a cap), it is a majority of the legal work in many firms. Because the "not to exceed" budgets are seen as a "cap," only to be bypassed if there is clearly out of scope work required and the client agrees to pay more, it is critical that there is a detailed identification of what is in and out of scope and that these parameters are discussed with the client.

Detailing what is out of scope is absolutely critical because it ensures that the client, the firm, and all members of the project team are on the same page. Clients often assume certain aspects of the work are in scope while the firm/legal department assumes they are out of scope, thus causing significant friction in the lawyer-client relationship. While the lack of it can cause friction, the presence of a well-defined scope can also be an effective cross-selling tool for outside counsel because it shows the client that the firm understands all of the areas involved and has the expertise to handle the out-of-scope areas, where a less experienced law firm in that area might not have identified those avenues of possibility.

- **Key Milestones and Dates.** This includes not only the legal key milestones or dates such as a hearing or a closing date but also the scheduling of regular status calls or quarterly financial reporting deadlines that are important to the client.

- **Budget/Fee Arrangement.** This includes either a detailed budget the law firm/legal department will use to manage the matter internally and/or a budget or fee arrangement requested by and provided to the client. Many law firms are starting to require internal budgets for matters over a certain size, even if the client does not request one. At this stage, budgets can be either extremely detailed or merely high level, depending upon the client's request and the law firm's data on typical fees and costs. In traditional project management, a detailed and firm budget is not created until the Planning Phase when there is more information about risks, variables and more. However, in the legal professions, there is often the expectation that a detailed budget will be provided with the scope of work document. Chapter 7 will cover the process of creating budgets in detail.

- **Key Resources.** This means the key members of the legal services delivery team in and outside the law firm, legal department, or client organization. In a law firm, these can include partners, associates, counsel, paralegals, subject-matter experts, or others, and, in the client, it can also include key professionals whose expertise may be necessary for the matter (scientific or medical staff for a mass tort or intellectual property matter, for example). A matter's key resources might also include members of a particular business unit who will be members of the project team. Other key resources can include expert witnesses, outsourcing vendors, etc.

- **Major Project Risks.** Project risks are any factor that could affect one's ability to have the project meet the expectations or objectives of key stakeholders. Project risks include not only legal risks, but can also include broader risks such as an aggressive opposing counsel, a difficult judge, failure to obtain necessary financing or regulatory approvals, "bad facts" uncovered in discovery, etc. These can affect the budget, timing, or schedule for a matter—or even the very goal of the matter itself.

- **Assumptions and Constraints.** In traditional project management terminology, assumptions are factors assumed to be true that must be validated throughout the life of the engagement, also called the project life cycle. These can be *factual assumptions* regarding the facts of the matter that if proved untrue could result in expansion of the scope and additional tasks to be performed. These can also be *procedural or strategic assumptions* regarding the opposing parties' litigation or negotiation tactics, which are factored into the tasks to be performed, and the time estimates provided.

  For legal matters, assumptions are those aspects of a matter that have been assumed in order to meet the budget provided or to meet the client's expectations. Assumptions are often detailed to provide a balance for some of the higher impact project risks, especially if those risks are not highly likely to occur (this will be explained more in chapter 5 on project risk analysis as part of the Planning Phase). Assumptions might address the division of responsibilities between the in-house and outside counsel, the amount of gigabytes of information, or the number of custodians for e-discovery purposes.

Constraints are limitations that affect the project parameters or one's ability to complete the project and meet the client objectives for budget or other outcomes. A good example of a possible constraint to a law firm is a law department's outside counsel billing guidelines, which often limit the professionals that can work on the matter or the steps that can be undertaken (such as a number of depositions or the number who attend each). For a law department, a constraint might be limited staff or budget for the legal matter.

By gathering the information presented in the nine elements above, a firm or legal department can handle a matter more efficiently and, barring any unforeseen risks, to perform well within budget. Effective scoping of a legal matter can:

1. Increase predictability of legal costs for the client.
2. Avoid misunderstandings about assumptions (and for law firms, prevent write offs resulting from these).
3. Help manage scope creep.
4. Open a dialogue with the client early in the process, which makes conversations throughout the engagement easier.
5. Prevent client dissatisfaction.
6. Improves matter profitability (for law firms).
7. Reduce legal costs (for law departments).

A project charter/scope of work document template is included in appendix 3–2.

Law Firm Implementation Example

The BakerManage™ process combines the information identified by this section in a Statement of Work that provides a detailed description of the matter and formally defines what is within and outside of the scope of the matter. It documents the initial high-level requirements, measurable objectives, and related success criteria of the client. It should also include the assumptions (factors known to be true that must be validated throughout the project life cycle), risks (uncertain events or conditions that could have a positive or negative effect on the outcome), constraints (factors that limit the options), and exclusions from the services to be provided (what is out of scope). If there are any expectations regarding the budget or expenses identified in the stakeholder analysis, this information is also captured in the Statement of Work. The Statement of Work is a supplement to the standard engagement letter form which normally includes a very high level statement of the services.

The process of building a project charter involves the project team and/ or the lawyers working on the matter discussing each of the nine areas above and documenting it for the matter. After the draft project charter is created, the best approach is to meet with the clients (internal or external) to discuss. For some clients, this meeting should also involve a review of the budget (including assumptions and risks) to help educate the client on all work necessary to complete the engagement. Then, a final version of the project charter can be agreed upon. In some instances, lawyers in firms use the document more like talking points with their clients and do not share the formal document with them. However, it is likely that clarification of expectations, scope, and other details provided through the process of developing a project charter will become the expectation in most lawyer-client relationships in the future.

Law Firm Implementation Example

BakerManage™ is a hybrid of the waterfall process used in traditional project management techniques. "Waterfall" refers to steps for implementation that are sequential and flow downward from a higher level of specification (project identification) to a more detailed level (project definition and execution). This technique is used to develop the scope, expanded phases and tasks (and in some cases subtasks), associate the time and resources (which includes rates) necessary for completion, and identifying a schedule for completion of the tasks. Assumptions and risks captured in the Statement of Work can also be elaborated at the phase, task and subtask level to capture the limitations and constraints of the budget estimate. All of this information is captured in a project budget and project schedule as part of the BakerManage™ Development Phase.

To develop systems for similar matters, a template can be formed including the standard documents for the "typical" stakeholders for those types of matters, common risks, assumptions and constraints, etc. Then, for each specific matter, the standard template documents can be modified as appropriate.

A project charter/scope of work statement can help:

- set expectations on the front end—anticipating obstacles, contingencies, etc.—and creates more realistic expectations and understanding on both sides;
- enhance understanding of the client's situation, objectives, and expectations;
- define those items that are in and out of scope at the outset and easier to manage throughout (this, in turn, lowers legal budgets and helps to insure fewer write-offs and enhanced profitability/productivity);
- initiate conversations early in process so they are easier to have throughout;
- eliminate confusion to prevent later billing disputes over fees;

- enhance communication within the project team;
- integrate new members to the project team because the baseline information, understanding, and analysis exist in a reviewable written document;
- staff projects more efficiently and effectively due to more advance planning to anticipate needs on project;
- create processes and checklists for current and future matters; and
- provide information to use for next project.

To recap, the key parts of the Engaging Phase are

- identifying and analyzing stakeholders,
- defining client expectations, and
- preparing the project charter or scope of work document.

Whether one embarks upon development of a full scope of work document or simply applies some of the recommended approaches, there should be obvious improvements to getting started on the matters where they are used.

Chapter 5

Planning the Matter

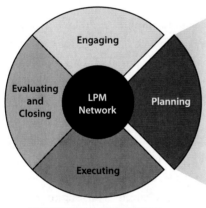

Activities & Processes
- Determine deliverables/work product
- Establish work assignments and other resources needed
- Determine budget
- Develop detailed matter schedule
- Develop communication plan
- Create change management plan

Deliverables & Work Product
- Deliverable/work product list
- Work assignments (task plan)
- Approved budget
- Updated matter timeline
- Project plan

Engaging

Evaluating and Closing

LPM Network

Planning

Executing

Figure 5-1
The Planning Phase of LPM

The Planning Phase is one of the most critical parts of legal project management (LPM). Even with the emphasis on LPM in many law firms and legal departments today, most of the focus has been on the steps in the Engaging Phase, especially regarding the scoping of work, and the development of a budget, which is sometimes based on a full breakdown of the work and other times based more on past experience with supposedly similar matters. More organizations are expecting their lawyers to develop project plans because without a project plan there is a higher likelihood of not meeting client expectations and of less efficient delivery of legal services. This can be detrimental to the client and outside counsel. The project plan is what enables a lawyer to not only develop an accurate budget but then, manage to the budget.

The project plan, if properly created, should form the basis for active management of the matter throughout its life by meeting client and key stakeholder expectations and providing the groundwork for more efficient and effective legal services. However, because lawyers often score high on the "urgency" trait mentioned in chapter 4 (and described in detail in chapter 12), many lawyers dislike planning and are reluctant to spend time on functions that do not seem mission-critical.

Plans can vary from one organization to another. Some legal organizations develop a granular budget with a lot of detail at the task level, but historically even they have not managed to the budget in an organized or disciplined way. However, legal organizations are now beginning to develop detailed budgets or plans, and to manage to them also. This is sometimes to deal with financial issues that have arisen with a lack of project management on matters or, for law firms, in an effort to differentiate themselves from competitors. To manage matters effectively to a detailed (and usually tight) budget, for example, one needs the task level detail, timelines, and tools like communication and risk plans. In fact, this level of detail or plans is now required by a growing number of clients. This chapter will explain how to develop these detailed plans to guide a matter throughout.

Law Department Notes

One of the most significant ways in-house counsel's dual responsibility (i.e., a company employee and a member of the bar) manifests is in the planning phase of a matter. In-house lawyers that understand the strategy and operations of the business are best positioned to articulate and monitor their company's definition of success. While lawyers (internal and external) may have *legal* definitions of success (e.g., X settles the case for less than $500,000), it is the business that has the ultimate say in what defines a successful outcome. For example, an acquisition transaction may involve entering a new market or adding to an existing revenue stream, which require a different level of due diligence (and associated costs) and communication with staff (e.g., human resources, information technology, and corporate communications). If the client is selling its core operations in a one-off transaction that results in an extraordinary accounting item, they will approach the same deal in a completely different way than if the client were a private equity firm where such acquisitions are routine. In other words, while the same set of operative facts may exist over a wide range of situations (e.g., a mergers and acquisitions (M&A) deal), it is the client's business context that determines how the matter should be managed. Thus, in-house counsel's deep understanding of context puts them in the best position to appreciate and guide the planning of the matter.

Overview of Project Plan

The main areas covered in a project plan are listed below. Each will be explained in detail later in the chapter.

- **Schedule.** This begins with breaking the work down into its component steps and then determining the level of resource (legal professional or other) needed for each step and the time required. It is designed to be a tool that includes all the steps in the matter from start to finish, including any that may change during the matter, such as if a motion for summary judgment is denied in a litigation matter versus if it is won.

- **Resources/Staffing Plan.** This includes who will perform each of the items on the schedule and when, which is beneficial to both the team and the client. This helps everyone on the project team know who is doing what throughout the matter and ensures appropriate staffing and no redundancy. This includes professionals and staff in the legal organization and outside who are necessary to complete tasks, including outside experts, vendors, such as for e-discovery, etc. It provides a way of communicating with the client about timing, delays, the impact of scheduling changes, and more. It also ensures that nothing falls through the cracks in the project team or between the team and the client.

- **Communication Plan.** This identifies all the key stakeholders with whom the team needs to communicate, what type of communication is preferred, who is responsible for the actual communication, and how it will occur.

- **Risk Management Plan.** This involves identifying the likely project risks and the probability and potential impact of each. Following the identification of risks, this plan involves developing strategies for addressing each risk.

- **Change Management Plan.** This involves identifying the approach to handling scope changes, which may involve formal processes or may simply be a policy statement. Most law firms do not actually do change management plans yet, but some clients have a formal change process where they require compliance of their outside counsel.

- **Budget.** A complete and thorough budget can be developed once the firm has analyzed the project and developed the work breakdown structure. The budget is based upon the schedule for the work, the anticipated risks, the level of communication needed, etc. This includes the basis for the fee and/or detailed budget. This is covered in more detail in chapter 7.

Law Firm Implementation Example

BakerManage™ encourages continued management by the team and the client by making all planning information available on a SharePoint site that is accessible by the legal team and the client. After the BakerManage™ Statement of Work is developed, the legal team prepares the project plan for the engagement which includes the list of tasks (or Work Breakdown Structure), the project schedule which includes the resources and timelines for the completion of tasks, the project budget which identifies the estimated hours for completion and rates of resources, and the communication plan which identifies the responsibilities of both the firm and the client for continued communications throughout the life of the project. All of this information is made available to the project team and to the client through a SharePoint site.

- **Project Plan** – The BakerManage™ Development Phase incorporates all planning concepts and methods including the stakeholders, statement of work, budget, schedule and communication plan. The schedule is developed as part of the budget development process.

- **Resources/staffing** – Information is incorporated into BakerManage™ Development Phase schedule for the project that shows the phase, task (or subtask), estimated time for completion, deadline, status and comments for issues related to the task. All individuals who are assigned work are identified on the schedule next to their task (or subtask).

Law Firm Implementation Example (cont.)

- **Communication Plan** – The BakerManage™ Development Phase also includes the creation of a communication plan. The plan is intended to include who is responsible for the plan, the content and requirements of client reports, the recipient of client reports, the frequency of client reports, any special billing requirements of the client, other communication specifications provided by the client, whether or not internal team meetings will be conducted on a regular basis and internal matter requirements such as weekly status updates and daily time entry. BakerManage™ templates are included in Appendix 3.
- **Risks and Assumptions** – Matter level risks and assumptions are identified in the BakerManage™ Development Phase Statement of Work. When the budget is developed, phase and task level assumptions and risks are also identified to clarify expectations with the client.
- **Change Management Plan** – BakerManage™ incorporates a Change Control Log, which is designed to capture changes to the Statement of Work. The log serves as a method to track what are essentially change orders throughout the engagement that will impact the scope, tasks, budget and schedule.
- **Budget** – The budget is developed in the BakerManage™ Development Phase prior to initiating work. This ensures that the statement of work is consistent with decisions by the client regarding the phases and tasks to be handled by the firm.

Each area of the project plan will be covered in detail below or in another subsequent chapter.

Schedule and Work Breakdown Structure

The first step in the Planning Phase is to build a schedule of the work. In project management terminology, a schedule is a listing of a project's milestones, activities, and deliverables, usually with intended start and finish dates. Those items are often estimated in terms of resource allocation, budget, and duration, linked by dependencies and scheduled events. Before a project schedule can be created, the person or project team developing the schedule should have a work breakdown structure (described below), an effort estimate for each task, and a resource list with availability for each resource. These tools can be used in discussions with the client. To the extent that decisions are made by the client with regard to the scope of services, these should be documented in the project charter or scope of work document referenced in chapter 4.

Thus, to develop the schedule, one typically begins with breaking the work for the legal matter into its component parts and then identifies the resources needed for each task in the matter. In most businesses or other organizations using project management, the breakdown of the work is called a Work Breakdown Structure (WBS). It is a decomposition of the work into deliverables or phases to be executed by the matter team to accomplish the project/matter objectives and create the deliverables (called a progressive decomposition in traditional project management terminology). The WBS serves two main purposes. First, it is used to develop more accurate budgets for legal work by enabling the lawyer to understand the costs of the work. Second, when developed at the granular level, it can be used to manage the team doing the legal work and ensure that no tasks are missed and there is no redundancy.

The WBS organizes and defines the total scope of the project and each descending level represents increasingly more detail, the documentation of which is commonly referred to in legal organizations as "templates" or "checklists." See figure 5–2. One of the reasons for this terminology is that several of the major legal-specific budgeting or project planning tools call them "templates."

While developing the initial WBS for a particular area of legal work can be time-consuming, once formulated, a standard WBS for that type of work can be maintained in the organization's knowledge management system. As new, similar matters are opened, the WBS can be modified or tailored to a given client situation. As a result, many practice groups are developing these templates for the areas of work that are most common in their area or that have the most replicable elements.

As LPM matures in a legal department or law firm, more of these templates will be developed and will provide excellent resources for the design of future engagements. It is highly recommended that these resources be shared with the client to help customize the engagement for the specific needs of the client. For example, it is easy to develop a standard template for litigation that can be tailored to a specific matter or modified to develop a more elaborate template for specialized litigation such as securities, intellectual property, or products liability.

To develop a WBS, the work required for the matter is broken down into phases or deliverables. While some in traditional project management suggest that all work has to be (and can be) broken into deliverables and sub-deliverables (rather than phases) down to the task level, more legal organizations are using phases rather than deliverables. In large part, this is because litigation was the first practice in most legal organizations to use LPM extensively, and litigation is usually planned by phases; the Uniform Task Based Management System (UTBMS) codes (commonly called "task codes") were first developed for litigation and are based on phases; and many of the publicly available technology tools for LPM (called project management information systems) are based on phases.[1]

Nevertheless, to develop a WBS for a matter, one can use phases, deliverables, or a combination of both. The first step is to identify the main phases or deliverables for the matter. Then, each phase or deliverable should be broken down into sub-phases or sub-deliverables. This deconstruction is repeated until each has reached its lowest level and cannot be broken down further. The end result is called the task or activity level.

At the task/activity level, certain criteria need to be addressed, such as estimated costs, time, duration, staffing or other resource needs. It is at this

---

1. *Project Management Information Systems*, WIKIPEDIA, http://en.wikipedia.org/wiki/Project_management_information_system (last updated Oct. 5, 2013, 11:06 AM).

level where experience level and type needed to perform the task (e.g., a paralegal, a fifth-year associate, or a partner) and how much time the task should take (e.g., three hours) can be identified. Figure 5–2 illustrates the process of breaking the work down.

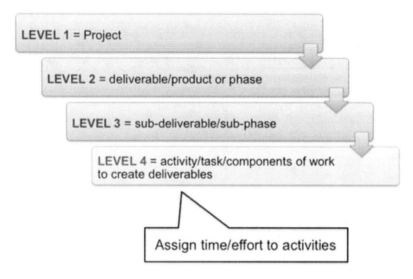

LEVEL 1 = Project

LEVEL 2 = deliverable/product or phase

LEVEL 3 = sub-deliverable/sub-phase

LEVEL 4 = activity/task/components of work to create deliverables

Assign time/effort to activities

Figure 5-2
Process of Breaking Work Down into Component Parts

Law Firm Implementation Example

The detail provided in the BakerManage™ budget can be gauged for the needs of the legal team and client. For some matters, phase and task level budget development may be sufficient. For a more reliable budget, the activities or subtasks should be developed to identify the work at a more granular level. This method is preferred when developing a budget for a matter that will eventually become a fixed fee arrangement.

The following examples (figures 5–3 – 5–5) provide sample WBSs or templates from various firms or planning tools. Appendix 3–3 provides a form to prepare a WBS. Figure 5–6 is an example of a WBS or phase/task/activity breakdown used in BakerManage™ and shows how subtasks or activities can be tied to the American Bar Association UTBMS. Figure 5–7 is an example of a WBS or budget outline for a litigation matter using the task codes as a starting point. One advantage of the WBS using the UTBMS codes is that it provides a guideline for timekeepers to make time entries to the correct code sets. It also provides the information necessary for automated budget tracking.

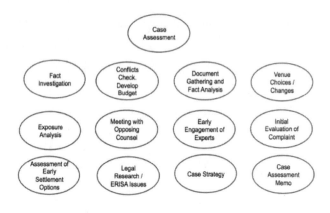

© 2014 Legal Project Management Institute. All rights reserved.

Figure 5-3
Sample Work Breakdown

Figure 5-4
M&A: Tender Offer—Beginning of a Work Breakdown Structure

Source: Engage, Thomson Reuters

Figure 5-4 (cont.)
M&A: Tender Offer—Beginning of a Work Breakdown Structure

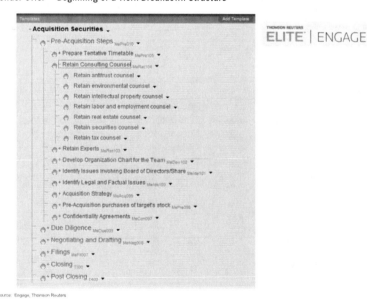

Source: Engage, Thomson Reuters

Figure 5-5
M&A: Tender Offer—Beginning of a Work Breakdown Structure to Task Level

Baker, Donelson, Bearman, Caldwell & Berkowitz PC
Legal Project Management Office
BakerManage- Budget Designer Process Map / Task List Outline

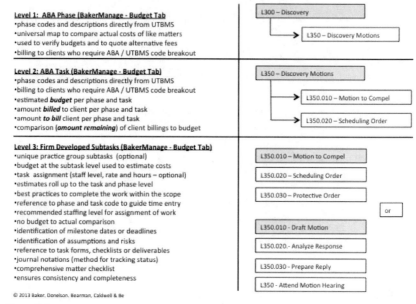

Level 1: ABA Phase (BakerManage - Budget Tab)
•phase codes and descriptions directly from UTBMS
•universal map to compare actual costs of like matters
•used to verify budgets and to quote alternative fees
•billing to clients who require ABA / UTBMS code breakout

Level 2: ABA Task (BakerManage - Budget Tab)
•phase codes and descriptions directly from UTBMS
•billing to clients who require ABA / UTBMS code breakout
•estimated **budget** per phase and task
•amount **billed** to client per phase and task
•amount **to bill** client per phase and task
•comparison (**amount remaining**) of client billings to budget

Level 3: Firm Developed Subtasks (BakerManage - Budget Tab)
•unique practice group subtasks (optional)
•budget at the subtask level used to estimate costs
•task assignment (staff level, rate and hours – optional)
•estimates roll up to the task and phase level
•best practices to complete the work within the scope
•reference to phase and task code to guide time entry
•recommended staffing level for assignment of work
•no budget to actual comparison
•identification of milestone dates or deadlines
•identification of assumptions and risks
•reference to task forms, checklists or deliverables
•journal notations (method for tracking status)
•comprehensive matter checklist
•ensures consistency and completeness

© 2013 Baker, Donelson, Bearman, Caldwell & Be

Figure 5-6
BakerManage™ WBS

Phase L100 - Case Assessment, Development And Admin.
   Task L210 - Pleadings
      Subtask □ Answer - Research and draft pleading
      Subtask □ Answer - Send draft pleading to client for review
      Subtask □ Answer - Finalize responsive pleading for filing and service
Another example of progressive decomposition below takes the deliverable and identifies all of the steps necessary to complete the deliverable, as follows:
   Prepare Answer
      □ *Review complaint and evaluate claims and defenses.*
      □ *Perform research on defenses.*
      □ *Prepare draft Answer.*
      □ *Discuss with client*
      □ *Finalize Answer, file and serve on plaintiff*

Figure 5-7
Sample WBS Using Task Codes

Another technique to create a WBS is process disaggregation where one breaks up legal projects into subsidiary pieces and then identify the staffing and time necessary to complete each piece. Regardless of the approach used, the end product of this process can be referred to as a WBS, a playbook, budget plan, or schedule. The result should be balanced—that is, detailed enough to accurately estimate the work but capable of being implemented without increasing the amount of time necessary to manage the engagement. In other words, an overly detailed WBS can be too detailed and impractical to implement.

After developing the WBS for a matter, the next step in developing the budget is to estimate 1) how much time or cost each task will take and 2) the experience level of person, if necessary, needed to do the work. In developing a WBS for a *new* matter for an organization, one would typically begin to identify the *specific* staffing for the matter. On the other hand, if preparing a detailed budget for a *potential* matter, such as to win work from a prospective client, one would prepare a schedule and budget based, instead, on categories of staffing. For example, one would estimate that a particular matter would need a senior partner for certain activities, a senior associate for others and perhaps a junior associate for still others.

Resource/Staffing Plan

The resource plan involves assigning specific people or other resources to the schedule developed for a particular matter and confirming their availability to perform the assigned work. The result is a master plan document that shows all the steps or tasks in the matter, who is handling each one, the due dates, the dependency relationships between tasks, and more. The resource assignment process is critical for detailed budgeting. But its primary purpose in most organizations is to keep the project team on track to meet all objectives, including financial ones. The resource plan (who is available to do the work) and schedule (who is doing what and when) are important to discuss at regular project team meetings since most schedules and assignments change in the course of a legal matter that extends over a long period.

Law Firm Implementation Example

BakerManage™ and other LPM software tools identified in appendix 2 permit users to select resources from the firm's database of timekeepers so that by the selection of the individual, users can see standard rates and ultimately the impact on the budget. As identified in the description of available LPM tools, some tools are even providing the user with information on the timekeeper's workload and availability in order to identify whether or not the timekeeper has the capacity to take on a new project.

Another tool for resources planning is called a RACI (responsible, accountable, consulted, informed) chart, which ensures that everyone on the project team knows who is handling each deliverable and what role they have with regard to each. It is a simple chart that documents each activity, task, or workstream (as corporations often call it) and defines responsibilities and assignments. Responsible is who is involved in working on the activity, and there may be more than one person. Accountable is "whose head will roll" if something goes wrong with the activity, and there is typically only one person accountable. Consulted refers to who has input on the activity (such as preparing a pleading). Informed refers to who needs to be copied or in another way provided communication about the activity or step.

Law Firm Implementation Example

Information similar to the RACI diagram is captured in the Baker-Manage™ schedule which is developed during the first phase of the project implementation. Rather than using a RACI chart, the Baker-Manage™ schedule identifies each individual's task or activity that they are responsible for in the engagement.

Aileen Leventon of QLex Consulting has helped many lawyers understand the value and use of RACI charts. Her guidance is as follows:

There are typically four classes of stakeholders in a RACI chart and the related document, a communication plan:

- **Responsible.** These individuals are responsible for (a) completing all assigned work, (b) utilizing effective two-way communication, (c) informing the team leader of work progression and (d) understanding and carefully monitoring how their work intersects with or is relevant to others' work.
- **Accountable.** This individual ultimately bears the weight of the success or failure of the matter and is accountable for the totality of the project. There is only one person who is accountable, while many may be "responsible" or play other roles. Throughout the course of the matter, this person must receive regular updates from those who are "responsible" and respond to updates with timely, specific and clear feedback. Changes that impact the project plan, particularly changes to the "Shared Understanding" documents, are at the core of these communications.
- **Consulted.** These are individuals (often within the client organization) who have veto rights. They are consulted in advance to determine which actions have an impact on project constraints. Likewise, they must be consulted about the project's evolution and be given a meaningful opportunity to drive the development of objectives, constraints, and assumptions (i.e., the "Shared Understanding").
- **Informed.** These individuals are directly affected by or have related interests to the matter. Those who are "informed" simply need to be kept abreast of the project's progress so they can adjust their activities and expectations. They may receive information after an event occurs.

To depict these roles and responsibilities, it is useful to construct a RACI chart, which is a matrix that matches (a) major project activities with relevant stakeholders and (b) each person's involvement in the communication plan. The RACI chart is a common project management tool. It should be created in the first instance by the project manager or team leader and, in larger projects, each subproject leader may organize a separate RACI chart for an area of responsibility.

Note that lawyers can perform multiple RACI roles for various parts of the same matter. For example, if you are running the e-discovery portion of a litigation matter, you may be "responsible" for responding to e-discovery; simultaneously, if the law-and-motion team is litigating a protective order concerning e-discovery, it is likely that you will only be kept "informed." Consider how this applies to all members of the team, including stakeholders who must be notified about status or consulted regarding disrupted activities due to pending litigation.

RASCI Chart: Links the "who" with the "what" (resources + scope)

WHAT	WHO			
	Relationship Partner	Junior Partner	Mid-level Associate	Junior Associate
Conduct due diligence	I	C	A/R	R
Structure transaction	A/C	R	I	S
Negotiate transaction	A/C	R	R	S
Closing	I	A/C	R	S
Client Communications	A/R	R	I	S
Post-closing	A/i	C	S	R

Associate activities with people and their roles
R = Responsible **A** = Accountable **S** = Support **C** = Consulted **I** = Informed
Each activity must have someone who is Accountable and only one person. Others may have multiple roles

Figure 5-8
RASCI Chart

Figure 5–8 is an illustration of a RACI chart for a transaction. (Note that this particular chart is called RASCI because it includes an optional role, *S*, for support.) The "What" column lists key phases. Depending on the complexity of the matter, each phase may require a separate RACI chart; likewise, if it is necessary to work at a more granular level, activities can be further detailed or divided.

To date, RACI charts are not used extensively in law firms, but they are used in many businesses, and law firm use will likely increase as more law departments are using them. In legal departments, where there is less hierarchy on legal teams or between legal teams and their business counterparts, it is a very valuable tool to make sure everyone knows who is handling what. In addition, legal departments have found it helpful to prevent "land grabs" among law firms where a matter involves outside counsel from more than one law firm.[2]

RACI charts are developed at the outset of a matter when the project manager, or in some situations the entire project team, identifies that activities that need to be completed at a matter or phase level and who is in each category of the chart. Once the assignments are made, it also identifies the necessary communication that needs to occur (such as keeping those "informed"). A template for a RACI chart is provided in appendix 3–4.

---

2. In-House Legal Department Representative Presentation at Managing Litigation, West LegalEd Workshop (Sept. 11, 2013).

Law Department Notes

The resource/staffing plan is critical to in-house counsel. First, there should be a clear allocation of work between in-house, the law firm, other third parties (e.g., legal process outsourcers, litigation support vendors, accountants, and financial advisors), and client personnel. Second, each party must understand its unique roles and responsibilities, which can be documented in a RACI chart or through another accessible tool. Finally, there should be an acknowledgement that, over time, there will be changes in resources, skills, and roles. As these changes occur, it is important to reconsider the overall resource distribution: the impact on projected costs, budgets, fee structures, and timing. How changes in resources or personnel will be addressed should be specifically called out as a process in the initial plan. .If the fee structure and workflow are based on *specific* assigned personnel and the continuity of law firm resources, inside counsel must address and monitor any changes in personnel or their associated billing rates in outside counsel guidelines, e-billing rules, and compliance systems.

Communication Plan

Project planning requires more than analyzing the steps required for the work and preparing a budget. One purpose of the plan is to determine the information needs of the project stakeholders and to define a communication approach that meets the stakeholders' needs and expectations, as well as one that stays within budget. Thus, to prepare a full project plan for a significant matter, a communication plan is a critical element.

Developing the communication plan involves considering what types of communication are necessary with each of the high or elevated stakeholders, particularly those in the client organization. In some types of matters, they are referred to as the "working group" (typically the key stakeholders who are multiple counsel representing the various parties in complex

Stakeholder Role	Communication Deliverable	Frequency / Deadline	Method	Responsible	Recipient Response
Client	Status report	Weekly	Conference call	Client responsible partner (CRP)	Approval
CRP	Draft interrogatory	Once, not later than Aug 1	Email	Senior associate	Revision / sign off

Figure 5-9
Sample Beginning of a Communication Plan

matter). Communication to these individuals takes place through e-mail distribution lists, extranets, or other channels. The development of a communication plan ensures that all the critical stakeholders are covered, even if they are not part of the working group, and that the communication is the appropriate type and level for each of them.

The communication plan involves addressing the following questions:

- Who needs to know what?
- When do they need to know it?
- How do they want to get it?
- What are they supposed to do with it?

It should cover all the key stakeholders and the key deliverables.

Many firms prepare a budget before they have prepared a communication plan. However, the best practice is to at least identify the main elements of the communication plan that will be expected by the client and other key stakeholders (such as a judge that may be known for requiring higher levels of activity than ordinarily expected) prior to preparing the budget. If the client expects a biweekly status call, this will require more time included in the budget than a matter where the client expects only a quarterly status call. Status reports that are delivered in person will cost more than those submitted via e-mail. Sometimes law firms communicate according to the communication plan but have to write off the time spent doing so because it was not anticipated in the budget. Without an organized and proactive approach to communications, law firms typically under-communicate both with contacts in and affiliated with the client organization and within their own project team.

Communication plans not only help to determine what the costs will be for certain communication expected by the client stakeholders, opposing parties, or others, they also ensure sufficient communication to keep the project on track and to meet client expectations. There should be a person responsible for each deliverable, similar to the assignments for a RACI chart. The communication plan is discussed and updated at regular meetings. Commonly, the communication plan is a part of the project plan and is developed by the project manager.

To prepare a communication plan, one should begin with the stakeholder analysis or grid prepared in developing the project charter/scope of work document. Once the key stakeholders (typically those who are in the high and elevated boxes in the matrix) are identified, the type of communication appropriate for each and the frequency/method of communication per stakeholder should be addressed. See figure 5–9. The communication plan should be regularly monitored for changes throughout the life of the project to ensure those responsible for the communication are handling it. The communication plan is one of the documents reviewed at regular project team meetings. A template for a communication plan is provided in appendix 3–5.

Figure 5–10 is an example of the communication plan used in BakerManage™.

Figure 5-10
BakerManage™ Communication Plan Example

Law Department Notes

It is essential to proactively identify recipients and providers of information and the way in which these stakeholders are answerable in the context of the matter. This is addressed in a communication plan, a document that articulates how the team communicates, who communicates to whom, and what the preferred medium for communication is. A communication plan is distinct from an ad hoc or crisis-driven explanation of how the team negotiates information, as it is deliberately considered and designed at the beginning of a matter. To formulate a communication plan, one needs to discuss needs, expectations, preferences, and constraints with the right people. The very first step is to identify who these "right people" are. In-house counsel is in the unique position to distinguish and manage internal stakeholders.

While part of outside lawyers' expertise is to identify and guide external stakeholders (such as the lawyers representing other parties in the transaction, the judge, or the regulator) and understand how each party relates to the matter, outside counsel rarely has the visibility or experience to make these determinations as effectively.

Risk Management Plan

A project risk, as described in chapter 4, is an uncertain event that, if it occurs, has a positive or negative effect on the prospects of achieving project objectives. It is any uncertainty that could affect one's ability to have the project meet the expectations or objectives of key stakeholders. Project risks include not only legal risks but broader risks such as an aggressive opposing counsel, a difficult judge, failure to obtain necessary financing or regulatory approvals, "bad facts" that are uncovered in discovery, etc. These can affect the budget, timing, or schedule for a matter—or even the very goal of the matter itself, such as acquiring a company.

Wherever possible, it is important to identify and analyze project risk prior to committing to a budget. For example, an overly aggressive plaintiffs' counsel can increase the cost of a case. If a key witness is not available for deposition or trial, that circumstance can change the course of the litigation dramatically. In an acquisition, if due diligence uncovers information that substantially delays the closing, the fees can be much higher. The process of analyzing project risk begins with the identification of possible project risks when developing the project charter. However, all information is not necessarily available at the time the project charter is developed, so this will need to be reevaluated when developing the project plan to determine if there are any additional risks. Categories of project risk are shown in figure 5–11 below.

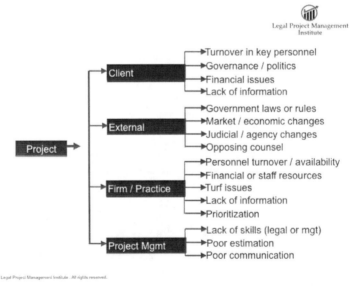

Figure 5-11
Possible Project Risk Categories

Once a list of all possible project risks has been developed, each risk must be analyzed in terms of its probability of occurrence and of its potential impact if it does occur. Some risks would have a very high impact if they occurred, but their probability is so low that it might be worthy to discuss with the client but not factor the actual risk into the budget. Others may have lower impact, but are so likely to occur that a cushion should be built in the budget for them or, at least, discussed with the client to explain how the budget will be affected if they occur. Figure 5–12 shows an analysis of risks for a litigation matter.

The following are examples of potential risks in a litigation defense matter from an actual implementation with a legal team:
- *Number of plaintiffs and co-defendants represented by other parties*
- *Level of aggressiveness of plaintiff's lawyers*
- *Extent of liability exposure - number of incidents, severity of injury, etc.*
- *Document intensity*
- *Claims of spoliation/fraud*
- *Corporate negligence issues*
- *Punitive Damages claims*

The following are examples of high probability risks that could result in increased expenses in a Litigation matter:
- *High probability risks (and included in the budget)*
- *Standard discovery disputes*
- *Multiple rounds of foreseeable discovery*
- *Vigorous adversary who will not cooperate*
- *Court-ordered hearings that are continued*

Lower probability risks (that might be discussed with the client but most likely not included in the budget):
- *Time related to compilation, processing, or review of electronically stored information (ESI)*
- *Bankruptcy filing*
- *Removal/remand to/from federal court*
- *Discovery of significant undisclosed facts that require a material amendment to the pleadings, etc.*
- *Appellate work, whether interlocutory or after final judgment*

Figure 5-12
Risk Analysis for Litigation Matter

After all risks are identified and analyzed, the information gathered should be plotted on the Probability/Impact Matrix, also called a Risk Analysis Matrix (figure 5–13). This matrix is done in the project planning phase but is continually evaluated by the responsible lawyer, project manager, or project team to determine if any factors have changed as the matter proceeds or information is gathered. For example, opposing counsel might take action in a way that is unlike their behavior in past matters, or there may be information uncovered in the discovery process that identifies several additional risks that were not evident at the outset of the matter. A template for evaluating risks is provided as appendix 3–6.

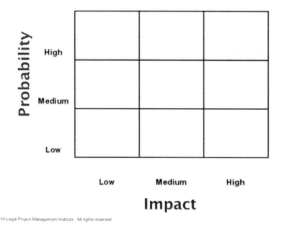

Figure 5-13
Probability/Impact Matrix

The Probability/Impact Matrix is a very powerful tool, especially for lawyers. First, lawyers typically are risk averse. In addition, for decades, as described in chapter 1, lawyers in private practice have not had to take many risks regarding the scope of the work, the timing, how long it took to complete tasks, the complexity of the work, etc. because clients paid by the hour and if the matter took longer, the lawyers simply billed more time and made more money. Now that clients expect their outside counsel to assume some or all of the risks associated with the cost of the matter, it is incumbent on the law firm to analyze the risks and determine which risks it will assume (e.g., as part of a fixed fee price or "not to exceed budget") and which risks it will not.

Without doing a thorough risk analysis, many lawyers are providing their clients with scope of work documents and/or budgets that have long lists of assumptions attached. Essentially, they are trying to "assume away" any risks to them. In the authors' experience, clients do not like this approach. Clients expect their outside counsel to assume some appropriate risks. In fact, as mentioned earlier, if a lawyer is hired on the basis of representing that it has significant experience in a particular area, the client expects that the lawyer will understand many of the risks involved and the ones that commonly occur should be incorporated into the budget.

Once the risks are mapped on the Probability/Impact Matrix, the next step is to evaluate the risks that are high probability and high impact and those that are medium or low probability but high impact. The client may expect high-probability risks to be included in the budget since they are often using the initial budget to make decisions like whether to pursue the matter (defend the lawsuit rather than settle, make a deal, etc.). If it is likely to occur (i.e., high probability) and the risk was not included in the budget, the client may not be pleased if they rely upon, what they assumed, was a thorough and realistic budget. On the other hand, in a competitive bidding situation to win the work, one could use the risk analysis in discussing the bid with the client to explain the probability of the risk and why it is not accounted for in the budget. If one does not do that and includes the costs associated with the many risks in the budget, the estimate one provides may be way more than the competitors'. Risks that are low probability but could have a high impact should be explained in the assumptions in the scope of work statement. Essentially, the process of analyzing the risks helps determine which risks to factor into a budget, which to discuss with the client, which to minimize or mitigate in some way, etc.

As an additional level of risk-management planning, some organizations list the risks by their risk score (a weighting of the probability versus impact) and keep them on a list that they review regularly at project team meetings. This list is called a risk register. Risks, which are uncertain possibilities, sometimes become "issues" in the project, meaning the risk is now a reality that the project manager or team will have to deal with to meet the matter objectives.

After a lawyer or project manager has analyzed the risks (in terms of probability versus impact), he or she should use the matrix to do two tasks: (1) develop a risk register with a ranking of the risks and (2) determine which risks will be assumed in the budget provided to the client and which will not (and therefore, need to be discussed with the client). The matrix is an important tool for communicating with clients about the types and levels of risk, making determinations who assumes the risk and finally, determining if there are any mitigation or other strategies to deal with the risk. After the plan is developed, in the Executing Phase, it is not uncommon for multiple risks to become reality. When that occur and the risk is now an "issue," it is tracked using an issues log.

Maintain inventory of all risks identified—updating probabilities, impacts, and controls if changes occur.

Risk Analysis Worksheet by Risk ID				
Risk ID	Risk Scenario	Probability	Impact	Score
A	Key stakeholders unavailable during project definition phase	2	3	6
B	Opposing counsel submits an unexpected motion	2	2	4
C	Loss of key team member in middle of project	1	3	3
D	Critical expert witness unavailable when needed for preparation	1	3	3
E	Change in key contact at regulatory agency	2	1	2
F	Scope changes require additional tasks and resources	2	3	6

Focus attention on the risks with the highest indices.

Risk Analysis Worksheet by Score				
Risk ID	Risk Scenario	Probability	Impact	Score
A	Key stakeholders unavailable during project definition phase	2	3	6
F	Scope changes require additional tasks and resources	2	3	6
B	Opposing counsel submits an unexpected motion	2	2	4
C	Loss of key team member in middle of project	1	3	3
D	Critical expert witness unavailable when needed for preparation	1	3	3
E	Change in key contact at regulatory agency	2	1	2

Figure 5-14
Giving Risks Priorities—A Risk Register

Change Management Plan

During every legal services engagement, things change that affect the course of the matter. The most common types of changes are those in scope, timing, and resources available, one or more of which typically occur during the course of significant legal matters. Some examples of each of these types are as follows:

- changes in the *scope* of the work
  - o changes in the client organization, opposing counsel, governing bodies (judiciary, regulatory agencies, etc.)

- o changes in information available (e.g., bad facts are uncovered in discovery, the volume of e-discovery changes as information is uncovered, or due diligence raises issues for additional negotiations in an acquisition)
- changes in the *resources* available, and/or
  - o lawyers leave or are unavailable (on other projects)
  - o client involvement in handling legal work increases or decreases
  - o key witness disappears or is otherwise unavailable or uncooperative
- changes in the *timing*, as a result of
  - o filing deadline changes
  - o opposing party requests
  - o market conditions for financing and equity offerings
  - o competing business opportunities
  - o judicial schedules

One tool for dealing with changes is the Change Impact Table below (figure 5–15). The way to implement this chart is to identify the changes likely to occur and the possible impact on the project from each change (e.g., could make the matter take longer, cost more, affect the client's business negatively, affect employee morale, etc.). Once the first two columns have been populated, the last column is used to identify a strategy or approach for dealing with the change if it occurs.

Possible Change	Possible Impact	Approach
1.	1.	1.
2.	2.	2.
3.	3.	3.
4.	4.	4.
5.	5.	5.

Figure 5–15

Change Impact Table

The change management plan may include specific steps to be taken if identified changes occur or it may simply be a process for documenting changes when they occur and obtaining necessary approvals (such as for additional costs to be incurred on the matter). Some companies have change order processes and require their outside counsel to submit change orders if any aspect of the matter changes, such as alternative resources need to be deployed on a matter (different staffing than was originally expected) or a delay results in the timing and/or budget changing. Even if clients do not require a formal change order process, lawyers should err on the side of communicating with their clients anytime there are significant variations from the project plan and/or budget estimates or quotes. The BakerManage™ process includes a change control log that is used to guide lawyers to communicate changes and record team recommendations and client approvals. The BakerManage™ change control process is described in more detail in chapter 9.

Goal of Project Planning

In summary, the project plan should guide a lawyer or project team in the active management of the matter through completion. Developing a project plan and managing the matter using it should result in many benefits. A primary benefit is more efficient delivery of legal services. Types of efficiency are discussed in more detail in the side bar which follows.

Increased Efficiency—A Key Goal of Project Planning

Everyone involved with LPM talks about "efficiency." But what does "efficiency" really mean? There does not seem to be much concrete discussion of what that concept does and does not mean and how to achieve it.

We want to start a dialog about this subject so that we all have a similar understanding about what we mean by "efficiency" and so that we avoid some problems developing because of different assumptions about the term.

What "efficiency" always includes:

1. planning-related efficiency: the elimination of wasted time due to inadequate communication about (1) what tasks need to be done by what members of the team and what tasks don't need to be done or are being done by others, (2) how long each task is expected to take based upon the scope of the task, and (3) the sequencing of the work so that tasks are done in the order that eliminates overlap or the need to redo certain aspects of the work.

2. timing-related efficiency: starting and stopping tasks requires more time than proceeding on a consistent timetable. The obvious example is preparing for a trial; if the trial is postponed, a good deal of the preparatory work will need to be repeated. Drafting documents can be similar; if you start

Carl W. Herstein and Joseph R. Sgroi are the chief value partner and the associate chief value partner, respectively, at Honigman Miller Schwartz & Cohn LLP. They are responsible for leading initiatives to enhance and expand the value provided to Honigman's clients. This piece was created for use in Honigman's "Sustained Effort" program, part of its ongoing LPM implementation.

drafting a set of documents and then have to put them aside for several days or more partway through, you will probably end up repeating some of the work. Another aspect of timing-related efficiency is doing work on an urgent basis. While sometimes urgency does improve focus, eliminates stops and starts, and keeps the scope of work limited to that which is essential, it often results in poor sequencing of tasks, duplication of effort because more people need to be involved than is ideal, and miscommunication because of stress and lack of time.

3. process-related efficiency: having forms, checklists, precedents, and technological tools in place avoids the need to create things from scratch, or to think through problems that have already been solved. This is why knowledge management is an important aspect of LPM.

4. staffing-related efficiency: using the appropriate personnel for the tasks at hand. We know that those with experience doing tasks usually do them in less time; we also know that those who are specialized have knowledge and skill that eliminates the need for research or analysis, at least to a degree. It is also the case that people who are used to working with one another, understand each other's expectations, and communicate well with each other, will get things done more quickly. Using an ideal combination of people can increase efficiency. On the other hand, poor delegation skills, inadequate communication, personal friction, inexperience, or a mismatch of talent and skill to the task, will result in considerable waste and duplication of effort.

What "efficiency" can often include:

1. goal-related efficiency: understanding the client's ultimate goal, and how we can best achieve that goal, is also a critical aspect of efficiency. For instance, it may be the case that the client's goal is to settle a litigation matter early to, among

other things, avoid negative publicity. Understanding that goal and designing a strategy—and the allocation of effort and time—consistent with that goal leads to the greatest opportunity to achieve an efficient result. However, it should also be recognized that pricing certain goals, such as early settlement, can be counterproductive if things don't work out as planned. In that case, for example, work that might have been done more efficiently early in the case but was postponed in the hope of avoiding it altogether may have to be done later in a hurried and poorly planned manner.

2. cost-/benefit-related efficiency: limiting the scope of work to those tasks that are most likely to have appropriate results. This is a very tricky concept of efficiency but is one of the most often discussed, usually in the context of the lawyers "who leave no stone unturned." What is "efficient" in any given case will usually vary depending upon the amount of money (or other thing of value to the client) that is at stake, the client's tolerance for risk, the particular lawyer's judgment about the risk, and the client's goal. The more that is at stake, the lower the tolerance for risk. This is what we are talking about when we speak of proportionality. It is also true that some lawyers (and clients) will evaluate the same risks differently. It is critical that the lawyer and the client be in agreement on the level of risk that both are comfortable with and that the lawyer and the law firm be similarly in agreement. That is because our reputation rests on providing a certain level of service. Even if a particular client is comfortable in taking risks that we as lawyers recommend against, in some cases, we as a law firm should not agree to proceed in that way.

What may be included in "efficiency" but is best thought of in a different way:

3. Does "efficiency" equal "speed?" While we all think of efficiency as equating at some level with getting things done more quickly (as with the "efficiency experts" of old who were always pictured with a stop watch, timing how long it took to complete a task), we submit that this is a problematic way of looking at efficiency in terms of legal project management. All things being equal, the person who can write the same letter or brief or contract more quickly but with the same quality as another person is more efficient. But while we should all strive to work with focus and diligence, it is a simple fact that some people do things more quickly than others. With a group of highly talented lawyers, people with similar experience will probably accomplish tasks at a reasonably similar pace. Although those who work more deliberately may want to consider ways to accomplish the same amount in less time, they should not do so at the expense of the quality of their work.

4. Does "efficiency" also mean spending less time on a task? Assuming that all the other elements of efficiency mentioned above have been taken into account, we would say that the answer in almost every case should be no. If the scope of the task is clear, proportionate to the problem, and necessary to the overall work, it should be done well—meaning to the standards of excellence of the firm. This can be a difficult point to address because one often sees statements like "we need a Chevy and not a Cadillac" for this task, or the work on this task only needs to be "good enough." The problem stemming from statements such as these is that it is hard to know what they mean. Making choices about what work should be done in light of the potential risk and cost makes sense; not taking the time to write a careful agreement does not. If a quality problem comes up later, no one will accept the argument that the work was only intended to be "good

enough," while if a problem comes up due to a scope of work that was reasonable under the circumstances, it at least ought to be.

There are no "right" or "wrong" answers regarding the definition of efficiency in legal organizations or to how it is used. There are so many possible ways to define it or achieve it so the authors wanted to offer some "food for thought" for legal organizations who want to consider different types of efficiency for which to strive.

Chapter 6

Budgeting for the Matter

Budgeting a Legal Engagement

While chapters 6 and 7 are predominantly written for a law firm's perspective, in-house counsel may find it helpful to understand how budgeting and pricing are approached by law firms. Although legal project management (LPM) is a relatively new approach to planning and managing legal matters, lawyers have been developing budgets for clients for decades. In most matters, budgets were only developed at the request of a sophisticated client, whether a corporation with internal budget constraints or an individual with limited resources. The resulting budget prepared by the lawyer was typically based on high-level phases of the engagement with lump-sum figures for the cost of each phase. Rarely, if ever, did lawyers provide detail regarding the tasks to be completed, the resources to perform those tasks, or the time to complete the tasks.

In the past few years, more and more clients are not only asking for but demanding detailed budgets for the engagements. Additionally, alternative or value-based billing has become more popular. This has placed increased pressure on lawyers to not only develop more budgets (and reliable ones) but also to demonstrate that they are able to manage to them. At the same time, many lawyers lack the information infrastructure resources to provide lawyers with assistance to develop accurate budgets for the following reasons:

- Many lawyers plan their matters based upon intuition and are without historical information regarding the time required to complete tasks or the potential variables that can increase time estimates.
- Due to the fact that most legal matters have historically been "block billed,"[1] most law firms cannot provide their lawyers with historical data and comparisons to assist lawyers with budget development.

Lawyers are not trained to price their matters, and some firms do not have sufficient numbers of dedicated business analysts to assist lawyers with this time-consuming process.

- Since budgeting is a relatively new focus of clients and most lawyers do not have a lot of experience doing it, lawyers are required to expend a considerable amount of time mapping out the case and estimating the cost of their services.

---

1. "Block billing" describes a method for identifying the work performed by a timekeeper who is billing by the hour. Rather than distinguish each task and the amount of time spent on the task, all the tasks performed in a single day are lumped into a narrative with a total number of hours for time spent that day. The narrative may be short clauses describing the work or may be a lengthy narrative supporting a significant amount of time spent during the day. This type of time entry makes it difficult to determine how much time, over the course of an engagement, is attributable to phase or tasks.

Law Department Notes

For decades, general counsel have had to demonstrate the value of the legal department—as a staff function that supports the core business. Of course, in their supporting role, lawyers help generate revenue; improve corporate balance sheets through recoveries and handling matters that reduce liabilities; creatively structure transactions; and enhance their company's strategic position in a market. Nevertheless, legal work is seen as a *cost* of doing business—it is a means rather than the end itself. From an accounting perspective, legal expense is a general and administrative expense (SG&A on the profit and loss statement) and, as such, must be managed.

Even when it is cost-effective to handle work in-house, the general counsel is under pressure to increase productivity and keep costs down. The legal department is not exempt from corporate hiring freezes and the general counsel may be limited in their ability to add new staff to meet the growing demands for legal services. This translates to in-house law department budgets that are fixed, frequently cut, and sometimes slashed drastically during the course of the year. In-house counsel, consequently, shares these pressures by demanding budgets from third-party service organizations such as law firms, which make up nearly 50 percent of a typical department's budget.

Historically, clients relied upon a lawyer's judgment and guidance with regard to the costs of legal engagements. Now, clients have become more sophisticated and data on pricing has become more readily available through companies like TyMetrix, Serengeti, and Peer Monitor, to name a few. As a result, budget development has become more critical for client satisfaction both from the standpoint of providing a realistic expectation of cost and as a tool for both the client and the lawyer to gauge management of the matter. Whether developed at the request of a client, for a response to a request for proposal, or for an alternative fee arrangement, budgeting is a powerful tool that can help a lawyer cement trust with the client. Budgeting is also a process now expected by in-house counsel for the matters they manage using a mix of internal and external resources.

Law Department Notes

Larger corporate legal departments, with their own chief operating officers and dedicated finance staff, have resources to focus on the cost of legal services and the management of law firms. Even so, many in-house lawyers resist relying upon these resources and may not invest the time to learn effective budgeting and resource management techniques since they still view their primary role as practicing lawyers.

Nevertheless, both in-house and outside counsel must figure out how to contain the cost of legal work, which, without the right skill set, is a particularly frustrating endeavor. For example, how can in-house counsel analyze the budgets they request from law firms without acquiring the financial and management skills to do so? To reach common ground on costs, legal service value, and business objectives, all lawyers must commit to acquiring these basic business skills.

LPM provides lawyers with a roadmap to develop a detailed and reliable budget. Drawing upon this roadmap, in this chapter, a six-step LPM budget approach will be outlined. The following approach is based upon the methods applied by Baker Donelson, using its BakerManage™ system. This six-step budget approach also tracks the techniques described in chapter 4 (Engaging Phase) and chapter 5 (Planning Phase). Additionally, chapter 8, covering the Executing Phase, demonstrates how the budget can be managed and monitored for a client and lead to innovations in alternative fees.

Six-Step LPM Budget Approach

The six-step process for budgeting developed by Baker Donelson includes the following steps:

1. Confirm the scope of the engagement.
2. Identify the framework for budget development and tracking.
3. Create a "playbook" for the matter.
4. Identify resources, rates, and time estimates.
5. Identify task-level assumptions, risks, and constraints.
6. Collaborate with the client and implement the budget.

Each of the steps is detailed below.

Step 1—Confirm the Scope of the Engagement

Earlier chapters of this book have been dedicated to the process of legal project management that includes development of a scope or statement of work, essentially identification of the detailed scope of the engagement. Even if an estimate does not implement all of the steps recommended in this book, at a minimum, the scope of the engagement must be clearly defined. A clearly defined scope protects both the firm (by clearly communicating the constraints of the budget) and the client (by confirming the work to be completed for the proposed budget).

Historically, the "scope" of the engagement was typically captured in engagement letters, in a firm's file opening system as the "nature of the matter," or in legal team memorandums as a one-sentence or one-paragraph explanation of the lawyer's or firm's role in the engagement. Articles and guidelines for engagement letters typically advise that it should include the duties of the firm, lawyer, and client; identify what the lawyer will do for the client; identify the nature of the matter (usually in one sentence—i.e., "serve as local counsel in the above referenced matter"); name the expected adverse parties; and identify how fees and expenses will be charged. However, many engagement letters are not very detailed. Even this level of detail and a corresponding phase-level fee estimate cannot set reasonable expectations with the client regarding the details of the services to be provided. Instead, a more detailed scope document should be prepared that is consistent with the Engaging Phase outlined in chapter 4 or in the BakerManage™ system as the project's Development Phase.

In LPM implementations, most lawyers do not intuitively understand the additional information that should be developed for "scope." In short, the BakerManage system captures the following information for a scope statement:[2]

- detailed explanation of the matter—for example, if a transaction, the proposed parties and structure; if litigation, a summary of the significant claims or defenses
- the client's strategy and objectives
- the client's expectations with regard to cost and expenses
- factual, legal, or procedural assumptions that are being made by both the client and the lawyer
- based upon the lawyer's prior experience or analysis of the matter at hand, identification of potential risks related to the particular case and potential increased costs resulting from lags in time, unavailability of resources, e-discovery, an uncooperative or vigorous opposing counsel
- any issues or responsibilities that are outside the scope of the firm's responsibilities and will be addressed by the client.

This information will form the foundation for the budget to be developed. Without this level of detail, budget estimates will typically be based upon the lawyer's and the client's prior experience in (or worse just recollection from) similar cases and may fail to accommodate the unique aspects of the case at hand or sufficient detail to be accurate. Additionally, as mentioned in chapter 4, defining out of scope is as important as defining what is in scope.

---

2. This information is also discussed in detail in chapter 4 (Engaging Phase) and chapter 5 (Planning Phase).

Law Department Notes

As employees of a company and members of the bar, in-house counsel's interests lay both in fostering the company's success (e.g., financial, reputation, compliance with law) and in providing quality legal services. The very notion of in-house counsel emerges from this dynamic: companies need lawyers who are both well versed in legal work and have a deep understanding of its relevance to their company's culture, structure, operations, strategy, and goals.

When the cost of legal services diverges from a company's focus on financial discipline, there will be conflict between lawyers and clients. The company may want to pursue a transaction or they may be faced with a litigation defense that has not been factored into the company's budget for legal services. The legal work will be done, but the legal department will also have to address budgetary constraints. The in-house counsel must find ways to address the issue of containing legal costs, which sometimes means passing pressure onto outside counsel who "blows" the department budget. However, if the legal department looks at all the work for which it uses law firms and has a good sense of this overall portfolio, then it is in a position to coordinate with firms to reallocate work, so the total law firm spending is consistent with the corporate budget.

Law firms may be required to cut matter budgets that are on track or to defer work to another financial reporting period or budget year. When law firms are asked to cooperate with General Counsel's corporate financial constraints, it may create tensions between the legal team and the client.

Law Department Notes (cont.)

Defining the scope and managing client expectations requires an understanding of the strategy and objectives for legal work—what is the business rationale? In other words, the legal work is derived from a business objective, which indirectly ties into the corporate financial statements. On the profit and loss statement, a business goal may be demonstrated in revenue generation (e.g., acquiring income-producing assets such as a business, contract, or intellectual property license) or cost reduction (e.g., divesting property, discontinuing operations, or reducing staff). On the balance sheet, the business purpose may be to reduce liabilities (e.g., reflected in reserves as a result of the settlement or disposition of litigation).

Litigation defense may seem to be only peripherally related to a business purpose. However, litigation is grounded in relationships between parties *who have a business arrangement*, whether it is a contract or a commercial connection. It is only when this relationship fails, and after all other consensual options are exhausted, that litigation emerges. Once litigation is in full force, lawyers tend to think of it as a legal battle. It is essential to remember that a business relationship—and a business issue—is at the heart of all litigation. The thread that connects strategy to objectives to financials to all forms of legal work, including litigation, is the client's business rationale.

To make it easier and quicker for lawyers to develop the scope of a matter, it is helpful to develop a standard set of questions that have been customized for each matter type or practice area, as described in chapter 5. Then, these questions can be used as a starting point for each new matter in that area. For example, it can be very effective for those lawyers who handle particular matter types or those in the same practice group to brainstorm to identify the key questions that should be asked of a client when undertaking that type of matter. Beginning your conversations with new or prospective clients with these additional questions can aid in development of more reliable budgets. These brainstorming sessions can also be used to identify assumptions and risks related to budgets developed for a particular practice area.

The level of scope detail outlined above also helps lawyers to satisfy their ethical obligation with regard to any matter responsibilities that are assumed by the client. As provided in chapter 11, under the ABA Model Rules of Professional Conduct, a lawyer may limit the scope of the engagement as long as there is "informed consent." ABA Model Rule 1(e) defines "informed consent" as "the agreement by a person to a proposed course of conduct after the lawyer has communicated adequate information and explanation about the material risks of and reasonably available alternatives to the proposed course of conduct." If a lawyer does not clearly identify this, he or she should not be surprised when the client assumed certain work was in scope for the budget provided—which is a cause of many law firm write-offs today.

Step 2—Identify the Framework for Budget Development and Tracking

As previously stated, due to lack of specific training, time, and resources, most lawyers will fall back on intuition to estimate the potential costs of representation. However, accuracy demands that more thought and structure be placed on legal budget development. For example, when evaluating the cost to construct a home, consumers rarely rely on the contractor's lump sum estimate. Instead, most homeowners want to understand the hard costs (labor and material) and soft costs (not related to a particular task, such as professional services, overhead, etc.). Additionally, more sophisticated consumers may want to identify the costs of phases such as lot clearing, pouring the foundation, framing, roofing, and electrical in order to ensure that funds are available. Similarly, in many types of legal engagements, the lawyer-client relationship will improve if the client has a better understanding of cost of the phases of the matter, and then, if requested, the cost of tasks to be performed.

The phases of a matter may be mapped by either significant scheduling milestones or by significant deliverables as described in chapter 5, when developing a Work Breakdown Structure or template for the work. For example, in a transaction, phases may be based on milestones such as structuring, drafting, and negotiating documents; due diligence; financing; and closing. In a litigation matter, scheduling milestones may track the court deadlines for answer, discovery, motions, pretrial, and trial. To budget for a matter means breaking the work into some level of component parts—high level or more granular as described in chapter 5.

When legal organizations first started to develop budgets, they could only do it by evaluating prior matters in their own organization because there were few tools for budgeting and matter analysis and little public data existed. Today, there are other alternatives. Regardless of the type of matter, a starting point for developing a budget is to decide what framework will be used for budgeting—whether it is developed within an organization, the company whose budgeting tool is being used, or another source. One resource lawyers have used extensively in developing budgets was developed by the ABA, Association of Corporate Counsel, and PriceWaterhouseCoopers, called the UTBMS "task-based billing codes" or simply task codes.

Step 3—Create a "Playbook" for the Matter— Assignments or Subtasks

Identifying the framework for budget development and tracking has become easier because the UTBMS codes are an excellent resource for launching a budgeting program. The next step of budget development can be more challenging and time-consuming but, once completed, creates a powerful resource for accurate and reliable budget development. This step is a budget template that can also be used as a "playbook" for managing a team and for communicating with clients all of the work that is required in a legal engagement. This is particularly important when the client may not be experienced in a particular type of legal work.

A "playbook" is a notebook containing the description and diagrams of the play of a team. It is most often associated with a football team, where plays are run in sequence to achieve the desired result—scoring a touchdown. The management of a legal engagement is very similar, although most lawyers carry their "plays" around in the heads and rarely communicate them in detail to team members. Imagine the success of a football team if the quarterback was the only member of the team who knew the entire play and individual team members were given their assignments but never understood each play's objective.

The accuracy of a legal budget can be improved by the development of a legal playbook from both the standpoint of identifying all of the steps and resources to complete the engagement and from the standpoint of providing the team with a clear understanding of the budget's objectives. This is also called a Work Breakdown Structure and schedule, as described in chapter 5. Many lawyers already possess resources that can be used to create a playbook, either in the form of checklists or outlines identifying all the deliverables at various stages of the engagement. These resources can be used to expand the UTBMS phase and task codes into additional steps to manage the engagement.

As described in detail in chapter 14, some firms have also taken this evaluation a step further to identify methods to streamline and implement efficiencies in all processes composing the management of a particular legal engagement. This technique is called process mapping and is used to identify those components of a legal engagement that can be standardized to promote quality, consistency, and efficiency. The process map can be developed by gathering all of these team members in a room and walking through the management of the engagement from beginning to end. By evaluating the legal matter step by step, including the administrative and the legal processes, a detailed playbook can be developed that provides the entire legal team with clear goals and objectives.

Step 4—Identify Resources, Rates, and Time Estimates

After the assignments or tasks have been identified in the matter playbook, the next step is to develop the schedule to correlate resources and time estimates to each task or subtask. This step in budget development first requires identification of the method of the budget estimate—that is, either top-down or bottom-up estimating.

Top-down estimating is essentially backing into a budget number. This may be required if the client has a reasonable idea of the cost of the legal engagement. The approach may also be required when responding to a request for proposal that includes historical information on legal spend. The top-down approach identifies a fixed price for the engagement and distributes that amount across the phases in the matter, then further distributes phase amounts to the tasks to be completed in that phase. Then, finally, allocates task amounts to the resource assignments. Time estimates are then developed by dividing the allocated dollar amount by the rate for the assigned resources. While these time estimates may not be representative of reality and are not as reliable as bottom-up estimating, top-down estimating is faster in most cases. In addition, even if it is not representative of the true costs of the matter, law firms are sometimes using top-down estimates because they have no choice if they want to win the work but to prepare a quick and not granular budget. The downside, of course, is this has been the cause of many law firm write-offs as mentioned earlier.

Bottom-up estimating starts at the resource assignment level and identifies the realistic amount of time required to perform an assignment or subtask. By applying rates to the time estimates, a budget amount can be developed at the lowest levels of the budget. These figures are then consolidated for all subtasks and rolled up into a total budget for a task, and likewise rolled up for a total estimate for the phase, and ultimately the matter. This method of estimation is generally the most reliable but is also the most time-consuming, because it requires budget estimators to consider the appropriate resource and appropriate time necessary for the completion of all assignments. In addition, because there are often tasks in a matter that are done simultaneously, budgeting at the bottom-up level can result in a higher budget than would actually be required.

Regardless of whether the person developing the budget is using top-down or bottom-up estimating, the assignment of resources and time estimates are closely intertwined. As a result, when applying either budget method, the estimator should identify who customarily performs the work. Most lawyers can estimate whether certain tasks are more appropriately performed by assistants, paralegals, junior, mid-level, or senior lawyers. When the budget or playbook is actually implemented, the lawyers will have a plan in place to staff their matters, and, depending on availability, time may be adjusted up or down depending on the availability of resources. For example, a lower-rate resource may require more time to complete the task.

Once the resources are identified, the time estimates for tasks can be developed in at least two ways. First, it can be done through the professional judgment of the managing lawyers based upon their prior experience. Second, it can be developed through evaluation of the amount of time required on prior matters. To the extent prior matters are utilized, the estimator should give consideration to the unique aspects of the case that may have impacted the time spent on the matter. These estimates should also be vetted with the proposed resources and other professionals (e.g., head of that practice in the legal department or firm) to ensure that the estimates are reasonable.

Step 5—Identify Task Level Assumptions, Risks, and Constraints

During the scoping process, general assumptions and risks were identified concerning the planning of the engagement. The next stage of budget development is to evaluate the assumptions, risks, and other constraints at the task and subtask level. Once identified, it is critical to communicate this information to the client so that all parties have reasonable expectations regarding the budget estimate.

Assumptions, risks, and constraints are defined in detail in chapter 4, but for purposes of review, they are defined as follows:

- **Assumptions** are factors known to be true that must be validated throughout the project life cycle. These can be factual assumptions regarding the matter that, if proved untrue, could result in expansion of the scope and additional tasks to be performed. These can also be procedural or strategic assumptions regarding the opposing party's litigation or negotiation tactics, which are factored into the tasks to be performed and the time estimates provided.
- **Constraints** are factors that limit the options available when handling a matter such as timelines, deadlines, client requirements or demands or regulatory issues.
- **Risks** are variables that may be encountered during the matter that could increase the estimated cost of tasks and assignments or otherwise cause a lawyer or project team not to meet the client's expectations.

The objective at this stage of estimating is to identify any assumptions being made with regard to the budget. Figure 6–1 illustrates some examples of budget assumptions:

<u>Transaction</u>

    Phase - Negotiation, Revision, Responses

        Task - Negotiate Purchase Agreement

            · *Resource: Shareholder*
            · *Time Estimate: 12 hours*
            · *Assumption: The parties previously prepared a term sheet that identified material terms and only non-material terms remain to be negotiated.*
            · *Assumption: The parties will only review and revise the agreement 3 times.*

<u>Litigation</u>

    Phase - Discovery, Disclosure, Inspections, Inquiries and Evidence

        Task - Depositions and Fact Witness Statements

            · *Resource: Shareholder*
            · *Time Estimate: 24 hours*
            · *Assumption: only 4 fact witnesses will be deposed each taking approximately 6 hours.*

Figure 6-1
Sample Budgeting Assumptions

Step 6—Collaborate with the Client and Implement the Budget

One of the primary goals of legal project management is transparency and better communication with the client. For this reason, it is critical to communicate the basis for the estimates, assumptions, and potential risks. Some lawyers may be uncomfortable providing a client with a more in-depth level of detail. They may provide phase-level estimates without the detailed tasks, subtasks, or resource assignments. However, lawyers implementing a legal project management approach who have shared the detail with clients are typically pleasantly surprised with the results. Clients have more confidence in the estimate, are better equipped to communicate the basis for the costs within their own organization, and have confidence that the managing lawyer has set clear goals for the legal team that will result in controlled costs. In fact, law firms are increasingly expected to communicate this level of detail with sophisticated clients. Moreover, law firms who have provided this type of detailed budgeting have won work as a result of the added level of communication and the transparency of this approach.

Additionally, it is critical to communicate the budget to the legal team. Communication of the budget and playbook will help to ensure that each team member understands the time allocated for his or her assignments and that there is no duplication of effort among team members. This will also help the legal team understand the importance of managing the work to the budget and notifying the managing lawyer when task or subtask estimates are not accurate or are exceeded.

In conclusion, project communication about budgeting avoids later problems. Almost every lawyer has experienced the repercussions of communicating an inaccurate budget figure to a client. The result is often uncomfortable conversations at the conclusion of the matter (if not before) regarding why the cost exceeded the estimate. This can result in write-offs or write-downs, whether by request of the client or initiated by the law firm to prevent damage to the relationship. Alternatively, a well-prepared budget and detailed communication about the budget with the client are insurance that the lawyers have clearly communicated the limitations (i.e., out of scope, assumptions, and risks) inherent in the budget. In the event a variable changes, both parties have agreed and understand that budget adjustments might be necessary (assuming the work is not priced based on a fixed fee or portfolio approach that includes changes like these). Following this six-step approach outlined above will help avoid problems and enhance lawyer-client relationships.

Development of Task-Based Billing

In the mid-1990s, in response to years of block billing using narratives that typically included a wide range of tasks, U.S. law departments and insurers desired to better understand the services provided by outside counsel. A joint committee composed of the ABA, the Association of Corporate Counsel, and PriceWaterhouseCoopers was formed to create a unified and standard billing system. The work of this committee resulted in a task-based billing system that permitted a more detailed classification of services performed. Templates were developed for litigation, project (transactions), counseling, and bankruptcy. Later, the LEDES oversight committee[1] assumed responsibility for maintenance of the system and developed what is now identified as the Uniform Task Based Management System (UTBMS). This committee later created additional templates for patent, trademark, and e-discovery.[2]

The ABA or UTBMS codes have been adopted by firms in the U.S. as the framework for billing and budgeting of matters. Other firms have further refined these codes to develop unique practice-specific

---

1. LEDES™ refers to the Legal Electronic Data Exchange Standard, which is a file format used by the legal industry for exchanging electronic billing and matter information. The 1998 standard requires the following information and other information to be included in formatted file: invoice date, invoice number, client ID, law firm matter ID, invoice total, billing start date, billing end date, invoice description, line item total, line item date, line item task code, line item activity code, timekeeper ID, timekeeper name, timekeeper class, and other information. The LEDES oversight committee has assumed responsibility for maintenance of the UTBMS codes (formerly the "ABA codes," which were jointly developed by the ABA, ACC, and PriceWaterhouseCoopers).

2. *See* UNIFORM TASK BASED MGMT. SYS., www.utbms.com (last visited Nov. 3, 2013); *Litigation Code Set*, ABA, http://www.americanbar.org/groups/litigation/resources/uniform_task_based_management_system/litigation_code_set.html (last visited Nov. 3, 2013).

codes after years of use of the ABA or UTBMS codes. For those legal organizations embarking on LPM and more rigorous budget development and tracking, the ABA or UTBMS codes are an excellent starting point for developing your organization's customized code sets. The transaction code set is relatively simple and includes 16 components. The litigation code sets divide a litigation matter in to five phases that include the following:

- Case Assessment, Development, and Administration
- Pretrial Pleadings, Interlocutory Applications, and Motions
- Discovery, Disclosure, Inspections and Inquiries, Evidence
- Trial Preparation and Trial
- Appeals

Within each of these phases, work is further elaborated into two to eight tasks. These case outlines can be used to either prepare estimates for the work to be performed at a high level or to develop specific assignments and resources to be completed for each task.

An additional benefit of budgeting utilizing task-based billing is the ability to automate budget tracking. Once phase and task codes are created, timekeepers log their time by phase and task code in order to track the work against the matter plan. If the firm applies task-based billing consistently across the firm, it will also promote the creation of a database of historical information that can be used for future budget development and comparison for like matters. With each completed engagement, lawyers and firms will increase the accuracy of their budget development.[3]

The code sets developed by the ABA and LEDES oversight committee include a Phase Code, Phase Description, Task Code, Task Description, and a definition explaining the type of work anticipated to be allocated to each code. The definitions help to ensure that time is being input accurately by all timekeepers. Implementation of these

---

3. Most billing systems also accommodate "matter types" which are used to distinguish the types of matters within a certain practice area such as those developed by the North American Industry Classification System, http://www.naics.com/.

codes may reveal that some lawyers rely upon their secretary to select the correct code. This practice can result in inconsistencies and inaccuracies, because the lawyer or other timekeeper doing the work is in the best position to correctly categorize the work. If the codes are being used to manage budgets and track historical performance for future budgeting purposes, timekeepers must be encouraged to make their own code selections, whether on a paper timesheet or in the time-entry software.

The benefits of task-based billing are illustrated by the following example of a block-billed time entry for a litigation matter representing two and a half hours of work:

Correspondence regarding meetings next week; review litigation budget from prior case as format and commentary for AAAA budget; telephone call to J. Smith with XX Healthcare regarding discovery responses, left message; telephone call to P. Hooper, lawyer for Industrial regarding need for documents and identity of individual to sign; correspondence to J. Smith regarding questions to be answered for discovery responses of AAAA; correspondence to S. Richards regarding contact for AAAA; telephone conference with S. Richards regarding history of AAAA; prepare correspondence to Client, S. Richards regarding same; prepare correspondence to T. Simpson of WWWW (formerly AAAA) regarding need to discuss discovery responses of that defendant.

Using the UTBMS Litigation Codes, the following is a breakout of the same two and a half hours of work:

(L110 Fact Investigation/Development)—(.4)

Correspondence regarding meetings next week; telephone conference with S. Richards regarding history of AAAA;

(L150 Budgeting)—(.3)

Review litigation budget from prior case as format and commentary for AAAA budget

(L120 Analysis/Strategy)—(.2)

Correspondence to S. Richards regarding contact for AAAA; (L310 Written Discovery)—(1.4)

Telephone call to J. Smith with XX Healthcare regarding discovery responses, left message; telephone call to P. Hooper, lawyer for Industrial regarding need for documents and identity of individual to sign; correspondence to J. Smith regarding questions to be answered for discovery responses of AAAA; prepare correspondence to T. Simpson of WWWW (formerly AAAA) regarding need to discuss discovery responses of that defendant.

Chapter 7

From Budgeting to Pricing the Matter

Once a budget is developed, many law firms automatically adopt it as their price for that matter. In doing so, they are unconsciously making a number of pricing decisions. Better outcomes can be achieved if important decisions related to pricing and budgeting are made strategically and not based simply on the cost of the work. The budget is essentially a firm's "cost" to do the work (assuming costs of personnel, running of the organization, and profit margins are included in the budget developed through hourly rates). The price, on the other hand, may be higher or lower than the budget or cost.

To understand these pricing decisions, one needs to:

1. understand the components of a price and
2. explore different approaches that can be used to set the price of a product or service.

Colin Jasper contributed this chapter. Jasper consults to leading law firms in the United States, the United Kingdom, and throughout Asia. As the director of Jasper Consulting, his focus is on assisting professional service firms to create greater value for their clients and to capture a fair share of that value for themselves. His articles have been published in a range of journals and magazines, including *Professional Service Firms Journal* and the *Journal of the Professional Pricing Society*.

The Components of a Price

First, the price of any product or service has two components—a price level and price structure. The price level is *how much* the firm charges (e.g., $5,000 or $6,000). The price structure is *the means by which* the firm charges (e.g., fixed fee, hourly rate). The primary pricing structure used within the legal profession has been hourly rates for many decades. However, over recent years, clients have increasingly sought alternative fee structures or "value-based fees" such as fixed fees and success fees. Once a firm has created a budget (what the matter will cost), decisions still need to be made regarding how much to charge (i.e., fee level) and the basis upon which to charge it (i.e., fee structure).

Approaches Used to Set Price Levels

There are three common approaches used by organizations to setting prices:

- **Cost-plus pricing.** This approach looks at the costs involved in producing a product or service and adds an appropriate profit margin to create a price. Provided a cost is estimated accurately, one will make money on every "sale" or in the case of lawyers, matter.
- **Market-based pricing.** The second approach to pricing comes from a very different perspective. This approach takes the view that, in a competitive market, it does not matter how much it costs to produce the service but what is important is what price it will take to win the work. With market-based pricing, one should identify competitors, assess what they are charging, and, depending on the relative market position, determine a price. If the quality of what is being offered is slightly superior, then the price may be slightly more. Notice that with this approach to pricing, one does not need to develop the cost of the offering. However, one must have additional services or products to offset any money lost on market-based price for that service or product.

- **Value-based pricing.** The third approach to pricing is the most talked about and the least understood. The heart of value-based pricing is to understand how much the product or service is worth to a client, then set the price accordingly. The more valuable the service, the more one may charge. If the client perceives an offering to be less valuable, one must lower the price. The price is based on the client's perception of value.

While different views exist regarding which is the most appropriate method of pricing, contemporary pricing theory in the business world and with major professional services firms is very clear. All three methods must be evaluated for each engagement. In setting a price, one cannot ignore costs, competition, or the client's perception of value. While this makes pricing more complicated, lawyers will achieve better outcomes if it is able to take a more integrated approach.

The Limitations of the Hourly Rates

When creating budgets for matters, most law firms multiply the amount of time required from each timekeeper against their hourly rate. While this has historically been a time-efficient means of creating an estimate, the limitations of using this approach for pricing should be understood. While hourly rates may have been established taking into account the cost of individuals (i.e., by applying a multiple to their salary costs), market pricing (i.e., what hourly rates the firm's competitors are charging), and value to clients (i.e., how much does the firm think its clients will accept), it implicitly assumes that these do not vary from one matter to the next. This clearly is not the case, as these points below illustrate:

- For matters that involve high leverage (i.e., few hours of partner time relative to other timekeepers on the matter), a much higher profit per partner (PPP) is achieved than for low-leverage matters. In these instances, a higher discount may be offered and still be highly profitable to the firm (when assessing profit based on PPP).

- Likewise, when a partner is working alone on a matter, these matters may be profit destroying, even at full recovery. That is, the revenue obtained may fail to cover the partner's compensation.
- Firms often describe matters that do not result in full recovery as unprofitable. Given that hourly rates include a profit margin, this is not necessarily the case.
- The nature of competition can vary considerably between matters. For some matters the firm is asked to submit a competitive bid, often competing against with other firms prequalified as capable of doing the work. In these situations the firm may need to discount rates to compete and win the work. For other matters, the client may only be dealing with one firm with certain capabilities, relationships, or experience on related matters. When this differentiation occurs, the firm may capture a greater return.
- Some matters are highly valuable to clients (such as major litigation and significant mergers and acquisitions activities), while other matters may be regarded as more routine (e.g., leasing, small-scale disputes). This will impact how much the client is willing to pay for the matter. As a provider of services, it is inappropriate for the firm to ignore these factors when developing a price. The firm should not recommend that the client spend more on a matter than it is worth. Similarly, where the firm believes that a matter may have significant financial impact on a client, it is the firm's responsibility to guide them accordingly and ensure they invest in the appropriate amount of legal work.

The Pricing Decisions

Having created a budget for a matter, the firm must evaluate the two pricing decisions:

1. what fee structure to use
2. what fee level—that is, how much to charge

Clearly the decision regarding fee structure impacts how much to charge. If the basis of the fee is hourly rates, the firm can provide a budget as the fee estimate. This is a best guess regarding the price of the matter using the agreed-upon hourly rates. If, however, the firm is charging based on a fixed fee or a success fee, then the amount the firm charges should be higher to account for the risk assumed by the firm. With hourly rates, the client assumes all the risk associated with uncertainty. With fixed fees, the risk is now transferred to the firm. As in every type of business, with risk should come reward. Many clients will say they do not mind paying a premium for certainty—although in today's cost-conscious market, it may only be a slight premium.

In such cases, rather than automatically adopting the budget as the price (irrespective of the fee structure), the firm should identify the most appropriate fee structure and then decide on the appropriate fee level. It is these decisions that are the difference between budgeting and pricing.

Fee Structures

The range of fee structures available to firms is limited only by the imagination. The most common types of fee structures are:

- **time-based billing** - including hourly rates, blended rates, discounted rates, and volume-discounts.
- **fixed fees** - including a fixed price for a defined matter, task-based fees, and retainers.
- **success fees** - including project success fees, contingency fees, and performance-based billing.

- **hybrid structures** - including capped fees[1] (hourly rates to a defined fixed fee) and collars[2] (hourly rates with performance billing around an agreed estimate).

The key difference between these fee structures is who carries the risk associated with the conduct of the matter. With time-based billing, the client assumes all the risk associated with uncertainty (unless there is a cap on the matter). If it takes longer, the client pays more. If it is completed more efficiently, the client pays less. With fixed fees and success fees, a significant amount of risk is transferred to the law firm.

In relation to fee structures, the key challenge for law firms and clients alike is to jointly determine the most appropriate fee structure for a given matter or set of matters. Given that time-based billing has been so dominant over recent decades, insufficient thought has been given to when alternative fee arrangements are more appropriate. The better a firm understands when to use each fee structure—and how to proactively manage them—the more successful the firm will be in collaborating with clients to design the most preferable fee arrangement. Outlined below is a broad indication of when each fee structure is appropriate and, equally important, the different ways matters should be managed depending on the fee structure chosen.

---

1. Some matters are more difficult to predict and the client may be more comfortable with a billable hour arrangement, but the client may still want to cap its legal spend. In this situation, capped pricing is used and the client and the law firm agree that the fee will not exceed a certain dollar amount. Bonuses can also be factored into this approach. If the matter settles before the fee cap is reached, the client only pays for the time it took to settle. MICHAEL D. BURKS & DAVID A. RUEFF, VALUE-BASED LEGAL SERVICES (NOT JUST ESTIMATING HOURS AT STANDARD RATES) (Sept. 2012).

2. Collars may either be collar up or collar down. A collar up implies that there is an amount set as the budget. If the firm goes over the limit, it cannot charge for any additional work until it reaches a certain amount over the limit (the collar amount). At that point, the law firm is allowed to charge a certain percentage of the amount over that limit. Example: The budget limit is $1 million. The collar is $100,000 and the percent is 60 percent. The amount from $1 million to $1.1 million cannot be billed. If the firm goes to $1.2 million, then it can bill 60 percent (40 percent discount) of the $100,000 that is over $1.1 million, or $60,000. A collar down is the same as a collar up only it also rewards the firm for being under the limit. Example: If the firm only bills $800,000, it would get a bonus of $60,000 or 60% of the difference between $800,000 and $900,000. *Id.*

The Use of Time-Based Billing

While some commentators feel strongly about eliminating the billable hour, there are clearly times when it is appropriate. Clients will often wish to engage a firm to assist them on a matter, but no one—neither the firm nor the client—can accurately scope what is required to complete the task. This may be in an adversarial situation, where costs depend on the behavior of the other party. It may be at the beginning of a dispute, where the desired or possible outcome of the matter are not certain. It may be in a broader relationship context where the client wishes to appoint firms to a panel without defining the specific volume of work that will be involved. In each of these situations, firms and clients should reach agreement on pricing at the beginning of the process, even though it may not be possible to cost the work. This is the ideal situation to use time-based billing.

When using time-based billing, it is equally important to both parties that it is managed appropriately. To this end, firms must acknowledge that clients don't like surprises. When time-based billing is used, estimates should be provided and be used to actively manage the work within the estimate. The two biggest criticisms from clients regarding hourly rates are (1) the law firm's lack of accountability (i.e., it is the client's position that a firm bills what they think the matter requires) and (2) the disconnect between cost and value. This leads to surprises and unexpected invoices, which, in turn, lead to fee disputes, client dissatisfaction, and write-offs. When work is being done using time-based billing, estimates should be provided using the techniques identified in chapters 4, 5 and 6. Additionally, the work should be managed against the estimate, and the client should be kept up to date regarding costs and necessary adjustments to the budget prior to incurring the costs, as described in chapter 7.

The Use of Fixed Fees

Fixed fees are appropriate when the work can be clearly scoped in advance and can be reasonably controlled by the firm. Some clients seek fixed fees even when significant uncertainty exists regarding the scope, but such a fee structure may not be in the client's best interests. While law firms may agree to a fixed fee, the fee should account for the uncertainty. Clients may prefer the lower time-based estimate and assume the risk. Similarly, when the law firm anticipates that the scope may be expanded, it may not be in the best interest of either party to enter into a fixed-fee arrangement. While some clients may ask for a fixed fee to cover an entire litigation matter, clients rightfully retain the option of settling at any point. When using a fixed fee for an entire litigation matter, they might jointly agree to a process to reduce the price if the matter does not go to trial. In many cases, hourly rates can be used to determine the alternative price, but this requires the firm's timekeepers to continue to record their time on the matter, even if operating under a fixed fee.

When fixed fees are being used, it is essential that both parties agree at the beginning of the matter what is included, and excluded, from the scope. In addition, it is essential that firms track work against the agreed scope and actively manage variations. Work on variations should not commence without providing the client with a price for the variation and having obtained prior approval from the client to proceed.

The Use of Success Fees

Success fees are appropriate when:

1. the lawyer's contribution is key to success,
2. the client would like the outside lawyer's outcomes aligned with its own, and
3. the lawyer can reasonably evaluate the chances of success.

Also, success fees ideally are used in an area involving multiple matters handled on a fixed fee basis to even out the risk carried by the outside counsel on any given matter.

When entering into success fee arrangements, both parties should discuss a broad range of possible outcomes and their implications. Without this agreed-upon understanding, clients may refuse to pay the agreed fee for a successful outcome because it occurred in a much faster time frame than expected. In addition, a lawyer may seek to withdraw from a matter prior to completion because the ongoing costs no longer justify the expected fee, assuming they can ethically do so.

The Use of Hybrid Structures

The greatest innovation in fee arrangements is the use of hybrid structures. This requires breaking down a matter or bundle of work to determine which parts should be charged based on time, fixed fees, success fees, or a combination.

Clients expect that their lawyers are familiar enough with the cost of their services to craft arrangements that meet the needs of the client and the matter. In many cases, clients are surprised and disappointed when they realize that their lawyers do not know how to cost or price their services. Historically, this has been due to the fact that clients and firms rarely collaborate to clearly identify the scope of the proposed pricing arrangement at the outset. Without absolute clarity regarding what the client is trying to achieve through an innovative fee arrangement, the lawyer is shooting in the dark and often unable to price in a manner that is fair and attractive to both sides.

In today's market, most clients seek greater certainty in the cost of legal services, but this means different things to different clients:

- To some, it means the quoted price will not be exceeded (solution: fixed fees on all matters).
- To some, it means greater consistency from one matter to the next (solution: task-based fees[3]).
- For others, greater certainty means achieving the client's internal budget targets (solution: retainer).

When a client requests an alternative to time-based billing, the firm must partner with the client to evaluate the nature of the matter and to explore the broad range of fee options in order to identify which meets the client's specific needs.

---

3. A fixed fee for a matter requires the specific scope of the matter to be agreed upon. Negotiating the scope for the matter is just as important as negotiating the fee. By comparison, task-based, or event, fees relate to projects that are replicated rather than one-off matters (e.g., preparing commercial leases, managing small litigation claims). Task-based fees are typically negotiated once and applied multiple times.

Comparing Hourly Rates, Estimates, Fixed Fees, and Capped Fees

The most commonly used fee structures are hourly rates, estimates, fixed fees, and capped fees. Despite the frequency with which these fee arrangements are used, many lawyers fail to understand the implications of the choices they make. Some lawyers resist providing capped fees because the risk is one-sided. But if the cap were high enough, why wouldn't one agree? Below is an example of how the fee structure can impact the fee level.

The example in figure 7–1 includes an assessment of the cost of an engagement based on hourly rates. In the example, the best guess is that the matter will cost $50,000; however, if things go smoothly, it may cost $45,000 or even as little as $35,000. On the other side, if things don't go the as expected, the fee may increase to $55,000 or even as much as $65,000.

- If the fee is based upon hourly rates, the client pays based upon the time necessary to complete the engagement times the firm's agreed hourly rates. The agreed price is effectively the curve.
- If the fee is based upon an estimate, the best guess is $50,000. It may be more, it may be less, but this is the best guess. The firm can manage the client's expectations by continually updating the client about increases or decreases based upon activity in the matter.
- If the fee is capped, the cap should be $65,000. Anything less will be a discount off of the expected hours (possibly in addition to already discounted rates).
- If the fee is fixed, it should be slightly above $50,000. At $50,000, the expected return is exactly the same as a fee based upon hourly rates. On some occasions the firm may make a premium, on other occasions the firm may incur a loss. But the difference between hourly rates and a fixed fee is the firm's assumption of risk—and, as mentioned earlier, with risk comes reward. How much above $50,000 depends on the firm's assessment of the risk. If the risk is high, the firm may increase the fixed fee to $55,000. If the risk is low, the firm may accept a slight increase to $51,000.

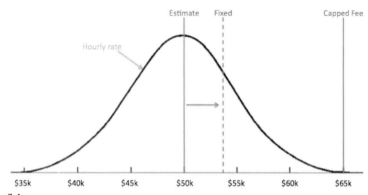

Figure 7-1
Comparing Hourly Rates, Estimates, Fixed Fees, and Capped Fees

Dealing with Uncertainty

One of the biggest challenges to pricing legal services is dealing with uncertainty. If the fee is based on hourly rates, the client bears the uncertainty. However, clients are requesting estimates at an increasing rate and are treating these estimates as capped fees in order to ensure their lawyers behave in an accountable fashion. Whether providing estimates, fixed fees, success fees, or capped fees, one must assess the various uncertainties that exist and determine how to deal with each from a pricing perspective.

Chapter 5 outlined how to create a risk management plan, including

- identification of project risks and
- the preparation of a Probability/Impact Matrix.

Once these steps are undertaken, the firm can make appropriate decisions regarding how to deal with project risks, see figure 7–2. If the impact is low, regardless of probability, the firm would generally assume this risk in its pricing model. If the impact is high but the probability is low, the firm may explicitly exclude this risk through the stated assumptions. If the impact is high and the probability is high, the firm should collaborate with the client to identify the most appropriate way of dealing with the risk. While the client may want the firm to be responsible for the risk, the client may not want to pay a higher price associated with the firm including this within the scope.

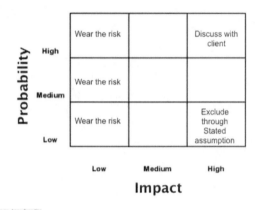

Figure 7-2
Probability/Impact Matrix

Other strategies for dealing with project risks include:

- **hybrid fee structures.** Carve certain risks out of the price and charge the client on an hourly rate basis if they occur.
- **staged pricing.** Provide a price only for what is known and visible now, with an agreed-upon process for providing a price for subsequent stages.[4]
- **conducting research.** Prior to pricing a matter, undertake research to determine if the risk does exist, and if so, quantifying its impact.

---

4. If the entire matter cannot be predicted with a level of certainty, the matter may be estimated by phases. This approach permits the firm and the client to enter into an alternative fee arrangement for preliminary phases of the case, with an agreement to reevaluate later phases when more facts and information are available regarding the opposing party's strategy. Matters that often fit into this category are litigation, mergers and acquisitions, and large commercial transactions. Clients benefit from this approach because they do not bear the risk of a windfall to the firm if the matter settles early before completion of all the phases. Conversely, the firm benefits, because they are not at risk for a fixed fee prior to gathering valuable information during discovery and motion practice. Burks & Rueff, *supra* note 2.

The bottom line is that it is imperative to determine the cost of the matter (as outlined in previous chapters on budgeting) and then, decide what will be the price of the work. This will depend on whether you will attract the work at a price higher than, the same as, or perhaps only lower than the cost/budget. As mentioned above, cost is only one of the factors to consider in setting price.

Law Department Notes

Before the practice of law began its transformation into a business (circa 1980s), it was appropriate for law firms to render simple bills "for services rendered," which the client paid without much inquiry. When the learned profession of lawyers organized into large law firms, there was a parallel change in the role of in-house counsel to manage law firms. Legal departments grew in size and their scope of responsibility increased. Based on legitimate needs to understand details and support bills, clients began to challenge fees for legal services.

One might ask: What happened to the legal profession in the U.S.? Where is the lawyer as counselor, the professional who places the client's interest first? Although the industry has indeed changed, the lawyer-client relationship has not—and cannot sustainably be a mere vendor-supplier relationship. Trust is the basis of the lawyer-client relationship, which requires transparency. If either party engages in tactics that undermine trust or transparency, cost-effective client representation is rendered impossible.

Chapter 8

Executing the Matter

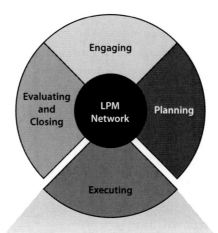

Activities & Processes
- Monitor work completion, adherence to matter strategy
- Aquire resources to perform work assignments (tasks)
- Modify matter timeline
- Communicate with stakeholders early and throughout the matter
- Manage scope changes with client and other key stakeholders
- Monitor against budget

Deliverables & Work Product
- Updated matter timeline
- Updated deliverable lists and budget
- Change requests

Figure 8-1
The Executing Phase of LPM

The Executing Phase includes two main aspects: *doing* the legal work for the matter and *managing* the legal work as a project. Lawyers leading major engagements have always spent time managing their matters; historically, though, they did not spend much time on the role of managing a project. The market today requires a greater level of proactivity to meet clients' expectations for efficiency and effective management of their work, and clients increasingly expect lawyers use the same project management tools that they do.

The four most important parts of the Executing Phase, in addition to doing the legal work, are

- dealing with changes in scope ("scope creep") because, inevitably, changes will occur in the course of the matter (at least in larger matters);
- managing communications with the various stakeholders throughout the engagement (this is covered extensively in chapter 9);
- managing the project team, including setting up your project management information system for the matter;
- monitoring budget to actual.

Each is covered below.

Dealing with Scope Creep

At the individual lawyer level, the most difficult of the five areas of the Executing Phase is dealing with "scope creep." Scope creep refers to uncontrolled changes or continuous growth in a project's scope. Definition of scope at the outset is important to develop and manage a budget—to ensure all parties to the matter are on the same page and that no party is taken advantage of. Scope creep is difficult for lawyers because it often means they need to have a difficult or awkward conversation with clients regarding changes in the engagement/project. For example, historically, the lawyer defined the matter and budget at the outset of the matter. Then, something changed and the lawyer simply did the necessary work to deal with that change without communicating to the client the impact of the extra work on the budget or cost of the matter. Then, at the end of the engagement, the client sometimes believed it have been overcharged when it is in excess of the original budget, when in fact, the lawyer provided additional services that were not included in the scope for the original budget. The lawyer and client were not on the same page, and conversations about these gaps can be awkward, or worse.

Part of the Executing Phase is dealing with scope changes pursuant to the change management process developed during the Planning Phase. It is important that changes are documented and the resulting effect on the project objectives is monitored. This information will also be invaluable at the end of the matter, when it comes time to identify lessons learned from this matter, because this will provide guidance on dealing with future projects.

For lawyers managing a project, there are several courses of actions when changes occur. These include the following:

- "Just do it." Do the additional work or handle the matter despite the changes that will make it cost more, even if the additional costs cannot be charged to the client. Since it is difficult to have conversations with clients about costs and resources, "just do it" is a common lawyer approach. However, it is important to let clients know that the firm has absorbed the cost so that they can recognize and appreciate the added value the firm is providing.
- Fully discuss with the client the changes required and the impact they will have on the matter. Collaborate with the client—both the in-house counsel and the business unit that owns the matter—to determine how the work and the costs will be allocated among the law firm, the legal department, and the business unit. Decision trees as illustrated below can be used for this communication.
- Refuse to change the scope of the assignment without a change in cost (if that is possible) and risk alienating the client (i.e., take only the agreed-upon six depositions in the original budget and not the 15 that are now deemed necessary). This last option is rarely a viable one for lawyers. The lawyer should also evaluate the ethical considerations associated with refusals to address additional issues that arise in the representation. ABA Model Rule of Professional Conduct

1.2(c) provides that a lawyer may limit the scope of the representation if the limitation is "reasonable" under the circumstances and the
client gives informed consent.

It is also important that changes are discussed with the project team or designated decision-making individuals so that changes are not ignored when
they happen or avoided until it is too late when either the law firm must
write off its bills (for outside counsel) or in-house lawyers have incurred
costs that are unsupported by their organization.

In addition, tools such as decision trees can be used by lawyers to explain
changes that might occur or are occurring to their internal or external
clients. Figure 8–2 is an example of a decision tree where a particular company expects its outside counsel to provide on each case that helps them
look at their portfolio of matters in terms of total risk and costs (legal fees
and settlement). Figures 8–3 and 8–4 are examples of decision trees used
to explain to the client the possible paths the matter could take (and the
resultant impact on cost and timing).

Lawyers are increasingly using tools like decision trees, Gantt charts, and
other visuals to explain to clients the potential risks, changes, and other
factors that can affect the outcome and costs of a matter.

Figure 8-2
Decision Tree Example for Litigation

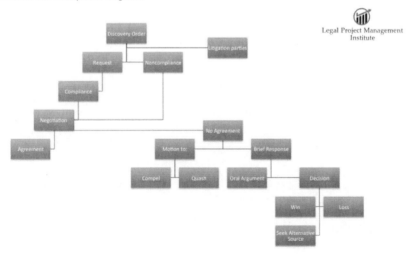

Figure 8-3
Decision Tree Example for Discovery

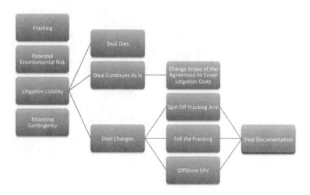

Figure 8-4
Decision Tree Shows Impact of Fracking Uncovered in Due Diligence

Law Firm Implementation Example

In the BakerManage™ Execution Phase, a Change Control Log is implemented to track changes to the original Statement of Work. The content of the log includes: (1) a detailed description of the issue or change; (2) a description of the team recommendation to the client including impact on the project plan elements (i.e. budget and schedule); (3) record of the client's decision; (4) confirmation that the decision has been implemented; and (5) confirmation that any necessary updates to the project plan (i.e. budget and schedule) have been implemented. This information is recorded in the Change Control Log (see below) and is made accessible by the project team and the client.

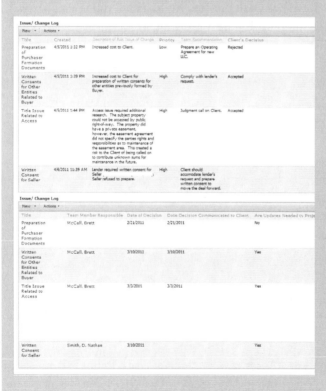

Managing the Project Team

Managing the Project Team has three main elements:

- regular communication within the project team
- keeping everyone on the project team on track regarding assignments (for which many organizations use RACI charts—see chapter 5).
- effective delegation and supervision of the project team.

Regular Communications Within Project Team

One of the goals of project management is controlling the work to meet client expectations, as outlined in the project plan. Control can only be accomplished if there is regular communication with the project team to ensure that they are adhering to project requirements and are made aware of changes. The communication plan prepared in the Planning Phase (and updated regularly) should include regular team meetings and other communication processes (such as use of e-mail distribution lists for what are sometimes called "working group members" on a matter) to accomplish this goal. The recipients of project communications typically include key stakeholders in the law firm, the law department, or the client.

A sample agenda for regular project team meetings would often cover the following areas:

- Discuss status of timeline and deliverables.
- Discuss budget versus actual costs incurred.
- Discuss any change requests/orders.
- Discuss action items and issues.
- Identify any changes to the stakeholder analysis.
- Identify any changes to the risk management plan.
- Update communication plan.
- Update the overall project plan.

The project manager, or someone designated, should keep track of the new or revised information on all of the topics above, update any team members who missed the meeting, and post the information on sites such as intranets for the matter team or extranets for the client, matter team and others (such as co-counsel).

"Regular" meetings may be weekly, biweekly, or monthly depending on the particular matter. For example, in a very large matter with many individuals on the internal team and a lot of changes occurring to the matter, the team may meet weekly or more frequently for a short meeting to keep the project on track. For a matter that has a very protracted timeframe for resolution, the team might meet just once a month or quarter. The timing should be based upon the number of people working on the matter, time and price sensitivity, complexity and duration of the matter, and reporting requirements of the client, among other factors.

Other project management methodologies, such as Scrum (described in chapter 18), recommend even more frequent and structured team meetings. The Scrum approach to project management (which is commonly used in nonlegal projects) calls for a daily "scrum"—a very short yet intense meeting, to encourage communication among team members regarding progress on project tasks and goals for completion prior to the next meeting. Where the matter justifies it, daily meetings are an excellent way to ensure that project team members are regularly exchanging information about new developments or changes. The meetings do not have to last more than a few minutes and can be used to update all team members on the prior day's activities and the team's goals for completion of work for the upcoming day. This may not be feasible for lawyers who manage multiple cases in a single day, but more regular team meetings, whether daily, every other day, or weekly, is advisable for any case.

These project meetings might be led by the partner in charge of the matter, a designated project manager, an associate fulfilling many of the project manager roles, or another member of the project team. The agenda might change with the needs of the engagement, but can be used to ensure that the entire team is made aware of changes and that the project plan is being regularly updated, including the budget. Chapter 17 describes the different roles needed to implement project management in a legal organization and the role of a project manager on a matter.

Keeping the Team on Track: Assigning and Managing Resources

As described in chapter 5, a common tool for managing a project team, including client stakeholders, is a RACI chart. This is a tool for ensuring that everyone on the project team, and sometimes within the client organization as well, knows who is responsible for each task or deliverable and what everyone's role relative to that task or deliverable is. To track the relationship of a stakeholder to a task or deliverable, one should incorporate a Resource Assignment Matrix or RACI chart, an example of which is in figure 8–5. It is significant to note that only one person at a time can be assigned to an accountable, *A* position. The list of deliverables from the work breakdown structure is used to generate the RACI chart and then the assignments are made by the project manager or within the project team. RACI charts are used to assign lawyers and staff and to manage the flow of work. They are also used to ensure appropriate communication with all of those involved in developing the deliverables.

Deliverables	Client	Partner	Sr. Attorney	Associates
Engagement Letter	I	A	R	I
Budget/Costs	I	A	R	I
Pleadings	I	C	A	R
Brief	I	A	C	R
Trial Prep	C	A	R	R

Figure 8-5
Sample Resource Assignment Matrix/RACI Chart

Though a RACI chart provides a clear visual representation of the work to be done and by whom, law firms have different ways of managing resources on their matters. Some firms have highly sophisticated centralized workload assignment systems so that, for every new matter, individuals are assigned tasks based on their current workload, their skill set, the next level of developmental need (as many firms outline in their benchmark or competency models for younger lawyers), and more. Associates are sometimes afraid to say no to any partner requesting assistance. A formal work allocation or assignment system can ensure associates are busy but not unnecessarily overworked in the early years of their career. However, such a system will require a significant cultural change in many law firms. There are still partners, who see associates making significantly more money than they did as a young lawyer, and are of the belief that associates should be prepared to work long hours.

Other firms still use a "free agency" system of managing associates—that is, any partner can grab an associate for a matter, regardless of that associate's other work, interest (or lack thereof) in that area of work, etc. However, for effective project management (and more profitable and happier lawyers), a more formal approach is desirable (i.e., one that identifies who is available for the team and when, what their skill sets are, who is responsible for what).

Law Firm Implementation Example

In regards to assignment of tasks, BakerManage™ utilizes a Share-Point Schedule to manage work assignments, responsibilities and assignments. An example of this tool is shown below.

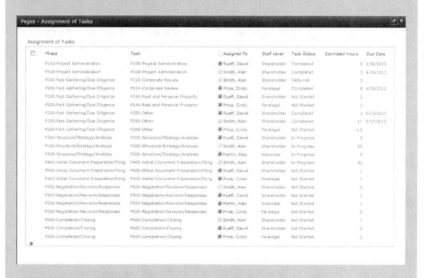

As one can see from this included example, each phase of action for the legal matter is broken down to the individual or staff level handling that action. It also includes the hours to be allocated to this action per staffing level/individual. While this covers the main aspects present in a RACI chart, and resembles the example provided regarding firms utilizing workflow capabilities, BakerManage™ provides a deeper understanding of the workload surrounding the task, itself, and also allows this aspect to be paired with other important project management tools, such as budgeting.

Figure 8–6 is an example of the staffing assignment process in Thomson Reuters' Engage™ planning tool, which is used as a lawyer or project manager builds a budget in Engage. The possible resources for a given matter are listed and their pricing or cost information can be used to build the budget, as well as to identify who is responsible for which tasks in the matter.

Figure 8-6
Staffing Assignment Process in Engage™

Another legal project management (LPM) tool by ERM Legal Solutions called Lean4Legal™ has a screen called Engagement Manager (figure 8–7) that displays information needed to monitor details of an engagement at a high level. These and other tools described in appendix 2 provide an efficient way for a lawyer or project manager to monitor and manage a matter throughout the Executing Phase. Each provides dashboard-type screens that can enable the user to have information about the matter's budget, staffing, task completion, deliverable status, and more, depending upon the tool and the information the user wants to track or monitor.

Figure 8-7
Engagement Manager Screenshot from Lean4Legal™

Monitoring Budget to Actual

Throughout the management of the matter in the Executing Phase, the lawyer in charge of the matter or the project manager is also monitoring the project budget against the actual time and expenses spent. This could be considered a part of the Executing Phase or, when it is done to determine the final budget vs. actual numbers, a part of the Evaluating Phase to be discussed in chapter 10.

Many law firms now have tools that enable them to compare the budget they created at the outset or a revised budget of a matter to the time and expenses actually spent. This enables the project manager, responsible partner, or others involved with managing client expectations to have timely information to:

- communicate with the client stakeholders responsible for the budget;
- make decisions when the scope or other parameters of the matter are changing; and

- change staffing or other assignments, if necessary, for the next part of the matter so that they can stay on budget or minimize write-offs if it is a fixed-fee matter or cap.

The images below are screen shots from various budgeting tools providing a visual representation of a matter's budget-to-actual comparison. These types of reports can enable a responsible lawyer or project manager to monitor progress during the course of the matter.

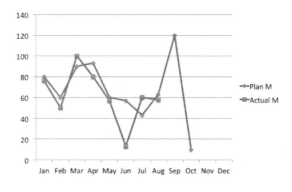

Figure 8-8
Budget Versus Actual – Flextronics Acquisition of ABC Corp.

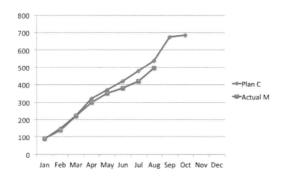

Figure 8-9
Budget Versus Cumulative Actual

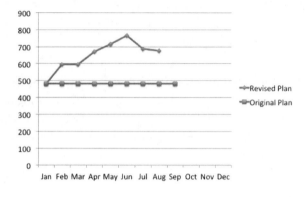

Source: ERM Solutions

Figure 8-10
Total Budget Change by Month

THOMSON REUTERS ENGAGE™

| Matter | Phase |

Calendar　People　Budget　**Budget To Actual**　Disbursements　3rd Parties　Management

As of 12/13/2011

View Period		Hours	Fees	Disbursements	Total		
Matter Total ▾	Budget	10,961	5,062,695	453,700	5,516,395	Agreed Fee Budget	$4,525,262
	Billed	2	219	0	219	Budget Blended Rate	$462
	Unbilled	0	0	0	0	Actual Blended Rate	$125
	Remaining Budget	10,959	$5,062,476	$453,700	$5,516,176	Budgeted Leverage	1.18:1
						Actual Leverage	0.00:1
	Percent Remaining/Over				91.77%		
	Billing Adjustments	0	0	0	0		

View Time Range							■ Budget	■ Actual	■ Variance	
Monthly ▾	Amount	Hours								
	05/10	06/10	07/10	08/10	09/10	10/10	11/10	12/10	❯ ❯❯	
Case Assessment (L100)	$93,974	$246,013	$247,042	$239,550	$31,461					$918,740
	$0	$0	$0	$0	$0					$0
	$93,974	$246,013	$247,042	$239,550	$31,461					$918,740
Pleadings and Motions (L200)				$99,133	$249,370	$175,097	$114,510	$54,408		$741,950
				$0	$0	$0	$0	$0		$219
				$99,133	$249,370	$175,097	$114,510	$54,408		$741,731
Discovery (L300)						$2,243	$16,663	$57,419		$1,514,430
						$0	$0	$0		$0
						$2,243	$16,663	$57,419		$1,514,430
Pre-Trial and Trial (L400)										$1,887,575
										$0
										$1,887,575
Total	$93,974	$246,013	$247,042	$338,683	$280,831	$177,340	$131,174	$111,827		$5,062,695
	$0	$0	$0	$0	$0	$0	$0	$0		$219
	$93,974	$246,013	$247,042	$338,683	$280,831	$177,340	$131,174	$111,827		$5,062,476

Figure 8-11
Budget to Actual Screenshot

As shown above in figures 8–8 through 8–11, these systems have become more sophisticated over the past three years and not only depict budget to actual but also spread that information over the active life of that matter. This information helps the client to plan both logistically and financially. These charts provide information that help to determine performance, and also provide information regarding when signficant portions of funding will be required for the matter. BakerManage ™ includes a similar tool that can be displayed as either a ledger or as a Gantt chart (figures 8–12 and 8–13).

Budget To Actuals Over Time

Client:
Matter:

Phase	Total Budget	Total Actuals	3/1/2011 Budget	3/1/2011 Actuals	4/1/2011 Budget	4/1/2011 Actuals	Budge
(Unknown) - (Unknown)		$414.14					
T020 - Project Execution	$1,180.00						
T030 - Project Closure Phase	$330.00						
T110 - Project Development	$640.00	$630.00		$315.00		$315.00	
T210 - Corporate Review	$528.00	$2,182.00		$1,091.00		$1,091.00	
T220 - Tax	$1,337.00	$288.00		$144.00		$144.00	
T240 - Real & Personal Property	$2,759.50	$2,428.00		$1,214.00		$1,214.00	
T270 - Regulatory Reviews	$410.00	$1,536.00		$768.00		$768.00	
T410 - Prepare Title Commitment	$360.00	$1,718.00		$859.00		$859.00	
T430 - Prepare Closing Documents	$480.00	$8,592.00		$4,296.00		$4,296.00	
T440 - Prepare Closing Statement	$180.00						
T510 - Review Lender's Note and Deed of Trust	$240.00						
T511 - Amend Contract to add Correct Seller and changes	$480.00	$252.00		$126.00		$126.00	
T610 - Conduct Closing	$960.00	$672.00		$336.00		$336.00	
T620 - Disbursements from Escrow	$246.00	$1,000.11		$402.50		$402.50	

Figure 8-12
BakerManage™ Budget to Actual as Ledger

When lawyers first started using budget to actual tools, the tools only showed the percentage or actual dollars spent of the total budget. These tools have evolved to spread budgets over time and to show actual dollars spent over time. This added level of information helps clients forecast their legal spend throughout the fiscal year.[1] The budgeting tools for lawyers—both

---

1. The measurement that still remains to be captured is percentage of work complete. Traditional project management includes formulas based upon "earned value" (EV), which are used to estimate or forecast project performance. Project success measurements, such as cost variance (CV), schedule variance (SV), schedule performance index (SPI), cost performance index (CPI), and others use EV in their calculations. EV is the value of work completed expressed in terms of the approved budget for that work—that is, budgeted cost of work performed. It is calculated using the actual percentage of work completed times the budgeted cost of the project. This calculation is compared with planned value (PV), which is the value of work that should have been completed at a certain point in time and actual cost. In manufacturing

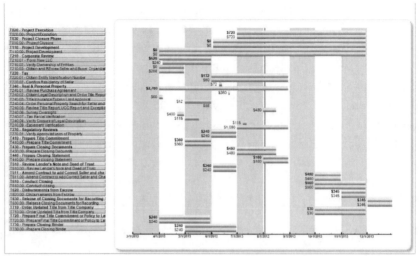

Figure 8-13
BakerManage™ Gantt Chart Budget Over Time

in-house and outside—are continuing to evolve and become more robust. This is evident in appendix 2, where the various LPM and/or budgeting tools that are available currently and their features are presented in greater detail.

It is important to note that these systems are only effective if lawyers and other team members enter their time on a regular basis, preferably daily. This is especially true if the client will have access to these reports. Once a client views this information, they will have an expectation that the information is current as of the date and time that the report is viewed. Firms

and other industries, the identification of actual percentage of work completed may be an objective measurement that can be easily identified. However, in professional services, like the practice of law, the measurement of actual percentage of work completed is subjective and more difficult to identify. Requiring lawyers to periodically estimate the percentage of work complete and input the estimate into a project management information system again would be subjective and would not result in a valuable measurement. Additionally, the comparison of budgeted to actual hours does not necessarily provide this measurement—because actual hours may not equate to the percentage of work completed. In the opinion of the authors, at this stage of LPM maturity, this measurement would require an additional level of administrative work on the part of legal teams and would not result in significant value. As LPM technology becomes more sophisticated, these types of measurements might become more feasible. In the interim, legal teams and clients can determine project performance by comparing budget performance to actual performance, which is typically at least accurate at the end of phases of work or completion of project deliverables.

implementing this type of system must be prepared to require legal teams to update their time on matters at the end of the day to provide the client with real-time information. This information provides clients with a current snapshot of their legal spend. Many clients prefer this type of system because it helps to avoid surprises and gives them confidence that the budget is being closely monitored by the law firm.

It must be noted also that this type of system does not replace monthly billing. Lawyers should not be concerned that they lose the ability to adjust billing or narratives at month's end. Since billing narratives are not shown in these types of systems, lawyers will continue to have the ability to make necessary adjustments to the bill prior to it being sent to the client.

The Role of a Project Management Information System in the Executing Phase

An important tool for monitoring and managing matters during the Executing Phase is a project management information system. A project management information system (PMIS) is a technological system used to collect and capture information related to a project. A PMIS is typically accessible by the entire project team and is used to "help [to] plan, execute, and close project management goals."[2] Today, Web databases, shared workspaces, and extranet sites sites can be used for a PMIS, as well as any of the publicly available tools shown in appendix 2. In application, PMIS systems may differ in scope, design, and features depending upon the project or the organization's operational needs and requirements.[3]

Setting Up the PMIS

After a project plan is developed, most of the legal project team's time will be spent on what is identified in the Legal Project Management Institute's model and BakerManage™ system as "executing." Prior to these phases, and after the project plan is fully developed and finalized, the team

---

2. *Project Management Information Systems*, WIKIPEDIA http://en.wikipedia.org/wiki/Project_management_information_system (last updated Jan. 9, 2013, 4:27 AM).
3. *Id.*

will have identified the information that will need to be tracked, managed, and communicated using a PMIS. The PMIS may be nothing more than a spreadsheet, shared document, or internal blog that is shared by the team to record status. However, it may also be more robust in the form of integrated software tools and data transfers to *pull* information necessary for evaluation of performance (such as time entry and financial information) and to *push* summary performance information to team members, the client, and other stakeholders.

Many detail-oriented lawyers already manage their matters with checklists, calendars, spreadsheets, form libraries, and informal meetings and conferences. A functional PMIS will enable the legal project team to also utilize these techniques in a shared environment, and to integrate team calendars for deadlines and availability, to have continuous access to the status of tasks and responsibilities, to monitor the status of the project budget, and, most importantly, to have a controlled and recorded mechanism for communication among team members, the client and other external stakeholders. The legal PMIS should also include the matter engagement letter, project plan, and information about changes resulting from new information or client-approved deviations from the original project plan.

Even if the firm has a template for a PMIS—such as a standard extranet for providing project information, the project plan and client's communication requirements may require customization of the template. For example, the goal with Baker Donelson's development of BakerManage™ was to create an "off-the-shelf" extranet that could be used in any matter, regardless of type. However, based upon the matter type or communication requirements identified by clients, such as reporting of key metrics related to their cases, the BakerManage™ extranet may be modified to provide the frequency, content, and accessibility required by clients.

Monitoring Performance

A key benefit of legal project management is a predictable fee and efficient resolution of the matter. Once the client's expectations and goals have been codified in the matter scope and tasks, the project budget and the communication plan (called the baseline in project management terms), the PMIS should be continually accessible to the project team in order to keep information up to date and current. The benefits of legal project management can only be achieved if the project manager or managing lawyer continually monitors actual performance against this baseline and identifies leakage (such as excess time spent on tasks with a budget constraint, expansion of scope, etc.) and deviations immediately.

Whether rudimentary or sophisticated, a legal organization's PMIS should enable the project manager to closely monitor it. The project manager should monitor to identify the need for curative actions, to take proactive steps to avoid material deviations from the plan, or, if necessary for the successful completion of the matter, to ensure that deviations are approved by the client.

- **Tasks.** The PMIS should be regularly updated with current information on the status of tasks, particularly when new issues arise that require additional tasks or when team members anticipate a deviation from planned tasks.
- **Calendar and Timing.** Based upon the project plan, the PMIS should identify delivery dates for various tasks. Team members should each be responsible for managing their tasks and regularly updating the PMIS with the status of their assignments to show conformance with deadlines. In addition, the responsible lawyer must be prepared to address internal constraints such as resource availability or unforeseen external constraints such as third-party delays or tactics by opposing counsel. Although these constraints may be unpredictable, by closely monitoring the status of tasks and timing, their impacts can be limited.
- **Budgets.** Typically, budgets are managed by evaluation of monthly billing statements. As stated in chapter 6 on budgeting, managing a project on a daily or weekly basis (versus managing by a monthly pre-bill), will greatly improve the firm's performance, because problems can be identified before significant excess time is logged against the client's matter. These deviations may be caused by inefficient team members, duplication of efforts, performance of tasks that are out of scope without client approval, or the failure to communicate client changes to the remainder of the team. To the extent supporting technology is available, actual billings should be shown in contrast to the budget to provide the project team and client with real time information on the project

team's performance. "Real time" for purposes of budget to actual billing comparisons will be based upon the frequency with which the project team members enters their time—whether it is daily, weekly. or monthly.

- **Team Performance.** The key to managing resources is communication. Communication can only be accomplished if the team regularly communicates either through meetings or through the PMIS. Clients may be reluctant to authorize regular team meetings out of fear that it will increase the cost of the matter.[4] The PMIS can provide an alternative by providing the team with a platform to update each other on performance. This will also provide a record for the project manager of the team's regular activity and conformance to the project plan. One key piece of information in the PMIS will be the estimated time for completion of tasks. This guideline can result in immediate savings to the client because team members will have a clear understanding of the project manager or managing lawyer's and the client's expectations with regard to the amount of time required to perform task.

Reporting Performance to the Client

Regular reporting to the client is a critical component of any LPM implementation. The status report should include quantifiable measures of progress and confirm conformance with the original plan approved by the client. The regularity of the reports to the client should be identified in the communication plan identified in chapter 9. However, it is highly recommended that status reports be provided to the client more regularly than client billings in order to provide the client with the information necessary to justify project billings.

Status reports may include the following information:

- Updated status including budget, calendars and schedules, and tasks

---

4. Although not relevant here, chapter 18 provides a counterargument to this assumption by clients. Regular meetings, which allow the team a specific time to address problems and questions, may in fact reduce costs to clients caused by legal team members and client representatives addressing issues with telephone calls and e-mail correspondence in an ad hoc manner. Scheduled meetings will confirm that everyone is available to discuss an issue and that the solution or resolution will be communicated to the entire team.

- Identified changes from the last report, including issues that may have been analyzed or addressed since the late report
- Key metrics identified by the client that communicate performance of the team (such as the number of completed due diligence items, documents drafted for a transaction, or the status of discovery, motions, or trial preparation in litigation)

In addition to budget-to-actual performance and depending on the complexity of the project, clients may also want to see the ratio of partner time versus associates and paralegals to confirm that the firm is appropriately staffing the matter and adhering to the original staffing or resource plan. For example, figure 8–14 is a screen shot from the Thomson Reuters' Serengeti system and shows the distribution of timekeepers per invoice.[5]

TIMEKEEPERS - Name

Timekeeper Rates: Timekeeper_Rates(1).xls [download]

Timekeeper	Rate	Hours	(%)	Adjustment	Total	(%)
Bill Smalls (LA)	$250.00	6.1	(34.3%)	--	$1,525.00	(27.0%)
Merrit Johnson (AS)	$375.00	2.6	(14.6%)	--	$975.00	(17.3%)
Dale Crunkett (PL)	$250.00	3.6	(20.2%)	--	$900.00	(15.9%)
Roar Amundsen (AS)	$350.00	2.3	(12.9%)	--	$805.00	(14.3%)
Anna Hart (PT)	$450.00	0.6	(3.4%)	--	$270.00	(4.8%)
Christopher Martin Madill (PT)	$450.00	2.6	(14.6%)	--	$1,170.00	(20.7%)
Total:	$317.13	17.8	(100.0%)	--	$5,645.00	(100.0%)

TIMEKEEPERS - Classification

Classification	Rate(Avg)	Hours	(%)	Adjustment	Total	(%)
Associate (AS)	$363.27	4.9	(27.5%)	--	$1,780.00	(31.5%)
Legal Assistant (LA)	$250.00	6.1	(34.3%)	--	$1,525.00	(27.0%)
Paralegal (PL)	$250.00	3.6	(20.2%)	--	$900.00	(15.9%)
Partner (PT)	$450.00	3.2	(18.0%)	--	$1,440.00	(25.5%)
Total:	$317.13	17.8	(100.0%)	--	$5,645.00	(100.0%)

Figure 8-14
Serengeti System for In-house Counsel to Review Their Outside Counsel Matter Staffing

Examples of Legal Project Management Information Systems

In the past two years, project management information systems have seen significant advancement. Systems are being developed by corporations, law

---

5. This image is taken from the Thomson Reuters presentation titled "The Report Cards You Don't See, Maximizing In-House/Outside Counsel Relationships" Bernadette Bulcacan, for the LawVision Group's Practice Management Professionals Roundtable (May 13, 2013).

firms, and third-party software vendors to address the needs outlined in this chapter. Appendix 2 includes information about many of these systems that are currently available to track legal matters. These systems are available for license by outside law firms or legal departments for implementation or are provided by law firms for their clients. These systems provide a wide range of available functionality that includes financial dashboards, project management data collection, automated alerts notifying users of milestones, etc. The following questions can be considered with regard to functionality when evaluating these systems.

General Questions
- How long has your system been available to consumers?
- What is the general scope of functionality of your product or purpose?
- What is the platform used to develop your application?
- Provide a summary of current functionality in the product.
- Provide a summary of proposed functionality in the product.
- How many customers (firms) and users are utilizing the software? Within those Firms, can you identify on average the percentage of lawyers using the product?
- How are the license fees for your product structured? By number of timekeepers, users or lawyers?
- Does your system communicate directly with Firm systems or does it require an intermediary database to pull information from Firm systems?

Project Plans
- Does your system provide a step-by-step approach for development of an entire project plan (work breakdown structure, schedule for the work, communication plan, etc.)?
- What are the components of the project plan in your product?
- How are changes to scope handled in your system?

Budgeting
- Do you provide template budgets, task lists or checklists with your product?
- Does your system accommodate phase and task coding?
- Does your system accommodate subtask coding?
- Does your system allow budget to actual comparisons? And do these indicate percentage of work completion or just the % of budget used.

Communication and Access
- Is your system open in the law firm intranet or does it require a separate login?
- Is your system open to client access through an extranet? Does it require login for client access?
- What information is available for client access?
- How is communication with other legal team members or the client addressed by your system?
- Does your system permit project plans, budgets or other project information to be exported to a report or document?

Figure 8-15
Survey Questions for Evaluating a PMIS

Responses to these questions and screen shots for several products are provided in appendix 2.

In addition to the systems outlined in appendix 2, corporate systems have also been developed to help track very large portfolios of matters for companies, such as in the bankruptcy and asset-recovery area. These systems are designed to allow in-house law and operations departments to monitor the status of matters and confirm that outside lawyers are not exceeding a previously agreed-upon threshold of fees. Outside law firms are required to update these systems on a regular basis either by manual data entry or by automated data feeds drawn from files uploaded to a central storage site designated by the client. Many in-house counsel are also utilizing third-party software applications that draw upon e-billing information to analyze the performance of their outside counsel. For example, figure 8–16 identifies a management dashboard provided in Thomson Reuters' Serengeti product.[6]

In summary, the Executing Phase means ensuring the legal work is managed as a project to accomplish the lawyer and client objectives of efficiency, effective communication and desired outcomes for the legal work. The most important aspects of the Executing Phase are to (1) manage the matter and the project team using the project plan, (2) monitor changes or variations, and (3) deal with changes or variations in the matter that will inevitably occur.

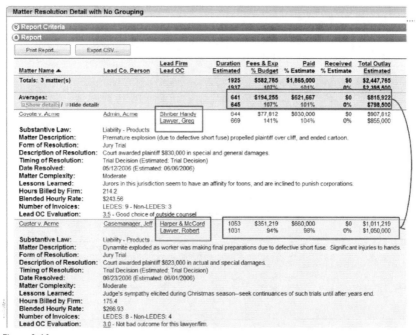

Figure 8-16
In-House Counsel Dashboard for Managing Matters

---

6. This image is taken from the Thomson Reuters presentation titled "The Report Cards You Don't See, Maximizing In-House/Outside Counsel Relationships". *See id.*

Chapter 9

Communication Management

The Need for Enhanced Communications

As detailed in chapter 5, the communication plan can be created by the project team and reviewed with the client contact or client team so there is buy-in from both sides. Formalizing how the team and the client will communicate project status and other information will result in cost savings for the client. For example, wasted time may occur when the following communication issues arise:

- Documents or information related to the matter are not provided to the outside counsel on a timely basis.
- An associate or paralegal has to contact the client multiple times to obtain an important document or case information.
- The client does not review and organize information prior to providing it to the outside lawyer.
- Firm lawyers constantly check in with the client team or conduct too many internal meetings on the status of the matter—each "check-in" costing the client (due to past abuses, many clients refuse to pay for these "internal conferences" among the project team lawyers).
- Firm lawyers fail to provide the client's legal team with timely information regarding a change in strategy or new information related to the case.
- Legal team members duplicate efforts because they are unaware of the work being performed by another team member.

- Legal team members overwork an issue (called gold plating in project management terms) because they have not been provided clear guidance on the issues in the matter.
- The client and the outside lawyer waste time try to catch one another by telephone (each call requires the lawyer to review his notes on the matter and confirm what needs to be communicated; by contrast regularly scheduled calls will ensure that this preparation time occurs only once).

Through producing and adhering to a comprehensive communication plan, and thus avoiding the situations above, law firms can focus on increasing and improving communication with the client and legal/project team.

Lawyers are known for their communication skills in many settings. They are known as effective advocates, skilled debaters, and competent drafters of complex documents. As a result, many lawyers believe they are skilled in the kind of communication necessary for effective project management, and yet many are not. There are various types of communication issues that arise that require better project communication.

As covered in chapter 12 on lawyer personality traits, lawyers can tend to avoid difficult conversations which can cause problems when managing matters. Lawyers are typically anxious to begin a new client relationship and thus do not want discussions about cost or "what could go wrong" to impede that new relationship in any way. As a result, they often avoid discussions about the client's expectations and objectives at the outset of a matter—or throughout a matter as circumstances change. Risk-averse lawyers would like to assume (and, as discussed in chapter 1, used to be able to assume) that cost is not a factor for accomplishing what is required in a matter, regardless of whether the client was informed at the outset that the cost, time, or scope could escalate beyond the original forecast. For these and many other reasons, lawyers need to learn the basic steps in project communication that are critical to success.

Current Methods of Communication with the Client

Historically speaking, a law firm's communication with its client tended to be very informal and mostly reactive. Typically, law firms would begin a relationship with an in-person or telephone meeting, followed by routine correspondence to confirm the client's formal engagement of the firm (sometimes called an engagement letter), which essentially just confirmed the law firm was the counsel of record for privilege and confidentiality. Other communication between the firm and its client dealt primarily with the necessary legal documents required for the engagement. Letters and e-mail correspondence with attachments have mostly handled this communication. For a litigation matter, such documents would include pleadings in the form of a complaint, response to a complaint, motions, briefs, and other discovery-related information. For a transactional matter, this might include opinion letters about the likelihood of certain options or the legalities of a deal, a letter of intent, or closing documents.

Another typical type of communication is monthly bills from the law firm to the client organization. These ranged from short descriptions to multipage documents in which each activity undertaken for the client was detailed. Many lawyers did not utilize their billing or communication about costs as the form of relationship management it should be. While some lawyers or firms had "rules" that they would not send out invoices without a cover letter explaining the activities covered in the invoice, many did not consider taking time to do this for every invoice, and clients were expected to simply pay the bill, though some did so grudgingly. For example, in one client interview conducted many years ago, an executive in the client organization stated, "A law firm should not send me a bill more frequently than other forms of communication."

In the last decade or so, clients began to expect regular written updates on the status of matters, particularly when the matters were very large or in the case of large portfolios of matters that could have a significant financial or liability impact on the client organization or corporate budget. Today, updates, status, or case management reports are expected weekly, monthly, or at some other interval. Or they can be posted on a law firm extranet for the client to access on a 24/7 basis. Many law firms are using their extranets as a major way of communicating with clients, including project documents such as budgets or status reports (often with confidential password access for only some members of the client's team), the main legal documents for the matter, links to resources, Q&A repositories for commonly asked questions (so) the clients do not get charged for their employees asking the law firm the same question over and over, etc. One law firm's usage of extranets increased from approximately 60 to 350 client extranets over a period of two and a half years of legal project management (LPM) training wherein lawyers were taught how to enhance their communications with their clients.

To date, the obligations of ABA Model Rule of Professional Conduct 1.4 regarding client communications have been interpreted loosely, and the requirement that a client remain "reasonably informed" has not included guidance on the frequency or depth of communication between the law firm and its client—as long as the lawyer does not fail to provide certain official legal notices to his or her clients or to communicate vital information necessary for the client to make decisions on the matter. In fact, for the most part the ABA Model Rules of Professional Conduct are designed to protect the consumer of legal services, especially the less sophisticated ones, as highly sophisticated in-house counsel in some cases have more specialized legal experience than their outside counsel.

ABA Model Rule 1.4 – Communications
a) A lawyer shall:
   1) Promptly inform the client of any decision or circumstance with respect to which the client's informed consent, as defined in Rule 1.0(e), is required by these Rules;
   2) Reasonably consult with the client about the means by which the client's objectives are to be accomplished;
   3) Keep the client reasonably informed about the status of the matter;
   4) Promptly comply with reasonable requests for information; and
   5) Consult with the client about any relevant limitation on the lawyer's conduct when the lawyer knows that the client expects assistance not permitted by the Rules of Professional Conduct or other law.
b) A lawyer shall explain a matter to the extent reasonably necessary to permit the client to make informed decisions regarding the representation.

Figure 9-1
ABA Model Rule 1.4

An interesting issue arises as to what "reasonably informed" means and whether a lawyer should be expected to provide a client with a process map, project charter or plan, or other document providing a high level of detail as to the steps in a matter of this type. For example, if a lawyer has a reasonable expectation that certain actions will be taken by the plaintiff's counsel and does not plan for that in the fee estimate provided to the client, is that keeping the client "reasonably informed"? If a lawyer should have done a risk analysis as described in chapter 5 to identify possible project risks that could cause the project costs to escalate or a deadline to be missed, has he or she "reasonably informed" the client?

There is also the question that, if some firms start to provide that level of communication, will it become the "standard of care" for all lawyers doing similar work? Such a scenario presented itself in regard to LPM as one risk management expert suggested a few years ago: "Project management will become the 'standard of care' as to how legal matters are managed."[1]

The field of project management brings a level of structure and process to legal work that has never existed before. In essence, with every LPM implementation, the industry is educating its clients on the best practices for evaluating and managing a legal matter. With this increased knowledge comes a higher expectation of service and, over time, the possibility of an elevated standard of care. While the industry is not there yet, the term "reasonably informed" may evolve to incorporate the enhanced practice techniques associated with LPM and new technologies for communication.

Current Methods of Communication Within the Legal Team

Communication within the legal team is another part of the important communication process for LPM. The legal team includes all of the members of the law firm working on a legal matter, but can also include members of the client's legal team (if any) and any outside vendors or contractors working on the matter. In some large matters, the inside legal team of in-house counsel and business executives and the outside team of their outside counsel, opposing counsel, and certain vendors are called a "working group," and they communicate through various mediums described below.

---

1. One firm using LPM to develop detailed project plans, provide real-time budget-to-actual status, and weekly case management updates to the client found that the client now expects this type of information from all of its outside law firms.

The communication for the legal team inside the client's primary law firm typically includes e-mails, memos, drafts of legal documents to be filed or negotiated with others on behalf of the client, and all meetings, whether in person or via video or phone. The more recent addition to the communication schema has been the use of intranet and extranet sites (i.e., virtual team rooms) where the internal team can share information and collaborate within the "four walls" of the firm or can expand that range to perform the same functions with an external team. For several years, Internet websites have been used to share and exchange information regarding a legal engagement. For example, for development projects, mergers, or other transactions, documents such as due diligence information, draft agreements, and final agreements were made available on a hosted website that was accessible by all parties and their counsel as early as 2003. These sites were typically hosted either by a title company, law firm, or one of the parties to the transaction. In addition, since the late 1990s, court filing systems have migrated to electronic filing systems, which make all court filings accessible over the Internet.[2] These types of systems have evolved with advances in software applications, such as Microsoft SharePoint.

During the Planning Phase of LPM, a client is provided with significant detail about the matter in the form of the Work Breakdown Structure (WBS), budget, RACI (responsible, accountable, consulted, informed) charts, etc. This sets a standard for the remainder of the matter requiring mechanisms to share information more readily with clients throughout the engagement. This is where tools such as extranets can provide the platform for communication. Since content on a SharePoint site can be audience targeted (i.e., information can either be displayed or hidden based upon a user's login credentials), the same site can be used to communicate with both internal (within the firm) and external stakeholders (clients, vendors, and local counsel).

Firms are now creating extranet sites (referred to as dashboards below) that include a wide range of matter management information that can be

---

2. Public Access to Court Electronic Records (PACER) is a service that provides the public with access to case and docket information for federal appellate, district, and bankruptcy courts. PUBLIC ACCESS TO COURT ELEC. RECORDS, http://www.pacer.gov (last visited Nov. 11, 2013). Many state judicial systems have also developed similar tools for state court matters.

shared with clients and the legal team in real time. This information can include:

- project documents—it is important to provide the project team and, increasingly, the client team access to the documents developed to manage the project, including, but not limited to, the project charter/scope of work document, the project plan, schedule, budget, team calendars, and matter status;
- publication of billing guidelines or guidelines for outside counsel for the entire legal team—it is important that every member of a project team understand the client's formal and informal billing guidelines (often called outside counsel guidelines);[3]
- documents and pleadings prepared for the matter;
- calendars showing milestones and deadlines;
- schedules or assignment matrices;
- budgets compared with actual legal spend;
- customized reporting requested by the client—as firms are now capturing many types of new data related to the matter, this information can be presented in a way that is more familiar to the client, such as report formats that mirror what the in-house lawyer must provide to management; and
- other communication tools such as blogs or wikis.

As identified in appendix 2, which provides examples of currently available project management information systems, this same type of information can also be communicated in a web-based software application. Whether using a firm-based system or third-party software, these sites are connected

---

3. There are many instances of law firms having to write off time on legal matters because a member of the project team was unaware of the billing guidelines and completed work that was out of scope, which needed preapproval or could not be billed. As attested to by e-billing companies auditing legal bills, the performance of legal work not covered under the guidelines has cost law firms thousands of dollars. To help ensure that out-of-scope or unauthorized work is not performed, some project budgeting tools actually imbed these guidelines into the client's matter information. This functionality prevents the firm from assigning work to a resource that is not yet approved to work on the matter. If someone starts to assign a task to someone who is not approved to work on the matter, the system will flag that action and alert the person to obtain approval or use another timekeeper who is approved.

to firm financial, time-entry, and resource databases in order to provide the client with real-time information regarding the status of the matter.[4]

Clarifying Expectations with a Communication Plan

When a lawyer begins a more formal project management approach as described in this book, the communication plan is a critical element of the overall project plan. Although, technically, the communication plan begins after the project team develops the WBS and schedule, it is important that the lawyer determine the client's expectations for communication prior to providing a fee quote or budget. As mentioned in chapters 5 and 6, whether a client wants a weekly or monthly, oral or written status report can have a significant impact on the budget. In addition, when attempting to determine stakeholders during the Engaging Phase, a common question is, who needs to be copied on correspondence for the matter. While this question helps determine whether there are any additional stakeholders not previously identified, it also helps to clarify who needs to be added to the regular communication channels and procedures in the communication plan.

Encouraging Efficiency by Improved Communication with the Client and Legal Team

In order to promote efficiency and the free flow of information between the client and legal team and avoid the pitfalls identified above, the following meetings should be considered with any communication plan:

1. **Initial Meeting with Client.** First, the project team should meet to discuss the new or potential engagement, develop a list of questions and information needed from the client or others, and begin to consider

---

4. In addition to communication, these systems also present opportunities for more efficiency—both the client and legal team members have access to more information regarding the matter. By sharing information on a real-time basis, legal teams can avoid duplication, gold plating (overworking an issue), and miscommunication.

the possible stakeholders for the project. Then, it is best to meet with the client[5] to identify and confirm requirements, expectations, and objectives so the team can develop the project charter or scope of work document as described in chapter 4.

In some situations where the lawyer or firm is trying to win the work during the Engaging Phase, whether through a request for proposal or other process, the client contacts may not meet with the lawyer or may not divulge full information about the matter or their company. However, whenever it is allowed and feasible, for prospective or new clients, it is preferable to meet with them to begin the process of defining expectations, objectives, requirements, success factors, and more.

2. **Project Kickoff.** After the project plan is drafted, it is best to review it thoroughly with all members of the internal legal team in order to confirm goals and expectations and ensure everyone is on the same page.[6] After making all necessary edits and revisions to the plan, it should then be reviewed with the client's internal team or, at least, the primary contact. After that meeting, the conversation with the client should be documented and any additional revisions made to the plan.

3. **Periodic Meetings with the Team.** The team should meet periodically to review the project plan and identify changes. The frequency of these team meetings depends on the nature of the project, its size, and duration. For some projects, there should be at least a weekly, very quick (sometimes just 10 minute) "check-in" meeting. For other projects, a monthly, one-hour meeting is necessary to review the project plan and other documents to discuss new information and changes. A

---

5. The "client" may be one person who is the main or primary contact, or that contact may simply be the person through which one will interact with all the other stakeholders within the client organization. In some cases, the "client" is actually a board or committee, not an individual. Regardless, it is important to at least attempt to have a meeting to go over all of the information necessary to develop the project charter.

6. Some firms have learned the value of this type of meeting the hard way. After spending a considerable amount of time developing a detailed project plan and schedule for an alternative-fee matter, the lead lawyer for the engagement failed to share any of the information with his team. As a result, none of the team members had any idea of the expectations of the client or the budgetary constraints that had been placed on the work. As a result, the project experienced cost overruns and resulted in an unprofitable matter for the firm.

sample of a project team meeting agenda is provided in chapter 8 and appendix 3–7. The deliverables from these meetings can include an updated project plan, a revised issues list or risk register, an updated stakeholder analysis, or a status report to be provided to absent team members or the client.

4. **Dashboards.** Many law firms and software vendors have developed dashboards for internal or external use to manage legal projects. These performance-reporting systems are designed to provide up-to-date intelligence and drive decision making. They are often the "home page" for linking to other applications or to access deeper analysis of data. These dashboards typically include the content described above and show a single screen with various metrics and measures of financial or other data, such as numbers of matters in a portfolio of work for a single client. The financial information can include budget-to-actual, profitability measures, or other financial levers that affect profitability such as the leverage, effective rate, realization, work in process etc.

5. **Periodic Meetings with the Client.** These are important to review project status and confirm expectations. Lawyers are very familiar with "matter status" or similar meetings to discuss matter strategy. However, historically, these meetings did not provide much detail about matter management. With some lawyers, there was an attitude that it was their responsibility to handle this and they did not need to involve the client or seek their input or opinions. Today, many clients want ongoing communication about matter management (now called project management) issues. Some want to be actively involved in decision making, and others simply want to be informed on a periodic basis or if the matter is off track in some way.

These periodic review meetings can have an agenda similar to the project team meetings (appendix 3–7). Others are focused on a specific issue like dealing with budget variations, scheduling issues or other scope changes. It is typically a good idea for a project team to have a preliminary meeting prior to the client meeting so whoever is representing the project team with the client is fully prepared and that all members of the project team are on the same page.

Law Department Notes

For both in-house lawyers and outside counsel, periodic meetings are excellent opportunities to informally take the client's "pulse" about how the matter is proceeding. Use these interactions to assess if the initial business goals and assumptions are still relevant, paying particular attention to changing circumstances and related implications. While the broad strokes of good project management include planning and executing, a critical aspect of LPM is defining, channeling, and monitoring the fluctuating route to success. During status and review meetings, determine

1. if there are new internal stakeholders,
2. whether any of the stakeholders who were instrumental in defining goals and objectives have new positions or roles, and
3. if there are other business initiatives that are pertinent to the matter at hand.

6. **Project Closure Meetings.** These are important to identify lessons learned, improved procedures, form document changes, and improved management practices. At the end of each matter, the project team should conduct an end-of-matter debrief or "after-action review" meeting. This process is described fully in chapter 10. In very large matters that have an extended timeline, interim reviews can be done prior to the end of the matter. For example, it might make sense to conduct a review at the end of each phase of a lengthy litigation matter to capture lessons learned while they are fresh in the mind instead of waiting until the end, when one risks forgetting the important ideas for improvement gathered earlier on in the matter.

As shown above, improved communication using legal project management is a function of both providing the client and legal team with more information and the use of technology. Early adopters of LPM who utilized Microsoft Word or Excel templates to capture and share project information experienced frustration as they found these formats to be extremely time-consuming and labor-intensive to update. With advancements in technology through SharePoint and the software applications identified in appendix 2, project management and communication is made much easier for lawyers and clients. By implementing the approaches outlined in this chapter, communication can be enhanced for the project team members and clients.

Law Department Notes

Given the ever-changing dynamics of legal matters, it is necessary to skillfully balance objectives, constraints, and stakeholder demands with agility and skill. But even a highly nimble team—one that adeptly manages uncertainty and complexity—will fall if communication is inadequate. The timely delivery of information is the lifeblood of a legal matter and a formal communication plan is its circulatory system. To achieve and sustain a shared understanding between counsel and client, which grows out of such effective communication, the legal team needs to implement a practical strategy to share information about real-time developments and changes with appropriate stakeholders throughout the matter's life cycle. A formal communication plan allows the initial shared understanding to evolve—instead of disintegrate—with the changing circumstances of the matter.

Some communication requirements and stakeholder patterns are unique to client organizations. In-house lawyers interface with many different individuals, including each other, the CFO, various business units, and law firms. The next several paragraphs are dedicated to what is special about and relevant to in-house interactions.

To quickly gauge an understanding of the company's stakeholder topography, pick a typical matter and guess how many internal stakeholders there are. Now, complete a RACI chart as described in chapter 5. Be sure to consider whether individuals from the finance department or other business units belong in this chart. There will likely be a greater number of stakeholders than first guessed. Keep in mind that each matter has stakeholders outside the organization, as well. This exercise is a reminder that solid communication must be shared with a wide variety of individuals who will either be consulted, informed, or otherwise a part of the communication plan.

Law Department Notes Cont.

To assess an understanding of transparency and accountability, consider the frequency with which law firms submit bills compared with the company's reporting needs. Instead of accepting law firm bills whenever they arrive, well-run corporate legal departments systematically monitor legal fees by asking firms to commit to a calendar that supports the company's financial reporting cycle and their department's budgeting cycle.

How effective is team-wide, department-wide, or organization-wide visibility into what others are doing—and why? Consider how increased visibility could impact delivery and response to information. Imagine the implications of this at the departmental or organizational level. Transparency isn't a measurement of the sheer volume of active communication; it also isn't everyone knowing everything all the time. Instead, transparency is the deliberate flow of communication to the right people at the right time. Accountability naturally emerges in a transparent environment.

Effective communication does not just increase efficiency internally. Understanding one's own process is essential for in-house counsel to get what they need when working with outside counsel, as well. It is wishful (and false) thinking to assume that a law firm or any other third-party vendor can understand processes, needs, or concerns without being told so directly. By communicating proactively and often with outside counsel, in-house counsel can help law firms embrace specific internal preferences and procedures.

Chapter 10

Evaluating and Closing the Matter

Activities & Processes
- Monitor scope, budget and relationships throughout executing phase and after
- Meeting of the matter team (end of matter briefing or "after action review")
- Revise matter strategy for future similar matters
- Administrative close
- Deliver final work product
- Archive reusable work product/ create "reusable" assets
- Obtain client acceptance/approval
- Obtain final payment

Deliverables & Work Product
- Update plan and budget
- Change orders
- Final budget-to-actual
- Exemplars, templates and model documents saved to knowledge management system

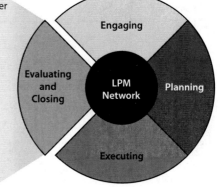

©2014 Legal Project Management Institute. All Rights Reserved.

Figure 10-1
The Evaluating and Closing Phase of LPM

The final phase of the Legal Project Management Institute's framework is the Evaluating and Closing Phase. This phase includes the following key elements:

- **monitoring the matter throughout**—including monitoring budget to actual, key milestones for progress with the client's objectives, scope

179

changes, and changes in other areas identified in the project plan such as staffing or risks or stakeholders

- **evaluating the matter**—at the conclusion to identify "lessons learned" and to debrief what worked well and what could be improved the next time a similar matter is undertaken

- **closing the matter**—including sending a final invoice, closing the matter in the accounting system where appropriate, and identifying "reusable assets" or documents that can be turned into best practices or model documents to use in similar matters (knowledge management resources).

Monitoring Matter

Monitoring was covered in the Executing Phase, chapter 8. In traditional project management, monitoring is covered as a separate phase that is illustrated as a circle around the outside of the other phases since it goes on throughout a project. We find with lawyers and legal project management however, that it is primarily done as part of the executing/doing of the legal work and managing the work as a project. Secondarily, it is critical that the project is monitored/evaluated at the end of the matter to understand what worked well and not as well, what factors affected the project outcomes and what metrics are relevant to evaluating the success of the matter.

Evaluating the Matter: End of Matter Debriefs

The area most frequently neglected by lawyers is the end-of-matter "debrief" or "lessons learned" where the project team discusses what worked well (or did not) in the course of the engagement. As will be covered in chapter 12, lawyers typically score high on a personality trait called "urgency" and usually, at the end of a matter, are eager to move on to their next billable project for clients and do not want to spend what is often "non-billable" time debriefing what they might have done differently. In addition to the urgency trait, lawyers are typically low on a trait called "resilience," which means they do not like admitting they made mistakes dislike criticism. As a result of these factors, many lawyers avoid spending time on this important step at the end of a matter. For this reason, innovations and improvements may be lost at the end of a matter simply because the legal team does not take time to evaluate their performance.

Law Firm Department Notes

Lawyers who advise companies that buy and sell businesses can help reduce the cost and increase the efficiency of executing transactions if lessons learned from a matter are exported to ongoing operations and corporate development practices. Examples include: Are there protocols for organizing materials that facilitate the preparation of disclosure schedules or integrating a company's records after closing? Should there be a process to expedite the preparation of Hart-Scott-Rodino filings?

For interim reviews, consider addressing e-discovery and the number of custodians. These meetings tend to generate fresh, problem-solving ideas. Any lessons learned can be put to immediate use for increased efficiency for the duration of the matter. In response to the trend of legal departments moving e-discovery in-house, an adoption of process mapping techniques can streamline the process and be used to assure consistency across matters and among law firm practices.

Despite the fact that in-house counsel does not differentiate between billable and non-billable time, they are likewise time and resource constrained. They score high on the "urgency" spectrum and are under pressure to do more with less. In-house lawyers typically jump from one matter to the next without pausing to take a breath, let alone reflect.

However, without a proper debrief or follow-up, in-house counsel can miss significant opportunities to add legal and business value. The impact of identifying and implementing improvement processes range from more efficiently using resources to significantly reducing costs.

The matter debrief is critical to enhancing the handling of future similar matters or of future matters for the same client even in different areas.

It is also a critical process for gathering data about the costs of matters, changes that occurred that affected achievement of project outcomes, issues that affected stakeholder expectations or relationships, and more. An end-of-matter debrief should be attended at least by key members of the project team. It does not have to take long, but it should at least cover what worked well and what should be changed for the next similar matter. An end-of-matter debrief can be conducted using a detailed checklist of questions or topics. A sample list of questions is provided in figure 10–2.

- What worked well on the matter?
- How did our matter team work together?
- What could each of us individually have done better?
- Did we meet the client's expectations and achieve their goals?
- Did we complete the matter by the deadline (if applicable)?
- How close to the schedule completion date was the project actually finished?
- At completion, did the project meet client's expectations without additional work?
- What templates, best practice documents, tools or techniques were developed that will be useful on our next project?
- What did we learn about:
  - **Scoping** a project that will help us in our next project?
  - **Staffing** a project ...?
  - **Scheduling** a project ...?
  - **Budgeting** a project...?
  - **Managing** a project...?
  - **Monitoring** a project ...?
- If we had the opportunity to redo the project, what would we do differently?

Figure 10-2
End of Matter Review—Sample Checklist

Sometimes, however, it is difficult to convince lawyers to spend sufficient time to conduct a thorough debrief at the end of the matter. One may need to start with a simpler, quicker process. One method for this is called a Plus-Delta Analysis. The "plus" (+) stands for "what worked well" during the matter. The "delta" (Δ) stands for change or "what could be changed for the next similar matter." In this instance, list some things that worked well on a recent matter and some things that should be changed for similar matters in the future or for other work with the same client. This can be done with a flip chart where one would simply draw a T shape in a project team meeting and ask everyone to share at least one example of a "plus" and a "delta" (similar to the approach with the T chart used for defining in and out of scope).

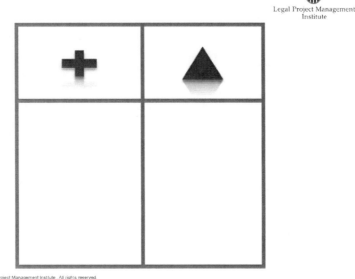

Figure 10-3
Plus/Delta Chart

Lawyers in law firms are starting to be asked by their clients to participate in a matter debrief with the client team or to provide their debrief information on ways to improve the matter handling to the client. Clients want to use this information to enhance the handling of their matters in the future. Even if a client is not asking to have a debrief session with a lawyer, the lawyer can differentiate himself or herself from other lawyers by offering to do a debrief with them or offering suggestions for improving the way the matters are handled based on the debriefs done within the legal organization or project team.

Law Department Notes

Matter debriefs are particularly important to in-house counsel because they mark opportunities to
1. gather feedback about how cross-functional teams worked internally and
2. identify the quality of the inside-counsel/outside-counsel relationship and areas for improvement.

This second point is critical. In-house counsel must *assess both process and strategy*, then clearly communicate *to the law firm* things that were done well and articulate why certain dynamics or deliverables were problematic. If the debrief surfaces specific feedback that could increase outside counsel's efficiency or effectiveness, it is in-house counsel's responsibility to share that information with the correct individuals at the firm.

Another closure tool is a client evaluation. Many times, clients may not feel comfortable vocalizing criticism of the legal team face-to-face. For this reason, BakerManage™ includes a client evaluation that can be completed by the client at the conclusion of the engagement. The evaluation form addresses overall performance of the matter, additional recommendations for improvements, and specific observations regarding members of the team.

The evaluation includes questions such as:

- Did the lawyers do an early case assessment and communicate the goals and objectives of the engagement?
- Did all team members return phone calls and/or e-mails promptly?
- Did the firm understand the business needs with regard to the engagement of the matter?
- Did the lawyers quickly focus and resolve key issues while consistently maintaining high-quality legal services?
- Did the lawyers demonstrate a comprehensive knowledge of legal subject matter and provide well-reasoned advice?

- Did the firm provide appropriate staffing and resources to deliver the required services in a timely manner?
- Did the firm prepare an estimated budget for the engagement and identify any risks that could negatively impact it?
- Did the lawyers develop and provide a clear understanding of the scope of the engagement, including stakeholder requirements?

Once the form has been completed, the firm should review the information to identify any additional lessons learned or recommendations for improvement captured in this form. This is also an excellent way for associates and staff to receive instant feedback on their performance and ways to improve.

Capturing Knowledge/Reusable Assets

At the conclusion of a matter, if not earlier, it is important to identify documents or other information that can be turned into best practices or model documents to use in similar matters. In traditional project management terminology, these are called "reusable assets" or "organizational process assets." In legal project management, this includes talking about what information was developed or gathered during the matter that needs to be captured, categorized, and otherwise made accessible to lawyers who will work on similar matters in the future. One of the best ways to increase efficiency is to not have to "reinvent the wheel" when handling a matter by accessing information that was developed in the past on similar matters. As will be described in chapter 15, legal organizations in the U.S. have struggled for many years with prioritizing resources and time to be dedicated to knowledge management (KM), as contrasted with the strong commitment made by U.K., Canadian, and Australian firms to support KM through full-time lawyers working on developing and harnessing the knowledge in their organization.

Law Firm Implementation Example

In the BakerManage™ model, changes are addressed in the Execution Phase using a change control log. Additionally, a lessons learned log is used throughout the matter to capture improvements identified by the client or the team for later engagements. These may be administrative improvements, procedural improvements, improvements to forms, etc. This information is evaluated in the BakerManage™ Closure Phase. In addition, in that phase, there is first a client meeting to review lessons learned, then a client evaluation is conducted to provide immediate feedback to the team regarding its performance and then an internal team meeting to evaluate the lessons learned, the client evaluation and implement any identified improvements to resources and procedures.

Closing the Matter

Closing the matter has a series of very important steps that are often neglected or considered less important. Of course, it includes providing the final work product to clients and ensuring they are satisfied with the legal services provided. In some firms, this includes providing the client with an end-of-matter survey or post-engagement questionnaire to elicit any feedback about the legal work or service provided. The closing of a matter also includes sending the final invoice and obtaining payment.

Also, while many lawyers consider this an administrative matter, it is also important to close the matter in the accounting system where appropriate (for lawyers in private practice). Many lawyers in firms dislike closing matters because they fear that it will convey to a client disinterest in working with them in the future or make it less likely the client will hire them again. However, risk management professionals in a law firm and in legal malpractice insurers know that it is important to ensure that the client knows that a matter is complete and there is no expectation that the firm or lawyer is continuing to work on that particular matter. It does not preclude the lawyer from working on future matters, but it signifies that the closed matter is now completed and that the lawyer is no longer retained to work on it. It is also important to close matters to prevent later strategic or business conflicts from preventing a lawyer from taking work from a company that is adverse to the first client in some way. Many firms have been conflicted out of handling matters because of a matter opened long ago and never closed.

The approaches in the Evaluating and Closing Phase can be used at the end of a matter or series of matters. Many can also be used at various points or stages of a matter—particularly a lengthy matter where lessons learned from an early stage may help avoid problems or increase efficiencies at a later stage.

Section 3

Considerations for Lawyers Implementing LPM

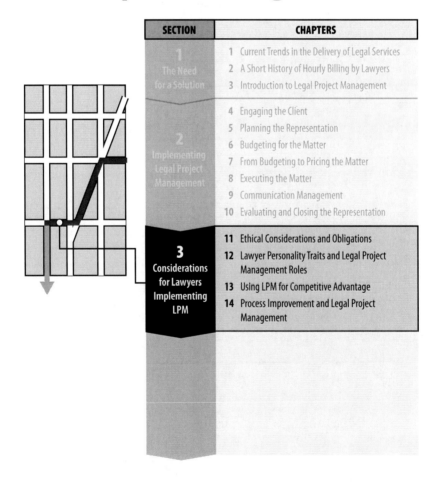

Chapter 11

Satisfying Ethical Considerations and Obligations Through Legal Project Management

Several books and guides have been written over the past few years on various models of legal project management. However, there has been no discussion of the important relationship between project management techniques and a lawyer's ethical obligations. This chapter will discuss the ethical rules that bind lawyers and will identify how a project management model can encourage adherence to these ethical standards.

The Project Management Institute (PMI) has promulgated a Code of Ethics and Professional Responsibility that apply to project managers.[1] The following excerpt explains the purpose of the code:

> As practitioners of project management, we are committed to doing what is right and honorable. We set high standards for ourselves and we aspire to meet these standards in all aspects of our lives—at work, at home, and in service to our profession.
>
> This Code of Ethics and Professional Conduct describes the expectations that we have of ourselves and our fellow practitioners in the global project management community. It articulates the ideals to

---

1. *PMI's Code of Ethics and Professional Conduct*, PROJECT MGMT. INST., http://www.pmi.org/About-Us/Ethics/Code-of-Ethics.aspx (last visited Nov. 6, 2013).

which we aspire as well as the behaviors that are mandatory in our professional and volunteer roles.

The purpose of this Code is to instill confidence in the project management profession and to help an individual become a better practitioner. We do this by establishing a profession-wide understanding of appropriate behavior. We believe that the credibility and reputation of the project management profession is shaped by the collective conduct of individual practitioners.[2]

The project management ethical standards are effective guidelines for business ethics. However, lawyers must adhere to and are bound by the rules of professional conduct in their jurisdiction of licensure.

For purposes of the evaluation of lawyer ethics as it relates to project management in this chapter, the ABA Model Rules of Professional Conduct will be used as a reference. Lawyers reading this book are encouraged to compare their own state's rules with the ABA Model Rules in order to confirm whether or not there are additional requirements that may be applicable to project management practices.

The ABA Model Rules and applicable state rules provide mandatory requirements for lawyers with regard to issues such as scoping, budgeting, quality, and communication. This chapter will summarize the applicable ABA Model Rules and describe how they must be considered with regard to the application of any project management framework. Additionally, figure 11–1 at the end of this chapter provides a summary of these Rules, the content of the Rules, and the legal project management process areas addressed by the Rules.

Project Scope

Project scope is defined as "the work that needs to be accomplished to deliver a product, service, or result with the specified features and functions."[3]

---

2. *Id.*
3. PROJECT MGMT. INST., A GUIDE TO THE PROJECT MANAGEMENT BODY OF KNOWLEDGE (PMBOK GUIDE) (4th ed. 2008).

As discussed in chapter 4, "scope" is essentially defined as the work needed to accomplish the client's objectives and expectations. Providing scope detail to a client should include clarification of not only the scope, but the other elements of the project charter or scope of work document as described in that chapter . This means addressing the other elements of the "triple constraint," (see chapter 18) such as expectations with regard to cost and time. It should include communication of the potential risks and any assumptions made with regard to a budget. Historically, this information has been captured in an engagement letter that might provide one sentence describing the nature of the matter to be undertaken by the legal team. Project management techniques call for a more detailed discussion to confirm the expectations of both the client and the lawyer for a legal engagement. Project management principles also support recording this information in a scope or statement of work document or agreement, something more detailed than an engagement letter.

ABA Model Rule of Professional Conduct 1.2, "Scope of Representation and Allocation of Authority Between Client and Lawyer," also encourage this type of dialogue between the lawyer and client at the outset of a case. The Rule reads as follows:

> (a) Subject to paragraphs (c) and (d), a lawyer shall abide by a client's decisions concerning the objectives of representation and, as required by Rule 1.4, shall consult with the client as to the means by which they are to be pursued. A lawyer may take such action on behalf of the client as is impliedly authorized to carry out the representation.

The Rule requires that the lawyer "abide by the client's decisions concerning the objectives of the representation." This infers that the client will be provided with sufficient information to make decisions about the details of the representation.

Rule 1.0(e) of the Model Rules confirms the level of detail required. The client must be provided more information than the standard one-sentence engagement letter to describe the scope of the engagement. The Rule provides as follows:

(e) "Informed consent" denotes the agreement by a person to a proposed course of conduct after the lawyer has communicated adequate information and explanation about the material risks of and reasonably available alternatives to the proposed course of conduct.

While most lawyers satisfy this requirement in verbal discussions with the client, details regarding the scope should be confirmed in writing and made available to the client to ensure that over time or during the course of a lengthy engagement all parties remember the original plan for the representation.

Once the scope has been defined, legal project management involves an evaluation of the tasks to be completed. The client may determine not to perform certain tasks (such as timely due diligence in a short-term transaction or expensive discovery in a minor litigation matter). To the extent that the client desires to limit the scope of the lawyer's representation, Rule 1.2 provides as follows:

(c) A lawyer may limit the scope of the representation if the limitation is reasonable under the circumstances and the client gives informed consent.

The comments to Rule 1.2 provide that scope limitations must be confirmed by agreement when the client has limited objectives or where "specific means" are excluded, as follows:

Agreements Limiting Scope of Representation. [6] The scope of services to be provided by a lawyer *may be limited by agreement* with the client or by the terms under which the lawyer's services are made available to the client .... A *limited representation may be appropriate because the client has limited objectives for the representation.* In addition, the terms upon which representation is undertaken *may exclude specific means* that might otherwise be used to accomplish the client's objectives. Such limitations may exclude actions that the client thinks are too costly.[4]

The comments to Rule 1.2 also place restrictions on the ability of a lawyer to limit the scope of the legal services.

> [7] Although this Rule affords the lawyer and client substantial latitude to limit the representation, the *limitation must be reasonable under the circumstances.* If, for example, a client's objective is limited to securing general information about the law the client needs in order to handle a common and typically uncomplicated legal problem, the lawyer and client may agree that the lawyer's services will be limited to a brief telephone consultation. Such a limitation, however, would not be reasonable if the time allotted was not sufficient to yield advice upon which the client could rely. *Although an agreement for a limited representation does not exempt a lawyer from the duty to provide competent representation, the limitation is a factor to be considered when determining the legal knowledge, skill, thoroughness and preparation reasonably necessary for the representation.*[5]

As highlighted above, limitations must be reasonable under the circumstances and must permit the lawyer to provide competent services.

With regard to the informed consent identified in Rule 1.2(c), the Rules further support the development of more-detailed statement of work or scope of work documents. Rule 1.0(n) defines "writing" as it relates to informed consent:

---

4. American Bar Association, Model Rules of Professional Conduct, Comments to Model Rule 1.2 (2013)(emphasis added);
   http://www.americanbar.org/groups/professional_responsibility/publications/model_rules_of_professional_conduct/model_rules_of_professional_conduct_table_of_contents.html.
5. American Bar Association, Model Rules of Professional Conduct, Comments to Model Rule 1.2 (2013)(emphasis added);
   http://www.americanbar.org/groups/professional_responsibility/publications/model_rules_of_professional_conduct/model_rules_of_professional_conduct_table_of_contents.html.

(n) "Writing" or "written" denotes a tangible or electronic record of a communication or representation, including handwriting, typewriting, printing, photostating, photography, audio or videorecording, and electronic communications. A "signed" writing includes an electronic sound, symbol or process attached to or logically associated with a writing and executed or adopted by a person with the intent to sign the writing.[6]

In summary, Rules 1.2(a), 1.2(c), 1.0(e), and 1.0(n), support the development of a written statement or scope of work document that confirms the client's decisions concerning the objectives of representation, the means of the representation, and any reasonable limitations on the scope of the engagement. In order to clarify and confirm the expectations of both the client and lawyer, a detailed scope of work document should be prepared that includes a scope statement, communicates assumptions and risks, and identifies expectations related to budget and time.

Project Budgeting

A legal project management approach to budgeting encourages the elaboration of the tasks to be completed, estimation of the time necessary to complete the tasks, and identification of the resources required to complete the task in the time allotted. Legal project management cautions against general estimates based upon prior experience. General or "finger in the air" estimates fail to communicate to the client the basis for the fee estimate. These goals are consistent with the ABA Model Rules that identify the elements to be considered in the development of a fee arrangement. Rule 1.5 provides as follows:

---

6. American Bar Association, Model Rules of Professional Conduct, Model Rule 1.0(n) (2013);

http://www.americanbar.org/groups/professional_responsibility/publications/model_rules_of_professional_conduct/model_rules_of_professional_conduct_table_of_contents.html.

(a) A lawyer shall not make an agreement for, charge, or collect an unreasonable fee or an unreasonable amount for expenses. The factors to be considered in determining the reasonableness of a fee include the following: (1) *the time and labor required, the novelty and difficulty of the questions involved, and the skill requisite to perform the legal service properly*; (2) the likelihood, if apparent to the client, that the acceptance of the particular employment will preclude other employment by the lawyer; (3) *the fee customarily charged in the locality for similar legal services*; (4) the amount involved and the results obtained; (5) *the time limitations imposed by the client or by the circumstances*; (6) the nature and length of the professional relationship with the client; (7) *the experience, reputation, and ability of the lawyer or lawyers performing the services*; and (8) *whether the fee is fixed or contingent.*[7]

The key guidance to take away from this Rule for budget development is that a legal budget should take into consideration the time and labor required, the difficulty of the questions, the skill required to perform the task, the fee customarily charged, the time limitations imposed, the experience of the lawyer, and the fee or pricing arrangement agreed upon with the client.

In chapter 6, a step-by-step approach has been provided for development of a budget or fee arrangement with a client. After development of an initial draft of a reliable budget, the next step in the budgeting process is confirmation of the estimate against historical information regarding similar matters. As identified by Rule 1.5(a), this approach is consistent with a lawyer's ethical obligations—the fee should be consistent with what is customarily charged.

Legal project management encourages sharing the details of the budget with the client both at the outset of the engagement and during the engagement as a measure of the actual performance against the agreed-upon budget. Rule 1.5(b) supports this approach:

---

7. American Bar Association, Model Rules of Professional Conduct, Model Rule 1.5 (2013)(emphasis added);

   http://www.americanbar.org/groups/professional_responsibility/publications/model_rules _of_professional_conduct/model_rules_of_professional_conduct_table_of_contents.html.

(b) The scope of the representation and the basis or rate of the fee and expenses for which the client will be responsible *shall be communicated to the client, preferably in writing, before or within a reasonable time after commencing the representation* . . . . Any changes in the basis or rate of the fee or expenses shall also be communicated to the client.[8]

To the extent that there are changes in the engagement, legal project management also encourages tracking such changes and communicating to the client the impact on the budget prior to incurring additional expenses and costs outside of the agreed-upon budget. This approach is supported by the language of Rule 1.5(b), which provides that "changes" shall also be communicated to the client.

Project Communications

One of the most consistent complaints about lawyers by their clients is their failure to communicate on a regular basis. Most lawyers communicate with their clients by telephone or by e-mail. The only summary of performance typically provided to a client is in a bill every 30 days or by a status or matter management report, if required by the client. As discussed in detail in chapters 5 and 9, regular and detailed communication regarding performance is imperative to successful matter management. The communication plan involves how much information is sent to whom, in what format, and how often. The object is to create a bridge among clients, legal teams, and other stakeholders.

Communication is an iterative process that is modified and refined as the matter progresses. A communication plan should be developed to address both internal communications among legal team members and administrative personnel and external communications with the client and external

---

8. American Bar Association, Model Rules of Professional Conduct, Model Rule 1.5(b) (2013)(emphasis added);

http://www.americanbar.org/groups/professional_responsibility/publications/model_rules _of_professional_conduct/model_rules_of_professional_conduct_table_of_contents.html.

stakeholders. Rule 1.4 confirms that these recommendations are consistent with a lawyer's ethical obligations to communicate with the client.

> (a) A lawyer shall: (1) promptly inform the client of any decision or circumstance with respect to which the client's informed consent, as defined in Rule 1.0(e), is required by these Rules; (2) reasonably consult with the client about the means by which the client's objectives are to be accomplished; (3) keep the client reasonably informed about the status of the matter; (4) promptly comply with reasonable requests for information; . . . (b) A lawyer shall explain a matter to the extent reasonably necessary to permit the client to make informed decisions regarding the representation.[9]

Model Rule 1.4 (a) provides that a lawyer shall "promptly" inform the client of decisions, consult with the client regarding the means of the representation, keep the client reasonably informed about the status of the matter, and provide sufficient information to permit the client to make informed decisions. The satisfaction of these requirements can be confirmed by working with the client to develop a communication plan that addresses each of these issues.

Additional ABA Model Rules also provide guidance on other communication responsibilities unique to lawyers. Model Rule 1.6 addresses confidentiality:

> Rule 1.6—(a) A lawyer shall not reveal information relating to the representation of a client unless the client gives informed consent, the disclosure is impliedly authorized in order to carry out the representation or the disclosure is permitted by paragraph (b) . . . (c) A lawyer shall make reasonable efforts to prevent the inadvertent or

---

9. American Bar Association, Model Rules of Professional Conduct, Model Rule 1.4 (2013);
   http://www.americanbar.org/groups/professional_responsibility/publications/model_rules _of_professional_conduct/model_rules_of_professional_conduct_table_of_contents.html.

unauthorized disclosure of, or unauthorized access to, information relating to the representation of a client.[10]

Model Rule 5.1 addresses communication with internal stakeholders:

Rule 5.1—(a) A partner in a law firm, and a lawyer who individually or together with other lawyers possesses comparable managerial authority in a law firm, shall make reasonable efforts to ensure that the firm has in effect measures giving reasonable assurance that all lawyers in the firm conform to the Rules of Professional Conduct.[11]

Model Rule 5.3 addresses communication with internal stakeholders:

Rule 5.3—With respect to a nonlawyer employed or retained by or associated with a lawyer: (a) a partner, and a lawyer who individually or together with other lawyers possesses comparable managerial authority in a law firm shall make reasonable efforts to ensure that the firm has in effect measures giving reasonable assurance that the person's conduct is compatible with the professional obligations of the lawyer; (b) a lawyer having direct supervisory authority over the nonlawyer shall make reasonable efforts to ensure that the person's conduct is compatible with the professional obligations of the lawyer . . . .[12]

Model Rule 7.1 addresses false advertising regarding the lawyer's services:

---

10. American Bar Association, Model Rules of Professional Conduct, Model Rule 1.6 (2013)(emphasis added);
   http://www.americanbar.org/groups/professional_responsibility/publications/model_rules _of_professional_conduct/model_rules_of_professional_conduct_table_of_contents.html.
11. American Bar Association, Model Rules of Professional Conduct, Model Rule 5.1 (2013)(emphasis added);
   http://www.americanbar.org/groups/professional_responsibility/publications/model_rules _of_professional_conduct/model_rules_of_professional_conduct_table_of_contents.html.
12. American Bar Association, Model Rules of Professional Conduct, Model Rule 5.3 (2013)(emphasis added);
   http://www.americanbar.org/groups/professional_responsibility/publications/model_rules _of_professional_conduct/model_rules_of_professional_conduct_table_of_contents.html.

Rule 7.1—A lawyer shall not make a false or misleading communication about the lawyer or the lawyer's services. A communication is false or misleading if it contains a material misrepresentation of fact or law, or omits a fact necessary to make the statement considered as a whole not materially misleading.[13]

Each of these Model Rules have applicability to LPM and lawyers implementing LPM can seek guidance from the Rules and their comments.

Project Quality

Traditional project management is used by many industries to manage production of a tangible product. There is a significant focus on quality planning, quality assurance, and quality controls to produce a product that meets the client's standards and specifications. Processes are monitored continually using tools such as quality audits and process analysis to measure the quality of the final product. Unlike a manufacturer, the lawyer provides an intangible product in the form of professional services. Therefore, most legal project management (LPM) models, including those addressed in this book, do not incorporate a specific process focused on quality assurance or control.

The concept of quality is, however, inherent in the ethical rules that govern the practice of law. ABA Model Rule 1.1 requires a lawyer to provide competent legal services and defines "competence" as follows:

A lawyer shall provide competent representation to a client. Competent representation requires the legal knowledge, skill, thoroughness and preparation reasonably necessary for the representation.[14]

---

13. American Bar Association, Model Rules of Professional Conduct, Model Rule 7.1 (2013)(emphasis added);
http://www.americanbar.org/groups/professional_responsibility/publications/model_rules
_of_professional_conduct/model_rules_of_professional_conduct_table_of_contents.html.
14. American Bar Association, Model Rules of Professional Conduct, Model Rule 1.1 (2013)(emphasis added); http://www.americanbar.org/groups/professional_responsibility/

While a specific process for quality is not contained in a typical LPM model, the entire LPM process is designed to help lawyers ensure that they are providing competent services. Project management techniques promote quality and competency through the use of budgets, task lists, checklists, forms, and collection of lessons learned, all which foster consistent and continuously improved legal services. Process improvement techniques also foster quality through improvements in the legal service delivery model (discussed in chapter 14).

Additionally, process improvement and project management tools also help to ensure there is balanced focus on quality. Overworking matters or "gold plating" occurs when research or work passes the point at which any additional time adds real value to the result. The use of tasks lists and other legal guidelines can help ensure that an appropriate level of quality is provided to the client, without overdoing it for a given matter's or client's requirements. As discussed in chapter 14, the quality of legal services can also be continually improved through the use of process analysis.

As stated in the introduction to this chapter, the Project Management Institute has developed a code of ethics for project managers, which is referred to as the PMI Code of Ethics and Professional Responsibility.[15] Unlike other industries using project management techniques, lawyers must also adhere to professional ethical standards and requirements. Whether designing a LPM model for implementation or adopting those outlined in this book, lawyers should first review the ethical requirements of their own jurisdiction to ensure that any LPM model is sensitive to these requirements. Thereafter, not only will legal project management approaches help a lawyer comply or even exceed the required ethical obligations, they can help a lawyer excel in client service and communication.

---

publications/model_rules_of_professional_conduct/model_rules_of_professional_conduct
_table_of_contents.html.

    15. *PMI's Code of Ethics and Professional Responsibility*, *supra* note 1.

Figure 11-1: ABA Model Rules and LPM Process Areas

Rule	Title	Information	Project Knowledge Area
		Client-Lawyer Relationship	
Rule 1.0	"Confirmed in writing"	(b) "Confirmed in writing," when used in reference to the informed consent of a person, denotes informed consent that is given in writing by the person or a writing that a lawyer promptly transmits to the person confirming an oral informed consent. See paragraph (e) for the definition of "informed consent." If it is not feasible to obtain or transmit the writing at the time the person gives informed consent, then the lawyer must obtain or transmit it within a reasonable time thereafter.	Scope and Communication
Rule 1.0	"Informed consent"	(e) "Informed consent" denotes the agreement by a person to a proposed course of conduct after the lawyer has communicated adequate information and explanation about the material risks of and reasonably available alternatives to the proposed course of conduct.	Scope and Communication
Rule 1.0	"Writing" or "written"	(n) "Writing" or "written" denotes a tangible or electronic record of a communication or representation, including handwriting, typewriting, printing, photostating, photography, audio or videorecording, and electronic communications. A "signed" writing includes an electronic sound, symbol or process attached to or logically associated with a writing and executed or adopted by a person with the intent to sign the writing.	Scope and Communication
Rule 1.1	Competence	A lawyer shall provide competent representation to a client. Competent representation requires the legal knowledge, skill, thoroughness and preparation reasonably necessary for the representation.	Quality

Rule	Title	Information	Project Knowledge Area
Rule 1.2	Scope of Representation and Allocation of Authority Between Client and Lawyer	(a) Subject to paragraphs (c) and (d), a lawyer shall abide by a client's decisions concerning the objectives of representation and, as required by Rule 1.4, shall consult with the client as to the means by which they are to be pursued. A lawyer may take such action on behalf of the client as is impliedly authorized to carry out the representation. A lawyer shall abide by a client's decision whether to settle a matter. In a criminal case, the lawyer shall abide by the client's decision, after consultation with the lawyer, as to a plea to be entered, whether to waive jury trial and whether the client will testify. (b) A lawyer's representation of a client, including representation by appointment, does not constitute an endorsement of the client's political, economic, social or moral views or activities. (c) A lawyer may limit the scope of the representation if the limitation is reasonable under the circumstances and the client gives informed consent. (d) A lawyer shall not counsel a client to engage, or assist a client, in conduct that the lawyer knows is criminal or fraudulent, but a lawyer may discuss the legal consequences of any proposed course of conduct with a client and may counsel or assist a client to make a good faith effort to determine the validity, scope, meaning or application of the law.	Scope
Rule 1.3	Diligence	A lawyer shall act with reasonable diligence and promptness in representing a client.	Quality
Rule 1.4	Diligence	a) A lawyer shall: (1) promptly inform the client of any decision or circumstance with respect to which the client's informed consent, as defined in Rule 1.0(e), is required by these Rules; (2) reasonably consult with the client about the means by which the client's objectives are to be accomplished; (3) keep the client reasonably informed about the status of the matter; (4) promptly comply with reasonable requests for information; and (5) consult with the client about any relevant limitation on the lawyer's conduct when the lawyer knows that the client expects assistance not permitted by the Rules of Professional Conduct or other law. (b) A lawyer shall explain a matter to the extent reasonably necessary to permit the client to make informed decisions regarding the representation.	Communication

Rule	Title	Information	Project Knowledge Area
Rule 1.5	Fees	a) A lawyer shall not make an agreement for, charge, or collect an unreasonable fee or an unreasonable amount for expenses. The factors to be considered in determining the reasonableness of a fee include the following: (1) the time and labor required, the novelty and difficulty of the questions involved, and the skill requisite to perform the legal service properly; (2) the likelihood, if apparent to the client, that the acceptance of the particular employment will preclude other employment by the lawyer; (3) the fee customarily charged in the locality for similar legal services; (4) the amount involved and the results obtained; (5) the time limitations imposed by the client or by the circumstances; (6) the nature and length of the professional relationship with the client; (7) the experience, reputation, and ability of the lawyer or lawyers performing the services; and (8) whether the fee is fixed or contingent. (b) The scope of the representation and the basis or rate of the fee and expenses for which the client will be responsible shall be communicated to the client, preferably in writing, before or within a reasonable time after commencing the representation, except when the lawyer will charge a regularly represented client on the same basis or rate. Any changes in the basis or rate of the fee or expenses shall also be communicated to the client. (c) A fee may be contingent on the outcome of the matter for which the service is rendered, except in a matter in which a contingent fee is prohibited by paragraph (d) or other law. A contingent fee agreement shall be in a writing signed by the client and shall state the method by which the fee is to be determined, including the percentage or percentages that shall accrue to the lawyer in the event of settlement, trial or appeal; litigation and other expenses to be deducted from the recovery; and whether such expenses are to be deducted before or after the contingent fee is calculated. The agreement must clearly notify the client of any expenses for which the client will be liable whether or not the client is the prevailing party. Upon conclusion of a contingent fee matter, the lawyer shall provide the client with a written statement stating the outcome of the matter and, if there is a recovery, showing the remittance to the client and the method of its determination. Client-Lawyer Relationship.	Budgeting, Scope, Communication

Rule	Title	Information	Project Knowledge Area
Rule 1.6	Confidentiality of Information	(a) A lawyer shall not reveal information relating to the representation of a client unless the client gives informed consent, the disclosure is impliedly authorized in order to carry out the representation or the disclosure is permitted by paragraph (b). . . (c) A lawyer shall make reasonable efforts to prevent the inadvertent or unauthorized disclosure of, or unauthorized access to, information relating to the representation of a client.	Communication
	Law Firms and Associations		
Rule 5.1	Responsibilities of Partners, Managers, And Supervisory Lawyers	(a) A partner in a law firm, and a lawyer who individually or together with other lawyers possesses comparable managerial authority in a law firm, shall make reasonable efforts to ensure that the firm has in effect measures giving reasonable assurance that all lawyers in the firm conform to the Rules of Professional Conduct.	Communication
Rule 5.3	Responsibilities Regarding Nonlawyer Assistance	With respect to a nonlawyer employed or retained by or associated with a lawyer: (a) a partner, and a lawyer who individually or together with other lawyers possesses comparable managerial authority in a law firm shall make reasonable efforts to ensure that the firm has in effect measures giving reasonable assurance that the person's conduct is compatible with the professional obligations of the lawyer; (b) a lawyer having direct supervisory authority over the nonlawyer shall make reasonable efforts to ensure that the person's conduct is compatible with the professional obligations of the lawyer . . .	Communication
	Information About Legal Services		
Rule 7.1	Communications Concerning a Lawyer's Services	A lawyer shall not make a false or misleading communication about the lawyer or the lawyer's services. A communication is false or misleading if it contains a material misrepresentation of fact or law, or omits a fact necessary to make the statement considered as a whole not materially misleading.	Communication

Chapter 12

Lawyer Personality Traits and Legal Project Management Roles

Larry Richard[1] has studied lawyer personalities since his Ph.D. dissertation more than 20 years ago. He has gathered personality data on thousands of lawyers, using instruments ranging from the Myers-Briggs Type Indicator to the Caliper Profile and the Hogan Assessment. The data from all three instruments confirms that lawyers are different from the rest of the public. For example, on the Caliper Profile, a personality estimation tool that impartially judges competencies, as well as recognizes hidden and dormant qualities, lawyers' scores are outside the general population norm on 6 of 18 traits.

"Managing lawyers is like herding cats," Richard likes to say. Richard bases this statement on the fact that he has been studying the personality traits of lawyers for the past 20 years, and has measured dozens of traits among thousands of lawyers. Research confirms that lawyers share quite a number of personality traits that distinguish them from the general public.

---

1. Larry Richard, J.D., Ph.D., is the founder of and principal consultant at LawyerBrain LLC, a consulting firm that focuses on improving lawyer performance through personality science. He is a leading expert on law firm leadership practices and change management in law firms and the nation's leading expert on lawyers' personalities. He can be reached at drlarryrichard@lawyerbrain.com.

A special thanks to Larry Richard for contributing to this chapter. This chapter is based on numerous articles and presentations by Richard on this subject. Additional information can be obtained on his website, www.lawyerbrain.com.

These "lawyer personality traits" have broad implications for the management of lawyers, the cultivation of rainmakers, the retention of associates, and a range of other critical issues in the day-to-day practice of law. This chapter, however, will focus on the traits primarily as they affect legal project management (LPM).[2]

Personality exerts a potent influence on virtually all aspects of law firm life. In recent years, managing partners and others leading lawyers within those firms have come to appreciate the importance of understanding these factors and how it affects the ability to lead and manage the firm professionals. While Richard uses many types of assessments to help a legal organization deal with its issues, the one that is most instructive for LPM is the Caliper Profile. The Caliper Profile was developed by the Caliper Corporation, based in Princeton, New Jersey. This profile has been in use for over 40 years, and over four million professionals, business managers, salespeople, and other executive level individuals have been profiled with this tool.

Lawyer Traits

Since his original 1998 research, Richard has profiled over 5,000 lawyers using the Caliper technique. Lawyers exhibit distinct and persistent patterns that offer insight into why it is sometimes difficult for law firm leaders and managers to get their partners to go along with even seemingly simple management decisions. Lawyers' scores are outside the norm on six Caliper traits: skepticism, urgency, sociability, resilience, abstract reasoning, and autonomy. Each will be described below. The Caliper Profile compares an individual's results or scores with the general population that is normed at 50 for each trait. So, the data below for lawyers studied shows their average score vis-à-vis the general population.

---

2. For more information about how the traits affect other law firm roles or operations, see the article "Herding Cats," Larry Richard, 29 Rep. to Legal Mgmt. 2 (2002).

Skepticism

The first trait relevant for LPM is skepticism. This trait indicates one's inclination to doubt or question others' motives. People who score high on this trait tend, of course, to be skeptical, even cynical, judgmental, questioning, argumentative, and somewhat self-protective while people who

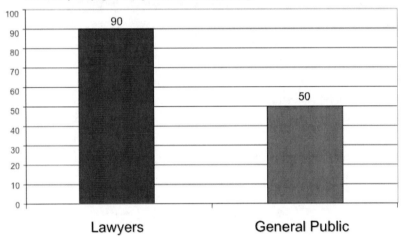

Skepticism

Symptoms of highly skeptical people? Pervasive questioning of facts and authority, sometimes cynical, judgmental, argumentative, and self protecting.

Source: Dr. Larry Richard, LawyerBrain LLC

Figure 12-1
Skepticism Trait Data

have a lower score end to be accepting of others, trusting, and give others the benefit of the doubt. The data gathered by the Caliper Profile research has shown that a high degree of skepticism is a "performance inhibitor" in some jobs. Highly skeptical individuals tend to be guarded and doubting of others' intentions. Lawyers score a 90 on a scale of 0 to 100, compared with the general public score of 50.

These high levels of skepticism explain many of the oddities and frustrations encountered in trying to manage lawyers. On the one hand, skepticism is a trait that can prove extremely beneficial to a lawyer. A lawyer's role is often to protect his or her client from the legal claims or directives of another party; for example, lawyers must ensure their clients do not sign documents that will be detrimental to the clients, etc. As a result, to a degree, skepticism is a valuable trait that is almost a hallmark of what lawyers are known for—not taking things at face value, looking for the inconsistencies, errors, or fallacies in a contract, a deal, or a pleading, for example. This trait can be particularly important for lawyers practicing in arenas such as litigation, tax, or mergers and acquisitions.

However, one of the challenges of personality traits is that the average person tends to use his or her stronger personality traits across all situations, rather than turning them on and off at will. Thus, if the profession attracts highly skeptical individuals, they will be skeptical not only when they are representing or protecting a client but also in other roles that might actually require *lower* levels of skepticism. In other words, the skeptical litigator may be well suited for adversarial encounters, but this same litigator will maintain the skeptical stance when attempting to build a rapport with a new client or in project team meetings, despite the fact that these situations may be performed more effectively in a climate of trust, acceptance, and collaboration.

Consider a scenario in which skeptical lawyers participate in a brainstorming session to identify stakeholders. Instead of letting various project team members contribute their suggestions of possible stakeholders for discussion, an extremely skeptical lawyer often leads with comments like "you are wrong" or "that is a stupid idea." Obviously, this creates an environment where open, candid dialogue is difficult and new ideas rarely surface.

Urgency

This trait measures the tendency to take quick action in order to obtain immediate results. It is a measure of an individual's sense of immediacy and a need to get things done, and high scorers on this attribute tend to be driven to act quickly, and those having high scores on urgency tend to exacerbate the need for immediate completion and tend to focus on this need with an air of impatience. Low scorers tend to be have demeanors which are considered patient, contemplative, measured, or in no particular rush. The lawyers score roughly 20 percent higher on this trait than the general public (71). Urgent people charge around like they are on their way to a

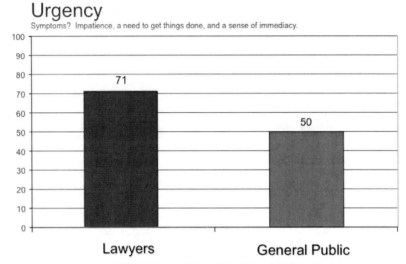

Urgency
Symptoms? Impatience, a need to get things done, and a sense of immediacy.

©2002 by Legal Management, July/August, "You've Got Personality" by Dr. Larry Richard

Source: Dr. Larry Richard, LawyerBrain LLC

Figure 12-2
Urgency Trait Data

fire. The urgent person often interrupts or finishes others' sentences, jumps to conclusions, and can be impulsive. As this person is results oriented, the urgent person tends to have a highly intense behavioral style, and efficiency and economy in everything is highly prioritized—from conversations to case or project management and relationships.

Urgency, like skepticism, is a trait that helps lawyers in many ways. Clients often expect their lawyers to be prepared to "jump over the moon." Lawyers exhibiting the trait of urgency adopt this as a default method of not only dealing with clients, but anyone they come in contact with. While clients generally appreciate lawyers moving their matters at a faster pace, urgency can have a negative impact on a lawyer's relationships with colleagues or support staff. Urgent people are sometimes brusque and poor listeners, and can be annoying to many people. This can add a level of tension to meetings, a level of frustration to supervisory relationships, and a sense of oppression to interactions with those considered to be in less powerful positions than the lawyer.

Project management is premised on the processes of taking time up front to identify client expectations and objectives, to discuss the details of the engagement, to carefully scope the work, and to develop a detailed project plan for the life of the matter (subject to changes of course). As was mentioned in chapter 4, highly urgent lawyers do not like planning and see it as a waste of time, thus the high urgency trait runs counter to the very foundation of LPM.

Another potential downside of this trait emerges most significantly in interpersonal relationships. Urgent lawyers who try to be "efficient in relationships" may eventually realize how oxymoronic this idea is. It takes time to build trust relationships with members of a project team and other stakeholders. Highly urgent lawyers often want to rush meetings or other communication and may not spend the necessary time to create the engagement and "glue" for a team to work well together.

To see the problem with high urgency and LPM, consider the following:

- Analyzing a process takes time and patience.
- Identifying how to streamline that process takes even more time and patience.
- Monitoring and controlling to that new process takes yet even more time and patience (and attention to detail).

A lawyer with a high sense of urgency is unlikely to want to spend the time analyzing a process or developing a project plan, as such a lawyer would rather get to work on solving the client or legal issue.

Sociability

High urgency may also explain why lawyers also differ from the general population so dramatically in the trait of sociability. Sociability is described as a desire to interact with people, and it can manifest itself in the ease of initiating new, intimate connections with others. Low scorers are not necessarily antisocial, rather, they are simply uncomfortable initiating intimate relationships. Because of this, low sociability scorers are more likely to rely on relationships that already exist, such as those that have surpassed the "getting-to-know-you" part; such as spouses, friends, and family members.

Sociability

Desire to connect with people, comfort in initiating new relationships with others, having emotional conversations with others.

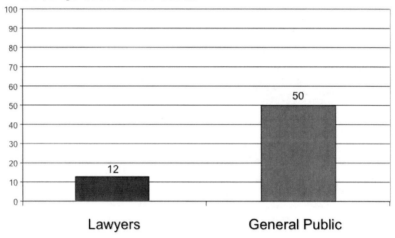

Source: Dr. Larry Richard, LawyerBrain LLC

Figure 12-3
Sociability Trait Data

Additionally, at work, low scorers are less inclined to enjoy interacting with others and may prefer to spend more time dealing with information, intellectual pursuits, or other interactions that emphasize the mind rather than the heart.

Is it any wonder that lawyers score low on sociability? The law is a profession devoted to logic and the intellect. Almost every law firm has standards of intellectual rigor that can be seen in their hiring processes and in the adulation paid to intellectually superior lawyers. It is difficult, if not impossible, to find a law firm that pays equal attention to the importance of relationships, that rewards and supports the cultivation of "quality time" among its professional personnel, or in any way measures one's people skills. Lawyers have an average sociability score of only 12.8, compared with an average of 50 for the general public. Take out the rainmakers in firms and the average score is 7! Rainmakers scored nearly *three and a half times higher on sociability* than the service partners, but their scores are still low compared to similar roles in the corporate world.

Low sociability scores have broad implications for many aspects of law firm management (practice group leadership, client retention, support staff turnover, and rainmaking, to name a few). However, because LPM is essentially about effective communication and management of expectations, sociability is a critical trait. Whether it is in communication in a project team, mentoring and supervising others, teamwork generally, or having a difficult conversation with a client about scope changes, low sociability can hinder a lawyer's effectiveness.

Resilience

Another important trait on which lawyers depart from the general norm is called resilience or ego strength. People who are low on resilience tend to be defensive, resist taking in feedback, and can be hypersensitive to criticism. Conversely, for a high-resilience individual, such as a typical successful salesperson, criticism or losing a pitch hardly fazes them. In fact, a very high-resilience individual, after having a prospective client reject his pitch, might well react with "That guy doesn't get it," rather than be concerned that his pitch or product was not top-notch or the right choice for the prospect.

Nearly all of the lawyers Richard has profiled (90 percent of them) score in the lower half of this trait, with the average being 30. The range is quite wide, with quite a number of lawyers scoring in the bottom tenth percentile. This information provides an understanding that, despite the outward confidence and even boldness that characterizes most lawyers, they are more sensitive under the surface. These lower scores suggest a self-protective quality. This may explain why so many partners' meetings get sidetracked into defensive exchanges and why a simple request to turn in timesheets is often met with a defensive tirade.

A critical task in project management is dealing with scope changes throughout a matter. Almost every matter has things happen that were not anticipated and, in some cases, that means the lawyer needs to talk to the client about the impact that change has on budget, timing, achievement of the client's objectives, and more. A low-resilience lawyer does not like to have these conversations. When faced with the news that a matter is off track or may encounter some issues in the future, a client will oftentimes get upset with the lawyer—a situation that a low-resilience lawyer

Personal Resilience

Symptoms of low resilience? Defensive, resist accepting feedback, and hypersensitive to criticism.

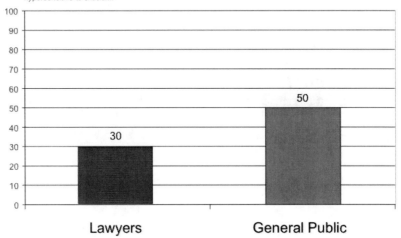

Source: Dr. Larry Richard, LawyerBrain LLC

Figure 12-4
Resilience Trait Data

hates. Furthermore, the prospect that a matter may be off track can make a low-resilience lawyer second-guess previous choices. They do not want to focus on what should have been done differently, and, therefore, typically do not want to conduct an end of matter debrief.

Abstract Reasoning

Another trait that is arguably stereotypical of lawyers is called abstract reasoning. This trait indicates the potential to solve problems and understand the logical relationships among concepts. People who show a high level of abstract reasoning are typically capable of understanding complex issues and integrating information.

Lawyers exhibiting this trait have the ability to detect and theorize fact patterns and "cause-and-effect" relationships that may not be apparent to the typical observer. However, this heightened awareness may also cause lawyers to focus on issues that may have no relevance or importance. This trait, along with skepticism, is at the heart of what most lawyers are known

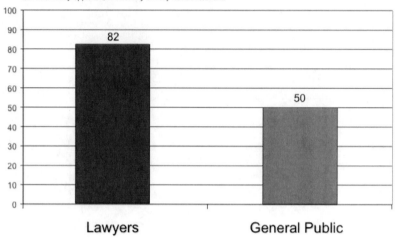

Abstract Reasoning

Ability to detect and theorize fact patterns and cause / effect relationships, that are not readily apparent, which may or may not be relevant.

Source: Dr. Larry Richard, LawyerBrain LLC

Figure 12-5
Abstract Reasoning Trait Data

for and, in many cases, is high on the list of criteria for hiring. It is sometimes described as "judgment" that clients say they seek from their lawyer and trusted advisor. As a result, it is considered a strength for many lawyers.

At the same time, lawyers trending high on the trait of abstract reasoning may also exhibit "analysis paralysis"—in which an individual or group cannot make a decision due to being overwhelmed by too much information, too many choices, or other related issues. Very high levels of abstract reasoning can cause project teams dominated by lawyers to spend too much time analyzing stakeholders or risks, or too much time debating options, instead of simply selecting a path or set of tasks to implement. This trait, combined with the natural risk aversion of most lawyers, can prevent necessary change and has been the cause of some failed attempts to implement LPM in organizations. Lawyers score an 82 in abstract reasoning compared with the general public score of 50.

LPM also involves a willingness to consider how matters can be handled better or differently. While this is not equivalent to full-blown process improvement as described in chapter 14, the process of breaking the work down into its component parts or conducting after-action reviews to identify ways to improve future matters is challenging for lawyers who are low-resilience and high on the abstract reasoning scale/spectrum. Most clients are familiar with some lawyers' tendency to overanalyze issues or challenge another lawyer's conclusions simply because it is inherent in their nature to do so. Thus, if lawyers suggest that they deliver their legal services differently (i.e., they have evaluated the process and identified a more streamlined approach to improve it), other lawyers may either reject the suggestions for improvement or continue analyzing them to the point where nothing is changed.

Autonomy

The final trait returns to the "herding cats" trait itself—autonomy. The data suggest that lawyers' autonomy scores generally average at the 89th

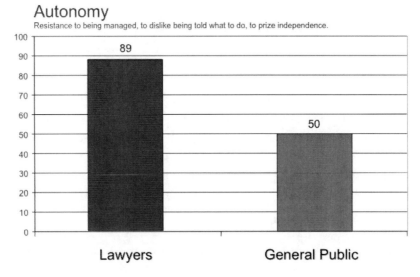

Source: Dr. Larry Richard, LawyerBrain LLC

Figure 12-6
Autonomy Trait Data

percentile. In other words, it is common for lawyers to resist being managed, to bridle at being told what to do, and to prize independence.

High levels of autonomy might not have been much of a problem when most legal matters were handled by general practice lawyers or when lawyers rarely worked as part of a team on large matters. However, today, many lawyers work in firms or as part of legal teams with significant amounts of management of their work. This can be an uncomfortable environment for those lawyers who still crave autonomy. Imagine being a project manager trying to get lawyers to work together who believe at their core that most projects are better done by a single individual (often them!) and that teamwork is a waste of time.

Managing a Team of Lawyers

So what do all of these traits together mean for legal project managers and for LPM initiatives in a law firm? First, it is important to recognize that personality traits are not, as Richard likes to say, a "jail sentence." While the traits described in this chapter are inherent in most lawyers, all professionals have personality traits that may not be consistent with the requirements of their job. Therefore, the first step is acknowledging that these traits exist and then try to work with and around them rather than simply ignoring them. This means identifying which lawyers exhibit the varying traits and to what degree and determining what effect on the project, organization, or one's personal role might result from these traits. For example, if a lawyer acting as the lead of a project team resembles the stereotypical lawyer described above, that lawyer will need to recognize the various viewpoints and traits of the project's stakeholders—the lawyers, nonlawyer team members, and clients alike. Self-awareness of both the strengths and potential weaknesses of these traits is important to be an effective project manager. If a legal project manager is not a lawyer, it is important to understand the above-mentioned personality traits to be better prepared to manage or lead lawyers.

The second step is for the project manager to recognize these traits in himself or herself and to try to ensure the traits do not cause issues in project management activities. According to Daniel Goleman, author of the best-selling 1995 book *Emotional Intelligence*, "emotional self-awareness" is the single most important emotional competency. Goleman's research found that people who regularly and consistently spend time trying to understand themselves, seek feedback about themselves, and gain insight into their own inner emotional life are found to be more successful in their professional and personal lives. Goleman's research indicates that this generalization applies with even greater force to those in leadership positions. In fact, emotional self-awareness is an inherent quality of effective leaders. Self-awareness is at the core of emotional intelligence, or EQ as it is called. Project managers—lawyers or not—need high levels of emotional intelligence to manage the team dynamic, communication, and relationship issues that typically arise in LPM. While lawyers are not known for high levels of EQ, the good news is that it can be learned. The foundational step is improving self-awareness.

Other practical suggestions of how the traits can be managed are as follows:

- When trying to develop new or creative approaches to a matter or project with highly skeptical individuals, brainstorming techniques that require the setting aside of "black hat" thinking[3] are recommended. For example, such a technique would be useful in initial discussions so that all the possibly great ideas are not rejected or shot down before they can even be debated. Or, solicit ideas individually prior to a team meeting so team members who are not skeptical lawyers do not disengage due to fear of being criticized by a lawyer who loves playing devil's advocate in every team meeting.
- It is important to illustrate to highly urgent lawyers how time for scoping or project planning sessions will enhance client relationships, reduce write-offs or result in other tangible outcomes. This will help combat their impatience and reluctance to spend time planning.
- The fewer highly autonomous lawyers in a project team, the better.

---

3. EDWARD DE BONO, SIX THINKING HATS (1999).

- Where possible, time or other limits should be placed on certain analysis or discussion sessions to avoid the paralysis and push to "get more evidence" when working with lawyers who are very high on abstract reasoning.
- It is important to pair the right personality for the right roles on the project team. For example, not every lawyer fits the stereotype, and some are higher on sociability or lower on autonomy (and likely already are seen as great team players in the organization).
- Lawyers found at the extremes of the above-mentioned traits may never "get it" and may need to be managed carefully.
- Teams should be balanced with "personality diversity" much like the organization does with other kinds of diversity. For example, a team should not consist entirely of "off the chart" skeptics, because such a situation would result in difficulty in engaging in any new approaches to matters.

In conclusion, it is most important to keep in mind that many of these six traits make lawyers successful as lawyers. However, at times, it is important to assist lawyers in "taking off the lawyer hat" and operating with the behaviors or traits more evidenced in leaders and managers in the business world and that are suited to effective legal project management. This can be done as lawyers better understand their traits and the impact of these traits on LPM, as self awareness is key to adapting so one can be more successful at LPM.

Chapter 13

Using Legal Project Management for Competitive Advantage

There are several aspects of using legal project management (LPM) for competitive advantage. These are applicable to the law firm readers of this book, not the law department readers though they may be interested in how law firms use this. The two discussed in this chapter are:

- using LPM to win specific business and
- using LPM to position the law firm as efficient and differentiate it from other law firms.

LPM and Client Development

As described in chapter 1, many companies are now asking their outside counsel to demonstrate how they are using LPM, legal process improvement, or other approaches to increase their efficiency or to add greater value to companies' legal work for which they are retained. Many requests for proposals for hiring law firms include specific language about the firms' LPM capabilities. The ability to manage engagements efficiently and effectively

---

This chapter was contributed by Wendy Bernero, who has more than 20 years of experience serving in senior administrative roles within major law firms. She currently serves as Chief of Strategic Initiatives of Proskauer Rose LLP.

across offices and practice areas, and in collaboration with a client's in-house legal and business teams, can be an important differentiator.

The following true story illustrates how incorporating work plans, budgets, and timelines in a new business presentation can mean the difference between winning and losing a major client assignment—even for "bet the company" work. The general counsel of a major financial institution's commercial and investment banking division (CIB) received a Wells notice from the Securities and Exchange Commission (SEC), following weeks of responding to regulatory inquiries. At that point, she reached out to her two "go to" law firms for securities enforcement and litigation work. In calls with the lawyers who serve as her principal contacts, she outlined the issues at hand and scheduled times for each to meet with her team to discuss defending the CIB in this important matter.

Both law firms under consideration were prestigious New York–based firms with a deep bench of former SEC enforcement and Justice Department officials. Both had worked with the CIB in the past and had the experience, expertise, and knowledge needed to provide the sophisticated counsel that the CIB required. The two firms took different approaches to their meetings with the CIB, and those choices directly impacted their chances of being retained for this important, high-stakes matter.

Firm A Approach

Firm A, which has a renowned securities, white-collar, and regulatory defense practice, assembled the team that would handle the engagement, briefed them on the matter at hand, and solicited their input on possible approaches to the representation. The meeting resulted in the development of a list of questions to send to the general counsel prior to the meeting. The questions not only focused on the details of the legal situation facing the CIB but also solicited information about the staffing and other resources the CIB planned to assign to the matter, allocation of responsibilities among the internal and external teams, and upcoming deadlines. Firm A also asked the general counsel to share her thoughts on the CIB's selection criteria for this engagement.

The general counsel answered all of Firm A's questions and provided important information about selection criteria. She relayed information including the following: (1) the post-downturn financial condition and outlook for the CIB was still weak, and (2) the financial institution as a whole was about to undergo another government "stress test," making this a challenging time to reserve for a large potential liability. As a result, not only was the CIB highly motivated to resolve this matter as expeditiously as possible, it also needed to carefully manage the legal costs of its defense. The general counsel added that the typical legal spend on a matter of this magnitude and importance could be as injurious to the bank as the investigation itself. She encouraged Firm A to focus some of its presentation on budget, cost, and project management. Based on this advice, Firm A's presentation to the CIB followed this agenda:

1. Introductions
2. Firm A's understanding of the situation
3. Discussion of suggested approaches
4. Decision-tree mapping of possible pathways the matter could take
5. Scope of work, suggested team, and allocation of responsibilities
6. Timetable for initial phases of matter
7. Budget and costs
8. Next steps

Firm B Approach

Firm B was also recognized as a top player in the securities enforcement bar and was very confident that it would win this mandate from the CIB. After all, it had a strong track record of recent successes representing the CIB and other investment banks in similar matters. Surprised that an advance meeting was requested, Firm B's relationship partner for the CIB invited a few partners with the requisite skills and experience to join him at the CIB meeting and asked his marketing team to compile attorney biographies, practice descriptions, awards and rankings, and track record of success into a pitch book to take to the meeting. Firm B's presentation to the CIB follows this agenda:

1. Introductions
2. Firm B's regulatory defense experience and credentials

3. Initial thoughts on situation facing CIB
4. Discussion and next steps

The Client Decision

Following the law firm meetings, the CIB general counsel convened the six-person CIB team to discuss the presentations and make a decision. At first, the team was divided based on initial reactions to the two presentations. The confidence and "take no prisoners" style of Firm B's lawyers, as well as its recent track record, were reassuring. At the same time, Firm A had strong credentials and capabilities, combined with a collaborative style. In addition, its focus on results, budget, and matter management was compelling.

To make the decision, the general counsel wrote the decision criteria on the conference room whiteboard. While writing, she mentioned that while Firm A had asked for the criteria and tailored its approach to meet it, Firm B had not. The chief financial officer pointed out that nothing in the criteria pertaining to costs and project management should be a surprise to anyone making a new business presentation these days—even for "bet the company" matters. After a brief discussion, the group agreed that overall Firm A was the best choice to handle this critical engagement.

Key Takeaways for Client Development

This is a true story and it has several important points for using LPM in client development efforts:

- Clients expect their lawyers to have in place strong matter management practices and processes that facilitate efficiency, quality control, and responsiveness—even for "bet-the-company" or other high value matters.
- Before making a new business presentation, always request information about the decision criteria.
- In a new business presentation or "beauty contest" setting, lawyers' ability to "talk the talk" of project management and convincingly demonstrate how they will "walk the walk" can make the difference between winning and losing new engagements.

- All lawyers on a presentation team must have at least conversational knowledge of basic project management terms and tools.
- All new business presentations at minimum should include a matter scope outline, timeline, work allocation proposal, and a discussion of fees and cost, including a proposed budget. Greater success may also be realized if the lawyers invest time in the development of a decision tree to explain possible courses of action to the client team.

The bottom line is that legal expertise is not sufficient to win a client's business. Many clients assume that a law firm bidding for the work has the expertise to address the legal complexities of the matter. Clients now also want to see that their law firm is sensitive to their financial and business challenges and will be good stewards of client resources.

Additionally, lawyers must not only "talk the talk" but must demonstrate the expertise to "walk the walk." Too often, lawyers will use LPM in client presentations as a way to differentiate themselves from their competition; however, they undermine the value of LPM when the client asks the key question, "How many cases have you implemented this in and what kind of results did you have?" Unless the lawyers have implemented LPM, all they can say is that they think it is a great process and are looking for a case to implement it on. Therefore, any business development presentation must demonstrate proven experience with planning the engagement as outlined in this book and implementing the tools necessary to manage to the plan.

In order to ensure continued business from the client, project management tools, such as lessons learned, should also be implemented in order to ensure that the relationship does not end with one matter. A heightened focus on client value and continuous improvement will cement a partnership with the client that can go beyond the matter at hand.

LPM to Position a Law Firm in the Marketplace

There are now many examples of law firms using LPM to differentiate themselves in the competitive market for legal services. Almost weekly, there is an article about law firms using these techniques to increase efficiency, decrease costs of legal work, or enhance client service. The LPM efforts of at least 50 major law firms have been discussed when representatives of these firms have been speakers on one of the public workshops that have been offered on LPM by organizations like the ABA, West LegalEdcenter, Practising Law Institute, or Ark Group.

In order to realize the marketing benefits of LPM, those responsible for LPM implementation should work closely with the firm's marketing team to outline and develop a presentation that will win business. Based upon the experience of the authors conducting hundreds of presentations on LPM, the following is a recommended outline for a business development presentation that incorporates LPM, where a law firm has implemented these tools or approaches:

- Introduction of the lawyers identified as the subject-matter experts for the matter at issue and their understanding of the client's goals with regard to the matter
- Discussion of the needs of the particular case and a proposed strategy
- Brief discussion of LPM implementation of the firm, presentation of a proposed scope of work consistent with the strategy, and an associated plan (including budget, resource management plan, and communication plan for all stakeholders)
- Demonstration of tools that can be made available to the client for monitoring the legal team's performance or other aspects of the project scope and plan
- Discussion by the subject-matter experts regarding their use of the system and success stories or observations

A key point of these presentations is that neither subject-matter expertise nor LPM expertise is sufficient by itself; both are required to win the work and manage the work effectively. Subject-matter expertise should be presented in conjunction with the LPM expertise to manage the matter in a different and more effective way than competitors.

The examples and ideas above are just a few of the ways that an effective LPM approach can be used to help firms differentiate from their competitors to win business, improve their profitability to enable the firm to be more economically stable or to attract laterals or otherwise, enhance its competitive position.

Chapter 14

The Relationship Between Process Improvement and Legal Project Management

Overview

As discussed in chapter 1, global business activity, the 2008 crash of the financial markets, a maze of increasingly complex regulations, and rising legal costs have had a profound impact on the role of the in-house corporate general counsel. To a much greater degree than their predecessors, today's general counsel are expected to exert more extensive control over legal spend, drive greater effectiveness and efficiency in supporting their internal clients, and ensure more predictable and positive business outcomes. In short, they have been charged with accomplishing more for less money and with fewer resources than their peers of less than ten years ago. This has resulted in a

Joseph Spratt, communications director at Seyfarth Shaw LLP, and Carla Landry, senior consultant at LawVision Group, contributed to this chapter. Spratt leads a number of strategic programs designed to strengthen lawyer engagement and accelerate culture change within the law firm. He has worked extensively with the Association of Corporate Counsel (ACC) on its Value Challenge efforts and has helped develop curriculum for the ACC's Legal Services Management programs for in-house and outside counsel. Joe is a certified Lean Six Sigma Green Belt and serves as a member of the firm's SeyfarthLean Steering Committee. Carla Landry has worked in the legal industry for more than 20 years. She is a certified Yellow Belt in Lean Sigma/Process Improvement for Law Firms and works with firms to identify cost-savings opportunities through resourcing legal services and improving existing legal processes. Carla is also an adjunct faculty member at George Washington University, teaching Economics and Profitability of Law Firms as part of a master's program in law firm management.

groundbreaking shift in the way companies secure legal services, and has resulted in a growing demand by general counsel for greater value from law firms, consulting groups, and legal process outsourcers.

Legal process improvement and project management are becoming key ways that lawyers deliver outstanding results and client service. Naturally, legal expertise is the critical baseline skill that clients expect. They also have greater expectations that their lawyers have a deep understanding of their business and industry issues. Furthermore, clients expect their lawyers to find more-innovative approaches and an open mind on how legal services can be delivered in different and sometimes, non-traditional ways. In fact, as described in chapter 1, the Association of Corporate Counsel (ACC), launched a multiyear industry initiative, called the Value Challenge, designed to spur innovation and change in the delivery of legal services.

The "value drivers" of globalization, recession, regulation, and the rise of technology have also created a broad resurgence of process improvement approaches—in the legal profession and across a variety of sectors and industries. Perhaps the most well-known of these methodologies are Lean and Six Sigma, which experienced a first wave of popularity in the 1980s, primarily for their use in businesses with a heavy manufacturing and/or engineering focus. More recently, the service sector, notably the hospitality and health-care industries, has utilized process improvement initiatives to substantially increase, for example, guest or patient satisfaction and decrease patient deaths or serious complications, while controlling or reducing costs. The health-care delivery system, in particular, has used process improvement strategies to meet increasingly stringent standards that determine the level of reimbursement by government or insurers. The urgency to "get Lean" is experiencing a full renaissance among businesses around the world.

Within the legal profession, the rise of Lean Six Sigma has been pioneered by a number of law firms, notably Seyfarth Shaw LLP, as well as a number of legal consulting firms. Other law firms and legal consultants use variations or components of Lean Six Sigma to help drive value and efficiency. The intertwined concepts and terms of "process improvement" and "project management" are intrinsic to any business improvement methodology; while the concepts are different, the terms are often used interchangeably.

This chapter will provide some clarity, show how these concepts work in tandem, provide background on methodology, and share examples of how key process improvements have been implemented on behalf of some leading general counsel.

Relationship Between Process Improvement and Project Management

The terms "project management" and "process improvement" are often used interchangeably in the legal arena, yet these disciplines are distinct and different in several key ways. A number of law firms and in-house teams seek to choose one or the other discipline, rather than combining or integrating them. As we have defined, legal project management is a method for defining, planning, executing, and evaluating projects. It is a proactive, structured approach to planning and managing a matter, whether it is routine or extraordinarily complex. Project management is a role and set of skills that ensures, for a particular matter or engagement, the lawyer or team develop an accurate, realistic budget and actively manage schedules, staff, and deliverables throughout the life of the matter or engagement. It is applying new skills, disciplines, and approaches to the way the work is currently handled to ensure meeting the objectives of the client and the lawyers working on the matter and/or their firm.

On the other hand, legal process improvement helps determine the best way to carry out a work process to achieve efficiency, excellent quality of work and service, high probability of successful outcomes, and predictability. It involves changing the way work is currently handled in order to improve it.

To expand upon this, process improvement is the successful development of a replicable model—enhancing or reengineering a work process by analyzing its existing state, identifying areas for increased efficiencies, and eliminating waste or rework to deliver desired business outcomes. It frequently involves the assessment and articulation of a current, flawed state, and—fairly distinctly from project management—it also involves the planning of an unknown, improved, and ideal future state.

Based upon these pillars, a core part of process improvement is two approaches: (1) process mapping, or value-stream mapping,[1] which is the development of a visual tool that illustrates the steps or actions performed to achieve a specific end result and (2) root-cause analysis,[2] which is a problem-solving framework that begins by examining the highest level of a problem to identify its underlying causes. It is used early in process improvement to drill deeply into a problem, in order to identify potential new approaches to tackle a core issue. Like project management, process improvement solutions often incorporate a technology-based component for efficiency, a reengineering of workflow, and work allocation among providers.

Successful culture change management—the adaptation to "the new way work gets done"—can often mark the difference between success and failure of a process improvement initiative. Assessments of a process improvement initiative are often based on aggregate metrics of success, such as reduced cycle time (the ability to manage how long it takes to complete a set of tasks (e.g., a real estate financing transaction), decreased legal spend, or increased percentage of desired outcomes across a portfolio or collection of like matters (e.g., a company's or business unit's collection of employment litigation cases).

Project management efforts concentrate on a discrete scope of activity with a defined start and end; frequently, it is the desired resolution of a matter with parameters related to cost, scope, and time (the triple constraint). The key principles to effective project management are establishing well-defined and achievable expectations between client and firm and developing robust communication practices that are strategic, team-based, and administrative in nature. A well-developed project plan of actions, deadlines, accountability, and timing often serves as the "guiding light" tool or

---

1. Value-stream mapping is a graphical technique to analyze the flow of information required to deliver a service to the client. The method identifies both value-adding steps and non-value-adding steps to locate potential waste.

2. Root-cause analysis is a method to identify the cause of a repetitive problem in a process. There are several techniques to identify the "root cause," which include the fishbone (or Ishikawa) diagram. The fishbone analysis is a graphical illustration used to identify defects, potential causes, contributing factors, and those factors and causes that should be prioritized to remove or minimize the defect.

"playbook" (as described in chapter 6) for all team members. Metrics of success in project management are often specific and singular: adherence to budget, timely resolution of the matter, and desired outcomes achieved at the matter level.

A quick summary and comparison of the concepts appears below:

	Legal Process Improvement	Legal Project Management
Function	A replicable model (Example: How we at Law Firm ABC manage the process of commercial litigation).	A customized application (Example: The litigation matter of Company X v. Company Y)
Representative tools	Root-cause analysis Process mapping Data collection and measurement Improvement plan Change management plan Control mechanisms	Project charter / scope of work statement Project plan / schedule (including task list) Status/progress report Communication plan Budget dashboard
Representative metrics	Cycle time Cost improvement over a period of time (e.g., annual spend) Desired outcomes at the aggregate level (e.g., a portfolio or collection of like matters, such as employment litigation)	Project budget met Matter completed on time Desired outcomes at the matter level (clients, law firms, legal departments)

Figure 14–1

Summary of LPI and LPM Concepts

There is benefit in both methodologies and they support each other. Strong use of project management on a single matter can often isolate or highlight opportunities for a replicable process improvement (e.g., how to reduce the number of steps in document review, revisions, and approvals on legal briefs). Conversely, a large process improvement initiative (e.g., how a legal department selects, manages, and evaluates outside counsel or how to reduce the costs in handling a single-plaintiff employment case) will yield a number of distinct steps or phases requiring project management expertise (i.e., to manage to the new processes).

Technology solutions are being used to map, measure, and speed work-flow processes. The more-innovative law firms are developing robust and user-friendly client collaboration platforms, advanced mobile technology applications, and sophisticated knowledge management systems that store, aggregate, and anticipate a lawyer's or a team's document and information management needs.

The following figure illustrates some of the pieces that intersect when successfully driving efficiencies with legal process improvement.

Figure 14-2
Areas of Intersection for Legal Process Improvement

Process Improvement Methodologies

The core principles of Lean and Six Sigma, and the hybrid approach that combines both names, are described below.

Lean and Six Sigma

Legal process improvement draws techniques from both Lean and Six Sigma. Lean is a continual focus on increasing value and the elimination of "waste" in an organization. It is a process improvement philosophy that focuses on the identification and elimination of waste and "non-value-added" activities from that process. In essence, it is providing what is needed, when it is needed, and in the amount needed with the minimum materials, equipment, labor, and space.

Six Sigma is a statistical term that dates back to the 1800s and Carl Friedrich Gauss' concept of the normal curve.[3] Motorola developed the Six Sigma methodology in the mid-1980s as a result of recognizing that products with high initial quality rarely failed in use. Jack Welch and General Electric adopted it in the 1990s. Essentially, at Sigma One there are 690,000 defects per one million opportunities in a process. At Sigma Six that number drops to 3.4 defects per one million. The idea behind it is that 99.9 percent is good enough. Although developed in manufacturing, there is application to the services industry, where one would follow information flow, rather than material flow. If you can track it, you can measure it in any number of ways (e.g., quality, time, cost).

Together, these two methodologies (aka Lean Six Sigma) provide a powerful toolkit. Lean increases speed and Six Sigma increases accuracy. Lean Six Sigma methodology uses a set of five principles as a framework for process improvement: define, measure, analyze, improve and control (DMAIC). Putting Lean Six Sigma principles into legal industry use requires interpretation and adaptation along these lines:

- **Define the problem and why it needs to be solved.** In the legal market, the focus is on the problem of how to deliver greater value, as defined by the client. Because "client value" is often a subjective balance between cost/benefits, predictability of process/results, achieving desired outcomes, delivery of high-quality client service, and legal excellence, it is crucial to work with clients to articulate what success and value look like for a matter, project, or portfolio. This articulation of goals and expectations is called "voice of the client." See figure 14–5, called "Voice of the Client," which provides a short discussion guide for use in initial client conversations. This is similar to the Engaging Phase of project management where the lawyer meets with key stakeholders to

---

3. "History of Six Sigma," http://www.isixsigma.com/new-to-six-sigma/history/history-six-sigma/ (December 8, 2013)

ensure an understanding of their desired objectives, expectations, and success factors.

- **Measure the current performance of the process.** In Lean Six Sigma language, this is the identification of process "defects"—not just errors or mistakes, but any inefficiencies that detract from client value. Some common defects in a firm-client process or relationship include a lack of communication, unclear accountabilities, poor data input, undefined limits on research, lack of standard forms or poor-quality forms, inappropriate training methods, or just-in-time pressure. These can lead to cost overruns that include excessive staffing, multiple drafts or rewrites, additional billed hours or write-offs from the firm, etc.

  The measurement phase also seeks to find and assesses opportunities to reduce variation and to eliminate waste or, in the legal industry, items that do not provide value to the client. These can include activities required by regulation, for example, which are not valued by the client but must be accomplished. Lean Six Sigma firms, like Seyfarth, use process-mapping techniques to assess a current-state situation and identify defects and waste in a given legal process—such as commercial litigation, trademark portfolio management, or real estate financing—or a related subprocess, such as document approval. Data analysis is also used to confirm and pinpoint the scale or impact of inefficiencies.

- **Analyze the opportunities to reduce waste or variation.** Tools employed in this phase can include the use of Lean Six Sigma root-cause analysis tools (e.g., see side bar "Why Ask Why?") to help stakeholders and decision makers identify a trigger event, or series of events in workflow, where a change in process can create a positive impact on multiple subsequent steps. Process maps can often be used to visualize and pinpoint these high-impact opportunities for change. Solutions to some of the legal service–related defects can include developing client protocols, standard processes, standard operating procedures, standard forms, data integrity, quality control procedures, document preparation software, and standard forms of communication. Some of these types of documents or approaches are part of the knowledge management in some large firms.

Legal process improvement also analyzes "flow," the ability to move from one step to another continuously or with the least amount of waiting or turnaround time as possible. Complex legal projects or processes, such as a transaction or series of transactions, depend on a multitude of moving parts to flow on incredibly intricate timetables. Seyfarth has professionals trained in Lean Six Sigma, Agile project management, and legal process improvement and who have expertise in workflow design. They help their lawyers and clients develop solutions that address flow and quality issues at a macro and micro level. Their cross-discipline training complements the strategic and legal skills of lawyers, and their solutions will often include strategic, practical use of technology.

Why Ask Why?

The 5 Whys is a Lean Six Sigma tool used as a problem-solving method to identify the underlying causes of an issue. It is simple, effective, and doesn't require any special templates, technology, or extensive data analysis.

At its most fundamental, the 5 Whys are asking the question "why?" five times, applying the following "why" to the answer given. Asking repeated questions encourages a work team to probe their collective knowledge of a problem. The cycle of asking why also allows the team to probe the various layers of a problem until reaching a level where solutions and preventive measures emerge.

Let's take a basic example to illustrate how the 5 Whys can work:

- Why was the client unhappy about the X matter? *She thought the bill was too high.*
- Why was the bill too high? *We conducted a lot of research.*
- Why was so much research needed? *We wanted to cover every possible angle to ensure a victory.*
- Why did we have to cover every possibility? *We did not have clear priorities from the client, and we wanted to achieve the best result. We thought that victory was more important than the cost of research.*
- Why didn't we know that when we started? *We did not have a specific conversation with the client about her expectations on costs versus outcomes.*

This team discussion led to a firm-client commitment to have a specific matter planning conversation at the outset of all future cases.

On larger issues, the 5 Whys are often used as a first step, in combination with more intricate and sophisticated root-cause-analysis tools. Seyfarth uses root-cause analysis to explore larger client-satisfaction issues and in strategic planning conversations. More information about the 5 Whys and the use of other Lean Six Sigma tools can be found online. Look to reputable sources, such as iSixSigma and the Six Sigma Academy.

- **Improve the process by piloting, implementing, and validating process changes.** Project management concepts and practices play a pivotal role in successful implementation. Tools such as a project plan, communication plan, and reporting schedules are used to keep work teams on track, on time, and on budget. The improvement and implementation stage often includes establishing improved protocols, documenting new practices, conducting needed training, and other hands-on project management aspects. The process map serves as a road map for defining the new process and for training team members. At Seyfarth, where more than 300 legal processes and subprocesses have been mapped, many associates keep a copy of a process map throughout a matter to help them anticipate workload and deadlines. Figures 14–3 and 14–4 show examples of part of a process map for commercial litigation.

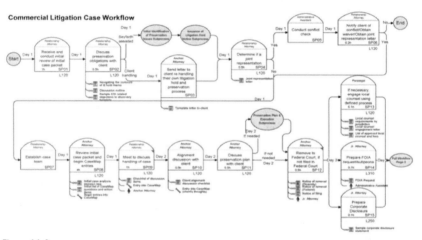

Figure 14-3
Sample Process Map: Commercial Litigation

One of the greatest challenges is that process improvement can often involve changing long-standing business practices—within a work team, between client and law firm, or throughout an organization. Consider the situation of many in-house lawyers who must move to working with a shared set of "preferred law firms" after having the ability to select their own outside counsel for many years, based almost entirely

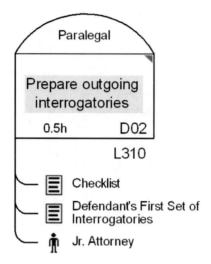

Figure 14-4
Task Map Legend

on personal relationships and experience. They may not be willing to change, even if they are mandated to do so. Changing motivations and behaviors can often determine the success or failure of an initiative. As a result, effective process improvement requires leadership and skills in culture change and change management. This is often the role taken on by senior leaders or champions.

- **Control the process to ensure improvements will be sustainable.** Using standard processes, forms, and communication helps provide an initial control over the new process. The collective results of process mapping, project planning, and project management help provide another level of infrastructure. Technology and reporting tools provide data for assessing progress and targeting improvements, offering another level of control. Finally, the control phase also includes the concept of "continuous improvement," or, to borrow a famous advertising tagline, "the relentless pursuit of perfection." A frequently used tool that helps facilitate continuous improvement is the after-action review, or "lessons learned," as described in chapter 10. It can be formal, or it can be a simple activity, in which key stakeholders assess what went well on a matter, project, or initiative, and what could be done more effectively.

Throughout any process improvement effort, it is important to circle back to the initial "voice of the client" efforts that established the initial goals and expectations. That will serve as a guiding light for success.

Voice of the Client

Some questions to consider while redesigning the process of delivering legal services and thinking through a client's objectives or voice include:

- What is unique about your business?
- How do you define success?
- What are your company's goals?
- What are your biggest challenges?
- How will legal outcomes support business strategy?
- What attributes are most important to you when working with outside counsel?
- What are your preferences for status reporting?

Figure 14-5
Voice of the Client Questions

To help provide more concrete information on how legal process improvement has been implemented, next are four short case studies. They provide brief overviews of successful process improvements that were implemented on behalf of some leading general counsel.

Process Improvement Case Studies

Improving Efficiency in Real Estate Practice

One of the most talked-about success stories of Lean Sigma application in the legal industry is the success of Morgan Lewis when it applied Six Sigma techniques to reduce the cost of delivering mortgage services. Ten years ago, Richard Sabat, a partner at Morgan Lewis and a Six Sigma Green belt, used Six Sigma principles to standardize procedures and improve efficiency in the firm's real estate practice. A big part of the application focuses on where waste was occurring in terms of quality, time, and cost.

Sabat started with measuring the number of word changes in documents, billing records, and associates' time records for purposes of identifying where duplication (i.e., waste) was occurring. Then, based on those findings, he instituted a plan to standardize procedures as much as possible. The goal at Morgan Lewis was to ensure that repetitive real estate transactions be done in as uniform a manner as possible. Then, with each new matter, one is expected to identify how it differs from the standard and focus on that. The idea is to have routine matters handled at the lowest possible level—by support staff, if possible—in order to reduce the cost of the service to clients.

Improving Litigation Management

One of the largest defense contractors in the U.S. consists of multiple business units, with employment counsel and human resources leaders across the country. The parent company sought a single law firm to handle this complex organization's high volume of litigation and counseling needs. Achieving greater consistency in practices, quality of outcomes, and efficiency were identified as key factors of success for the legal team, which has been a strong and vocal proponent of value-based approaches for many years.

They turned to Seyfarth Shaw, an Am Law 100 firm recognized for its pioneering use of Lean Six Sigma for the delivery of legal services, to manage its complete portfolio of employment litigation, including cases that go to trial, and counseling work for a flat fee. The work is part of a five-year relationship between client and firm.

Process improvement was key to meeting the client's objectives and delivering value. With input and support from Seyfarth, the in-house legal team conducted extensive "voice of the client" interviews with corporate and division counsel to identify issues and potential root causes at the portfolio and matter level. The firm then collaborated with the client to develop a standard trial process map to assess each case for its potential to go to trial on the front end and throughout the case. Furthermore, a new trial process was launched to align firm staffing on litigation matters to drive better outcomes in the most efficient and cost-effective way possible. The new process increased the law firm's ability to deliver high-quality work with the alternative fee arrangement.

The flat-fee pricing approach provides the client with greater certainty for its legal spend. A new trial approach triages cases and staffing based on potential risk, leading to improved outcomes. The firm has been able to create cost savings of 30 percent on an average per-matter basis for single-plaintiff employment litigation, based on a five-year track record of nearly 180 matters. This relationship has become a model of collaboration between the client and firm to strengthen efficiency, proactively target areas of potential risk, and improve litigation results.

Key components of the Lean approach are:

- **data analysis/risk identification.** The law firm's team tracks and organizes empirical information, giving the firm and the client an improved ability to analyze data critical to mitigating risk, avoiding litigation when possible and succeeding in circumstances when cases do go to trial.
- **use of project managers.** The project manager is responsible for organizing and coordinating team meetings, ensuring that deadlines are met, and having oversight of day-to-day cost management. The project manager uses tools to help analyze progress on individual matters and helps assess litigation and counseling-related activity so that the firm's lawyers can uncover or pinpoint emerging trends or issues for the client's legal team.
- **innovative tools.** Tools used in this engagement include a counseling log, a telephone hotline to provide employment counseling advice to the client's representatives, and Charge Tracker, a database that captures employment agency charges filed against the client and its subsidiaries. These tools help the firm and client monitor case activity in real time and retroactively.
- **trendspotting.** The law firm uses this data to spot trends that can help mitigate potential litigation, or can help the team succeed when litigation cannot be avoided. Results are also analyzed to help drive consistent practices throughout the complex structure of the client's organization. Finally, they are used to identify client-service enhancements and opportunities for continuous improvement.

Managing by Metrics: Global Trademark Process Improvement

An innovative relationship between a U.S.-based footwear manufacturer and Seyfarth was recognized by the *Financial Times* "Innovative Lawyer" report for "encouraging external firms to adopt (Lean) Six Sigma" and for "tying firm remuneration to outcomes it delivers." Over the past two years, the law firm, Seyfarth Shaw, has implemented a robust, integrated process for the client that is designed for progressive cost improvement; that is, the firm is responsible for delivering the same outcomes in year two at a lower cost than year one. The new process combines sophisticated metrics and the use of highly refined technology, including a proprietary client-firm mobile app to pinpoint intellectual property–related issues and opportunities. The new process has led to significant year-over-year performance improvements and annual efficiency gains of 15–20 percent in the management of a global trademark portfolio that grew 11 percent during the two-year period to exceed more than 4,000 marks and 800 domain names across 190 countries.

Key components are:

- **highly focused metrics.** Lean Six Sigma techniques, notably "voice of the client" and process mapping, helped the firm and the client identify a set of seven specific performance metrics, with aggressive year-over-year targets. These create a check-and-balance system to measure efficiency, responsiveness, quality of service, cycle time, and cost management. These metrics also ensure that the firm's efforts are completely aligned with the client's goals and expectations.

    Tracking productivity, costs, success rates, and response/renewal time is used by the client and the law firm to identify root causes and opportunities for continuous improvement; performance on selected metrics influence law firm compensation. The firm is incentivized and rewarded at a macro level for innovation, continuous improvement, and progressive cost reduction.

- **technology.** Technology tools contribute to achieving these metrics and reporting on them; technology is also used to address client service "points of pain"—those aspects of day-to-day management that can make or break successful firm-client relationships. Client-facing dashboards provide an at-a-glance indication of performance metrics.

Important metrics and reports are displayed in easy-to-understand charts and graphics. Client contacts can log in and quickly gain specific progress information at the portfolio level. Client dashboards and a wealth of other budget and management tools using real-time client data at the individual matter level are accessible to clients on the firm's robust and customized extranet platform.

Selection, Management, and Evaluation of Outside Counsel

A communications and aviation electronics company serving commercial and military customers around the world saw an opportunity to rethink systemically how its team could purchase outside counsel services and provide legal support to internal clients. The company turned to Seyfarth Shaw. The company's CEO had recently renewed the company's Lean quality and process improvement focus, and recognized the tangible benefits—predictable fees, consistency of processes, and a more efficient team—that the office of general counsel and the company could realize.

Using core techniques from Lean Six Sigma, the law firm led the law group through a value-stream mapping exercise to plot the client's then current state. Afterward, the law group developed a future state map, incorporating the use of knowledge management, process efficiencies, and best practices. The law group broke into four sub-teams to focus on specific areas that needed the most work to achieve the future state:

- **Engaging and managing outside counsel.** Responsible for creating a consistent engagement process, which supported the use of alternative fee arrangements (AFAs) for the first time.
- **Alternative fees.** Responsible for researching the uses and challenges of alternative fee structures and determining which specific alternative fee structures were best suited to the client.
- **Lessons learned.** Responsible for creating effective feedback loops to ensure candid conversations among the client's business leaders, its law team personnel, and outside counsel, and develop the tools to enable the "lessons learned" conversations to take place and be documented for use in the selection process on future matters.

- **Strategic analytics.** Responsible for determining data needed to support AFAs and the selection of outside counsel, and determining the appropriate method to capture and report on data.

Project management played a key role in the implementation of the new process. The teams followed the Lean DMAIC model as a blueprint. Significant milestone steps were supplemented by weekly team status meetings, monthly general counsel/core team reviews and "Quarterly Gate" reviews.

Each team developed its own charter, which included scope, goals, and deliverables. All of the teams conducted "voice of the client" interviews with nonlegal employees (human resources, corporate development, contracts) and outside counsel. They interviewed other corporate counsel, including representatives from a number of Fortune 500 companies. Each team was responsible for developing appropriate tools and templates.

Within a year, the client and law firm's consulting team completely reengineered how the law group selects, engages, manages, and evaluates outside counsel. In the first three months since the client started using the law firm's new AFA processes, the Law Group saved over $58,000 and the firm projected the client savings for fiscal year 2012 to be approximately $400,000 (eight percent of approximately five million dollars of outside counsel fees).

Managing a Large Portfolio of ERISA Litigation

An Am Law 100 firm recognized for its pioneering use of Lean Six Sigma for the delivery of legal services has managed a national portfolio of routine benefits litigation to help a global insurer achieve its goals for consistency and value across each matter. The firm has a long-standing relationship with the client, but prior to 2012, the law firm had never been involved with the client's routine benefits litigation portfolio. The opportunity arose when members of the client's in-house legal team shared the issues the company confronted while managing its large portfolio of litigation challenges to its denials of disability and life insurance benefits.

With significant investment by the law firm, the firm leveraged their unique approach to managing large portfolios and developed an innovative technological solution, called Portfolio Tracker, to help the client better manage and derive information from the portfolio. The firm enabled the client's in-house counsel to analyze macro- and micro-level data about cases and case trends that may have been left untapped by the sheer burden of managing case files the conventional way. To date, more than 250 individual lawsuits have been or are being managed through this portfolio approach.

The law firm applies a pioneering use of Lean Six Sigma to its client service model for large portfolios that allows it to create a highly effective, innovative, and integrated solution that builds and expands on its foundation of success. In collaboration with the client and lawyer teams, members of the firm's Legal Project Management Office and Legal Technology Innovations Office created a solution that has delivered tremendous business value for the client.

Key components are:

- **process improvement.** Prior to being engaged for this work, the team developed a process map for managing these cases, and since has, with the client, jointly reengineered it to create greater efficiencies, eliminate waste, and reduce costs at the individual matter and portfolio level.
- **technology.** The law firm's client collaboration tool helps increase productivity and enhance communication and coordination, execution and delivery, and management and control of the engagement. The firm's technology serves as a knowledge and project management hub that captures documents, as well as issues, process improvement ideas and responses, project plans, and reports. Portfolio Tracker is housed within this tool. The firm also use this platform to aggregate tasks, documents, and calendar entries across multiple matters. Templates, knowledge banks, and document automation are also part of the solution.
- **automation.** Many functions that were previously disparate and varied across matters and previous providers are now automated. The prior solution mandated manual case form reporting and no two forms were alike across various providers. Now, the law firm can automatically generate one consistent case-assessment form for any matter in the portfolio in a matter of seconds, using data captured in Portfolio Tracker.
- **improved quality and consistency.** Working closely with the client team, the firm created best-in-class documents and legal arguments and then took a standardized approach to their use where appropriate.

For example, the firm worked closely to devise the best possible settlement agreement, which has now become the standard, facilitated by a template, rather than having a different agreement for each in-house counsel.

- **continuous improvement.** Lessons learned are continually discussed and improvements in the approach are continually made. In the first six months of the engagement, weekly calls devoted to lessons learned with the client were held. The firm's core team now continues to hold weekly meetings focused on process improvement, where they continually review the process map, use of templates, review trends, and discuss client feedback.

As described in this chapter, process improvement and project management are important methodologies that support each other, regardless of which a lawyer uses first.

Section 4

Considerations for Organizations Implementing LPM

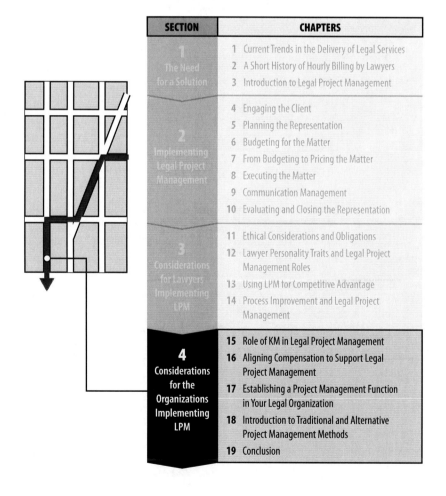

Chapter 15

The Role of Knowledge Management in Legal Project Management

Traditional Approaches to Knowledge Management in Law Firms

Law firms have been utilizing knowledge management (KM) for nearly 20 years and yet multiple definitions of the term still proliferate—"getting the right information to the right people at the right time" (IBM), "the capability of an organization to create new knowledge, disseminate it . . . and embody it in products, services or systems" (Nonaka), "the process of capturing, distributing and effectively using knowledge" (Davenport). As a result, it should not be a surprise that there is no single definition of knowledge management in law firms. However, the basic premise is the same regardless of KM's definitions and subtle, seemingly academic, distinctions. For law firms, KM means stop reinventing the wheel, reuse existing work product, capture what people know before they leave or retire, capitalize upon that knowledge for business advantage, and ultimately drive greater efficiencies into the delivery of legal services.

This chapter was written with contributions by Andrew Terrett, Sally Gonzalez and the book coauthors. Andrew Terrett is the Co-leader, BLG Adroit of Lean Project Management, and Director of knowledge management at Borden Ladner Gervais LLP. Sally Gonzalez is an independent consultant who is recognized as a leading expert in knowledge management, strategic technology planning, and process improvement for the legal services industry and formerly the CIO or similar roles with several Global 50 firms.

Historically, implementation of KM in a law firm is a multifaceted and complex endeavor including some or all the following key services:

- **Know-How**—capturing and maintaining forms, model documents, and guidance notes that can be tailored and reused from matter to matter.
- **Current Awareness**—keeping informed about changes in the law and sharing that knowledge across the organization quickly so that it can be integrated with currently active matters.
- **Expertise Location**—finding experts inside the law firm or legal department so that their knowledge can be shared and applied to the specific matter at hand.
- **Know Ourselves**—understanding specific areas of practice and understanding both the repeatable and unique processes and work steps involved in specific types of matters.
- **Develop Our Lawyers**—providing continuing legal education for fee earners on a formal basis and providing more informal, one-on-one coaching for newer lawyers to help them grow their legal and business skills more quickly.

Delivering these KM services requires human resources to perform KM work processes (e.g., capturing information and keeping it current in databases, updating model forms and templates, and maintaining professional development training materials and delivering classes). Many firms, especially those in the United Kingdom and Canada have traditionally funded dedicated resources to perform this work in the form of practice support lawyers, who are fully qualified lawyers who are embedded in practice groups and have little or no billable-hour commitments. In the United States, it has been more common for firms to staff KM on a part-time basis in the form of special-purpose committees or seconded lawyers assigned to specific tasks, such as creation of a specific model document and to look to technology to fill the gaps.

Today, all law firms view technology as a key enabler of their KM programs. The most successful firms have created tight alliances between their KM and IT professionals to deliver automated KM services such as online databases with model forms and templates, "Google-like" enterprise search to find and reuse existing work product and find experts within the firm, skills databases to profile internal and external databases, and intelligent systems to deliver current awareness based on an individual lawyer's interest and or practice affiliation. A few forward-thinking firms have focused on document assembly tools and many have focused their efforts around the redevelopment of the firm's intranet through "matter centricity," an approach that presents lawyers with all of the information about a matter aggregated from multiple systems (e.g., time and billing, document management, and marketing).

Like legal project management, a mature KM program including all of these elements combines people, process, and technology with a significant dose of behavioral change management, a Sisyphean task if ever there was one.

How Can KM Support LPM and LPI?

If we compare knowledge management with legal project management (LPM) and process improvement (LPI), we can see a commonality of goal—all are focused on more efficient work methods, improved quality, and thus the reduction of risk. And all three share change management as their biggest challenge. However, as illustrated by the table below, their purpose, methods, and approaches differ significantly.

	Knowledge Management	Legal Project Management	Process Improvement
Overall goal	More efficient work methods, higher-quality work product and reduced risk	More efficient work methods (i.e., "doing things right" as defined by approved, repeatable steps)	More effective work methods (i.e., "doing the right things" as defined by analysis of which work steps are needed and effective)

	Knowledge Management	Legal Project Management	Process Improvement
Purpose	To deliver information and resources needed by professionals to perform legal work	To provide structure and the efficient execution of work	To optimize production processes and thereby reduce costs and eliminate defects
Methods	Analysis of existing work processes, content development and maintenance, training, software implementation, and change management	Analysis of existing work processes, application of specific approaches, tools and skills to increase efficiency and improve relationships, training, tool development and deployment, and change management	Analysis of existing work processes, identification and realization of process improvement opportunities, change management
Who does it?	Practice-support Lawyers, KM team, librarians, and/or seconded lawyers	The matter-responsible lawyer, "first lieutenant," full- or part-time project managers or lawyers/project managers	Business analysts, whether internal or external
Biggest hurdle	Behavioral change / change management	Behavioral change / change management	Behavioral change / change management

Figure 15-1

Comparison of KM, LPM, and PI

Despite their differences, KM, LPM, and PI can be viewed as important allies. Properly structured as part of a unified function, they can work together to achieve their common, shared goal. Many project management or process improvement initiatives start at a practice group or matter level by identifying the types of work undertaken. Ideally, the work should be mapped out in detail. Undoubtedly there will be certain key points during the execution of the plan when KM is required to play a role. For example, in a transaction KM can provide access to key precedents; in a litigation, KM can provide access to external experts and to prior research on key legal issues involved in the litigation. Through legal project management, KM professionals can be much more tightly integrated into the delivery of legal services and more directly support the firm's efforts to improve profitability.

As stated above, a point of intersection between LPM and KM is resources and forms used for a particular matter. In chapter 10, this was referred to as organizational process assets (a term from traditional project management), also known as resources, templates and forms which can streamline the work of lawyers and legal teams. While LPM seeks to provide tools to plan, manage, and control an engagement, KM can provide necessary form documents, checklists, and research for the matter. However, KM must be conscious of the limited time that lawyers have to sift through a firm intranet or a warehouse of forms to identify a document or resource that may be useful in their engagement. The key is to make lawyers more efficient and not overwhelm them with an abundance of documents in the hope that a relevant document will turn up.

In addition, most KM document libraries are typically populated with specialized forms used by other lawyers on matters with their own unique issues. There is insufficient time for a lawyer to review a "form" document and identify any provisions customized for another lawyer's engagement. As a result, lawyers most often pull from their own library of forms that contain provisions that are familiar to them.

Nevertheless, with advancements in KM, there is a solution. Rather than forcing lawyers to cull through document libraries or using advanced search mechanisms to serve up a host of documents with potential key terms, the better approach will be to utilize matter intake information and provide a limited number of very relevant checklists, forms, and other resources that are unique to the engagement being managed by the lawyer. Additionally, the resources provided should be true forms without modification for another lawyer's engagement. If these considerations are included within the plan for integration of KM and LPM, the wealth of information collected over the years by a KM team will add even more value to the LPM and LPI implementations.

Good News, Bad News – KM Maturity is a Critical Enabler

The Good News: Law firms with mature Knowledge Management (KM) programs are well positioned to move ahead quickly as they adopt Legal Project Management (LPM) and Process Improvement (PI). As these firms apply LPM to identify repeatable work steps for specific types of matters, it is a relatively simple next step to leverage existing KM-based tools (e.g., forms, model documents, and guidance notes), processes (e.g., content management), and resources (e.g., practice support lawyers) to make specific work steps more efficient and less costly without sacrificing quality. In addition, as a firm embraces Process Improvement, it can look to its KM organization for essential skills and proven methodologies for foundational activities such as after-action-reviews and legal process analysis. This marriage of KM with LPM and PI is beneficial to all in that it enables the KM organization to focus on providing practical tools in support of specific LPM and PI initiatives and thereby support a firm's efforts to satisfy client demands for improved efficiency while maintaining the firm's profitability.

The Bad News: Firms that do not have existing KM programs in place will find themselves disadvantaged in their LPM and LPI initiatives until they build sufficient KM resources to support those efforts. As these firms begin to understand the repeatable work steps in matters, they will have to spend time and effort to create tools such as re-usable forms and model documents and establish the processes necessary to maintain the tools. Most importantly, they will have to build the human resources (i.e., practice support lawyers or their equivalent) necessary to support these tools and processes as well as the organizational support necessary to attract and sustain those resources. However, it is important that law firms not be overly daunted by these challenges. If they succeed in building a KM program that has the laser-like focus provided by LPM and LPI, they will find they are likely to achieve a much higher ROI on their KM investments than firms that lack this very practical focus for their KM activities.

Chapter 16

Aligning Compensation to Support Legal Project Management

The Challenges of Current Law Firm Compensation Systems

One of the more challenging issues law firms have faced in partner compensation systems in recent years has been how to motivate or incent lawyers to contribute to group activities and to collaborate. Almost every medium and large law firm in the U.S. had implemented some form of formal *practice* management system. Over the past decade or two, firms have established practice groups, client teams, industry teams, and other structures designed to help manage the practice, position the firm to attract more and better business, enhance morale, or take advantage of the benefits offered by a group. In doing so they have realized they needed to incentivize the lawyers to work in groups and collaboratively, rather than in silos, in order to make practice management most effective. Now, these and other issues affect how firms incentivize lawyers so project management is effective.

Joseph B. Altonji, a compensation and strategy expert with LawVision Group, and Carla Landry, senior consultant with LawVision Group, contributed to this chapter. Altonji is a Co-founder of LawVision Group and has spent nearly three decades consulting for law firms and their leaders, in the United States and internationally, including over 20 years with Hildebrandt International and then Hildebrandt Baker Robbins. Landry also contributed to chapter 11.

While most successful firms have subjective or "total contribution" compensation systems[1] designed to take into consideration numerous factors, including teamwork, commitment to the firm and management time. It remains the case that the two most critical compensation factors in most parts of the legal industry are personal performance measures—personal production (generally measured in terms of cash receipts for the lawyer's personal work efforts) and some measure of client generation, typically "origination"—regardless of the system structure.[2] Given the market for talent and "portable business," this situation is unlikely to change rapidly, and the key goal must be to balance personal performance with more team-oriented and other qualitative behaviors that are critical for succeeding in today's market and for practice management and project management approaches to work.

As firms begin to introduce legal project management (LPM) concepts and practices, the challenges to setting compensation become even more complex. While encouraging the teamwork and collaboration critical for LPM remains a challenge in heavily "numbers-driven" compensation systems, the next compensation issue facing firms implementing LPM is how to incentivize efficient and profitable management of matters. These questions force a firm to consider a different challenge—not so much how to incentivize nonnumerical factors but to make sure to focus on the *right* numbers.

There are two areas where the currently emphasized numbers fail to align properly with the goals of LPM in law firms, and they derive from the two most important numbers in most current compensation systems, at both the partner and associate levels. The first is partner rewards for

1. In LawVision Group's 2013 survey of law firm partner compensation systems, 87 percent of participating U.S. firms reported utilizing one form or another of a subjective compensation decision-making process. However, subjective processes vary widely in their degree of reliance on accounting data, with some giving significant weight to qualitative contributions while others vary only slightly from the results that might have been attained utilizing a formulaic approach. The strongest systems incorporate the data but also place significant value on other contributions.

2. A very limited number of firms, typically with highly institutionalized practices, have continued to be able to successfully operate "lock-step" compensation systems, which de-emphasize personal client control and demand homogenous lifetime performance from partners to ensure stability. However, due to the high expectations required for success, few firms can maintain this approach successfully.

"top line results" instead of "bottom line results" (i.e., profitability). The second area where law firm compensation and evaluation systems tend to diverge is in the mismatch between the significant emphasis on billable hours as the primary measure of personal productivity (especially at the associate level) and the obvious implications on improving efficiencies that can result in *reduced* time spent, at least on a matter level. Each will be addressed below.

The first issue derives from the focus in most firms on rewarding partners for "top line results" (absolute revenue) rather than "bottom line results" (profitability). Until recently (roughly, the last decade but increasing dramatically since 2008) this was of less significance because (1) realization rates across the board were substantially higher and (2) practice "value positions" within any given law firm were far more homogenous because the pace of standardization and commoditization had not yet become extreme. Both of these conditions no longer hold, and as a result, profitability differentials among practices with similar revenues are now significant. Differentials among individual partners in how effectively they manage their own individual practices are also significant, further enhancing the need to focus on profitability as part of the compensation decision.

While firms do increasingly utilize profitability data in setting partner compensation,[3] profitability remains a secondary factor in setting compensation for most firms. In part this stems from the still underdeveloped understanding of what "profitability" even means in a legal practice. Although this is gradually changing, historically law firms measured "profitability" in terms of whatever was left over for the partners, often without consideration of the value or cost of a partner's time and efforts. While profit per partner is still the dominant public metric in the profession, this measure of profitability is not economically sound, and at the practice/matter level can lead to extraordinary misallocation of resources. In the extreme, using this measure of profitability, partners who do all of their work themselves, assuming their rate is paid, will have the most "profitable" practices,

---

3. More than 40 percent of respondents to LawVision Group's 2013 Partner Compensation System reported that client and matter profitability had at least a moderate impact on partner compensation.

because their time is assumed to be "free." The profit margin on their work might be as high as 50 percent. However, a better answer for the client and for the firm in the long run might be a well-leveraged practice that has a more modest "margin"—but lower cost to deliver the service. Unleveraged partners, while maintaining a high margin, are effectively limited in the amount they can do for the clients.

Common Profitability Measures/Calculating Profitability

There are five common profitability measures. Allocation methods for calculating profitability are described more fully following the five measures.

- **Net Income.** This is the final, bottom-line dollar amount available for distribution to partners after all expenses have been paid. By itself, a firm's net income is a relatively meaningless number since the value itself, say $20 million, doesn't really indicate how a firm is performing. All it tells us is that the firm has $20 million in net income.
- **Net Income as a Percentage of Revenue (Profit Margin).** This figure is often quoted, yet has little use and is rarely understood. Because profit margin is significantly impacted by a firm's leverage structure, it's quite possible for a partner to earn more in a well-leveraged, low-profit-margin firm than a partner in a little-leveraged, high-profit-margin firm.
- **Net Income per Equity Partner.** This is one of the most commonly quoted measures of profitability (because of Am Law annual publications). While this number may be useful when comparing one firm to another, it is only useful if the calculation of net income and who is and who is not an equity partner is done consistently.
- **Profits in Excess of Partner "Salary."** The goal of this calculation is to determine how much excess profit a group, typically a practice area and sometimes an office, generates after the partners are paid some basic amount for their working attorney effort.
- **Net Income by Office/Practice/Client/Fee Earner.** This calculation is intended to reveal how much excess profit is being pushed to the bottom line after taking into account all costs associated with the group (or whatever is being analyzed).

Common Profitability Measures/Calculating Profitability (cont.)

There are three primary options for calculating profitability. As one moves down from one option to another, the level of detail increases, as does the need to develop additional assumptions. By and large, the choice of which option is best depends on the level of detail the firm wants and the amount of time to be spent on the analysis.

For a high-level planning exercise, a firm may simply calculate the contribution to overhead and partner compensation for each of its various practices and use that information to help identify which practices are contributing the most and may be good places for further investments. This means using one of the first two formulas below. The second one can be more difficult, as it requires agreement to more assumptions about allocations.

For matter profitability, a firm would typically use the third formula: fully allocated costs. Also, a firm may want to use this method for trying to determine how it should price its services in order to meet a profit target after paying all direct and indirect costs.

Formulas for calculating the three primary options follow (definitions for the terms used are included in the endnote):

- **Contribution to Overhead and Partner Compensation.** Revenue *less* Direct Costs *equals* Contribution

    Revenue
    (Direct Costs)
    Contribution

- **Contribution to Partner Compensation.** Revenue *less* Direct Costs *less* Allocated Overhead *equals* Contribution

    Revenue
    (Direct Costs)
    (Allocated Overhead)
    Contribution

Common Profitability Measures/Calculating Profitability (cont.)

- **Fully Allocated Costs.** Revenue *less* Direct Costs *less* partner Compensation (or Proxy Compensation) *less* Allocated Overhead *equals* Profit/Loss

Revenue

(Direct Costs)

(Equity Partner Compensation or Proxy)

<u>(Allocated Overhead)</u>

Profit/Loss

Definitions:

Revenue—fees collected from client

Direct Costs—costs associated with all timekeepers who are not equity partners (e.g., associate or paralegal compensation and benefits)

Overhead/Indirect Costs—all other costs that are not direct costs (e.g., rent, technology, administrative staff salary, and benefits)

Allocated Overhead—portion of total firm overhead expenses that are allocated to each timekeeper. Some firms calculate the amount of overhead allocated to timekeepers depending on title (e.g., partners could have a larger allocation of overhead than paralegals because it is assumed that they utilize more of the total firm overhead dollars).

Partner Compensation—compensation (or a proxy amount) and benefits attributed to each individual equity partner.

Measuring profitability and efficiency is important in firms seeking to be successful in their project management initiatives because project management is about the efficient and effective management of matters. Improving efficiency and effectiveness ultimately involves changing how things are done, which requires people—the partners in this case—to change their own behaviors. For example, partners need to care about using the best *and* most efficient lawyer or resource on the matter for the task to be done, rather than use "their favorite associate" on every project even when that person does not have the right level of competency or the right legal expertise for the matter and is therefore likely not the most efficient.

There are other issues that arise when partners do not have a direct financial incentive (i.e., compensation motivation) to operate in a way consistent with good project management. Examples include:

- A partner who is not concerned about associate inefficiency on a matter because write-offs/write-downs do not have a significant impact on his compensation. As a result, he does not spend the necessary time up front explaining a matter, providing clear instructions when he delegates, etc. When the associate is inefficient and some of his or her time needs to be written off, assuming the partner adjusts the client's bill appropriately, the partner sees little personal impact, at least in the short run.
- A partner who records more time to the matter for a given task than the task requires or that was budgeted when pricing the matter for the client, because the partner is not efficient or is not paying attention to the time spent on each task.
- A partner who has too much of his time on a matter to keep his hours high (which does positively impact his compensation, usually), rather than delegating to a more cost-effective resource for the work.

Each of these regularly occurs in many firms and has an impact on the management of matters.

The second area is in the mismatch between the significant emphasis on billable hours as the primary measure of personal productivity and the implications on improving efficiencies. Associates almost universally (and partners generally) have some level of billable hours target, goal, or expectation. In many firms, if an associate does not meet these targets, they are potentially vulnerable to losing their jobs, particularly if this failure to meet the target persists over time. In many firms, failure to meet the billable hours target makes the associate ineligible for bonuses (or some bonuses), even if he met many other qualitative goals or measures that the firm tells associates are important. Still other firms are even more direct and link bonuses and pay directly to the hours the associate works. Of course, all of this tells the associates that what is most important is their hours and their economic value, not the other areas that firm management might have articulated, but does not appear to, factor into the compensation decision.

The focus primarily on billable hours for associate performance is particularly a problem for LPM or any effort to increase efficiency on matters because, on the one hand, most firms today are talking extensively (through memos, firm meetings, etc.) about the importance of efficiency in handling clients' work and, on the other hand, they are specifically rewarding associates for their higher billable hours, as long as the firm can collect for those hours. In most firms today, there is no direct measure of an associate's efficiency, so they are essentially rewarding them for being inefficient, though no firm would state that it is consciously trying to do so.

Each of these issues can be addressed if partners, and ultimately all time-keepers on a matter, have the incentive to handle the work in an efficient way, in addition to meeting all the expectations for quality work and service.[4]

---

4. It should be noted, however, that the issue concerning hours probably cannot be fully addressed under most circumstances, and will remain a significant issue as long as the primary approach to billing clients for legal work is hourly. In a 100 percent fixed-fee environment, of course, the partners would clearly have an incentive to produce work efficiently, and this could be conveyed to the associates with appropriate incentives. However, there remains a question of capacity management, and as a result, a major increase in efficiency of, say, 25 percent would not result in any less pressure on the associates to work on client matters—it would simply translate into a reduction of 25 percent in the number of people employed to do the work (unless the firm had a matching increase in the number of matters the clients wanted handled). If an average associate is currently working 1,600 hours on client matters, it makes no sense to allow that to decline to 1,200 (from a cost management point of view), so the pressure to maintain client hours ("productive time") will remain. Absent a huge influx

Before addressing how to reward profitable and efficient management of matters, we should deal with some myths and misperceptions about compensation generally.

Compensation Principles

First, compensation is not simply a way of dividing the profits. It is one of the most powerful management tools available in any firm. While research shows that most lawyers are not primarily motivated by money (contrary to popular opinion), compensation does more than reward lawyers for their contributions. Because there is little hierarchy in law firms and little position power, compensation is often seen as a way the partners are ranked, recognized, and their success acknowledged.

Second, if a law firm has an "objective" or formula compensation system, it is almost impossible to consistently and fairly reward complex behavioral activities like teamwork, upfront planning on a matter (to prevent inefficiencies or client dissatisfaction later), quality, practice group management, lawyer development, and client relationship management and sharing. This is largely because those behaviors do not lend themselves to simple or quantitative measurement. As a result, since these are all critical activities in most firms, purely objective systems have largely disappeared, as noted earlier. However, a system does not have to be purely objective, in the sense that compensation can be set entirely by spreadsheet, for this situation to exist.

Subjective systems vary widely in the degree to which their outcomes mimic a purely formulaic approach. In the more truly subjective firms, perhaps two-thirds of the compensation allocation can be linked directly to the numbers, leaving a third available to differentiate based on more qualitative considerations. In others though, the numbers drive the outcome in all but name—making them essentially a formula in disguise. Conceptually of course, "profitability" does lend itself to quantification, and could be

---

of additional work to do, there are very strong countervailing pressures that will ultimately remain in place.

included in a formulaic or virtually formulaic approach, though this is not typically a statistic used in such systems.

Third, changing human behavior is very complex. It is not simply a function of the right compensation incentives. One must also recognize the impact of historical ways of operating and doing the legal work, firm culture, leadership, and other norms that affect behavior of lawyers. While compensation systems affect behavior and can dis-incentivize the right behavior, law firm culture and other factors can also affect how the lawyers will work in teams, collaborate, manage people and projects effectively, and more.

Metrics to Incentivize LPM

Increasingly, legal organizations are questioning what metrics should be used to measure the impact of project management—at an organizational, matter, and individual level. As described above, law firms are also responding internally to the market pressures described in chapter 1 by beginning to change the historical metrics of success. After years of increasing write-offs and write-downs, firms are now focusing on the impact of partner actions (or inaction, such as a lack of project management) on these losses. Historically, productivity reports in law firms focused on hours and dollars billed, and hours and dollars collected. Write-offs and write-downs, although shown in reports, were not necessarily evaluated as long as the billing or client lawyers had a threshold of collections in their column. Now that law firms are placing a greater emphasis on not only collections, but profitable collections, law firms are also analyzing data on the profitability of clients and matters.

For example, if there are $1 million in collections and $200,000 in write-offs for matter A, and there are $500,000 in collections and $50,000 in write-offs for matter B, matter B may be more desirable work, despite the lower total volume. These types of success metrics are not being reviewed solely at the matter level, but are also being reported and evaluated at the client level.

Law firms are analyzing some combination of the following metrics, some of these also illustrate an interest in improving processes in addition to managing projects:

1. write-offs
2. matter profitability
3. client profitability
4. unit cost of work
5. unit time to complete
6. total matter elapsed time—total matter elapsed time in some cases might not change, but the firm may be able to spend time on higher value functions that increase client satisfaction or increase the chance of achieving any bonus or success fee from the client, where applicable
7. client satisfaction—there have been several articles about Eversheds' project management success, and they use this measure, along with others
8. associate utilization
9. associate retention
10. adoption rates of project management or process improvement techniques (such as on tools like budgeting or matter management)—this may be too easily manipulated to be very useful but may have some value from a firm management perspective in terms of comparing how different practices use the techniques, etc.

Most law firms are not using these in a comprehensive fashion yet, but a growing number of firms are gathering information and starting to evaluate at least some of these. One of the challenges with these metrics is that there are many factors affecting outcomes. Often, it can be difficult to separate the impact of project management from other factors, like market competition for associates or overall demand affecting associate utilization.

Some firms are considering these metrics and others as part of partner compensation systems to drive partner behavior in the areas now desired in the "new normal" marketplace. These additional metrics include profit per practice member or per employee, matter contribution to profit/margin, profit per share of practice managed, total profit of work originated/

managed, unit cost of work originated/managed, etc. Depending on the individual's role in the project team or position in the firm, one metric may be weighted more than another.

Profitability is a measure of not only the collections versus write-offs but also the cost rates for all timekeepers on the matter versus the standard rates collected for those timekeepers. For example, if matter C is staffed with mostly partners with a lower cost-to-standard-rate margin, and matter D is staffed mostly with associates and paralegals with higher cost-to-standard-rate margins, matter D will be more profitable.

In most law firms, profitability goals are set at anywhere between 25 percent and 33 percent over the cost rate of all timekeepers, depending on the nature of the work. When firms evaluate alternative fee arrangements, such as fixed fees or capped fees, pricing managers and analysts will model the potential profitability by looking at the cost rate of all timekeepers, the number of hours related to those timekeepers, and the standard rate for all timekeepers. If the potential profit margin is lower than the goal, the matter should either be declined or staffing assignments must be reconfigured to reach the profit goal. In some matters, law firms may realize even higher profitability when large teams of associates, staff lawyers, and paralegals are responsible for most of the work and create significant leverage. Other matters may have lower profitability because partners perform most of the work and have no leverage to spread their costs.

With regard to client or matter write-offs and write-downs, project management provides a remedy. Project management empowers legal teams with a systematic method for scoping and clarifying expectations with a client before the matter begins and makes available the necessary tools for more accurate budget development and more efficient management of the matter. Project management budget development techniques, such as "what if" scenarios, can also assist with staffing models to ensure that the right mix of partner, associate, staff lawyer, or paralegals is established to meet the profitability goal.

Steps to Align Compensation and Metrics

With these points in mind, there are some steps that can be taken to align a legal organization's compensation incentives with the goals and activities of legal project management.

1. **Matter Profitability Data.** First, while most law firms have subjective partner compensation systems, as mentioned above, most firms also have a heavy emphasis "on the numbers." So, if firms can find the right metrics to measure that incentivize good LPM behaviors, these are likely to be taken more seriously by partners than more subjective criteria, such as teamwork. One of the most important metrics for this is matter profitability. Many firms have been analyzing information about client and matter profitability for years. Until recently, however, they had not used it directly in the partner compensation process.

   There has been a valid concern that too heavy an emphasis on profitability would result in a compensation process focused on individual partner profitability—"I made this much profit for the firm, so I should be paid that." Instead, use the profitability of the matters a partner manages as *one* of the objective criteria he or she is compensated based upon. Historically, the closest factor to this in many firms was realization, and in some firms partners would be penalized if their matters had significant write-offs/write-downs that affected realization. However, realization statistics are affected by many factors besides efficiency and LPM practices, and are a weaker measure of overall lawyer management effectiveness than are profitability measures.

   Several years ago, at least a dozen Am Law 100 firms started educating their partners about what matter profitability data meant and how they could affect the profitability of their matters. In some firms, they told them directly that within a few years they would be including this data in the objective information used for partner compensation. As noted earlier in footnote 3, a fairly significant number of U.S. firms are at least beginning to incorporate profitability measures into their compensation-setting processes. Other firms are still just teaching partners about it; however, they are having increasing numbers of conversations with partners when their matters have profitability issues to hold them more accountable and ensure they understand the impact of their decisions as they staff and manage their matters.

When partners believe that the profitability of the matters they manage is a significant factor in their compensation, it incentivizes more upfront project planning and better delegation (including clearer communication about the project, the specific assignment, any budget or other limits on the amount of time the task should take, etc.). It also incentivizes them to stay on top of what is happening on a matter (or to assure that someone does) to make sure the work is proceeding according to the project plan.

2. **Messaging in the Compensation Process.** It is important to carefully evaluate the organization's messaging to determine if the organization is sending mixed or even negative messages about the kinds of behaviors that are important for LPM. There are three main areas to review, as follows:

   o **Gathering Compensation Information.** First, look at the process for gathering information during the compensation process. Many firms ask their partners to complete a short questionnaire or a memo about their contributions, particularly those that will not show up in the objective data used by the compensation committee. Many firms also conduct interviews of each partner to elicit information that cannot be accurately or effectively obtained through memos or to have a more insightful dialogue with each partner than the information they gather in written forms.

   With either a questionnaire or interviews, it is important to be cognizant of the messages that are sent, and the expectations that are encouraged. For example, some firms that have implemented legal project management kept using the same historical questionnaire and/or interview guides that focus primarily on individual contributions and, directly or indirectly, top-line results, also sometimes called "volume revenues." Questions like "what are your personal goals for your practice?" and "what have you personally done to contribute to the firm?" often reinforce the perception that all that matters are individual contributions. Instead, ask questions that support the behaviors the firm is trying to motivate, such as "how are you improving the efficiency of the matters you manage?" and "how are you teaching other members of your team what the client's expectations for efficiency are?" or "how have you changed your approach to managing your matters to meet the current rate or efficiency pressures from clients?"

Many firms also utilize interviews with firm management, particularly practice leaders, as part of the compensation process. These are valuable for many purposes, but to encourage behaviors consistent with LPM, input about partners should be gathered from practice group leaders, the LPM initiative team, an alternative fee arrangements or billing committee (who in some firms have to approve all alternative fee arrangements, significant deviations from standard rates, significant write-offs, etc.), the CFO, pricing director, legal project managers (if any), and others who may have information about how each partner is on or off track in terms of the kinds of behaviors and attitudes the organization wants to encourage.

This input can be solicited and provided to the practice leaders for these partners or to another person actively involved in the compensation process, and does not mean having a meeting with the compensation body and the person in each of these positions. Each new behavior that is important to encourage for LPM to be successful should be evaluated or discussed in the compensation process so partners recognize there are different areas of emphasis and incentive from in the past. For example, in some firms implementing LPM the past few years, they changed the questions guiding their partner interview process. In others, they provided a memo from firm management at the beginning of the new year for compensation outlining the new metrics and behaviors that would be considered or expected.

o **Specific Messaging.** The second area concerns the need for clear, consistent, and effective messages to the partners with the compensation feedback. These themes or messages should be designed to guide partners toward their highest and best roles for the firm, *not* to justify or rationalize their compensation. The exercise of designing clear messages forces members of the committee to have very important conversations about what partners should be focusing on in the coming year, and how they can provide the greatest value to the firm (which, in turn, should enable them to earn more compensation). Then, these messages should be delivered in in-person meetings with a chance to explain and discuss them. Absent this step, it is virtually impossible to use the compensation system effectively as a management tool with the goal of changing behavior.

o **Feedback.** The third area involves the input into the feedback process. Post-compensation-setting messages should include feedback from the practice group leaders, LPM initiative team, the CFO, pricing director, office managing partners, client team leaders, or others who have had input in the process. The feedback can be in summary form as long as it is clear that (1) a range of peoples' input was solicited (the partner should know who they were), evaluated, and valued as part of the process and (2) the committee used its best judgment to weigh and consider this input in reaching its conclusions. The compensation committee should not fall victim to the idea of attributing feedback and avoiding personal responsibility for making tough decisions. The committee's role is to hold people to high standards and generally hold partners accountable. The key is to gather the feedback—and ensure that the partners know who has input—and concentrate on ensuring that the message given to the partner is the right message, regardless of whom it comes from.

In summary, using compensation as the powerful management tool that it can be is not easy. But, it is critical to the future success of law firms. If the compensation system is not aligned to include supporting more efficient and effective management of matters, many LPM initiatives may prove ineffective long term. This means tracking the right metrics and valuing behaviors consistent with effective LPM. However, aligning compensation with the evolving needs of a firm or legal department will be an ongoing, continuous process while the overall structure and performance of the legal industry is in flux. It is important to recognize behaviors that drive efficiency—but firms still must recognize and reward partners in a way that makes them competitive for talent, and like it or not the market remains very active for "portable books of business." Similarly, the tension between rewarding efficiency and the focus on hours as a performance metric will probably not disappear rapidly and certainly will not prior to a much more complete adoption of fixed- or project-billing approaches as the standard in the industry. So while this will be a work in progress, the key is to find a good balance now and to continue to refine the approach as the organization and the market evolves.

Chapter 17

Establishing a Project Management Function in Your Legal Organization

As discussed throughout this book, legal project management (LPM) is a new approach for lawyers. Law school curriculums and other programs for practicing lawyers have not prepared lawyers for the dramatic changes currently taking place in the legal industry that now require specialized training to implement project management techniques. So how can a law firm or legal department ensure lawyers have the necessary resources to address these types of issues and encourage processes and procedures for project management?

This chapter will cover three main topics: (I) the various roles that are helpful in implementing LPM in a legal organization, (II) the steps needed if one decides to establish a legal project management office (LPMO), and (III) the skill sets and resources necessary for supporting project management in legal organizations.

Key Roles for Implemention of a LPM Initiative

There are various roles that are important in implementing legal project management, at least at this stage of its evolution in legal organizations. The roles include:

- leader of the LPM initiative in the organization,

- project manager at the matter/project level,
- internal "consultant" to the project teams,
- trainer in LPM concepts and skills, and
- change agent.

One person can play more than one of these roles, but at least at this stage of LPM's implementation in most legal organizations, all of the roles are important. Each is described below.

Leader of LPM Initiative

In most organizations, the leader should be a senior in-house counsel, partner, or equivalent level and ideally a member of the organization's management. In a law firm, this would be a member of management or the executive committee. It is optimal if the leader can champion the initiative after the benefit and experience of early adoption of LPM in his or her own work.[1] The leader of the initiative in law firms has often been in charge of a committee or task force dedicated to rolling out pilot projects, exploring new tools or approaches, or getting buy-in of senior lawyers. These task forces or committees have worked best when they are composed of a multi-disciplinary team of lawyers and other high-level professional management from functions like knowledge management (KM), finance, practice management, business development, information technology (IT), and professional development. The leader has the primary role of championing the initiative, lobbying for resources (budget, dedicated staff, investment time, etc.) for the initiative, leading partner or senior lawyer retreats or meetings to develop buy-in, and more. In legal departments, the leader has often been one of the assistant or associate general counsel, assisted by other professionals with a background in project management or related subjects.

---

1. At Baker Donelson, this role was assumed by the firm's Chief Strategic Planning Officer, William Painter and author Rueff suported the initiative as the LPM Officer.

Law Firm Implementation Example

Based upon the Baker Donelson's decision to implement project management, in 2011, Baker Donelson shareholder David Rueff assumed the newly created position of Legal Project Management Officer in charge of leading a team of project managers in the Firm's newly created Legal Project Management Office. The scope of that office is consistent with the information in this Chapter. David's background in project management evolved from both his pre-law and law firm experience. Prior to law school, David was a Senior Systems Engineer for a computer hardware and software company. His experience with this company included the use of project management methods for software development. In his role with this company, David also provided technical consulting services for the implementation of a project management information system used to characterize hazardous waste sites. The system collected site specific information into a relational database (such as soil, surface hydrology, subsurface hydrology, contaminant measurements and surface mapping) and presented that information in a graphical display for evaluation when designing remedial solutions. As a practicing lawyer, David's exposure to project management methods grew in part from his experience managing a legal team administering grants for Hurricane Katrina. The grant management process required evaluation by a multi-disciplinary team of accountants, lawyers, engineers, environmental scientists, auditors, and project managers through an assembly line type process. Each point in the assembly line was required to receive input regarding the applicant's eligibility for assistance, evaluate that information and then approve the application for further processing. Due to the large number of grants (in the thousands), the limited budget for management of the grant process pursuant to federal guidelines, and the strict timelines for processing, all phases of the grant administration process, including legal, were required to detail their processes (i.e. the WBS referred to in chapter 4), identify the time necessary to administer the process, and identify the budget to administer that process.

> ## Law Firm Implementation Example cont.
>
> This "plan" had to be managed using a project management information systems built in a web based database. Additionally, the "plan" had to be re-evaluated every 30 days to confirm the size of the team and to identify areas for improvement and streamlining. This immersion into a true project management workflow is what prompted David's interest in obtaining the Project Management Professional (PMP) certification through the Project Management Institute. After David obtained the his PMP certification, the Firm's Chief Strategic Planning Officer, William Painter, recognized that these techniques might have broader application to both the management of alternative fee arrangements and hourly matters which lead to the development of the BakerManage™ process.

Project Manager at Matter Level

Many legal organizations are beginning to recognize the need for a project manager to be a part of the matter team, at least for large matters. These individuals lead the development of the project charter and project plan, plan team meetings (and sometimes run them), develop and manage the budget, monitor budget and other plans, identify issues, and interact closely with the partner/senior lawyer in charge of matter.

When a firm undertakes a new matter, there is typically a designation of various roles for the matter, such as the relationship/client, lawyer, the billing lawyer (i.e., the one who is credited with revenue from the matter), and the responsible lawyer (though the usage of these terms varies from firms to firms). In some cases, these designations may relate to the same lawyer, but when there are different lawyers assigned for each designation, the responsible lawyer (at least as how it is defined in most firms as the person managing the matter) is most likely the "project manager" for the matter. In a legal department, there is a designation of the lawyer in charge of the matter.

The person who serves the role of the project manager (PM) should perform the following actions:

- Facilitate development of the scope of work statement and project plan
- Monitor the budget, actuals, and changes in scope
- Track performance and provide feedback
- Resolve issues and manage conflict within the project team and with stakeholders
- Manage stakeholder perceptions and expectations
- Distribute information/communicate effectively
- Provide or arrange for substantive, procedural, or process training, as necessary
- Handle change requests (staffing, scope, resources, deliverables, timing, etc.)

The PM does not have to do all of these things but should ensure that someone on the project team is responsible for each of them. Through the PM's direct oversight of these responsibilities, or even through delegation of duties to another team member to assure coverage, the project is typically more successful in achieving objectives and should be shielded from the devastating effects that can result from changes within the matter.

The PM could be a lawyer or paralegal who is trained or at least knowledgeable in project management and who is already a member of the project team, and the role of PM will be another "hat" or role that person will play on the team. The matter PM could also be a professional with project management experience whose only role on the matter is to be the PM. In some organizations, PMs are former practicing lawyers, and in other organizations, they come from varied PM backgrounds, which might include technology, manufacturing, consulting or construction. The PM at the matter level would help the matter team through each of the phases of LPM, as described in the framework in chapter 3.

The PM may be an existing member of the legal team and not a full-time designated PM for the team. In these situations, legal organizations are still trying to determine who is the best person to play these roles. One major New York firm is having its paralegals obtain certifications in legal project management so they can act as PMs for their matters for a major financial institution. Other firms are training their senior associates or new equity partners to be the PMs on matters, while still others feel that every lawyer should have a working understanding of LPM to apply to their work whether they will play a role as a PM or as a lead partner on a role. While any member of the project team with enough experience and interpersonal skills can be the PM and every member of the legal team plays a role in project management, some roles work are better for certain individuals than others. For example, while the most senior lawyer on the project may have the gravitas to manage client relationships, develop budgets with appropriate assumptions, guide lawyers' time allocation to a project, etc., they often do not have the time for nor the interest in, developing plans and detailed budgets and managing the financial aspects of the work. If the PM is also playing a role in the substantive legal work, the PM will need to be careful to not be so focused on the "billable" work and ignore the critical project management tasks that are most pressing.

The PM functioning at the matter level may be assigned to a single client or large matter, to all the matters of a particular client, to a practice group for its matters, or to a client or client portfolio of matters (a group of matters that are related to a particular client). As a result, the PM may work on one very large matter at a time or for many matters, much like an account manager.

Internal "Consultant" to the Project Teams

This role is very similar to the project manager for a particular matter, but some firms, especially small to midsize firms, have only one project manager for the entire firm. In this case, the person cannot function as a project manager handling all the PM roles for all, or even most, of the firm's matters. Instead, the PM functions like an internal consultant to the matter teams, providing advice, helping them use tools and fulfilling other functions—depending on the number of teams using them and the priorities of each matter team.

Project Management Trainer

An element of almost every legal organization's LPM initiative is some type of basic education and skills training. The training may be conducted by outside consultants or it may be developed and taught by professionals in the firm or legal department. In some organizations, the head of LPM efforts has developed and led the training. In others, they have not done training with small or large groups but have taught the LPM skills through one-on-one coaching with the lawyers or paralegals. Dedicated PMs may not have the skills to teach others; however, some organizations expect those skills as part of what they seek when hiring a director of legal project management.

Change Agent

As mentioned in earlier chapters, legal project management is not a complex area to learn or apply. The biggest challenge facing legal organizations is the behavior change that is required—getting lawyers to do things differently than they have done in the past. As a result, a major role of many involved with LPM initiatives is that of change agent. Each of the roles described above involves an element of change management, whether it is getting lawyers to use different forms or systems, communicating differently with clients and the members of the project team, or other changes. It is very helpful if the person (or persons) leading the LPM initiative understands the processes and steps involved in change management and behavior change.

Currently, many legal organizations are hiring or trying to hire legal project managers who will fill one or more of the roles above. In some cases, the job description covered all of the areas above. However, be careful about expecting one person to fulfill too many of these distinct roles described above. It may doom a person to failure, especially in legal organizations where failure could set the initiative back and create more lawyer cynicism about the new approach. Sample job descriptions for LPM positions recently filled in law firms are provided as appendix 4. Many have the same title but different requirements or job functions.

Establishing a Legal Project Management Office

The next part of this chapter will provide a step-by-step approach for building, staffing, and operating an office dedicated to project and process management, budget development and oversight, and collection of lessons learned and resources. Many organizations have already accepted the value of project management in the technology side of their organizations and have established project management offices to oversee large-scale technological initiatives. Some legal organizations are now applying this management concept by creating a formal team whose sole responsibility is to foster the implementation of LPM.

The recommended steps include:

1. identifying key stakeholders for the LPMO and create buy-in,
2. identifying a consistent LPM approach for the organization,
3. developing the scope of services for the LPMO, and
4. assembling the necessary resources for support/staff the LPMO.

Identify the Key Stakeholders for the LPMO and Create Buy-In

A foundational tenet of project management is clarifying and confirming expectations with stakeholders. This is also critical in the creation and implementation of a legal project management office to ensure continued support, collaboration with other departments, and centralization of matter management resource development. The following charts (figures 17–1 and 17–2 below) identify the key stakeholders within the organization who should be consulted for law firms and corporate legal departments:

Law Firm

Stakeholder	Scope of Expectations
Managing Partner / Executive Committee / Chief Executive Officer	Are the policy and procedures consistent with the needs of lawyers and the goals of the organization?
Chief Financial Officer	Are the structure of the team, proposed resources, and budget for all LPMO activities supported by firm's revenue and profitability expectations?
Chief Operating Officer	What is the organizational placement of the LPMO, reporting structures, budget approvals, and required credentialing for the team?
Strategic Planning	How will the office interact and help further the short-term strategic goals and long-term strategic plan of the firm?

Stakeholder	Scope of Expectations
Marketing	How will the office collaborate with marketing to support new-client development and client retention?
Finance and Billing	Since budgeting and predictability is a key component of project management, how can the firm's financial reporting and billing systems be used to gather and present matter-level performance information?
Information Technology	A LPM implementation fosters an environment of innovation. How will these innovations be captured and implemented to meet the expectations of clients and lawyers? A project management information system (PMIS) is often selected and implemented by the IT department. How can a PMIS facilitate the LPM efforts in the firm? Should a PMIS be built internally or purchased from an outside vendor?
Knowledge Management	LPM is closely tied with knowledge management because it relies upon templates and resources created by others and, through lessons learned, fosters an environment of continued improvement. How can resources be fed to LPM implementations and improvements be cataloged within the firm's knowledge management framework?
Pricing and Procurement	More clients are including an in-depth evaluation of pricing in the selection of their outside legal counsel. How can the LPM budgeting process include the pricing evaluation techniques of a procurement department to ensure that the profitability goals of the firm are incorporated into matter management?
Training	How can LPM be incorporated into the developmental processes and training sessions for all new hires, associates, practice groups, and clients?

Figure 17–1

Law Firm Stakeholders for LPM Implementation

Legal Department

Stakeholder	Scope of Expectations
General Counsel	LPM offers a methodical framework to ensure consistency in the legal services provided to an organization. How can a LPM system be implemented within the corporate legal department and imposed on outside counsel to control legal spend while maintaining quality of work and service?
Business Department Leads	How can the business departments and legal department collaborate to improve the delivery of services within the organization?
Information Technology	How can a PMIS system be implemented within the company to improve communication among the business, management, and legal departments and provide real-time information on the cost and outcomes of legal matters and the performance of outside counsel?
Procurement	Just as with law firms, procurement identifies the specifications and evaluates the responses of requests for proposals (RFPs) for legal services. How can a system be established to clearly communicate this information to ensure comprehensive responses to RFPs and streamline the evaluation and analysis of law firm selection and management?

Figure 17–2

Law Department Stakeholders for LPM Implementation

It should be noted that obtaining the buy-in of all these stakeholders is not an easy task, and may require the formation of committees composed of some of these key stakeholders to create an internal support mechanism for LPM. Those corporate legal departments or law firms that have been leaders in LPM also had internal champions, such as practice group leaders, rainmakers, and key members of the management team, with the strategic vision to realize the benefits of a LPM approach.

The LPMO for one firm has been in existence for over two years, and has the following reporting structure:

- The team is led by a lawyer with experience in the practice of law, project management, and some technology.
- The LPM lead reports directly to the firm's chief operating officer.
- Budgeting planning and approval are coordinated with the firm's chief financial officer.
- Strategic vision and development are coordinated with the firm's strategic planning officer.
- The LPMO coordinates with the firm's technology committee to eliminate overlap and duplication with IT and KM responsibilities.
- The LPMO cooperates with the procurement officer to implement LPM concepts into fee arrangements.
- The LPMO coordinates with e-discovery initiatives that require the implementation of project management techniques to control costs.

Figure 17-3
Legal Project Management Hierarchy

Figure 17–3 shows this firm's LPMO organizational chart.

Whether developed by committee or by individual consultation, the goals of the stakeholder group implementing the LPMO should be the following:

- Develop, encourage, and/or confirm firm or organizational support for the initiative at all levels of management.

- Ensure consistency with the long-term strategic vision of the organization.
- Determine and implement appropriate communication to the business units, practice groups, and lawyers (as applicable).
- Coordinate with other functions or departments to confirm consistency with other initiatives.
- Educate lawyers on the importance and application of project management principles to achieve client value, cost savings, and predictability.

As part of building a consensus with stakeholders, law firms and legal departments trying to implement LPM understand that lawyers want and require real-world examples of how LPM can enhance their matter management, prior to investing the time to implement new methods into their practices. They may demand empirical proof that the methods work. Some may ask for data that demonstrates that cases managed with LPM are more efficient than those managed without LPM. Unless a lawyer has identical matters that can be managed side by side, this is almost impossible to demonstrate. However, similar proof can be obtained by testimonials from those within the organization and from other organizations that already apply project management techniques. These individuals should be able to provide examples and experiences of the benefits of project management and may even have a history of stronger profit margins and great client retention. Additionally, client testimonials regarding the benefits of LPM can provide another powerful source of evidence that the techniques can and will improve client retention and trust.

Identify a Consistent LPM Approach

The first step in implementation of a legal project management office is to work with the key stakeholders identified above to identify or develop a consistent framework for management or alternatives described, and closure. Firms and legal departments can use the method outlined in chapters 3 through 10, methods more aligned with traditional project management identified in chapter 18. There are several methodologies discussed in this chapter, which may provide guidance such as traditional or waterfall project management, Scrum techniques or Six Sigma. The approach may also need to be customized for the needs of different practice areas such as transactional versus litigation or matters that are heavily controlled by regulatory processes. Although a legal project management office could be established without this, it is unlikely that significant results will be realized without having an overall PM framework and approach that fits the organization.

In addition to the process and methodologies selected, lawyers and legal teams will require an easy way to implement them. This requires the creation of a project management information system that permits project information to be shared across the organization, including documents, budget status, and schedules. In chapter 8, a framework for a PMIS is described, and appendix 2 provides examples of software applications that can be implemented as a successful implementation tool. Some of these systems, as described in that chapter, also provide their own unique workflows for matter evaluation and management.

Develop the Scope of Services for the LPMO

Defining the scope of an LPMO within an organization is an iterative process that is likely to require regular reevaluation and possible reconfiguration. This is especially true if the LPMO team is leanly staffed in order to reduce the impact on the organization's bottom line. On a project basis, the primary objective of a LPMO is to implement LPM concepts that add value to client relationships and increase efficiency and value of legal matters. This includes creating methods for improved communication and more transparency between the lawyer and the client and for fostering improved communication between the lawyer and legal team. From the standpoint of the organization, the primary objectives of the LPMO are implementation of a LPM process and identification of quantifiable results from this process, such as enhanced client relationships, or improved profitability of matters or reduced legal costs.

The scope of the LPMO function can include training and consulting with legal teams on implementation, developing and cataloging resources, encouraging further innovation in legal practices and processes, and collaborating with clients to cement relationships. Organizations should also consider what other legal support services should be included in the LPMO, such as document review, litigation support, e-discovery, pricing and analytics, or practice group support in order to ensure that the concepts of project management are woven into the fabric of the organization. In some firms, the project management function is "housed" in the finance, KM, business development or practice management structure as it relates closely to each of these functions. In others, there is a separate LPMO.

Areas that may be part of the scope of the LPMO or the group leading LPM in the organization include the following:

1. consistent application of the PM methodology
2. promoting adoption
3. training
4. consulting and technical marketing
5. pricing and procurement
6. data collection and reporting

Each is covered in detail below.

Consistent Application of the PM Methodology

Once a project management methodology has been adopted and approved in an organization, it is the job of the LPMO to ensure that it is consistently applied. If the process and system are displayed to clients, it will set expectations as to the level of detail and type of information that will be regularly provided to communicate matter/project status. Lawyers and clients who are implementing the process for the first time cannot simply fill out forms and never look at the information again. Rather, they must be coached by project managers to provide more detail than they have provided in the past regarding the nuances in the particular matter, the strategy, and their expectations with regard to costs and expenses. This data will provide the baseline for improved management and controls throughout the life of the matter. They must also be coached to adhere continually to a project management framework by scheduling regular updates to the project management information system and sharing those updates with the team and the client.

Promoting Adoption

The selection of a LPM approach should promote procedures that will not increase the costs to the client or increase time for matter management. The idea is to make matter management more efficient. This can be accomplished by not only providing useful tools to gather and distribute matter information but also to improve the service delivery model. Clients (whether they be internal or external to the organization) will realize the benefits of a LPM approach by avoiding surprises and being constantly apprised of the issues in a case.

Adoption can also be encouraged by the creation of what traditional project management identifies as organizational process assets, discussed in chapters 10 and 15. LPM helps to capture the best practices of lawyers and teams. This information, in the form of case outlines, templates, checklists, and other documents, will create a database of historical information to improve future budget estimates and matter management. The LPMO can also work with practice groups to develop unique project management plans, process maps, and databases of tasks, risks, and budgets tailored to each area of practice.

Training

The LPMO should be involved in training initiatives for all levels of the corporate legal department or law firm. As the subject-matter experts for project management and the technology supporting the LPM techniques, the LPMO will be in the best position to clearly communicate techniques and justifications for implementation. Representatives or leaders of the LPMO should also be the primary contacts for implementation, including project plan and budget development (using LPM techniques) and the proper use of templates and resources. In many law firms, however, the talent management or professional development department will also play an important role in designing and offering the training.

As to the structure of training, there are many schools of thought regarding whether horizontal, vertical, practice group, or team training is the best method. This depends in large part on the culture and philosophy of the firm or legal department. The LPMO should be involved in leading decisions about training, often in consultation with the professional development department (at least in a law firm). The LPMO and the professional develop department should consider whether the training strategy will be different for each practice type, depending on needs, the sense of urgency and buy-in to LPM. One law firm, after several practice-group-level training sessions, decided to focus training and implementation on select legal teams in order to ensure that there were sufficient resources available for implementation, project planning development, and trouble shooting. This also focused the resources where they were most needed—that is, with teams who have embraced the techniques and were willing to make an investment in an improved service delivery model for the client.

Consulting and Technical Marketing

As stated above, the LPMO will assemble the subject-matter experts within the organization on legal project management techniques. As a result, the members of the LPMO may act as internal consultants to matter teams, practice group leaders, firm management, or others on implementation of LPM approaches. Project managers may work closely with lawyers, paralegals, and case assistants to develop project plans for litigation and transactional matters, budgets, and schedules and implement the tools necessary for managing to these resources. There is also an element of training in this consulting role, since every implementation presents an opportunity to train legal teams on project management.

The development of a LPM program or approach will also provide the firm with opportunities to differentiate its services from those of other firms through its focus on client value, predictability, transparency, and continuous improvement. Lawyers who are motivated by client development are likely to seek out the LPMO project managers to assist with demonstrations of the system and with implementation. This "technical" marketing role of the LPMO will require project managers to have the ability to develop customized presentations and to conduct those presentations for clients. It is also beneficial for these technical consultants to be on hand to answer questions from clients about customized functionality.

Pricing and Procurement

As the matter management consultants within the law firm or legal department, the LPMO should be actively involved in the development of reliable budgets. In some organizations, this is driven by the finance professionals, and in others, it is through the LPM professionals or LPMO. This requires a step-by-step process to evaluate the unique attributes of a matter (scope, assumptions, and risks) and to incorporate that information into the architecture of a detailed budget (i.e., the work breakdown structure). As outlined in chapter 7, the LPMO team should also work closely with the pricing or procurement departments or professionals to ensure that budget development is sensitive to market pressures. This can be accomplished by evaluating historical information of like matters while taking into consideration any distinctions in the scope, assumptions, and risks. Additionally, the LPMO should assist the procurement department with crafting agreements, engagement letters, and contracts for services to ensure that all project planning components are incorporated.

Data Collection and Reporting

Data collection and evaluation is one of the most important objectives of the LPMO, because it encourages the identification of trends and variables that will improve the next engagement. Data collection should include the following information: budgets (qualified by scope), standard assumptions, customary risks, and communication of anticipated deviations from the baseline budget established at the outset of the matter. In order to capitalize on this information, it may be advisable to dedicate particular members of the team who are solely responsible for monitoring matters to provide lead lawyers with periodic reports on performance and analytical information. Long term, it may also be advisable to retain business analysts whose sole purpose is to evaluate data and provide lawyers with key information regarding their practices.

Skill Sets and Resources Necessary for Supporting Project Management in a Legal Organization

In order to be successful, several of the law firms and legal departments that have been leaders in this area have found that legal project management requires a team of seasoned project managers to provide support within the organization. Other law firms have begun with a task force or committee led by partners and a director of project management (or person of similar title) leading their LPM initiative. In those firms, they have focused on training paralegals, associates, or counsel to be the project managers for matter teams. The information below will apply to those firms that plan to have dedicated project managers who are not "wearing another hat," such as functioning as a paralegal or practicing lawyer. Other firms that may not be ready for this approach or may prefer to have a member of the matter team perform the project manager role may find that their professionals will play one or more of the roles described in the "Key Roles for Implemention of a LPM Initiative" section, above.

For most law firms currently implementing LPM, the resources dedicated to LPM, at least initially, are mostly not billable. As a result, the creation of a formal project management office will increase overhead and expenses. Similarly, in corporate legal departments, in the early stages of implementing LPM, LPM resources for the legal department will not be a source of direct revenue for the company. In both cases, however, the efficiencies and cost savings inherent in implementing LPM approaches typically more than justify the additional expenditures. In addition, a few firms have begun billing for the time of their project managers. For example, Seyfarth Shaw LLP has demonstrated that they can cover the overhead, compensation, and benefits of their entire LPMO of approximately 20 people through time billed to clients. Some clients are happy to pay for a project manager on their matters when they see the PM adds value.

The LPM function should be staffed with individuals with a unique set of skills in technology, legal matter management, project management, presentation, change management/consensus building, and communication. Some firms, as evidenced by the case studies included in this book, have hired project management professionals to fill this role. Others have pulled from the internal resources of the firm by selecting practicing lawyers, paralegals, or professionals from finance, pricing, or KM.

In addition to the traits and skills identified above, selected team members for the LPM function should also have familiarity with firm processes and procedures related to billing, time entry, and reporting. Organizations should not look to underproductive individuals to staff this department or function. Likelihood of success can be increased in some organizations if team members have a proven track record and credibility with lawyers so this may justify drawing from within the organization to staff this new function.

Most importantly, LPM leaders should possess strong organizational and interpersonal skills. The skills or traits identified in the Project Management Institute's *Guide to the Project Management Body of Knowledge (PMBOK Guide)* for project managers are:

- leadership,
- team building,
- motivation,
- communication,
- influencing,
- decision making,
- political and cultural awareness, and
- negotiation.[2]

This is a tall order, and not every project manager will excel in all of these, but certainly the leader of the LPMO or LPM initiative in the organization should.

Regardless of the types of professionals selected to fill these roles, the following is a list of some of the recommended qualifications for the leader and team members of the LPMO. Although this may change as LPM becomes more accepted in law firms, currently the authors believe that the leader or leaders of a LPM function need to be either a practicing lawyer, with

---

2. Project Mgmt. Inst., A Guide to the Project Management Body of Knowledge (PMBOK Guide) (4th ed. 2008).

knowledge of the challenges associated with management of clients and billing, or a professional with significant experience in legal organizations that commands high levels of credibility with senior lawyers. In addition, the leader of the LPM function and the team members should have many, if not all, of the following qualifications:

- Project Management Professional certification or significant PM experience
- experience in budget development and management
- experience in the use of technology on matters
- experience with implementation of a PMIS
- experience with the implementation of LPM on matters
- adaptability, flexibility, and the ability to implement change

Team members might be practicing lawyers, paralegals, business analysts, or project managers from other industries or backgrounds.

The size of the LPM function will depend on the scope of services, training, and the level of implementation provided for legal teams in the organization, as well as the size of the organization. Organizations are cautioned to avoid training large groups of legal professionals without making the necessary resources available for implementation (tools, project manager assistance, etc.). Thousands, if not millions, of dollars could be wasted if lawyers and legal teams are trained but there is a lack of a formal PMIS to support implementation or other resources to aid with implementation. In fact, the training often creates significant buy-in and interest in using LPM approaches, and then, if the organization does not have resources to support actual LPM implementation, lawyers can become very frustrated.

As with most roles in legal organizations, the exact requirements of the job will vary from firm to firm and one law department to another. Sample job descriptions from several organizations are attached as appendix 4. The keys are to clarify expectations of key stakeholders up front so that the legal project manager that an organization hires to lead or support the LPM initiatives is able to be successful.

Chapter 18

Introduction to Traditional and Alternative Project Management Methods

The previous chapter outlined an approach to establish a legal project management function in an organization. One of the key elements recommended was developing a consistent framework or process for matter planning, management and closure in a given legal organization. The two legal project management models described in this book were drawn in part from traditional project management methods, but were modified to meet the needs of legal practitioners. The following chapter is meant to provide the reader with an overview of traditional project management and a comparison of traditional project management to alternative methods. This information may be used by the reader for the evaluation of alternative methods and techniques that may be applicable to their own organization or practice. An organization seeking to develop a method for LPM that fits their needs might use one of the two models discussed in chapters 3 through 10 or may want to develop one based on traditional or other approaches to PM described below. The organizations setting standards for project management and available certifications for both traditional and legal project management will also be discussed.

Historical Matter Evaluation and Management Techniques

Prior to the concept of formal project management in legal engagements, lawyers developed various techniques to manage components of their practices. These techniques included forms, checklists, and a library of legal research memoranda and model documents. These tools helped reduce the amount of rework in the management of a new engagement.

For example, transactional lawyers prepare checklists that typically identify deliverables, documents, and status, who is responsible (like the RACI chart discussed in chapters 5, 8, and 9), and any issues to be resolved. Due diligence is a subproject in every transaction and has its own set of checklists, review protocols, and timetables. An example of a skeleton checklist for a construction loan is provided below:

Documents	Responsible Party	Comments	Status
Commitment Documents			
Commitment Letter/Extension	Firm/Client	Signed and delivered	Final
Loan/Collateral Documents			
Construction Loan Agreement	Firm	Circulate a final draft	Draft
Promissory Notes	Firm	Final circulated	Final
Deed of Trust, Assignment of Leases, and Rents and Security Agreement	Firm	Lawyer to circulate final draft	Draft
Guaranty Agreements: Company, LLC Owner, LLC John Smith	Firm	Lawyer to circulate final draft	Draft
Environmental Indemnity Agreement	Firm	Final circulated	Final
Security Agreement	Firm	Draft circulated	Draft
UCC-1 Financing Statements Secretary of State Filing	Firm	To be prepared and filed	Draft

Tax lawyers may also develop forms that incorporate the current requirements of the U.S. Internal Revenue Code. The tax lawyer maintains an index of these forms and all lawyers working within the group are required to utilize these forms. The value of this type of practice is efficiency (not re-creating documents for every new client), consistency of service, and protection from potential mistakes or malpractice from a failure to address a required term or provision.

In litigation, early case assessment techniques are used to outline the legal issues in a complex case prior to development of a litigation strategy. This assessment may involve the identification of the supportive and problematic facts, inventory of key documents and witnesses, and research of the legal issues in the matter. Many litigation lawyers will capture information from case assessment, discovery and pretrial in the format of a trial notebook that evolves throughout the matter. A trial notebook is the lawyer's checklist for conducting the trial and making arguments throughout the case.

There are also software applications that provide tools for:

- storage of pleadings,
- organization of facts and witnesses chronologically,
- incorporation of deposition transcripts or videos,
- creation of a privilege log,
- enhancement of search capabilities, and
- sharing of case information across a legal team.

Although these are all valuable techniques, these tools do not promote planning, budgeting, and management of the team. There is no clarification of the client's business needs and goals with regard to the matter (i.e., what success is, expressed in both business and legal terms), the scope of the work that will be handled by the members of the legal team, and a process for determining how roles and responsibilities will be allocated. There is no evaluation of the key stakeholders or decision makers in the client's organization or how to reconcile differences among stakeholders.

The above techniques also focus more on deliverables and not on the work necessary to complete those deliverables. As a result, there is no way for a client to clearly understand how much work is required to complete each deliverable. A task-based checklist or plan developed with the project management techniques outlined in this book helps to communicate this information to the client and all the members of the legal team, which in turn builds confidence in any budget and timeline based upon those tasks.

The approach described for litigation is based on the view that handling a matter (a project) should begin with a baseline set of assumptions about an anticipated outcome. It also applies to transactional and regulatory matters. In this way both the client's goal is clear and the route – the proposed legal solution or strategy to achieve the client's goal – is also clear. Although changes may be required along the way, there is a well-articulated plan and tactics to execute that plan at the outset. As the matter evolves, it is important to monitor whether the baseline assumptions (derived from the initial stakeholders) continue to be valid. Although there will be many twists and turns resulting in modifications to the work plan, the goal and solution may not change materially. Traditional project management/waterfall techniques effectively address this context.

Project Management Approaches

In order to evaluate the best approach for an organization, it is important to understand the origins and objectives of project management. Modern project management began with the development of the Gantt chart in the early 1900s and over the last hundred years has evolved into a specialized discipline that is used by virtually every industry. In many industries or organizations, project management is defined as a systematic method to collect comprehensive specifications for a product, manufacture that product in the most efficient manner, and produce a result that is consistent with the client's stated requirements.

Although the "product" for a lawyer is legal services, lawyers also have similar responsibilities to deliver those services consistent with client requirements or standard practice. Traditional project management can provide a framework for lawyers to improve their management practices. Traditional project management (detailed in this chapter and appendix 5) involves a significant number of processes[1] that are designed to wrestle control of three variables that are used as a measurement of a project's success: scope (tasks to be performed), time (deadlines imposed on the matter), and cost (including the size of the team) (the triple constraint). These variables are depicted in figure 18-1.

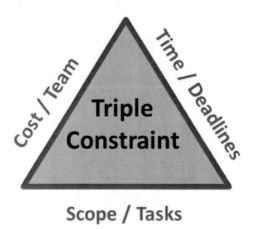

Figure 18-1
Triple Constraint

Changes in one variable will require an adjustment in the other variables. Project planning is about setting a baseline for scope, time, and cost and then controlling these variables during project execution. If a change requires one of the variables to be adjusted, then the other variables must also be evaluated for change and communicated to the client.

For example, as depicted in the first example in figure 18-2, if the scope of the project is expanded and cost remains the same, the time for completion

---

1. The discussion of traditional project management in this book is based upon the author's understanding of A Guide to the Project Management Body of Knowledge (PMBOK Guide), Fourth Edition. A Fifth Edition of the PMBOK Guide has been released by the Project Management Institute ("PMI"), and PMI has developed materials comparing the Fourth Edition to the Fifth Edition which can be found at the following: http://www.pmi.org/~/media/PDF/Marketplace/PMBOK_Guide_Fifth_Ed_Appendix_X_1.ashx (last visited December 11, 2013). For an understanding of PMI's current approach to project management, the reader is encouraged to review this material.

may need to be expanded (i.e., it will take the existing team longer to complete added scope or tasks).

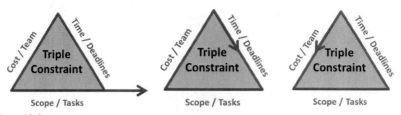

Figure 18-2
Triple Constraint Alternatives

In contrast to the current techniques of lawyers described at the beginning of this chapter, or the definition of legal project management provided in chapter 3 and explained throughout this book, project management outside the legal profession is typically defined as a systematic method to collect comprehensive requirements for a product or service based on a user's well-defined needs, develop a refined list of specifications for the output, manufacture that product (deliver the service) in the most efficient manner, and produce a result (output) that fulfills the client's requirements. There are different techniques and approaches to project management, even within the industries that have been implementing these concepts for decades. These include the "waterfall" (defined below) or the Project Management Institute's ("PMI") *Guide to Project Management Body of Knowledge (PMBOK Guide)*[2] approach, and "agile" techniques.

The most significant difference in these approaches is that in waterfall or traditional project management there is a large investment in upfront planning to develop a plan that can be used to manage the engagement to completion. The scope is controlled, and changes or dramatic deviations from the plan are not encouraged. The motto is "plan the work, work the plan." It is based on the notion that significant changes in direction should be resisted since they have a high likelihood of requiring modification of

---

2. PROJECT MGMT. INST., A GUIDE TO THE PROJECT MANAGEMENT BODY OF KNOWLEDGE (PMBOK GUIDE) (4th ed. 2008).

the plan that all the parties have embraced. If the goal and solutions do not change materially in a legal matter, this can be appropriate for those types of matters and many subprojects within a matter (e.g., due diligence, closing preparation, Hart-Scott-Rodino filings, patent prosecution, e-discovery, and drafting a motion for summary judgment).

On the other hand, there are times when the client's goal is clear but the best way to achieve it is not. This is particularly the case when there are competing stakeholders whose interests cannot be readily reconciled. For example, a company may wish to make an acquisition and be aware that the largest customer of the acquired party is likely to be displeased with the change of ownership. The expression of a potential dispute by that customer could have an effect on the negotiation, relationships with other customers, and, obviously, successful completion of the transaction. There are many ways to approach this set of facts, even though there is a willing buyer and seller who have the clear goal of wanting to do the deal. An iterative approach of developing a strategy, testing it, learning from it, and to move forward or retrench, would be appropriate in this context. No matter the scenario or the thoroughness in examining each option, and the order for executing any plan, iteration is inevitable. In order to address the disparate interests and needs of buyer, seller, and customer, it will be necessary to reevaluate after each stage of this dynamic scenario—and be nimble.

Agile techniques, which emerged to address the challenges with software development, spend less time on trying to develop the entire universe of specifications at the outset and acknowledge that the project is an iterative process. Agile techniques allow the product to evolve over time based on information that emerges during the course of the project. Planning is not diminished, but the plan, its assumptions, the Work Breakdown Structure, and the definition of a successful result are regularly reevaluated and tested and frequently reconsidered.

So which approach is most appropriate for implementation in legal engagements? The models outlined in this book are hybrid models. The BakerManage ™ model, for example, draws its phases from the waterfall approach but do not mirror it exactly and is designed to accommodate changes, no matter how significant, throughout the life cycle of the project. The tools developed with BakerManage ™ which are included in appendix

3 include agile-esque components which are designed to encourage regular communication between team members and the client regarding scope changes, completed tasks, matter status, and budget performance. The Legal Project Management Institute model is also a hybrid, which has elements of both traditional project management (because lawyers need to do a better job of upfront planning such as scoping, task assignments, and more) to form a baseline and Agile to be flexible enough to take into account the changes that will inevitably occur in most legal matters.

The authors developed these models after a thorough evaluation of various techniques including the work processes of lawyers discussed above. The following is a summary discussion of factors to consider when evaluating the right approach for an organization. Any of these techniques, a derivative, or a combination of certain attributes may be suitable for legal project management implementation.

PMBOK Guide Model of Project Management

Traditional project management is most often associated with the model advocated by the PMI. PMI describes a successful project as one that is completed within time constraints, within budget, with effective and efficient utilization of assigned resources, at the desired performance and technology level, and with the finished project accepted by the customer.[3] The PMI model of project management is codified in *A Guide to the Project Management Body of Knowledge* (*PMBOK Guide*). The *PMBOK Guide* is a management guide and international standard that provides the fundamentals of traditional project management.[4]

The following discussion is not intended to be a comprehensive restatement of project management as described in the *PMBOK Guide*, but is intended to provide an overview of the project management framework and to identify how each of the traditional project management processes is used to help define and manage the project. Figure 18-5 below identifies

---

3. To accomplish these goals, PMI identifies that a project manager should possess specific skills, which are covered in chapter 17. PROJECT MGMT. INST., http://www.pmi.org/default .aspx (last visited Nov. 7, 2013).

4. *Standards Overview*, PROJECT MGMT. INST., http://www.pmi.org/ PMBOK-Guide-and-Standards.aspx (last visited Nov. 7, 2013).

how the process groups and knowledge areas intersect as taken from the Fourth Edition of the PMBOK Guide. For more-detailed information on these processes, the *PMBOK Guide* is the best resource for definitions of these and other project management terms referenced below.[5] Also, appendix 5 provides an outline of the *PMBOK Guide, Fourth Edition* processes and some of the inputs, outputs, and tools used in each process.

The *PMBOK Guide, Fourth Edition* defines the 42 standard processes.[6] These 42 processes are distributed throughout five process groups and nine knowledge areas, each of which is defined and discussed in appendix 5.[7] The *PMBOK Guide* also identifies inputs, tools, and techniques for evaluation of data, and outputs that, if followed in this workflow order, allow for the cycle to continue with the inputs for the next process.[8]

Figure 18-3

The flow of this information is as follows:
→ process inputs
→ tools and techniques for evaluation of data
→ process outputs
→ inputs for the next process

Project management experts sometimes refer to this model outlined in figure 18–3 as waterfall project management because the steps for implementation are sequential and flow downward from a higher level of specification (project identification) to a more detailed level (project definition and execution).[9] Based upon the above overview and the summary provided in

---

5. *Id.*

6. Please note that the following discussion and appendix 5 are drawn from the Fourth Edition of the *PMBOK Guide* and do not incorporate changes in the Fifth Edition from July of 2013. *Id.*

7. *Id.*

8. *Id.*

9. *Waterfall Model*, WIKIPEDIA, http://en.wikipedia.org/wiki/Waterfall_model (last updated Oct. 27, 2013).

appendix 5, the following are some of the pros and cons of the *PMBOK Guide* approach as it was applied by the authors in the development of legal project management models. The following considerations outlined in figure 18–4 below, in the opinions of the authors, should be evaluated if an organization is considering implementing these specific techniques as recommended by PMI.

Figure 18–4 Considerations for Choosing a LPM Approach		
Pros	Cons	Reason
	Language and terms	Traditional project management has its own language and terms. This is one of reasons that lawyers have been reluctant to adopt all the technical components of traditional project management. Lawyers, who are still burdened with significant billable-hour requirements, are often unwilling to spend sufficient time to learn new techniques and terminology, and become proficient integrating those techniques in their practice. A more streamlined approach is needed for integration into the practice of law.
Detailed requirements gathering		The PMBOK Guide model of project management focuses on intensive requirements gathering at the beginning of a project. These requirements are then implemented throughout the life cycle of the project. This includes the evaluation of all stakeholders, which until recently has rarely been performed by lawyers, but which provides significant value.
	Detailed requirements gathering	Traditional project management includes 42 processes and is labor-intensive. It may not lend itself to full integration into a legal engagement. The purpose of the models outlined in this book is to draw from the best of PMBOK Guide, Fourth Edition project management and incorporate additional tools to create a system that can be integrated into existing matter management techniques.

Figure 18–4 Considerations for Choosing a LPM Approach		
	Monitor and control changes	Although the PMBOK Guide model includes methods for addressing changes, they are most often associated with changes for corrections, preventing defects (quality and risk responses), or at the request of the customer. The process is not designed to address dramatic changes in the product design or specifications. This is one of the pitfalls of implementing the PMBOK Guide model in legal matters. The scope or plan in a legal engagement rarely remains constant and new variables must be constantly be evaluated. This is why the authors' approach includes regular evaluation and revisions that are more typical of Agile.
Controlling scope creep		One of the challenges that lawyers face is providing a client with an estimate at the outset of case, but being required to take on new responsibilities as they arise throughout the matter. This may be necessitated by new developments in the case, or by a client off-loading internal responsibilities to the lawyer due to lack of resources. In either case, the lawyer cannot decline the expansion of scope; however, a change control regiment that involves evaluation of the impact on the budget and schedule is an excellent management tool for the client-lawyer relationship.
Communication		As identified by the stakeholder evaluation, project management has a heightened focus on planning communications. This aspect of matter management has been historically neglected by lawyers. Most in-house counsel surveys identify communication as one of the most significant areas of improvement for outside lawyers. By planning communications at the outset of an engagement, lawyers will avoid frustrated client or team members who are not receiving information on the status of the matter.
Risks		Lawyers have not historically communicated risks to clients in an organized manner. Rather, risks are communicated throughout the management of the case as they arise or as they appear inevitable. A better approach is promoted by project management. Risks are initially identified at the outset of the matter and communicated to the client to allow them to utilize the information in their evaluation of cost and strategy.

Figure 18–4 Considerations for Choosing a LPM Approach		
Task development		The concept of a work breakdown structure (WBS), discussed in chapters 4 and 5, is a valuable tool for attorneys to plan and budget an engagement. Historically, attorneys have budgeted their cases at the phase level, using general estimates without evaluation of the actual activities, resources, or time required to complete the work in a phase. The technique of developing a WBS will ensure that any budget is reliable and provides a management tool for performance to the budget.
Closing		Lawyers historically have not conducted a postmortem with their clients. There is significant value that can be derived on several different levels from an evaluation at the closure of a case. The client-lawyer relationship is enhanced by identifying areas of improvement. The legal team's performance can be improved by identifying necessary changes to forms and processes. The individual's performance can also be improved by an evaluation of adherence to the schedule, budget, and scope during the project.

Agile Project Management and Scrum Techniques[10]

Agile was originally developed for use in the software industry. The objective was to avoid setting all product requirements with the customer at the outset, but to allow those specifications to evolve as new functionality was delivered and tested by the customer. As a result, as discussed above, Agile techniques spend less time on trying to develop the entire universe of specifications at the outset and allow the product to evolve over time. There is a planning process at the outset, which is based on an iterative approach of testing assumptions, requirements, and the evolving definition of success.

---

10. The following discussion of Agile and Scrum is based upon author Rueft's application of these techniques in the development of project management software and the authors' evaluation of the application of Agile techniques to the practice of law. As a result, the approach described may not follow exactly the methods described in the materials cited in this section. The reader is urged to review the cited materials in this section to obtain an understanding of the approaches intended by the developers of Agile and Scrum techniques.

Knowledge Areas → Process Groups↓	Integration	Scope	Time	Cost	Quality	Human Resources	Communications	Risk	Procurement
Initiating	Develop Project Charter						Identify Stakeholders		
Planning	Develop Project Management Plan	Collect Requirements / Define Scope / Create WBS	Define and Sequence Activities / Estimate Activity Resources and Durations / Develop Schedule	Estimate Costs / Determine Budget	Plan Quality	Develop Human Resources Plan	Plan Communications	Plan Risk Management / Identify Risks / Perform Qualitative Risk Analysis / Perform Quantitative Risk Analysis / Plan Risk Assessment / Plan Risk Responses	Plan Procurement
Executing	Direct and Manage Project Execution				Perform Quality Assurance	Acquire Team / Develop Team / Manage Team	Distribute Information / Manage Stakeholder Expectations		Conduct Procurement
Monitoring and Controlling	Monitor and Control / Perform Integrated Change Control	Verify Scope / Control Scope	Control Schedule	Control Costs	Perform Quality Control		Report Performance	Monitor and Control Risk	Administer Procurement
Closing	Close Project or Phase								Close Procurement

Figure 18-5
Intersection of Project Knowledge Areas and Process Groups

The key principles of an Agile approach are provided in the following, AgileManifesto.org.[11]

We follow these principles:
Our highest priority is to satisfy the customer through early and continuous delivery of valuable software.

Welcome changing requirements, even late in development. Agile processes harness change for the customer's competitive advantage.

Deliver working software frequently, from a couple of weeks to a couple of months, with a preference to the shorter timescale.

Business people and developers must work together daily throughout the project.

Build projects around motivated individuals. Give them the environment and support they need, and trust them to get the job done.

The most efficient and effective method of conveying information to and within a development team is face-to-face conversation.

---

11. *Principles Behind the Agile Manifesto*, AGILEMANIFESTO.ORG, http://agilemanifesto.org/principles.html (last visited Sept. 28, 2013).

Working software is the primary measure of progress.

Agile processes promote sustainable development. The sponsors, developers, and users should be able to maintain a constant pace indefinitely.

Continuous attention to technical excellence and good design enhances agility.

Simplicity—the art of maximizing the amount of work not done—is essential.

The best architectures, requirements, and designs emerge from self-organizing teams.

At regular intervals, the team reflects on how to become more effective, then tunes and adjusts its behavior accordingly.

This may be translated to legal work in figures 18-6 and 18-7, contributed by Aileen Leventon of QLex Consulting Inc.

The Scrum process is a method of Agile project management techniques and was developed in the early 1990s by Ken Schwaber and Jeff Sutherland to aid with the management of product requirements, which are constantly changing.[12] The technique involves setting preliminary project requirements and then periodically evaluating those requirements in order to address necessary changes in product functionality.

Scrum techniques take a different approach from formal project management.[13] The Scrum method is most often applied with software development where requirements may not be fully identified at the outset of the project and may evolve as functionality is tested and refined.

---

12. KEN SCHWABER, AGILE PROJECT MANAGEMENT WITH SCRUM (Microsoft Press 2004), *available at* http://www.gobookee.net/agile-project-management-with-scrum/.

13. Again, the following summary is based upon David Rueff's experience with Scrum techniques that were implemented by a software development team for the development of BakerManage and may not follow exactly the model intended by the original creators of Agile and Scrum techniques.

#	Agile Principles Applicable to Software Developers	Agile Principles Applicable to Lawyers
1	Our highest priority is to satisfy the customer through early and continuous delivery of valuable software	Our highest priority is to satisfy the client through early and continuous delivery of valuable solutions. Legal solutions consider the business context, outcome, risk, resources and overall value to the client; solutions can be defined and are the basis of a project plan.
2	We welcome changing requirements, even late in development. Agile processes harness change for the customer's competitive advantage	Demonstrate skill and deliver value by responding to changing goals within an analytical framework that allows for evaluation and adaptation, but adopt an approach that minimizes impact on project plan and budget, particularly if fees are hourly-based. Communication is critical and be sure to differentiate between change for its own sake and change that materially affects goals.
3	Deliver working software frequently, from a couple of weeks to a couple of months, with a preference to the shorter timescale	Milestones and benchmarks in the project plan require ongoing reference to original plan and interaction with client to confirm status and validity of approach over time.
4	Business people and developers must work together daily throughout the project	Lawyers and clients, including business people, must come together frequently to assure that business goals and legal strategy are synchronized and remain so.
5	Build projects around motivated individuals. Give them the environment and support they need, and trust them to get the job done	Build projects around motivated individuals. Give team members the environment and support they need, and trust them to get the job done. Nevertheless set boundaries and establish a process so that team members must understand context, plan, budget and roles of the team and work together over the duration.
6	The most efficient and effective method of conveying information to and within a development team is face-to-face conversation	Information is provided and digested with reference to the project framework; this may not require face-to-face conversation, but reference to shared knowledge and workspaces are critical.
7	Working software is the primary measure of progress	The delivery of effective and relevant solutions is the primary measure of progress. Work product that exceeds scope or is not essential is not valuable.
8	Agile processes promote sustainable development. The sponsors, developers, and users should be able to maintain a constant pace indefinitely	Agile processes are sustainable and scalable. The project team should deliver more informed and efficient work product and solutions over time having learned to work to a plan and accumulated relevant knowledge. Consistency among team members and their accumulated knowledge reduces costs and increases value to client .
9	Continuous attention to technical excellence and good design enhances agility	Continuous attention to technical excellence and good design enhances agility . Team members learn to distill complex information and adapt to changing circumstances with minimal disruption to overall effort.
10	Simplicity—the art of maximizing the amount of work not done—is essential	Simplicity—the art of maximizing the amount of work not done—is essential. The ability to identify important issues and context is a highly valued skill and gives the client and the team the confidence to choose an approach that will minimize work that is not value-added or outcome-determinative.
11	The best architectures, requirements, and designs emerge from self-organizing teams	Using the agile framework, team members themselves should make decisions about roles, approach and strategy given their knowledge of the solution desired.
12	At regular intervals, the team reflects on how to become more effective, then tunes and adjusts its behavior accordingly	At regular intervals, the team reflects on how to become more effective, then adjusts its behavior accordingly. Self evaluation and team evaluation and self criticism are valuable processes; identification of defects and opportunities for improvement should be rewarded.

© 2009-2013 QLex Consulting Inc.   Aileen Leventon, Esq.   917-860-7043

Figure 18-6
Agile Software Engineering Principles Are Applicable to Legal Work

Figure 18-7

From QLex Consulting—Translating this to the legal context, Scrum may be suitable when neither the goal nor the solution for a matter are clear. Consider a situation in which a company has a seemingly unresolvable dispute with a high profile customer over an intellectual property license. From a legal perspective there are obvious contractual and IP licensing issues, and there may be regulatory and antitrust aspects as well. High profile customers raise issues of reputation, media coverage and require elevating the matter to the Board of Directors. There are may ways to address this. There are also numerous possible priorities, internal and external stakeholders. There may not be an optimal solution that satisfies everyone involved. What means should be used to address this and in what order? Clearly, this matter is not susceptible to a waterfall model of project planning even though it is possible to establish numerous well-defined work streams. It is appropriate for Scrum however, since each workstream can be tested, evaluated and iterated in response to the output of regular/daily scrums, backlogging and other techniques described here. With a fast-paced matter, the sprints are an apt ways of describing how lawyers approach a matter. Scrum emphasizes the discipline of a structured approach to mitigate lawyers' sense of urgency.

As provided above, the model for traditional project management focuses on upfront planning and implementation of those requirements by the project team. Scope creep or drastic expansion of the requirements is avoided.[14] With Agile or Scrum, changes in scope are embraced and the project plan is constantly reevaluated based upon the findings of the development team during the last development cycle.[15] The client regularly receives updates

14. SCHWABER, *supra* note 4.
15. *Id.*

regarding these findings in order to set new priorities. In short, the project plan in Agile or Scrum is constantly evolving.

In application, Scrum involves iterations or sprints to limit the work in progress. This permits the project team to focus on functionality that is immediately necessary. Depending on the organization, iterations may be one week, two weeks, or longer; however, a daily Scrum or team meeting is conducted in order to continuously clarify priorities and drive production.[16] In contrast to formal project management, the project plan in Scrum is not perfect. It is a starting point for development, and is designed to accommodate new design ideas as functionality is developed and rolled out to the customer.

A unique characteristic of Scrum is the daily Scrum that is intended to be a regularly scheduled short meeting with team members. The daily Scrum involves a meeting of the project team to identify the work completed since the last iteration, ask questions necessary for continued work, and to set priorities for the next iteration. The daily Scrum also helps to avoid context switching (jumping from one priority to the next without completion). The objective is to focus the project team on manageable chunks of work that can be completed by the next iteration.

Another unique characteristic of Scrum is backlogging. Certain functionalities may be backlogged while other functionalities are prioritized by the project team. The project team's work is limited to prioritized functionality for the upcoming iteration. In this way, the work of the team is focused on what is a priority for the client. Backlogged requirements are evaluated at the end of each iteration to determine whether or not they should be moved into the project team's development lane in the next iteration.

Ken Schwaber describes the technique as being used "to solve complex problems and drive better results—delivering more valuable software faster."[17] Schwaber, in his book *Agile Project Management with Scrum*, identifies the following benefits of the approach:

---

16. In the author's application of Scrum techniques, iterations were intended to be completed weekly, but varied from one to six weeks depending on the complexity of the functionality requested.

17. Schwaber, *supra* note 4.

- Effectively manage unknown or changing product requirements
- Simplify the chain of command with self-managing development teams
- Greatly reduce project planning time and required tools
- Build—and release—products in 30-day cycles so clients get deliverables earlier
- Avoid missteps by regularly inspecting, reporting on, and fine-tuning projects[18]

Based upon the above overview, the following is a summary of the pros and cons of the Scrum approach as it is applied to a legal engagement, in the authors' opinion. The following considerations should be evaluated if an organization is considering implementing these techniques precisely in legal organizations.

Agile Project Management Approaches—Pros and Cons

Figure 18–8		
Pros	Cons	Reason
Daily Scrum		Legal teams do not spend enough time communicating or, if they do, it is disorganized and rarely includes a formal agenda. More periodic meetings of the legal team will ensure that new issues are adequately evaluated and timely communicated to the client. This will necessarily also lead to regular updates to the project plan and budget prior to performing the work.
	Daily Scrum	Legal practitioners rarely have the luxury of focusing on only one project a day. Rather, some lawyers may touch over 15 different matters in a single day. Therefore, literal application of a daily Scrum for legal engagements may not be feasible. This may be especially true in matters that have starts and stops, where the matter does not involve a large team, or where lawyers are managing numerous cases at one time. A daily Scrum for each matter could eat up a significant portion of the workday.

---

18. *Id.*

Figure 18–8		
Setting priorities		One of the most interesting components of the Agile and Scrum processes is setting priorities at each Scrum meeting. This provides an opportunity for the lead lawyer to help team members set priorities on the next iteration of their work and to ensure that they adhere to the project's requirements and specifications. It also helps to manage possible distractions or "context switching" on the team's work. For example, team members who are participating in several projects may need assistance balancing their work demands.
	Project team oversight	Scrum calls for little to no interruption of the development team during an iteration. In legal engagements, the project team may be staffed primarily with associates, paralegals, and analysts. Lawyers are ethically obligated to provide proper oversight. If iterations involve communication with the client, this technique may not be feasible.
Addressing evolving project requirements		The Scrum technique is designed to accommodate evolving project requirements. This technique is an excellent way to address requirements in a legal engagement where all issues may not be identifiable at the outset of the case. For example, when significant discovery has not been completed, periodic evaluation of the project requirements will ensure that the strategy and plan are comprehensive.
	Backlogging	In the authors' evaluation and implementation of Scrum, as product functionality was developed, new requirements would be identified. The development team was required to prioritize development requests for the next iteration and backlog lower-priority requests, because the development team had limited capacity to manage a significant number of development requests at one time. In the management of legal engagements, lawyers rarely have the luxury of deferring requirements. Whether a transaction or litigation, party or court deadlines require that all requirements be managed within those deadlines. It may not be possible for issues or requirements to be backlogged.

The above comparisons provide a cross section of project management, Agile and Scrum techniques and are intended to provide a high level understanding of these alternatives. The reader is encouraged to review the cited materials in order to gain a comprehensive understanding of these approaches. Any one or a combination of the tools in these approaches may provide the reader with a model for implementation in their organization.

Standards, Certifications and Training for Project Management

PMI sets standards for project management to allow professionals to speak with common language, no matter the industry or geographic location.[19] This common language steers organizations toward repeatable processes to achieve predictable results. PMI has more than 700,000 members, maintains 250 local chapters in 70 countries, offers five certifications, and produces *A Guide to the Project Management Body of Knowledge* (*PMBOK Guide*) which provides an in depth description of the tools and techniques of project management.[20] Specific industries are represented within PMI by Communities of Practice, which are groups of professionals focused on implementing project management approaches in the same industry. These professionals share ideas, best practices, and other information to assist each other with project management implementation and to advance the professional development of their members.[21] Historically, Communities of Practice exist for construction, aerospace, finance, and other specialized industries. In September of 2010, PMI created a legal project management (LPM) Community of Practice to share information in this developing area.[22] PMI has been recognized as setting global standards for project management and due to its recognition of LPM, should be considered as an excellent resource for lawyers.

There are several other organizations that set standards and credentials for project management. These include the International Project Management

---

19. PROJECT MGMT. INST. http://www.pmi.org/default.aspx (last visited Nov. 2, 2013).
20. *Id.*
21. The Project Management Institute's Communities of Practice listing can be found at http://www.pmi.org/get-involved/communities-of-practice.aspx.
22. The Project Management Institute's LPM Community of Practice webpage can be found at http://legalpm.vc.pmi.org/Public/Home.aspx.

Association,[23] Office of Government Commerce in the United Kingdom,[24] and Project Management Association of Japan.[25]

For those interested in learning more about traditional project management and obtaining a comprehensive certification, the Project Management Institute offers several credentialing opportunities. Each of the law firm project management offices that are currently in place value PMI's Project Management Professional designation (PMP), as have some legal organizations seeking to hire a director of LPM. This credential recognizes demonstrated knowledge and skill in leading and directing project teams and in delivering project results within the constraints of time, cost, and scope (the triple constraint). Eligibility requirements include a four-year degree, three years of project management experience with 4,500 hours spent leading and directing project tasks, and 35 hours project management education.[26] Once certification is obtained, it is valid for three years. Upon expiration of the certification period, the holder must complete a certification application/renewal agreement and pay a renewal fee to obtain an extension of the certification for another three years.

With regard to certifications for Agile and Scrum, PMI offers a certification for Agile which is the Agile Certified Practitioner (PMI-ACP).[27] The Scrum Alliance offers a Certified ScrumMaster® (CSM) program.[28]

Various consultants to the legal profession have also developed short certificate programs that provide legal professionals with an understanding of the basic project management terminology, skills, and tools—as applied to lawyers. In early 2010, Susan Raridon Lambreth and Carla Landry, together

---

23. The International Project Management Association website can be found at http://ipma .ch/.

24. The Office of Government Commerce website can be found at https://www.gov.uk/ government/organisations/cabinet-office.

25. The Project Management Association of Japan website can be found at http://www .pmaj.or.jp/ENG/.

26. The Project Management Institute website can be found at http://www.pmi.org/ default.aspx.

27. The Project Management Institute website can be found at http://www.pmi.org/default .aspx and the information regarding the PMI-ACP certification can be found at http://www .pmi.org/Certification/New-PMI-Agile-Certification.aspx.

28. The Scrum Alliance website can be found at http://www.scrumalliance.org and the information for the Certified ScrumMaster® (CSM) can be found at http://www.scrumalliance .org/certifications/practitioners/certified-scrummaster-(csm).

with a team of certified PMPs created the first live project management certification program designed specifically for the legal profession. This two-day LPM certification course was taught publicly for the first time in June 2010, in conjunction with Pace University's faculty for project management. Since then, over 3,000 legal professionals in the U.S., Canada, United Kingdom, and Australia have completed one of the LawVision (or its predecessor) courses. In December 2010, consulting firm LegalBizDev launched its program that combines webinars, readings, and telephone coaching to certify lawyers in LPM .

In order to make LPM training more accessible to busy lawyers, in 2012 LawVision Group and the Legal Project Management Institute, launched the first e-learning courses in LPM. The two-course program enables lawyers and other legal professionals to obtain a certificate in LPM and is available through West LegalEdcenter or the Legal Project Management Institute.[29] The Legal Project Management Institute also offers an advanced certificate in LPM that combines live or online training with work on actual matters with a LPM Coach. The evolution of project management as a profession and discipline and legal-specific applications of project management and certifications is depicted in the figures 18–9 and 18–10.

ABA-accredited law schools are also creating courses on LPM to address the ABA's promotion of practical-skills training for law students. Author David Rueff teaches one of the first law school courses on Legal Project Management at the Mississippi College School of Law in Jackson, Mississippi. This ABA accredited law school recognized the advantages that project management can give to its law students who are graduating into a highly competitive job market. Boston University School of Management offers a "mini MBA" for corporate counsel, in conjunction with ACC, that includes these skills. Additionally, software vendors, such as those profiled in appendix 2, offer LPM software programs with their own LPM approaches.

To date, the legal industry has only scratched the surface of the value that project management techniques can add to the practice of law. This book was designed to help lawyers capitalize on approaches that have been

---

29. The two courses compose the LPM LaunchPad Certificate in Fundamentals of Legal Project Management (www.lpminstitute.net).

successful in many other industries, including other professional services firms. The methods outlined in this book have provided an approach for project management that has been tailored to the way lawyers work and that is similar to that applied in other professional services organizations like consulting, accounting, and banking. In addition, appendix 5 provides an overview of all of the areas of traditional project management, taken from the *PMBOK Guide, Fourth Edition*, not just the ones commonly being applied by legal organizations now.

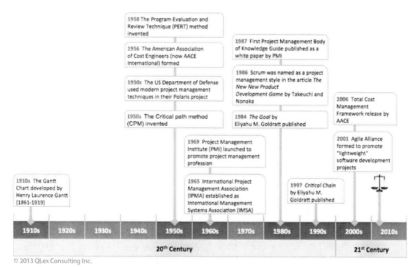

© 2013 QLex Consulting Inc.

Figure 18-9
Evolution of Project Management: Modern Historical Timeline

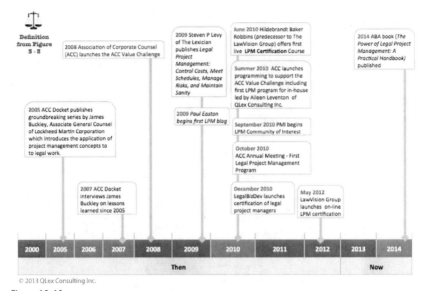

Figure 18-10
Evolution of Project Management: Modern Historical Timeline (Expanding on Scale Symbol Time Period)

Chapter 19

Conclusion

The purpose of this book has been to provide the reader with a step-by-step approach to implementing improvements into the practice of law and the management of law firms and legal departments. The book describes two models for project management that have been tested through implementation in many types of legal practices, from litigation and transactional to intellectual property and regulatory matters. These models are approaches that have been modified from traditional project management to fit the unique aspects of legal services. They are intended to draw from the best of the traditional PMI approach to project management, other project management theories, and historic lawyer matter management approaches. The intent with these models was not to diminish the effective ways lawyers practice, but to enhance these practices by providing a new, more structured and effective framework for relationship and team management.

The adoption of LPM is increasing rapidly. In programs for the International Legal Technology Association (ILTA) and Practising Law Institute (PLI) in 2011, the authors were part of programs in which audience polling showed that only a small percentage of firms were actively using legal project management. However, at a similar panel discussion at the ILTA conference and at the 2013 PLI Project Management for Lawyers program, it was evident that the number of LPM adopters had grown exponentially to then include a majority of the audience. Also, as evidenced by the case studies provided in this book, the number of firms and corporations implementing LPM has grown significantly and the level of that implementation has dramatically increased in scale and sophistication from one or two isolated projects to organization-wide initiatives. Also, as evidenced by the software vendor submissions in appendix 2, the sophistication of the tools is maturing rapidly.

Where project management in the legal profession will go next no one fully knows at this point. There are many ideas percolating around the profession. Some believe that use of approaches and techniques like those outlined in this book will become the "standard of care," much like in health care. Others want organizations like PMI, ABA, Association of Corporate Counsel, and/or others to develop standards with which all lawyers should comply, much like the ABA Model Rules of Professional Conduct.

At a minimum, it is likely that there will be several elements of this continued evolution, including the following:

- Legal project management will be a course in most law school curricula and in the development programs of law firms for younger associates.
- There will be more integrated efforts within legal organizations, involving knowledge management, technology, process improvement, and project management—rather than the stand-alone or, in some organizations, even silo functions, each tackling their own parts of changing the legal services delivery model.
- Every legal organization will have a project management information system, though of varying sophistication, that enables it to collect, analyze, and share information on matters.
- Tools will evolve to streamline front-end planning and budget development to make it easy and time efficient for lawyers to do.
- Analytical tools for evaluation of that data will result in more accurate pricing and create fee arrangements that can be customized based upon the matter and can assist the lawyer in managing to the agreed-upon fees.
- Task codes will become the standard for how all time is entered on matters—for both in-house (when they track time) and outside counsel.
- More law firms and legal departments will employ individuals as "legal project managers" who will have varying backgrounds (i.e., they might be lawyers, certified project managers, or other) who will have full-time roles helping lawyers manage their matters.

- Many, if not all law firms and legal departments will have administrative resources dedicated to developing and implementing LPM.

As detailed in this book, the legal professional has only scratched the surface of the benefits that project management brings to the practice of law. The benefits discussed in this book—enhanced client and project team relationships, predictability, transparency, efficiency, and consistency—all promote and encourage client satisfaction.

What does the future hold for LPM? Pandora's box has been opened and the legal profession cannot go back to where it was—which the authors believe is a very good change. While some may argue that application of more processes and routines will commoditize the "art" of the practice of law, in fact, it may be what saves the legal profession from cost and pricing pressures that already are driving rapid commoditization. And, as importantly, if executed well, LPM has the potential to rebuild the trust relationships between lawyers and clients, while also enabling them to be more creative, more innovative, and better lawyers.

Appendices

Appendix 1

Case Studies in Implementing LPM

Baker Donelson Bearman Caldwell & Berkowitz, PC

The Origins of LPM at Baker Donelson

Baker Donelson formed an alternative fee arrangements (AFA) committee in 2009 to encourage broader use of these types of engagements. The committee identified a need both for improved methods of pricing and for managing AFA engagements to promote more predictable returns. The committee also recognized that any solution implemented for effectively managing AFA engagements also should be implemented for any engagement regardless of pricing in order to provide more predictable costs and transparency for our clients for all matters entrusted to the firm.

One of Baker Donelson's shareholders, David Rueff, took a special interest in project management due to his pre-law background working for a computer hardware and software development company and due to his experience implementing project management principles to prepare task lists and budgets for a disaster recovery grant program. This immersion into a true project management workflow prompted Mr. Rueff's interest in obtaining the Project Management Profession (PMP) certification through the Project Management Institute (PMI). After Mr. Rueff obtained the PMP, the firm's Chief Strategic Planning Officer, William Painter, recognized that these techniques might have broader application to both the management of alternative fee arrangements and standard hourly rate matters.

After evaluation of these techniques, Mr. Painter and Mr. Rueff concluded that traditional waterfall project management would be too complicated and cumbersome for implementation by attorneys. At that time, there was no project management process designed specifically for lawyers and there was no commercially available software for legal project management. After Mr. Rueff obtained the PMP designation, Mr. Painter challenged him to evaluate traditional waterfall processes and derive a streamlined methodology for attorneys. The goal was to develop a process to collect more information for planning and pricing, provide tools for improved management to a budget and enhance communication with the client and legal team. Over the next three months, Mr. Painter and Mr. Rueff worked to design a project management process for attorneys. The resulting unique process, called BakerManage™, tracks the way attorneys work and includes three distinct phases - a Development Phase, Execution Phase and Closure Phase - with associated tools for each phase.

After initial implementation of the process using Excel templates, the firm realized that it could be streamlined and communication improved using SharePoint technology. In 2011, another committee was formed to develop the BakerManage™ process in the SharePoint environment. This committee included representatives from the firm's Information Technology, Billing, Knowledge Management, Pricing and newly-formed Legal Project Management Departments. Initially, the BakerManage™ Excel templates were migrated into SharePoint 2007. Additionally, data required for template creation, such as timekeepers and their standard hourly rates, was tied to existing Firm information systems. Likewise, once the budget was developed, the BakerManage™ SharePoint sites regularly communicated with Firm financial databases to provide a real-time budget-to-actual comparison. In 2012, the BakerManage™ process was streamlined and migrated to SharePoint 2010.

After developing BakerManage™, Baker Donelson hired subject matter expert Pam Woldow of Edge International to review the proposed process and conduct interviews with key stakeholders to identify significant challenges in their practices that could be addressed by LPM. Ms. Woldow gave the process a highly favorable evaluation. The Firm then asked her to assist in introducing and presenting the business case for legal project management to the Firm's management team in March 2011. Shortly thereafter, Baker Donelson's newly formed Legal Project Management Office, led by David Rueff and Felicia Morris, another Baker Donelson PMP, began implementation of the system with two client teams - one in bankruptcy and another in health care litigation. Team members were introduced to the business case by Ms. Woldow and Doug Richardson of Edge International and then trained on the BakerManage™ process and use of the SharePoint system. The Firm's training also involved the development of phase and task codes for each project team and the development of a template budget. Additionally, shareholders were trained by Ms. Woldow and Mr. Rueff at the firm's Shareholder Retreat in May 2011.

Concurrent with this training, the firm also implemented an AFA initiative led by Pricing Manager Mike Burks and Pricing Analyst John Christenson.

The firm established an internal policy requiring the implementation of LPM for AFA evaluations, proposals and budget management.

An ancillary benefit of LPM implementation has been the use of phase and task codes to track budget-to-actual at the phase and task level and to capture historical data regarding the phase and task level cost of an engagement. Historical data can be used for future pricing purposes. In the firm's pilot implementations in 2011, the LPMO developed customized phase and task code sets for budget tracking. The LPMO identified a significant lesson learned, that, while customized code sets might be useful for development of a matter specific budget, they made it almost impossible for one attorney's matters to be compared to another's if a different phase task code model was implemented. In current implementations, the use of Universal Task-Based Management System codes (also called ABA billing codes) is encouraged so that all similar matters handled can be compared across the firm.

Obtaining Stakeholder Buy-In

Firm Chief Strategic Planning Officer Painter was tasked with introducing the concept of legal project management to the Firm's attorneys. The presentation was made as a part of the presentation of the Firm's long-term strategic plan. Mr. Painter conducted Firm-wide sessions with the shareholders and also conducted on-site meetings with each of the Firm's offices. These presentations were essential to establishing the credibility of the initiative and educating attorneys on the need to implement project management principles. Additionally, Mr. Painter and Mr. Rueff conducted several presentations to the board of directors, Strategic Planning Committee, department heads, practice group leaders and office managing shareholders.

When the initiative was launched in 2011, there was initial concern among shareholders and management regarding the additional overhead created by the LPMO team members. As a result, in the first year of implementation, only one firm staff member was solely dedicated to the initiative. The main driver for this concern was a downturn in attorney productivity that also occurred during this time period. However, as the initiative began to produce success stories and as demand increased, the Firm approved additional dedicated resources.

In order to reduce the investment required by attorneys and encourage implementation, the Firm also took two aggressive steps. First, the LPMO was staffed with non-billable project managers to assist attorneys with project plan creation, budget development, matter site and extranet creation and on-going management. These resources were not charged to the client and proved to be critical to the successful implementation of LPM. Second, the firm provided attorneys with credit for time spent on the implementation of project management and the development of resources that could be used by other attorneys for implementation.

The BakerManage™ process was developed to be an off-the-shelf tool that can be implemented by all practice areas. However, one size does not fit all. Implementation by various attorneys and practice areas has been different and depends on a number of factors that included the needs of the engagement, the time for setup, the size of the matter or number of matters and the desire of the client to view matter status through the Firm's extranet portals.

An ancillary initiative of LPM and AFA implementation has been tasked based timekeeping and billing. The Firm first began to implement phase and task code timekeeping and billing with LPM implementations and AFA tracking in 2011. In 2013, the Firm began a mandated Firm-wide implementation of task-based timekeeping by all timekeepers. To date, over half of the practice groups have been trained and are utilizing phase and task codes for all new matters, with a goal of having all groups implementing them by the close of 2013.

Key Elements of BakerManage™

Baker Donelson implements legal project management in various forms with legal teams that either have a need to implement efficiencies or are trying to differentiate themselves from competitors. Implementation involves the development of a detailed project plan (scope, assumptions, risks and what is out of scope), identification of stakeholders, development of a communication plan, development of a detailed list of tasks tied to a phase and task code framework, and development of a reliable budget. All of this information can be shared with the client and is made available to the project team for the purpose of continued management of the engagement.

The key elements of Baker Donelson's project management process (shown below in the BakerManage™ process diagram) are: (1) Development Phase – identifying the client's needs through the creation of a detailed project plan; (2) Execution Phase – implementing the client's goals and regularly communicating with the client; and (3) Closure Phase – providing the agreed-upon solution and measuring client satisfaction.

Each of the BakerManage™ process phases includes a set of tools and templates for implementation of LPM. The Development Phase provides templates for Stakeholder information, a Statement of Work, Task List,

Schedule, Budget and a Communication Plan. The Execution Phase of BakerManage™ includes best practices for monitoring the scope of the project and a template for a Change Control Log (for scope and budget changes), schedules, budgets and communications. The Closure Phase includes templates for a Lessons Learned Log (to capture improvements for the next engagement) and Client Evaluation and encourages both an internal team and a client wrap-up meeting.

The LPMO has developed template budgets through Budget Designer, another tool developed by the Firm and described in more detail below, which can be used by attorneys to develop client or template budgets. The LPMO is also working to develop additional resources that can be used to streamline project plan development, including standard assumptions and risks by practice area.

LPMO Department Structure

The Legal Project Management Office (LPMO) was created in 2011 to lead the LPM initiative and reports to the Firm's Chief Operating Officer, and regularly consults with the Firm's Chief Strategic Planning Officer and Chief Administrative Officer. The Firm's Practice Support Department (for Litigation Support and eDiscovery) was later merged with the LPMO to provide additional technical resources and to implement project management principles in other legal service areas. The LPMO now has three separate Departments - LPM Support, Litigation Support/eDiscovery and Contract Counsel/Document Review. Each of these Departments requires a focus on project management principles to promote efficiency, predictability and transparency. The LPM Department includes attorney/project managers who are certified through the Project Management Institute as PMPs. The Litigation Support and eDiscovery department is led by a technical consultant who also is certified as a PMP. The Contract Counsel and Document Review Department is led by an attorney who is currently working to obtain PMP certification. All these team members were either drawn from within the firm or hired based upon a combination of legal, technology and project management expertise.

BakerManage™ Success Stories

In August of 2012, Baker Donelson received a Distinguished Peer Award from the International Legal Technology Association for outstanding achievements in the category of "Project of the Year." Baker Donelson received the award for its patent pending BakerManage™ system and for being one of the first firms to create and implement a Legal Project Management Office.

In 2013, Baker Donelson conducted an attorney retreat where a panel of BakerManage™ users spoke about their experiences implementing the system. One of the pilot teams described the use of the system to provide more regular communication to the client in the form of periodic reports on the status of a portfolio of matters. The LPMO developed a tool to capture periodic case management updates on all of these matters. Prior to implementation of this tool, it took two to three days for the large team of attorneys managing the portfolio to assemble these case management reports. Individual matter sites were developed to allow team members to input updates into BakerManage™. Other case information was also captured on the site, such as project plans and budget status. Once these sites and processes were implemented, the case management report could be produced at the click of a button. This tool enabled the legal team to provide the reports to the client every two weeks and significantly reduced the amount of time required to produce them.

Another success story involved the implementation of the BakerManage™ system for a client who desired a detailed budget and the ability to monitor budget-to-actual performance on a real-time basis. The LPMO's project managers worked with the legal team to develop a detailed budget and project sites for collection of project plans, documents, case management status and budgets. Team members were encouraged to log their time on a daily basis to phase and task codes so that budget-to-actual information was tracked in real time. The client was provided secure access to these sites, including the ability to monitor performance. The client logged in two to three times a week to check case status. Upon completion of the matter, the client commented that the system provided more information on case status than they had received from other law firms that had been managing cases for years. The client also commented during the closing phase that the BakerManage™ process was one of the reasons that the client was transferring five additional matters from other law firms to Baker Donelson. The client also stated that BakerManage™ set a new standard for case management that the client was going to request from its other law firms.

Implementation and Training

In 2012, the firm considered firm-wide training of LPM but determined that training should be focused on those teams willing to invest in project planning, budget development and use of BakerManage™ to improve communication with the client. To date, over 200 attorneys and staff members have been trained on LPM methods and have implemented BakerManage™ in over 1,000 cases. Implementation has taken various forms from project scope statements, phase and task code development, budget development and tracking, and client reporting to full implementation of the BakerManage™ model.

In 2012, the LPMO and Strategic Planning Office identified budgeting as one of the most critical but time-consuming components of project plan development. The firm's LPMO, worked with the IT, KM and Pricing Departments and with the firm's internal SharePoint and database developers to create a budgeting tool called Budget Designer to streamline the budget development process. The tool is accessible from BakerNet, the Firm's intranet, and provides attorneys with a way to develop phase, task and activity level budgets that can be used in BakerManage™ or as stand-alone budgets for any client matter. The system draws upon Firm financial data to populate tasks or activities with specific timekeepers and their rates. The system is also a repository for all budgets created by a practice group or individual attorneys. This tool streamlines budget creation by allowing attorneys to view existing budget templates as a starting point for budget development. Currently Budget Designer includes budgets for over 120 litigation and transactional matters and 30 practice group templates.

The LPMO is continuously educating clients, attorneys and staff on the benefits of LPM. The LPMO has conducted over 90 internal and external presentations since October 2011 including seminars and training sessions for the American Bar Association, International Legal Technology Association, Project Management Institute, Association of Corporate Counsel,

National Bar Association, West, Thomson Reuters, Practising Law Institute and Mississippi College School of Law.

Dealing With Potential Objections

To attorneys who claim that their clients are not asking for project plans or budgets so therefore LPM is unnecessary, the Firm responds- "Why wait for your client to ask for more efficient management practices? You should be leading this discussion." Baker Donelson encourages its lawyers to be proactive and to implement LPM and budgeting for all matters regardless of whether their client has requested the application of these tools. If the client has to ask, it may be too late. Many lawyers have responded by using LPM to successfully differentiate themselves with their clients and the firm has built on this success to convince others of the merits of legal project management as a highly effective tool to deliver client value..

In addition, the firm provides project managers to support LPM implementation for legal teams without any cost to the client. BakerManage™ extranets are also provided to the client at no extra cost. This is an acknowledgement that the client should not have to pay for the Firm or lawyers to implement more efficient practices.

Bilzin Sumberg Baena Price & Axelrod LLP

Bilzin Sumberg Background

Bilzin Sumberg is a South Florida-based commercial firm that distinguishes itself by offering sophisticated legal services along with significant value to clients. Client representation is approached with a clear understanding of client business goals as well as an understanding of the industries in which the clients compete, thus enabling lawyers to provide operational value to each client.

The LPM Path

Legal project management (LPM) is wholly complementary to Bilzin Sumberg's culture and management philosophy. One of the pillars of LPM is communication both with the client and among the team of attorneys working on the project. As the economic downturn affected clients and the firm's internal operations, a need was identified for a more systematic methodology with which to approach efficiency.

Two years ago, the Executive Committee decided that the annual partners' retreat would focus entirely on LPM and its related concepts. Prior to the retreat, Jim Hassett from LegalBizDev, was hired to work with three well-respected partners, each from a different practice group, with the intent to represent both transaction and litigation oriented practices. Two of the partners were practice group leaders and the third represented one of the firm's largest clients. LegalBizDev worked with each of these senior partners to develop LPM specific skills, team management, budget templates and communication strategies. The partners understood and welcomed the challenge of LPM coaching for the three months leading up to the retreat.

Building Consensus

At the retreat, Jim Hassett moderated a panel discussion of these three influential partners, highlighting their achievements and benefits for them individually and for the firm.

These in-house testimonials demonstrating success as a result of utilizing LPM methodologies were critical for building interest and support for the LPM initiative among the partnership. Several additional partners volunteered for LPM coaching immediately following the retreat. Then LPM coaching was offered to all partners firm-wide, with partners selected to ensure that partners from all six of practice groups were included. At the time of this writing, more than half of the partners in the firm have participated in coaching and programs are being implemented for associates. Including people at every level in LPM planning and implementation is key; those responsible for various tasks have the clearest understanding of how processes can be more efficient.

Next Steps

LPM and knowledge management (KM) are integrated at Bilzin Sumberg, and fall under an organizational umbrella that focuses on efficiency and profitability. LPM is one of Bilzin Sumberg's critical success factors, and all attorneys, both partners and associates, are evaluated on the basis of their efficiency. Various technologies and policies that are focused on maximizing efficiency have been implemented. Examples include:

- The firm-wide use of practice specific task codes with a mandate that lawyers assign the task codes, rather than delegating this job to their administrative assistants.
- Lawyers input their own time (this is mandated for associates and strongly encouraged for partners) so that data is more accurate.
- The scope of each matter is posted on the firm intranet to ensure that all members of the team are aware of the matter scope. New matters begin with team meetings so there is immediate communication among the entire team and a discussion of the proper use of task-based codes for that particular matter so all members of the team use the codes consistently.
- The development and use of forms that allow attorneys to produce documents relatively quickly without sacrificing the quality of legal services, benefitting the firm as well as the clients.
- Effective budgeting tools that provide clients with insight into both the legal strategy as well as an understanding of the ultimate cost. The use of the departmental task-based codes is the framework for budget templates.

These initial and ongoing investments in project planning and proper team management maximize communication that creates value for the client and provides for the reallocation of underutilized personnel that results in profitability for the firm.

LPM Highlights

LPM methodology has provided Bilzin Sumberg with the tools to identify deficiencies in the prior AFA pricing process and to develop a more accurate approach to budgeting and risk analysis. The improvement of budget management techniques, through tracking and frequent reporting, identifies potential losses on AFA matters due to "scope creep." The most significant improvement due to LPM efforts is better team coordination and much improved project management. The ultimate result is the project leader can manage client expectations and better communicate the status of a project. Together, the project leader and the client can make informed choices relating to the project's direction and the projected legal fees.

Sustainability

The Managing Partner and Executive Director were deeply involved in the LPM initiative from the outset. Without support from key leaders, an initiative of this dimension could not be accomplished. To promote sustainability, the next evolution in this initiative, Bilzin Sumberg has established an LPM committee that meets bimonthly to discuss best practices and the progress of each practice group specifically in regard to LPM, KM and efficiency. The partners and associates who comprise the LPM committee are responsible for communicating with each of their departments and their practice group leaders. LPM is discussed at every firm-wide and departmental partners meeting, practice group leader meeting and staff meeting.

Changing behavior is a difficult task, especially in a law firm, and can only succeed if top management is supportive and compensation systems are aligned with firm objectives. There is significant optimism and enthusiasm about Bilzin Sumberg's program, the benefits to the firm and, more importantly, increased value and transparency for the clients.

Borden Ladner Gervais LLP (BLG)—BLG Adroit: Lean Project Management Program

Overview

At BLG, we began investing in the development of legal project management (LPM) for our lawyers and other professionals in 2005, and were already using alternative fee arrangements (AFAs) for some of our largest clients. Until 2011, however, our efforts in regard to LPM and AFAs were mostly informal and unstructured. In the fall of 2011, the firm determined that a formal national LPM program should be developed to help BLG achieve four key strategic goals:

• Revenue generation and profitability, including revenue protection

- Practice optimisation and innovation
- Enhancing BLG's market profile for excellence and innovation
- Enhancing the value BLG brings to its clients, leading to increased client satisfaction

Our LPM program is named BLG Adroit: Lean Project Management (BLG Adroit) – with "Adroit" meaning deft, skillful and adept. BLG Adroit encompasses two methodologies: LPM, based on internationally recognized project management standards, and legal process improvement (LPI), a combination Toyota's "Lean" and Motorola's "Six Sigma" process improvement methodologies. Also within the BLG Adroit program are a growing suite of LPM and LPI tools for budgeting, AFA development and LPM and LPI techniques, including process mapping.

At BLG, we believe that the adoption of LPM and LPI methodologies will benefit both our firm and our clients by:

- Increasing the predictability of fees
- Improving the accuracy of cost estimates
- Improving the management of matters, budgets and AFAs
- Enhancing the collaborative and productive relationships between our clients and our lawyers
- Improving realisation rates and profitability

Getting Started

To develop and implement the BLG Adroit program, BLG's National Management Committee (NMC) created a program team headed by BLG's National Business Department Leader (a senior member of NMC) and two other partners, one from our Corporate Commercial practice group and the other from our Securities and Capital Markets practice group, and created a full-time National Co-Leadership role for two LPM/LPI professionals. One of the BLG Adroit National Co-Leader roles was filled by our existing National Director of Knowledge Management, a qualified solicitor (member of the Law Society of England and Wales) and a certified Project Management Professional (PMP) with significant project management experience. He also holds a Lean Six Sigma Green Belt certification from Six Sigma

Academy, and is currently working towards his Black Belt certification. The other National Co-Leader role was filled by a newly hired National Lean Project Management Counsel who is a seasoned lawyer (member of the New York State Bar) with over 25 years of commercial law and litigation experience in Canada, the U.S. and internationally, including the management of large projects and processes as a practicing lawyer in a U.S. law firm and an executive in-house legal counsel in Canada. She is also a graduate of Villanova University's Project Management Program and is currently working towards her Green Belt certification from Six Sigma Academy.

To assist us in our initial program development planning, and to help provide further training in LPI to our National Co-Leaders, BLG engaged Seyfarth*Lean* Consulting LLC, a subsidiary of Seyfarth Shaw LLP. Seyfarth Shaw is one of the most well-known and earliest law firm pioneers in the U.S. to adopt LPI along with LPM, having begun its "Seyfarth*Lean*" program in 2005.[1]

Helping Lawyers Understand how LPM/LPI applies to Legal Matters

Obtaining buy-in for LPM and LPI started from the top-down, with high-level, in-person "awareness" training delivered in early 2011 by the BLG Adroit National Co-Leaders to the firm's senior leadership (approximately 60 partners from all of BLG's six offices across Canada). An expanded version of this session was repeated in 2012 for substantially the same group of partners. Following the formal launch of the BLG Adroit program in the fall of 2011, the National Co-Leaders conducted in-person awareness training sessions for BLG's Professional Development Committee, all BLG regional Chief Operating Officers, and the senior members of each of the firm's key support departments (Finance, IT and Business Development, including the RFP team). At the same time, the BLG Adroit team began a broader introduction/awareness communications plan directed to all BLG personnel through national status up-date memos and quarterly national in-house newsletters, the first of which was published in mid-2012,

---

1. Seyfarth Shaw was recently recognized by BTI Consulting Group, which tracks the strength of law firm brands based on client interviews, as the leading law firm in the U.S. for using innovation to deliver legal services mapped to client needs (The BTI Brand Elite 18 2013 annual study).

followed by the development of an internal, bilingual BLG Adroit web-portal launched in the first half of 2013 that contains a large amount of self-help training videos and other educational materials, as well as tools, tips and examples of LPI and LPM projects and process maps.

During 2012, BLG'S lawyers and other professionals were provided with BLG Adroit's AFA Handbook and tools developed by the BLG Adroit National Co-Leaders and an AFA Committee of BLG lawyers, as well as BLG Adroit's proprietary budgeting template (developed in-house on the Excel platform) and budgeting software (BudgetManager) that integrates with the firm's time-docketing system (CMS – Aderant Expert). In 2013, BLG's lawyers were provided with an LPM Handbook developed by the BLG Adroit National Co-Leaders. Also in 2013, in-person training sessions on the budgeting tools and software were conducted by the BLG Adroit National Co-Leaders in each of BLG's offices. These sessions focused on how the key LPM and LPI elements -- process mapping, budgeting, the use of task codes in time-docketing and scoping, all done in close collaboration with the client -- aid in developing more accurate pricing, whether in the nature of budgets, quotes or AFAs, and improved matter management. In addition, during these sessions we began the introduction of the concept of the national use of standardized task codes for all time-docketing in all matters to enable the firm to collect useful historical data for future pricing purposes, and some of our practice groups have already moved to standardized task codes in time-docketing.

The BLG Adroit team's approach to training all of its lawyers and professionals in LPM and LPI is reflective of BLG's culture and is consistent with the more recent findings of most commercial LPM consultants, which is that the most effective training is "just-in-time" and "learn by doing" training (as opposed to mandatory classroom training in theory and principles). We are training our lawyers and other professionals on an on-going "as-needed/as requested" basis, working with groups of lawyers who express an interest in and/or are responding to a client demand for LPM or LPI techniques. The National Co-Leaders continuously work closely with groups of lawyers within many different practice groups on individual projects to facilitate the application of LPI and LPM techniques for specific client matters and matter types.

Early Successes

A number of projects have resulted in improved efficiency (cost-reduction or cost-predictability) and effectiveness of matter management for clients and have strengthened our client relationships, including in areas such as commercial real estate leasing, intellectual property, commercial litigation, annual renewals of securities registrations, mutual fund prospectus renewals, small commercial lending transactions, not-for-profit continuances and annual corporate maintenance, eDiscovery, small and mid-sized mergers and acquisitions and national client audit inquiries.

In June 2013, BLG and its client Healthcare Insurance Reciprocal of Canada (HIROC) were recognized as an Association of Corporate Counsel (ACC) Value Champion (the only Canadian organizations to receive such recognition in 2013), as a client-firm collaboration that delivered substantial value by cutting spending, improving predictability and achieving better legal outcomes using a fee model comprised of a base fee plus a performance fee determined by a number of specific "value criteria" including process management, responsiveness, predictable costs and final results[2]. This is an example of the type of arrangement that BLG is encouraging as part of BLG Adroit.

As our lawyers come to understand how LPM and LPI can assist in providing legal services, they find that when they explain to clients how these methodologies can help the client achieve better cost-predictability and management of the relationship between BLG and the client, leading to higher levels of client service and satisfaction, they see that the adoption of LPM and LPI is a highly successful business development tool.

Conclusion

Based on the design of the BLG Adroit training program as a combination of self-help tools and "just-in-time" in-person training, we are winning over our lawyers to the adoption of LPM and LPI techniques on a "one-by-one" basis, and with a firm of more than 750 lawyers and other professionals, this approach takes time. But we believe it is the right approach for our firm, and it is beginning to show results and to take root within the firm, as

---

2. See www.acc.com/valuechampions

more and more of our lawyers come to understand that in today's world, LPM and LPI provide the means to help them to deliver what our clients want and expect.

Dechert LLP

The Creation of Dechert's Project Management Team

In the wake of the 2008 economic meltdown, companies started tightening their belts on all fronts, including legal spend. Suddenly, clients were asking their outside lawyers to set budgets at the outset of projects, and to stick to those budgets. In addition, more and more clients were demanding alternative fee arrangements (AFAs) to enable the client to obtain predictability in costing out its legal spend. What many companies quickly discovered was that most law firms were ill-equipped to respond to these demands appropriately. Dechert LLP, however, recognized an opportunity to give our clients what they wanted, and so "Legal Project Management" was formed.

Initially, the road to success was quite bumpy. Traditional project management was not geared to appropriately manage legal matters, because often a formulaic approach to matter management is difficult to achieve in the legal arena. We, therefore, had to modify our approach and develop a new tactic, where certain aspects of traditional project management were blended with the firm's technology and processes in an effort to manage client costs while maintaining the firm's profitability.

To that end, we devised a system whereby the Project Management team leveraged historical data with similar objectives and assumptions to a current project to establish a budget and fee arrangement for clients that were objectively reliable. To do this, we linked the firm's project management capabilities to our financial systems to help the firm develop a project plan and budget for the client at the outset of an engagement, and to enable the Project Management team to monitor and manage progress on the engagement. The idea was, if the project began to veer off course from the established budget or fee arrangement, the Project Management team could immediately reach out to the legal team to address the issue head on, rather than wait until the completion of the project.

Once the Project Management team learned how to create plans and budgets for various matters, the next step was getting the lawyers in the firm on board with this new approach to legal engagements. In order to "sell" the concept of planning and budgeting matters to the firm's partnership, the Project Management team was presented as a service not only to the lawyers, but also to the clients. We began conducting presentations on the firm's project management capabilities, programs, and expertise to the various practice groups within the firm. By focusing on lawyers in practice groups, we could custom-tailor the presentation to their specific needs with respect to particular matters. We explained how AFAs could be managed to maintain the firm's profitability while providing clients with transparency, predictability and accountability. Concurrently, we engaged in open dialogues with the firm's big clients who were pressuring outside firms for a deeper commitment to cost savings, and offered to them the same services, including follow up reports after matters were completed to demonstrate how time was being managed and how their money was being spent. All of this has enabled Dechert to demonstrate to our clients a commitment to protecting their investment in us.

Dechert's Current Project Management Structure

Dechert's Project Management unit is currently housed within the Finance Department and is staffed with a team of professionals with various academic backgrounds, including degrees in law, business, mathematics and information systems. The group is lead by the Firm Wide Director of Project Management, who began her career as an attorney in a large regional law firm in Philadelphia and went on to spend 10 years as an in-house attorney at two Fortune 500 companies. Her client-based perspective, together with the other team members' wealth of professional experience in the areas of financial analysis, financial planning, budgeting and legal services, creates a diverse professional background to help the team fully understand the concepts of Project Management and how to effectively utilize these methods using the firm's technical resources – including our time tracking system, our accounting and billing program, and our system for aggregating baseline data from the billing program – to comply with the needs of their clients and meet the firm's financial objectives.

The Project Management team provides four basic services:

1. Pricing and Budgeting,
2. Matter Management,
3. Client Communication and
4. Education.

At the outset of a project, the Project Management team works closely with the Marketing department and the firm's lawyers to provide assistance with responses to requests for proposals, budget forecasts and developing complex pricing models for standard hourly rate matters, discounted hourly rate matters and matters involving alternative fee and value based billing arrangements.

In addition to providing pricing assistance, the team assists with matter management by providing customized reporting which is delivered as frequently as requested (weekly, bi-weekly or monthly) and can be as general or as granular as desired (down to the level of tracking how much time and cost each timekeeper is investing on each task). The team's reporting suite includes: budget verses actual statistics, financial trend analysis, profitability analysis, detailed narrative analysis, Gantt chart style work plans and detailed financial charting.

For clients who are interested in more detailed and frequent communication, the Project Management team provides direct-to-client reporting on a matter-by-matter basis or for an entire portfolio of issues. The team also works with the firm's lawyers to prepare client presentations on specific topics such as the client's legal spend or on more general topics such as the firm's approach to legal project management and legal cost issues.

Finally, the Project Management team provides both individual and group training to the firm's lawyers on subjects including team resource offerings and other topics such as how to develop a budget and work plan, the firm's pricing scenarios and alternative fee and value based fee arrangements, how to draft engagement letter pricing language, and the firm's financial requirements and profitability standards. Additionally, the team is working on long term projects such as constructing a pricing database that will allow the firm to capitalize on past experiences by serving as a centralized repository for pricing decisions. The pricing database will incorporate matter and task based analytics to serve as a tool to further guide the improvement of the firm's pricing strategies and pricing performance.

The Future of Dechert's Legal Project Management Department

The landscape of legal services continues to change and adapt to a new way of client thinking. Clients expect outside law firms to be more than mere advisors; clients seek lawyers who will be partners and collaborators, sharing in the risks associated with legal uncertainty, who are driven by the same desire to achieve cost-effective, positive outcomes. Although the structure of Dechert's Project Management team and systems are securely in place, we strive to continue our efforts in further evolving the Project Management initiative to meet the needs of our clients by remaining client-focused and flexible in our approach to pricing and managing AFAs.

In an effort to anticipate client needs, Dechert's Project Management team has developed training programs not only for partners, as mentioned above, but also for senior level associates who are on track to become partners. By providing training to these associates before they become partners, we aim to create a new generation of incoming partners at Dechert who, at the outset, are focused not only on a client's legal needs, but also on a client's business needs. This training, coupled with the Project Management team's continued efforts of providing quality pricing and matter management services to the partnership and client base, as well as creative alternative fee structures, will enable the firm to adapt more readily to the ever-changing needs of its clients.

Dechert's goal is to continue to maintain a level of reliability and transparency in order to enable its clients to understand the value of the services provided by Dechert, and ultimately how the client's money is being spent. Accordingly, in addition to providing clients with detailed reports outlining how a matter was managed at intervals throughout the course of a project, Dechert is engaging in a process to provide real-time reporting to certain clients to allow such clients to have accurate up-to-date data on a project at any given time. This level of transparency will demonstrate Dechert's commitment to the client's legal and business needs, and the importance Dechert places on communication and collaboration with its clients.

Conclusion

Changing long-standing practices can be very difficult. But the ability of a law firm to recognize the need to adapt to a changing environment with respect to client expectations is critical for success. Dechert's Project Management team has made great in-roads, both with Dechert's attorneys and also with our clients, by demonstrating the need to focus not only on the billable hour, but also on profitability and predictability through innovative means. Such efforts can lead to greater success, not only for the firm, but also for the clients we represent.

DuPont

Legal Project Management ("LPM") is a disciplined approach to the management of legal matters. It involves the application of knowledge, skills, tools and techniques to achieve project objectives. LPM is all about delivering legal services at a higher level of satisfaction to the client. This is accomplished through a gained understanding of the matter from the perspective of the client and using a disciplined approach to collaboration, communication and decision-making.

Tom Sager, Senior Vice President and General Counsel of DuPont, has thought a lot about the skills needed by the lawyer of the future to successfully serve the business clients of today. He truly believes project management is a skill set every lawyer needs to serve his/her client in the most effective way. In fact, as he started to look at what was going on in the legal industry and talk to others in similar situations, he came to the conclusion that all legal professionals could benefit from becoming more efficient in their work practices and more effective at serving the clients to meet the ongoing business challenges they continually face. It is more than just being an excellent legal practitioner, you need to understand the client and meet their conditions of satisfaction (including on time, in scope, on budget).

"The role of lawyers in the corporate setting is to respond to a client's need for legal support in maximizing shareholder value and supporting corporate stewardship. Often the lawyer must guide the client to articulate clearly the full range of business objectives and stakeholders in a situation. He or she evolves from the role of technical specialist and risk manager to a key participant in addressing business challenges and opportunities. In-house counsel is uniquely situated to meld legal strategy and tactics with the operational constraints that the business imposes.

For a company like DuPont, this requires stewardship of corporate resources through disciplined management of costs as well as the protection of its assets. Concurrently, counsel must model the behaviors that the client expects of other members of the business team: stewarding the client's resources and demonstrating accountability not simply for what is done, but also for how it is done. In-house counsel manages the delivery of legal services to the client, while guarding against being pulled to work on the interesting legal issues at the expense of tactically managing a cost-effective action plan that achieves the client's business goals. For these reasons, legal project management has come to the fore." (from a 2011 report for DuPont Legal authored by Aileen Leventon and James Buckley from QLex Consulting)

It was decided that after receiving the appropriate level of education and training, our legal staff would be required to utilize Legal Project Management principles for certain legal matters, initiatives and projects. Legal professionals would learn to develop effective project teams and lead them in a way that optimizes the use of time and resources; the emphasis would be on results, not activity. In March 2011, QLex Consulting (Aileen Leventon) was hired to design and deliver a basic training course for everyone in the worldwide Legal Function. The training was a total of four hours broken into two, two-hour sessions. Participation was mandatory for all legal professionals and administrative staff. The training consisted of lecture, facilitated discussion and table-top exercises. The training sessions covered basic project management concepts such as the role of the project manager, eliciting from the client their goals and objectives in context of the matter at hand, stakeholder analysis, and risk analysis. Each person also was exposed to a few basic LPM tools (project charter, RACI chart, task list and simple schedule tool). The hope was that everyone would leave the training with a learning they could immediately apply to something currently in their work queue.

The intent of the training was not to turn the lawyers into professional project managers, nor was it to provide a prescriptive project management methodology. The point was to help everyone in Legal understand the value in using a disciplined approach to managing their work and keeping the end goal in mind. It all begins with understanding the legal matter from the client's point of view, eliciting the client's objectives and goals through an intentional dialogue, and developing the scope of work based on this understanding. The schedule, budget and task list should be created with a focus on the scope of work and the criteria for success as defined by the client (a.k.a. conditions of satisfaction).

In order to drive the idea of using Legal Project Management to better serve our clients, we knew we had to do more than just training. We created a multi-dimensional change management plan that involved messaging, education, coaching, developing proof of concept, benchmarking and measuring results. This type of follow-up activity is critical in driving behavior change through a large, complex organization.

One of our most successful applications of project management to legal work is in the Patents organization. They are in the process of transforming their organization to becoming a world class leader in the way they deliver legal services to the DuPont businesses. There are multiple projects designed to improve their processes, improve their skills and abilities and better align with the needs of the businesses. They are using project management to drive these efforts towards sustainable results. Legal professionals manage the projects through the utilization of the tools and techniques on which they were trained and with the assistance of coaches provided through the Six Sigma organization. Coaches/mentors are essential for people trying to learn new ways of doing things.

We have also been successful in lowering outside counsel costs through the use of an enhanced budgeting process. The process focuses on fees, expenses, staffing and forecasting. It begins with a conversation between the in-house and outside counsel to discuss the legal matter in terms of the context of the situation, the objectives of the client, the conditions of satisfaction and scope of work. The budget is created based on this mutual understanding. Quarterly budget meetings are held to monitor changes in scope and assumptions. Changes seem to be the norm in legal matters so the legal team needs to be prepared to recognize the change and acknowledge the potential impact on the strategy, scope, deadlines and budget. It is critical to discuss the changes with the business client and articulate the risks and potential consequences.

As is typical of a law department, we do not have a cadre of project management resources at our fingertips to drive the change and provide one-on-one mentoring for everyone. Currently, there is one certified project manager devoted to our Legal Project Management initiative. Her role is to coach and mentor groups and people assigned to major initiatives and projects. (She is also the Knowledge Manager and Six Sigma Champion.) We do not have a formalized program although we have leveraged project management resources from another organization in DuPont with a formal Project Management Office and from the Legal Six Sigma team.

Back in the beginning of our journey, it was important that we acknowledged the fact that the cultural changes required to fully optimize the use of legal project management in the Legal Function were not going to happen quickly. Time and patience are necessary to evolve into this new mindset. We had to look at the anecdotal evidence to measure progress and keep the change management plan fresh and alive. One lesson learned is progress will not occur without direct involvement from management and people who can facilitate the change.

Fenwick & West LLP

At Fenwick & West we have conducted a number of experiments to find the right mix of project management support for our matter teams. The implementation approach that is appropriate for a project is dependent on the client's needs, the composition and working style of the team, and the particulars of the legal matter.

Initially we identified three in-progress litigation matters to serve as pilots. The overarching goal of the pilot projects was to determine how

LPM can facilitate enhanced monitoring of accrued legal fees and scope trends against budgeted assumptions and constraints, define success and ensure broad awareness throughout the team of the client's business goals, and seek out other practical modifications to the legal teams' systems and processes for managing matters.

The pilot teams (partners, associates, paralegals, and staff) took part in all-day training on LPM principles with a focus on high-impact techniques (scope management, work breakdown structure, risk management, communications) using their matter as the sample project. Following the session, the teams applied the knowledge gained directly to their matters. By the end of the process, each team contributed their experiences and feedback to the firm's combined learning which resulted in a set of best practices for future matters to employ.

In addition to the pilot teams, the firm also undertook a number of projects to supplement the attorney education effort, such as:

- <u>Investments in developing advanced internal PM expertise</u> Team members with the requisite baseline skills and qualifications were selected for in-depth training to act as project managers and are actively involved in matters that require specialized PM support.
- <u>Formalizing eDiscovery process best practices and process</u> Fenwick's soup-to-nuts eDiscovery service for litigation matters fits prominently into LPM by providing attorneys a structured process to follow over the life of the matter, ensuring optimal outcomes for clients.

In combination with Fenwick's long-standing and fully-adopted task-coded budgeting and financial reporting tools, this approach of optimizing process, providing targeted training, and utilizing state-of-the-art tools and analytics provides our clients the confidence that our matter management skills are as top-notch as our legal advice.

In summary, the foundation of our LPM service is built on:

1. <u>People</u>: Trained project managers are available to add a layer of oversight and monitoring of in-progress work against budgeted fees, and to track and respond to changes in scope.

2. <u>Technology</u>: Scalable tools and timely data to monitor work progress and budget performance across all matters.
3. <u>Education and adoption of best practices</u>: Consistent reinforcement of recommended steps and procedures.

Fredrikson & Byron P.A.

Driving Forces

At Fredrikson & Byron, in addition to excellent legal work, we have always prided ourselves on delivering exceptional client satisfaction and value. In 2012, the Board of Directors approved a formal knowledge and process management initiative named FredAdvantage™. The pillars of FredAdvantage are legal project management, legal process improvement, knowledge management and technology.

From the client perspective, the goals of Fred*Advantage* are to better integrate the voice of the client into matter planning, provide more predictable budgets, improve attorney communication with clients, and enhance the overall client experience. From the firm's perspective, the goals of Fred*Advantage* are to improve quality, consistency and realization.

Getting Started

The Fred*Advantage* initiative began with the selection and appointment of a cross-functional leadership team. This team includes an Administrative Director and two Lead Attorneys, one litigator and one transactional lawyer. The Director is a Six Sigma Green Belt with five years' experience in project and knowledge management. The Lead Attorneys are mid-level partners in the Securities and Intellectual Property Litigation Groups. In addition to the core leadership team, there is a Fred*Advantage* Committee that includes a member of the Executive Committee and the firm's COO, CFO, CMO, CIO and CHRO.

The Fred*Advantage* leadership team applied project management tools to create a charter and project plan for the rollout of our new initiative. The group identified critical stakeholders and risks, defined success, developed a communications plan, and established concrete objectives.

Three initial pilot projects were selected. The first pilot project consisted of regular small to mid-sized M&A deals for a single client. The M&A pilot group increased matter efficiency by developing checklists, deal sheets, a team intranet site and other LPI tools, and has instituted more regular internal communications among the group. The second pilot project was a patent infringement lawsuit. The patent infringement team implemented LPM and is providing regular project status reports to the client, including a comparison of the fees incurred to the budget. The third pilot project is for patent applications. This pilot group is using LPI tools to increase efficiency and uniformity in the preparation of patent applications.

Susan Lambreth, of LawVision Group, provided training to firm leaders and to the participants in the three pilot projects. The Fred*Advantage* leadership team received "train the trainer" coaching.

Branching Out

After the pilot projects were up and running, the leadership team identified additional projects in the Labor & Employment group and trained the members of those teams. The Administrative Director and Lead Attorneys serve as trainers, coaches and consultants for new and ongoing projects. At this time, the firm does not have full time project managers. The role of project manager is being filled by a member of each project team, often a junior partner or senior associate. To date, Fredrikson & Byron has trained about 60 people in LPM, including partners, associates, paralegals, and administrative staff.

The introduction of Fred*Advantage* required a coordinated effort to position the initiative, train participants, manage change, and develop supporting tools and systems. The supporting tools and systems included:

- LPM training materials for half-day sessions led by the Administrative Director and Lead Attorneys. Each participant receives a binder with course materials and additional resources. Template documents are made available on the firm's intranet.
- Handouts and presentation materials for use in raising awareness about Fred*Advantage* among firm attorneys.
- Software to support the development of project plans.

- Financial tools and process for producing budget vs. actual reports.
- Task codes for litigation, intellectual property litigation and employment litigation. Task codes for transactional matters are in process.

Results

Results are apparent in the year since the Fredrikson & Byron Board of Directors approved the Fred*Advantage* initiative. Firm management has actively encouraged the use of Fred*Advantage* tools and processes, and more lawyers are using LPM and LPI in their work. The IP Litigation Group readily embraced LPM and is using LPM to manage all patent litigation matters. The M&A and patent groups are working more efficiently and providing greater value by using LPI. Additional lawyers, paralegals and staff are being trained in other practice areas.

We are delighted with the results we have achieved since launching the Fred*Advantage* program. Client-attorney communications in matter planning and budgeting have been greatly enhanced. Matter management is going much more smoothly and predictably. And, most important, client feedback has been positive.

Honigman Miller Schwartz and Cohn LLP

Overview

In 2011, Honigman adopted a new strategic plan to achieve leadership in adapting to changes in the legal marketplace. As part of that plan, we committed to focusing on delivering clearly defined value to our clients on a consistent basis. We believe "value" means the combination of:

- **Outstanding Quality** – work that is well crafted, and reflects knowledge, experience and creativity.
- **Efficient Resource Allocation** – the right personnel at every cost level matched to the work.
- **Service and Communication** – the attention and information clients want, provided in a timely manner.

- **A Commitment to Help** – an understanding of the client's industry, business and needs, and a passion for helping achieve the client's business goals.
- **Price and Proportionality** – an understanding of the client's business objectives, with the fees and costs proportionate to their goals and fair and consistent with their needs.
- **Predictability** – a product that is consistent with what was agreed to, with changes due to changed circumstances communicated in a timely and thoughtful manner, and
- **Something Added** – delivering something above and beyond what is ordinarily expected, be it an unexpected solution or savings, making connections, or providing new perspectives.

Legal Project Management (LPM) was identified as a critical component in successfully implementing our plan to consistently provide outstanding value to our clients. In addition, although we have had extensive alternative fee arrangements (AFAs) in many practice areas for years, we saw a need to expand our capabilities in that area firm-wide, also requiring effective use of LPM.

While many of our lawyers intuitively used informal LPM methodology, we felt that was insufficient and that a formal, firm-wide embrace of LPM was necessary. Our strategic plan recognized that it is not possible to provide top-end value to clients without first understanding how to internally improve processes to drive efficiency, consistency, and quality. We also believe clients need easily understandable options, both with respect to the terms of the proposed engagement and the strategy to achieve their goals. LPM is at the core of achieving both these goals.

As part of the plan, the firm also created the positions of Chief Value Partner and Associate Chief Value Partner to locate responsibility for overseeing and sustaining our value oriented efforts.

Training and Implementation

In 2011, we took our first steps toward implementation. We began a roll-out of comprehensive phase/task based billing on a department by department basis to facilitate efficient and effective budgeting and monitoring against budgets firm-wide. We also selected software for both budgeting and project management purposes, and trained a group of personnel on using the budgeting software, so that they could assist attorneys with that aspect of LPM. We also developed a methodology and a form for doing fee estimates based on LPM principles that was implemented as a firm policy.

Our more visible LPM training and implementation began in 2012 with two 90- minute internal training sessions, conducted by our Chief Value Partner and Associate Chief Value Partner, on the fundamentals of LPM, including much of the theory behind LPM, and how it fit into our strategic plan. Each training session also featured a segment from a partner on a successful use of LPM at the firm. Those training sessions were open to all lawyers as well as a significant portion of our non-lawyer support staff, and were extremely well attended. Providing these in-house training sessions allowed us to lay the groundwork for our LPM efforts on an efficient and cost-effective basis. It also helped to increase the LPM expertise of some of our key people in connection with this effort.

The next step was involving certain "LPM champions" throughout the firm who we had identified earlier in the process. We asked them to help lead our effort by receiving more extensive LPM training to assist with department and practice group implementation. Those "champions" attended full-day training courses with a leading consultant and were tasked with beginning to implement LPM into their day-to-day practices.

Our plan was to make this the beginning, not the end, of training and implementation. One of the themes we had heard from others in the industry who had undertaken similar efforts was that they tended to fizzle out not too long after they began. We have continued to conduct monthly "Sustained Effort" meetings, which include attorneys and staff from across the firm's practice areas and at each of our offices. In these sessions we have (1) provided ongoing training on various LPM aspects, such as determining staffing needs and modeling budgets, as well as related topics, such as choosing the right AFA for different engagements; (2) discussed other "value" components that are closely tied to LPM, such as what "efficiency" really means; (3) shared best practices in implementing LPM in different practice areas, for varied clients, and at differing project size levels; and (4) shared successes and failures in LPM implementation. We have had engaging discussions about what improvements we can make, what resources the firm can provide, and what new or different approaches we can take to help ensure that our efforts are broadly successful. These Sustained Effort meetings have been a key component to keeping LPM in the forefront of everyone's mind and demonstrating how LPM can actually work in real life legal practice at our firm.

We have also successfully encouraged individual lawyers to become involved with other groups outside the firm that focus on LPM so they can bring that knowledge back to us. We also provide access to LPM related webinars and encourage participation in them.

In addition, our two Value Partners work one on one (and sometimes two on one) with our lawyers to review LPM plans, budgeting efforts, potential AFAs and the like, to help them work through the myriad situations that they face. This becomes a key learning experience both for the lawyers and the Value Partners.

Our departments have also integrated LPM into their plans. For example, the litigation department mandates the use of LPM and budgeting in all significant new matters, and we held a special additional training session in LPM for the real estate department, focusing on department specific examples of how LPM can be implemented. The implementation efforts at the department level will be gradually expanded to each practice group in the firm.

Lessons Learned and Early Successes

We believe that a key aspect of making LPM work is making our training effort as broadly based as possible. While our partners are the ones most often engaging with clients on issues such as scoping, staffing and budgeting, our associates, paralegals and non-lawyer staff, including various members of our finance, accounting and business development departments, as well as many of our administrative assistants and other support personnel, are essential to LPM success. Improved communication and coordination among our lawyers and staff, at all levels, make a difference. When each member of the team understands not only how LPM is employed but why, there is a deeper and more thorough understanding of what we are doing for our clients, what attorneys or staff are responsible for each piece of the project, how the timing of everyone's work interrelates, and how this all affects the budget. This is the key to harnessing the greatest benefits from our LPM efforts for both our clients and the firm: more accurate and predictable fee estimates, better efficiency and work product innovation, greater realization and profitability, and improved communication and collaboration.

We have now had the opportunity to fully implement LPM principles on a number of projects across a broad range of practice areas, both transactional and litigation, and for projects of varying length and size, and to track those matters from start to finish. It is clear that our efforts have resulted in a higher sensitivity to, and focus on, many of the principles of LPM and have helped to improve our communication both with our clients and among our attorneys on many of these issues that were often overlooked. However, LPM is a discipline, and it requires a disciplined approach and a sustained effort, so our journey has only begun.

Conclusion

Our efforts have gone a long way in what seems like a short time, and have started to show results across a wide variety of practices and clients. Our lawyers are actively implementing LPM into their practices and seeking out opportunities to educate clients on how our LPM and value-initiative efforts can benefit them.

Providing outstanding value to our clients on a consistent basis, and being able to communicate that value and how it is achieved, is a critical aspect of our strategic plan that cannot be realized without the implementation of LPM. And implementing LPM on a consistent basis throughout a law firm is something that requires discipline, buy-in and understanding from lawyers and staff alike, as well as a sustained effort to innovate and improve. We as a law firm are committed to this effort.

King & Wood Mallesons

Commencing the Legal Project Management Journey

In October 2010, global law firm King & Wood Mallesons (formerly Mallesons Stephen Jaques) wanted to explore using project management to help provide a unique and powerful client service experience. Their Director of Legal Logistics, Michelle Mahoney had just finalised a multi-national project for a global construction company where the client experienced a very positive outcome. Chairman of the firm's 'Practice Excellence Committee' and Partner, Peter Stockdale, then asked Michelle to investigate whether combining law with project management could deliver ongoing benefits for the firm and its clients. Michelle then outlined a plan based on client needs, including creating a Project Management Office (PMO), a centre of excellence to share learnings and a training programme for legal staff reinforced by a suite of support tools.

Next in the firm's Legal Project Management (LPM) journey was to fulfil the firm's position of deciding to staff its PMO with non-legal Project Managers, by recruiting its PMO members from the construction engineering and professional services industries.

In parallel, to support the embedding of project management skills within the firm, King & Wood Mallesons refreshed the professional development capabilities for its legal teams, by including project management as a required professional development capability for all Partners and lawyers working at the firm.

Then in 2011, the firm engaged leading LPM consultant and ex-lawyer, Pam Woldow from Edge International to facilitate some LPM workshops for four of the firm's major clients and to help inform the firm's LPM training content. The decision for the firm to take its initial steps of its LPM journey together with some of its major clients was a significant one. It became evident that when the client's and the firm's legal teams were brought together in the same room and were given the opportunity to learn how they could work more efficiently together – it was a powerfully positive experience for everyone involved.

Additionally, the firm also established an LPM training team that was made up of some of the firm's brightest and best senior lawyers who believed in the need for change and recognised the importance of building project management capability in-house to support the changing needs of clients.

That same year the firm also invested in an estimating and matter management tool; Thomson Reuters 'Engage' software, to provide its Partners and lawyers with capability to support them in running their matters as efficiently as possible.

An Australian first

In March 2012, the firm announced to the Australian market its investment in a LPM programme inclusive of a dedicated project management service for clients via a PMO, supporting project management tools, along with a commitment to train 480 of its Partners and senior lawyers in the firm's Legal Project Management methodology.

Recognising that the Australian legal market had become an increasingly sophisticated and competitive environment, King & Wood Mallesons understood it had to consistently demonstrate value for money and deep business insight to its clients, rather than rely on legacy relationships to generate business.

By investing in its LPM programme the firm now had a first-mover advantage; no other legal firm in the Australian market had created a project management training course designed and trained by lawyers for lawyers.

Clients viewed this announcement as an innovative move and one that was critical to effective practice management, as LPM enabled for the client's broader commercial objectives to be focused on, not just the provision of legal advice.

Specifically, by investing in an LPM programme the firm saw numerous benefits to its clients including:

- Providing accountability, predictability and certainty on cost;
- Creating transparency over how clients' matters were being managed and how the budget was tracking;
- Empowering clients so they could decide what work needed to be prioritised;
- Enabling clients to be able to make better and informed decisions on how they wanted their budget spent; and
- Giving clients confidence that their matters would be managed with exceptional service and value for money not just some of the time, but all of the time.

LPM had been viewed as a systematic and standardised approach for scoping, planning and managing legal work within an agreed time and budget, but what LPM meant to King & Wood Mallesons was about being known as a firm that could consistently deliver market-leading work to scope, on time and on budget for its clients. Clients had been clearly communicating that they wanted accountability, predictability and certainty on cost; LPM was an enabler for the firm's Partners and lawyers to consistently deliver to clients within agreed timeframes and without any surprises.

Responding to the challenge

The single biggest challenge for King & Wood Mallesons was to live and breathe project management and to embrace the change around embedding it. The firm wanted its lawyers to find value in the PMO and to innately want to use the frameworks and processes in place – and to do this on a regular basis. Attending LPM training meant for its Partners and lawyers to take time out of their busy schedule to do so. The firm responded to this challenge in two ways. One, by breaking down course content into components so training could be run across two sessions to free up time and secondly, by recognising Partners' and lawyers' time spent in training towards their billable targets.

Driving successful change in any organisation is challenging and in law firms it is no different. As King & Wood Mallesons was aware that its lawyers preferred to be trained by lawyers (as they knew what a lawyer's life was really like), the firm guided by its PMO, decided that by inviting some of their senior lawyers to inform the content and deliver the training, there would be a greater chance of success for buy-in from its legal teams. Additionally, by having the firm's own legal-based training team, it provided an excellent feedback channel as to what was working in the training and what could be improved. The feedback the PMO received about the firm's LPM training programme was overwhelmingly positive - the approach and the content had hit the mark for the firm's very busy lawyers.

Responding to feedback has been key in ensuring the quality of the training content has been upheld, with the PMO continuing to use both quantitative and qualitative feedback data to refine training content and add in new materials to keep the training content fresh and relevant.

Championing innovation

Since commencing its LPM programme in Australia, the firm has exceeded its training targets. Many of its clients' major matters have been supported, mentored or project managed through the PMO and the firm's LPM tool kit now includes over 40 templates and examples, along with standardised project management documentation for Partners and lawyers to use.

2013 has been another busy year for the firm's LPM programme, with the firm continuing to invest in project management capability by delivering training to senior legal staff as well as extending training to all legal teams and other key support functions across the firm. Furthermore, rollout of training on Engage, has evolved with the delivery of tailored team-based training, inclusive of both legal and support staff, to drive maximum skills uplift and efficiencies through shared learning.

This year the firm has also continued to run LPM training workshops with clients by providing Continuous Learning Education (CLE) training to clients on LPM key principles. Such is the demand for these skills that earlier this year, the firm was asked by a major client to co-develop and co-deliver a bespoke LPM training programme to help train 80 of the client's lawyers.

Additionally, this year members of the firm's PMO, who are certified Prince2, Australian Institute of Project Management and Project Management Professionals, have extended their capability to become Black Belts in Lean Six Sigma, to provide leading expertise on client's matters in both legal process improvement and efficiency.

Supporting a global powerhouse

When in late 2011, the firm announced its intention to combine with leading Asian legal firm, King & Wood, a new legal powerhouse, 'King & Wood Mallesons' was created. Centred in Asia, it was the first verein alliance law firm of its type in the world, combining a Chinese and Western law firm.

Recently, the firm has announced another combination, with international legal firm SJ Berwin to join the King & Wood Mallesons member firms, effective from November 1, 2013.

With this latest combination, King & Wood Mallesons will become a truly global legal powerhouse; made up of 30 offices around the world with 553 Partners and 2233 lawyers.

It's a combination that will not only serve to fuel the firm's commitment to continuous improvement, but will help to push the boundaries of project management through to process *efficiency*.

The firm knows from first-hand experience that LPM is a journey, not a destination.

King & Wood Mallesons is committed to LPM for the long term, both for its clients and its people.

Mayer Brown LLP

Approach to LPM

Mayer Brown has made a substantial investment in a global, integrated legal project management initiative that has included training for lawyers, licensing and launching of Thomson-Reuters' Engage project management software across Mayer Brown's global offices, and creating and refining the firm's proprietary tools, templates and protocols for scoping, estimating and managing client matters. The Engage software is allowing Mayer Brown to provide rapid updates to our clients on project plans and, for matters priced on an hourly basis, actual spending levels measured against budgets.

By way of background, Mayer Brown was formed primarily through a 2002 tie-up of the U.S. firm Mayer, Brown & Platt and the UK firm Rowe & Maw, and a 2008 merger with Johnson Stokes & Master (JSM), based in Hong Kong. (There are also predecessor firms in Germany and France and an affiliate in Brazil.) The combined firm is focused on serving the needs of large global companies in complex and critical matters.

Each of the predecessor firms had begun to reengineer its processes in the early 2000s, with Hong Kong focusing on optimizing execution speed and reliability, London focusing on knowledge management, and the U.S. emphasizing technology. By 2011, various Mayer Brown regions had in place country-based LPM training in a number of locales, alternative fee-arrangement protocols, an initiative in London in response to Lord Justice Rupert Jackson's review of the costs of civil litigation in the UK. There were also several technology initiatives related to LPM. The impetus for each project was that general counsel were seeking lower and more predictable costs for legal services.

Mayer Brown's leadership saw the need for something more ambitious and all-encompassing: a push toward greater efficiency in every aspect of the firm's operations, including its management of legal matters and its interactions with clients. As a result, they launched a global firm-wide strategic initiative titled the Drive for Efficiency, or D4E, now into its third year.

D4E is led by a D4E Core Team that includes equity partners from four practice groups and geographies and representatives from its Finance, Attorney Development and Information Technology Departments. The D4E Core team also includes the firm's Director of Pricing and LPM as well as a PMI-credentialed global project management professional. Our Director of Pricing and LPM is in our Finance Department, but we consider LPM as a strategic priority that affects everyone at the firm.

The D4E Core Team began its efforts by hiring a consultant and then, with our consultant's help, conducing a survey of partners to ask what they believed to be the principle areas where D4E could add value. Over 400 partners responded to the detailed web-based survey and provided hundreds of useful narrative responses. Based on those responses, the D4E Core Team set its objective as allowing the firm to offer lower and more predictable costs of delivery of legal services through:

1. Scoping and estimating
2. Alternative fee arrangements
3. Legal project management
4. Lower costs of production
5. Consistency

Because Mayer Brown is a global law firm with a substantial number of product lines designed for some of the world's most sophisticated legal buyers, the D4E Core Team needed to identify ways to provide tools and templates that are unique to specific practices. To do so, the firm designed "D4E Champions" from key practice areas to develop and refine tools, such as scoping and estimating checklists and engagement letter templates, for use in their practices.

Checklists are at the heart of Mayer Brown's approach to LPM. When a client seeks the firm's counsel, for example, scoping checklists help our lawyers get a comprehensive picture of the client's objectives, estimate billings more accurately, delegate work more effectively, monitor progress with greater specificity and communicate more effectively. At this level, Mayer Brown's LPM checklists emphasize how to conduct very specific operational steps at discrete points in the life cycle of similar kinds of matters.

In addition to practice-specific checklists, the firm has created an overarching six-point LPM checklist to be followed by lawyers in every client matter. The first step on that checklist, dubbed "Listen," underscores the critical importance of asking specific questions of the client before starting work to learn what the client hopes to achieve, how success will be defined and how important success is to the future of the client's business. While we considered using a more standard PMI-based approach, we decided that our client-service-oriented culture required an LPM methodology that is focused on client value instead of typical project success indicators. Mayer Brown was ranked #2 for client service in the 2013 edition of the BTI Client Service A-Team. The firm was praised for being efficient, providing value for the dollar and putting the right talent on matters, among other things.

The firm has also trained partners across all regions on scoping and estimating, alternative fee arrangements and legal project management. The training and the supplementary materials are available on our intranet site and have been replayed in meetings of senior associates and counsel. We have also made written materials available separately on, for example, alternative fee arrangements. This training has been supported by communications in our annual partner meetings, our firm strategy, our monthly partner meetings and communications from our Managing Partner encouraging the changes that we are creating.

As noted above, we have also implemented Engage from Thomson-Reuters. Engage is a matter management and budgeting system. Engage is integrated with our billing system and replaces spreadsheet that, while very flexible, are prone to error. We have loaded estimation templates created by D4E Champions into Engage along with templates provided by Thompson-Reuters. User support for Engage is provided by our Finance Department and we are finding growing user acceptance. This technology is a vital help in our legal project management efforts because it allows us to develop written plans in a consistent manner and to track how actual spend compares to budgeted spend.

We are also implementing projects to reduce the cost of delivery of services. However, these have tended to be targeted efforts, such as process optimization or automation for specific legal products. We are also working with various alternative approaches to staffing including contractors, staff attorneys and out-of-country resources. One key approach has been to solicit ideas from practice leaders on ways that with firm resources they can reduce their individual costs of production.

There has been little active resistance to the Drive for Efficiency. The greatest challenges thus far have been to implement Engage (which is still developing) and to create an LPM methodology that works for the way we serve our clients. Delivering those tools has enabled a change to offering lower and more predictable costs of delivering legal services. As a result, we have found that people are changing the way that they think and act.

We intend to continue to press forward on all five objectives. On legal project management specifically, we plan to both expand the number of LPM professionals on our team and also to build training for associates and to build legal project management skills into our "associate competencies" model. We also plan to further improve and document our tools so that we pursue legal project management in an increasingly consistent global matter. We see legal project management as a continuing core competency, much like talent management and substantive legal training.

Miles & Stockbridge P.C.

Overview

One of Miles & Stockbridge's first successes in project management and process improvement, branded "Project X", was a system developed in 2008 for budgeting and managing merger and acquisition deals. It incorporated not only a customized set of billing task codes, an internal tool to track budget-to-actuals, but also a proprietary process of prioritizing specific identified client needs for each acquisition to avoid wasteful diligence. Building upon the Firm's desire to develop and support additional value-based service offerings, as well as growing client demand for efficiency, predictability and shared risk, key members of Miles & Stockbridge's management team began exploring an even broader legal project management ("LPM") program in early 2011.

The Firm's goal was to create win-win scenarios for both itself and its clients, with a particular focus on engagements employing alternative fee arrangements ("AFAs"). The team quickly realized that while alternatives to the hourly fee may be the way of the future, LPM's biggest immediate return on investment was, ironically, on the traditional hourly fee engagement. With the overwhelming majority of engagements still falling under the traditional model, the Firm believed that LPM could help confront the shrinking realization rates facing the legal market. Therefore, the Firm's program was designed not only to help with the transition to alternative service delivery and pricing models, but also sought to equip its lawyers with the tools to create more competitive and predictable budgeting, while also protecting profit margins by reducing write-offs/downs and increasing realization.

Implementation

Formal implementation efforts began in earnest in early 2012, with strategic investments in technology, personnel and training. Miles & Stockbridge was an early adopter of the Thomson Reuters LPM software ENGAGE, knowing it was important to be up and running sooner rather than later with off-the-shelf software, rather than allowing internal application development and refinement to stall momentum. The technology was an immediate tangible use as a teaching tool, and helped accelerate subsequent roll-out and training exercises. The software package included a number of pre-configured matter templates, which could then be customized to form the basis of many practice-specific "work breakdown schedules". In most cases, these templates jump-started the laborious process mapping exercises.

Concurrent with the ENGAGE rollout, the Firm tapped an existing staff member as a project manager and pricing analyst to support the pricing, knowledge management, and technology needs of the firm's LPM efforts. The abilities to mine and analyze historical data, build pricing templates, and actively manage matters, fell into place and the Firm found it had a leg up on its LPM initiative, as well as a competitive advantage over its peers. Later in 2012, the Firm hired a director of pricing and practice management. It was felt that practice management, which already touched the functional areas of finance and marketing, would be the most efficient and effective structure to hold the Firm's pricing and project management roles. This non-lawyer support, along with a group of lawyers – deemed "LPM Champions" – formed the team tasked with spearheading Firm-wide implementation, which included five key aspects:

- The identification of key matters that would benefit from LPM and innovative pricing models, limited to 2-3 matter types per practice group
- The extensive mining of prior similar matters, leading to process maps, matter templates, and pricing structures
- The participation of an "LPM Champion" and extensive non-lawyer support on matters subject to project management
- The use of just-in-time, on-line training
- The automatic scheduling of follow-up meetings (not to exceed 60 days between meetings) for all matters under project management

Since LPM is truly a sea change for most legal practitioners, any law firm taking on an LPM implementation will quickly find itself faced with a monumental change management project. Those asking lawyers to dramatically alter how they think about and view their approach to meeting client expectations will undoubtedly be met with resistance. In many cases, LPM and attendant process improvement fundamentally go against past practices. As such, classroom training to a large audience was not viewed as an option. Instead, based upon the literature and reports from the field, the Firm embraced "just-in-time" training on actual client engagements in combination with individualized online training provided by LawVision. Individualized training was focused and started with a core group of LPM Champions, who were from a cross-section of departments, practice groups, and office locations. In doing so, the Firm sought to embed LPM experts and organically raise awareness throughout the Firm. By "riding shotgun" with the director and/or manager in just-in-time sessions, champion training was periodically reinforced via real-time training. Furthermore, taking a holistic approach, the core group also included members of the Firm's marketing department to expose them to the key concepts of LPM.

The Path Ahead

While many at the Firm have become certified in LPM, generally speaking, all lawyers were not expected to become project managers. Instead, lawyers were expected to attain enough of an understanding of basic techniques and concepts to allow them to tap into the Firm's extensive LPM resources. At the end of the day, certain phases of the LPM process require more lawyer attention than others. As such, lawyers will need to be equipped to define and capture client objectives, conduct stakeholder analyses, and set forth budget and scope assumptions. Nevertheless, a large firm cannot expect all of its timekeepers to support all of the day-to-day project management functions. Most lawyers would prefer to – and should - practice law. Staffing a team with a dedicated PM or firm LPM resource who serves up period progress reports, allows them to do so. At the same time, lawyers generally do not care to be "project managed". The Firm has found that flashing color-coded key performance indicators ("KPIs") in front of lawyers does not move the ball forward. Finding the appropriate balance between too much and just enough LPM is key. This can vary between geographic (office) locations, practice group, or even within a small practice area.

Early Successes

LPM has aided the Firm's new pricing team in offering legal services to both sophisticated corporate clients, as well as unsophisticated users of legal services, such as individuals or small companies seeking representation in mergers and acquisition transactions. By engaging the client and breaking down the work, clients are provided with greater visibility into costs, contingencies, etc. – putting them in the driver seat. Client communication plans, which now include the delivery of meaningful budget data, mean clients are no longer subject to "black box" billing routines.

Employing this approach, the Firm recently negotiated a "win-win" AFA with a Fortune 500 client in the form of a fixed-fee for a large portfolio of over 1,000 litigation matters. The LPM program also has borne fruit in the

Firm's rapidly growing Intellectual Property Practice Group. With patent reforms now taking shape under the recently enacted America Invents Act and firms scrambling to learn the new *inter partes review* procedures, our lawyers were prepared to map out the process and tailor project plans for its clients. Not only have these techniques permitted our Firm to creatively structure fee arrangements that focus on client value; they have created a "value-add" for clients by allowing our lawyers to impart knowledge about the process.

Conclusion

The benefits of the Firm's LPM program have begun to take shape. The Firm has taken to heart what clients are demanding – efficiency, predictability in fees and shared risk.

Norton Rose Fulbright

Overview

At Norton Rose Fulbright, we are committed to achieving our clients' business and legal objectives by providing legal services of uncompromising quality in an efficient manner consistent with our client's expectations. As part our commitment to a culture of on-going process improvements, we implemented workSMART, an efficiencies and innovation program driven by fundamental legal project management principles. Initially rolled out to our disputes practice, workSMART is a comprehensive and multifaceted program designed to improve the efficiency of every aspect of the legal services provided by the Firm from the time a matter is opened until resolution. workSMART is designed to provide lawyers the tools they need to offer our clients the quality of service they deserve, within budget and according to an agreed upon scope. The awareness of our clients' demand for transparency and cost reduction motivates lawyers to utilize workSMART resources throughout all phases of the dispute process.

Background and Scope

In 2011, a group of leaders in the Firm's disputes practice formed the Efficiency and Innovation Committee to develop a more systematic and process-oriented approach to the handling of litigation matters. The Committee's objective was to determine how current processes could be improved to better service our clients. As mentioned, one of the products of the Committee's work was the workSMART program, the purpose of which was to deliver the following benefits to our clients:

- Reduced costs while achieving the desired results
- Enhanced quality and consistency of legal services provided
- Improved communication and collaboration

The first phase of the program involved discussions with clients and a speakers series. We invited general counsel, consultants, and leading members of the Association of Corporate Counsel to address dispute partners regarding industry trends surrounding legal project management (LPM), pricing, budgeting, and other ways to reduce costs and add value.

The Committee then formed five working groups responsible for addressing the lawyers feedback and advice received from our clients and consultants. Each working group was led by two partner co-chairs and a project manager who supervised a team of lawyers and legal support professionals from the IT, Finance, Library Services, Litigation Support, and Marketing departments. These groups were further supported by professionals from the firm's Project Management Office.

The priorities of the working groups were driven by what we believe matters most to our clients: quality, efficiency, consistency, cost predictability, and effective and timely communication.

Scope of workSMART Program

The working groups were charged with developing practical strategies and processes in the following areas:

- Legal Project Management
- Knowledge Management

- Budgeting and Finance
- Client Collaboration
- Training and Adoption

Legal Project Management (LPM)

One of the primary goals of introducing LPM principles and protocols is to improve quality, consistency, and efficiency, thereby reducing our clients's overall legal spend. The LPM working group generally defined the scope of the LPM role as defined below.

- Assist in defining scope of work that is aligned with the client's expectations and desired outcome
- Assist in the preparation, management, and reporting of the matter budget
- Provide support in assembling legal teams to ensure alignment of resources and skill sets to the task
- Communicate project expectations and status to team, clients, and other stakeholders
- Proactively manage changes in matter scope, identify potential risks, and recommend adjustments
- Ensure legal staff are applying the right tools and processes to every task
- Coordinate with knowledge management to ensure resources are maintained and updated
- Conduct matter debriefs to improve processes

Knowledge Management (KM)

Through the KM working group, our lawyers developed a litigation Case Management Framework that incorporates practical tools, technology, practice tips, and preferred vendor relationships and pricing. This proprietary "just in time" Framework provides efficient access to the firm's knowledge management resources, including templates, forms, and checklists, laying the foundation for the "Norton Rose Fulbright" approach to litigation. The Framework is maintained on the firm's intranet and from within it provides links to related resources and tools. By providing a one-stop case management platform, our lawyers can focus their efforts on efficiently developing and executing case strategy, client collaboration, and tailoring our representation to meet the desired outcomes.

The KM working group also implemented more structure into maintaining key work product by assigning senior lawyers and partners to routinely review and update certain high-quality firm documents. This curated Litigation Forms Library can be used to quickly find relevant forms and templates and as a starting point for further research.

Budgeting and Finance

To increase certainty in our clients' legal spend, Norton Rose Fulbright's budgeting process leverages experience in similar matters as an input, and allows for analysis of various scenarios should changes occur to the original scope of work. Even in those matters in which clients do not mandate the use of task codes, the firm requires lawyers to use firm customized task codes to capture metrics that provide additional insight and allow for a more a more informed estimating and budgeting process.

The firm was an early adopter of the Engage budgeting and project management software. In collaboration with our clients, lawyers outline the engagement requirements, matter scope, and initial strategy. Engage then creates comprehensive matter-project plans and budgets, including complex alternative fee arrangements. Engage also generates reports that detail the current budget-to-actual spend, resulting in greater transparency for our clients.

Client Collaboration

Our client collaboration working group developed a proprietary dashboard to make case-specific information accessible to clients on a confidential and secure Internet-based platform. The dashboard is maintained on a firm-hosted secure Extranet and provides transparency to clients in the following areas:

- **Contacts.** Provides contact information for the Norton Rose Fulbright team and other parties involved in the case such as co-counsel, opposing counsel, third-party counsel, vendors, experts, witnesses, and the court.

- **Calendar.** Offers an online calendar with key events, including depositions, meetings, court dates, and case filing deadlines.
- **Status.** Provides periodic status reports and ready access to meeting agendas and minutes.
- **Tasks.** Includes a comprehensive list of action items related to case activities.
- **Documents.** Enables access to key documents associated with the case, such as discovery, expert documentation, correspondence, orders, pleadings, research, and transcripts.
- **Budget.** Offers the ability to track real time billing-to-date against the planned budget in both graphical and table formats.
- **Document Collaboration.** Serves as a platform to share and draft documents.
- **Billing.** Provides monthly billing information, including electronic copies of all invoices.

Training and Adoption

Recognizing that effective training and communication is essential to widespread adoption, and thus involved our professional development team in the development of the program. We divided our training program into two parts: general awareness training for all lawyers and just-in-time training for client-specific teams including lawyers, paralegals, and support staff.

Our general awareness training covered all aspects of the workSMART program, with the intention of providing our litigation lawyers with a foundation for future adoption. Following up on this general awareness training, we identified partners who were interested in piloting the workSMART program. Those partners and their teams underwent initial training on the fundamentals of LPM and the application of workSMART resources to their matters.

The training program will continue to evolve as we roll out LPM protocols beyond the firm's dispute practice. The training delivery methods will expand to include class room training on the effective use of workSMART resources, on-line training on LPM, and class room training in advanced LPM and budgeting.

Client Adoption and Feedback

Our workSMART program has received positive feedback from our clients. In particular, clients value the increased predictability of their legal spend and the improved communication facilitated by the program. In-house counsel appreciate the client dashboard for immediate and efficient access to case status and budget information.

Both our lawyers and clients have been impressed by the efficiency gains achieved through the application of our initial LPM program, and we have seen a significant increase in both interest and adoption of the workSMART resources. We expect the number of matters being managed through workSMART will continue to increase over the coming years as the program matures and training continues. As we move from the pilot phase to widespread adoption, the feedback from our clients and lawyers will continue to inform our ongoing process improvement initiatives.

Reed Smith LLP

By Vincent Cordo and Melissa Prince

Approach to Project Management

Like most other law firms, Reed Smith developed its legal project management department after the recession put tremendous pressure on many of the firm's clients and they began to seek a shift from an hourly based pricing model to a value based pricing model, increased financial transparency and process improvement.

Legal Project Management ("LPM") at Reed Smith involves the application of a structured approach to planning, pricing and managing legal matters so the firm keeps its service delivery model in line with client expectations. What sets Reed Smith apart from other firms is that it couples LPM and advanced Task Based Billing with cutting-edge technology and its systems are set up to manage large portfolios of matters, giving it the ability to manage volume better than any other firm. The firm has invested significantly in its resources –people, systems and repeatable processes – so that it can continue to do exceptional legal work and still provide the efficiency, cost effectiveness and the quality of services that clients are looking for.

While Reed Smith takes a flexible approach to LPM that is based upon each client's individual needs, the firm also focuses on being involved from the inception to the completion of each of its matters in the following ways:

1. **Defining the "What":** Setting Objectives, Defining Scope and Identifying Potential Outliers – One of the keys to a successful client relationship is understanding client needs. Each client has unique goals and business objectives and while one pricing structure may work well for one client, it may not work well for another client. For this reason, at the beginning of each engagement, the Reed Smith legal team sits down with each of its clients to have frank and detailed pricing discussions where the legal team asks questions such as what would the client consider a successful outcome of the matter, what are the client's priorities, both overall and for the matter, whether the client has specific pricing parameters/concerns, and the types of risks that are involved in the engagement. The answers to these questions help the firm to work to ensure that each client's goals and business objectives are captured by the most appropriate pricing structure and approach to matter management.

2. **Budgeting, Work Plan and /or Process Mapping Assistance** - The LPM team next works with the client to create a detailed budget, matter work plan and/or process map that breaks the legal work to be completed down at the task and timekeeper level and provides the estimated budgets and timeframes for each task.

3. **Matter Management**

(d) **Client-Specific Task Codes** – After a matter is underway, the LPM team develops customized client-specific task codes that serve two purposes. First, task codes assist the firm in building a historic pricing database to assist it in pricing similar matters in the future. Second, the LPM team uses task codes to implement internal and external matter management dashboard reporting.

(e) **Matter Management Dashboard Reporting** – for each client matter or portfolio of matters, the LPM team can provide customized matter management dashboard reporting that measures budget and work plan performance on a real-time basis and enables Reed Smith lawyers to have frequent communication with the firm's clients regarding how their matters are being managed. The LPM team can monitor metrics such as the number of hours spent on a particular task, the percentage of completion of work in relation to the scope of work and the budget and timekeeper staffing levels.

(f) **Weekly Team Meetings**- Throughout the course of an engagement, the LPM team assists Reed Smith's lawyers with matter management by meeting with legal team leaders on a weekly basis to go over matter financial performance, task completion and to proactively address issues such as risks to the budget, schedule and scope of work. By addressing these issues with Reed Smith's lawyers proactively, this enables them to in turn promptly speak with firm's clients and empowers the firm's clients to make day-to day business decisions affecting their matters and business objectives.

(g) **OuRSite** – Reed Smith's clients can monitor matter status and progress using the firm's ouRSite© platform, which is a state-of-the art case-management system built on the Microsoft's SharePoint platform. ouRSite© allows Reed Smith's clients to access to documents, financial information, billing information and other matter-related information for a client matter or portfolio of client matters. Within ouRSite©, the client has the ability to drill down and access work product and can monitor the statuses of its matters and how the Reed Smith team is progressing against the budget for its matters.

8. **Conducting After Matter Reviews** – At the end of each matter, Reed Smith asks its clients questions such as, did the firm meet the client's business objectives, was the client satisfied with the pricing for the matter and the end product, did the end product save or cost the client money, was the matter efficiently and properly managed and would the client utilize the firm for future matters. Reed Smith uses after matter reviews to learn from its experiences, increase client satisfaction, and focus on process improvements that can increase future performance, cost-effectiveness and efficiencies.

Seyfarth Shaw LLP

The "Voice of the Client" is a core principle of Lean thinking and one of the driving forces behind our Seyfarth*Lean* client service model. The basic premise of Voice of the Client requires you, as a lawyer or a firm, to step outside your own interests and view the world as your client does. While the concept sounds inherently obvious to professional services work, delivering on this premise demands a significant paradigm shift.

At Seyfarth, our ongoing listening and discovery processes helped us understand how profoundly our clients wanted and needed greater efficiencies and business value that went far beyond legal excellence. They identified issues and opportunities at every stage of a legal engagement that we knew we could address through process improvement and a strategic approach to project management.

This pivotal learning and change of perspective led us to completely integrate the use of legal project management throughout the life cycle of a client engagement and relationship. By changing the way we viewed project management toward more holistic and strategic applications, we have delighted clients, gained national recognition and made significant inroads in changing the culture and the business model at Seyfarth Shaw.

Our Approach

Project management at Seyfarth has become a driver in terms of excellence in client service and differentiation within the legal profession.

Our project management team helps facilitate our Voice of the Client process to define and articulate what value means for a particular client or situation. Through effective facilitation, the lawyers and the project managers develop a practical and strategic understanding of a client's legal and business issues.

The Seyfarth project management team, and their technology innovation counterparts, work in tandem with our lawyers and all other firm functions to design solutions and see them through final implementation.

Our approach is distinguished by:

- *Our track record and the increasing sophistication of project management and process improvement work we have done with clients.* We manage $300 million transactions or $30,000 compliance projects. We have included a sidebar article that briefly describes some examples.
- *Its flexibility.* Unlike other industries that employ project management disciplines, legal project management offers unique challenges due to the variation in legal services and the potential adverse forces, like the motives of opposing counsel, which can impact project scope, needed expertise, strategy and deliverables. The need for flexibility and adaptation is critical.
- In conjunction with our technology innovations team, we are rapidly evolving our project management philosophy to incorporate the concepts and methodologies of Agile project management, a discipline frequently associated with software innovation and development.
- *Our view that project management is a client-facing function.* Project management team members truly have a seat at the client's table and are an integral part of the Seyfarth legal and client service team. By being closer to the business, they can often pinpoint solutions that a partner or a lawyer may not know. As trained professionals in project management, they focus on the organizational management aspects of a project and information flow .
- *Our use of a dedicated group of professional project managers, so that our lawyers can focus more on substantive issues and strategy.* We currently have approximately 18 employees on our project management team. Our senior project managers are all PMP certified, Yellow Belt and/or Green Belt certified, and Agile or Scrum certified. Reflecting the level of achievement they have contributed to our client organizations, some PMs have been trained and certified by in Agile by our client companies.

Our approach differs from other approaches we have seen in the legal profession. For example:

- Our project management team is not solely focused on the pricing function of an engagement but rather the project planning and execution including facilitating alternative fee arrangements.
- Our efforts do not focus primarily on training lawyers to become project managers, although we do train them on the key concepts and to recognize when to engage the project management team.
- We do not think of our work as a set of tools or templates, but a fully realized strategic approach and cultural discipline.

Today, our project management team supports more than $55 million in revenue on a wide range of client needs in nearly all practice areas. Our project management team has supported more than 500 Firm clients in the past 18 months ranging from process improvement initiatives, providing technology solutions, project planning and execution and supporting our legal teams in a variety of ways. Based on the strength and success of our Legal Project Management Office, Seyfarth created the Client Solutions Group, which also includes the Legal Technology Innovations Office, a team of approximately 6 legal solution architects. These two groups collaborate extensively on developing and implementing customized solutions for clients.

Culture Change

Project management has been a driving force in changing the culture at Seyfarth to become a Lean organization. Originally a group of 6 to 10 that was established in 2004, the project management team was internally focused, dedicated to work like IT initiatives and office relocation/expansions. The team was pivotal in launching and driving many of the firm's Lean Six Sigma Green Belt process improvement initiatives.

As the firm's Seyfarth*Lean* efforts began to take root with clients in 2008, the team became heavily involved in collaborative process mapping efforts with client legal teams, adding a practical, valuable perspective to current-state assessment and future-state planning. Recognizing the opportunity to deliver higher levels of client service and efficiency, the team shifted almost exclusively to client-dedicated efforts in 2010.

For the project management team, the use of process mapping became a critical turning point. "For us, it was the game changer. It brought project management closer to the core business, and it was key to the firm's cultural transformation. The process mapping effort captures how we work as national client teams across function roles of lawyers, technologist, practice managers and project managers," said Kim Craig, director of Seyfarth's Legal Project Management Office.

The benefits of process mapping -- both in terms of creating efficiencies and in building more collaborative client relationships -- helped drive greater support and buy-in from Seyfarth partners. We have found building support and commitment among partners is never predictable or easy, but once we have 'won them over,' they often become our most enthusiastic advocates.

Some of the strategies that helped us over the years have included: demonstrating success on internal initiatives before working with clients; building some pivotal client relationships with progressive in-house counsel; introducing training first with executive leadership and a cross-section of partners from various practice areas; creating more practice-specific Yellow Belt training; and, gaining recognition and acclaim within the legal profession, which built momentum among clients and additional validation for partners.

Perhaps the most important element in driving culture change and partner support has been the consistent and passionate level of commitment from the firm's Executive Committee and its national practice leaders.

Key tools

In the course of pursuing our strategic approach to project management, we have created a vast library of tools and templates. While some are very specific in focus or customized for a single client, there are many that have very broad usage and illustrate how we integrate the use of technology:

- **SeyfarthLink,** our web-based client collaboration tool, helps increase productivity and enhance communication and coordination, execution and delivery, and management and control of the engagement. SeyfarthLink serves as a knowledge and project management hub that captures documents, as well as issues, process improvement ideas and responses, project plans and reports. We also use this platform to aggregate tasks, documents and calendar entries across multiple matters. Templates, knowledge banks and document automation provide enhanced efficiencies to the legal service delivery. Financial dashboards and reporting are also part of the solution.

- **Portfolio Tracker** is a database consisting of information for a bundled group of matters. It allows a client to view the status of all (or a subset of) matters and receive e-mail notifications upon new entries into the database, upcoming due dates and filing deadlines.. The database enables Seyfarth to generate and deliver customized reports on a host of metrics. It is comprehensive and includes critical information on every matter, including, for example, claim background, type of matter, location, business unit, resource assignments, links to documents and other information related to that matter. While the databases contain a great deal of information, custom views allow for "at a glance" consumption and a variety of options to filter the data. The view in the database varies based on the needs of the client and our teams. For example, it can be displayed by basic case information (for all cases), resource assignment views (a client can have a customized view that pares down the data so that their view contains only relevant cases for which they are responsible, which has been a huge delighter), Seyfarth attorney views, lawsuit information, state court information, etc. Through extensive collaboration with one client's in house legal team as well as its businesses, we customized approximately 120 database fields of key case information.

Continuous improvement

Another core premise of Lean thinking is continuous improvement, whether it is the Lessons Learned discussion at the conclusion of a matter or in the adaption of new ways to think and work. When it comes to project management at Seyfarth, we are rapidly moving to a specialized form of Agile project management.

Generally accepted project management techniques often use waterfall methods. This approach assumes that all aspects of a project can be planned at the outset from start to finish. However, legal work, by its nature, demands a more dynamic, flexible approach that matches strategy to the situation at hand.

We have found that Agile is a more flexible, highly evolved approach, often used in software companies. Characteristics of Agile project management include: self-organizing teams; planning by phase, rapid prototyping, daily stand-up progress meetings and so on. Agile project management reduces complexity by breaking down a project into manageable segments or short cycles. The central leader is a 'scrum master,' whose role is to ensure the team meets core requirements (e.g., adherence to a case strategy, or pre-defined outcomes for success) rather than completion of a task list. We think that Agile has tremendous potential to be adapted for the legal profession, and can serve as a model for complex litigation, cross-border transactions and other substantive legal processes.

Our firm's journey in value and innovation continues to lead us -- and our clients -- into exciting new territory. Project management has been a critical ingredient and catalyst for success. We have gained tremendous confidence in our ability to set and exceed the expectations of our clients, and to continually set new heights for us to attain.

Client successes with project management

Here are some examples of Seyfarth client successes, in which our project management team and our capabilities played a pivotal role.

Area of practice: Corporate

Achievement: Integrating Legal Project Management Into Complex Transactions

Client: Financial services provider

We were asked by a first-tier financial institution to help develop a strategic plan for the management of a significant cross-border reorganizational project involving several hundred millions of dollars in assets, more than 700 employees, and a fixed close date. The client's objectives for the plan included cost effectiveness, tactical demand on internal resources, and achievement of mission critical project milestones. We worked closely with the client to apply legal project management to this large transaction, developing an extensive and detailed plan for organizing, structuring, and approaching the client's new direction in international strategy. We leveraged the skills of one of Seyfarth's client-facing project managers to organize and manage key engagement activities. We then participated with the client in presenting the project plan, its goals, and the implementation strategy to multiple team leads across many different workstreams. As a result of our success in helping the client reach its planning objectives, we were appointed to serve as program director for the project.

Client successes with project management cont.

Area of practice: Labor and employment
Achievement: Meeting client challenges through process improvement partnerships
Client: Fortune 100 conglomerate

Our project managers led our attorney and client team through process mapping sessions. Collectively, we created a step-by-step record of the client's single plaintiff litigation process, identifying all resources, documents and best practices. We determined the required steps, sequence, task time estimates and appropriate resources to complete each task. We incorporated company-specific template documents, such as early case assessment templates, designed to eliminate duplication of effort across multiple matters. By establishing a systemic flow of tasks, we also identified stages in the process with the most risk. We then matched these stages with efficient solutions. Instead of individual experiences driving case progress, we established a shared set of documents and resources that could be used for similar cases. The new institutionalized process ensured greater efficiency and consistency across the company's external legal service providers and allowed our attorneys to focus on outcomes for the client.

Client successes with project management cont.

Area of practice: Intellectual property
Achievement: Reducing Cycle Time and Improving Productivity in the Trademark Process
Client: Global footwear maker and marketer

A project manager is an integral member of our client team. The project manager facilitated the creation of a detailed project plan and helped the team manage deadlines and milestones in the massive effort to transition the client's trademark portfolio (then approximately 4,000 trademark registration and application records) to Seyfarth. To ensure we stayed on track, our project manager facilitated weekly meetings to review status, discuss issues and share lessons learned to improve processes for the transition of the entire portfolio. In our initial discussions with the client, they emphasized the importance of transparency and real-time knowledge management capabilities. In response, our project managers directed the tailoring of our client collaboration technology platform.

Area of practice: Employee benefits litigation
Achievement: Effective portfolio management
Client: Premier insurer

This solution includes a number of innovative approaches that are facilitated by legal project managers and generate value in portfolio management, including process improvement, effective use of technology to help the client achieve its goals and continuous improvement. In addition, our project managers collaborated with technology architects to support the client team in automating many functions of the work, which were previously disparate and varied across matters and previous providers. For example, the prior solution mandated manual case form reporting and no two forms were alike across various providers. Now, the team can automatically generate one consistent Case Assessment Form for any matter in the portfolio in a matter of seconds, using data captured in Portfolio Tracker.

Client successes with project management

Project management through the life cycle of an engagement

Seyfarth*Lean* Phase	Seyfarth project management role
Voice of the Client	Facilitate conversation with client to define project scope, success metrics and strategy.
Solutions planning	Participate and facilitate client-planning sessions including who does what when.
Process improvement	Lead and facilitate current state process mapping sessions and Kaizen sessions to tear apart the current process and develop a future state improved process including templates, checklists, technology and right-sized staffing.
'Traditional' project management	Employ various project management planning tools including MS Project, Gantt charts, timelines and project workbooks to track issues, communication plans, financial management and status reporting.
Continuous improvement	Facilitate formal and informal lessons learned sessions with project teams inclusive of clients.

United Retirement Plan Consultants

By Russ Dempsey, SVP & Chief Legal Officer

*What were/are the driving forces that caused your law firm/
department to put a major emphasis on legal project management?
Was it to promote alternative fees, more reliable budgets,
[for Firms] to address write offs or write downs, [for legal
departments] to address outside counsel budget overages?*

Initially I was drawn to legal project management (LPM) because I believed LPM could help structure successful value-based billing engagements. I've been leveraging value-based billing models for several years and

LPM's promise to increase budgeting skills, improved communications and ability to stay to plan were key reasons to embrace LPM. LPM has proved out time and time again that it can deliver in those areas.

Secondly, I thought that LPM may help with increasing the effectiveness and efficiency in the delivery of legal services of the in-house legal team. We have used LPM in-house to perform work-flow optimization analysis, improve knowledge management, and manage projects. For example, better knowledge management now exists in the form of a developed SharePoint site for the legal team, an internal legal blog, and a legal Wiki site to provide information regarding frequently asked questions.

What have been some of your early successes from using project management on your legal matters?

One example of a success is from a fixed fee I structured when I negotiated for a series of commercial lease reviews. As I discussed the fixed fee with the firm, they justifiably were concerned about the possible impact of some problematic lease provisions, (e.g., escalation-of-rent clauses, building allowances and improvement), that threatened the firm's profitability on the fixed fee arrangement. The firm had worked with the company in the past and knew they there were certain lease provisions that we may negotiate aggressively, which jeopardized the fixed fee structure.

I worked with the firm to develop a Risk Chart that would help manage areas in the engagement that could generate excessive work. Ultimately, I secured a fixed fee that was in my company's best interest, and the firm had a mechanism to manage their time commitment on the engagement. I suggested we consider a Risk Chart, and begin by agreeing on the fee, scope of the engagement, major decision points, and the decision makers. Next, we documented the risks and likely consequences, assigned a probability to each risk, prepared mitigation strategies, noted the triggering events, and scheduled a project review. In the example engagement, we assigned percentages to the probabilities; however, I think for the Risk Chart T-shirt sizes will suffice – i.e. small, medium, and large.

Shortly into the AFA discussion, the firm quickly noted risks, intending to kick the engagement into an hourly rate. The purpose of the Risk Chart was to leverage project management concepts to create a tool that would preserve the alternative fee, rather than dictate the opt-out provisions of the AFA.

To mitigate the identified risks, I reviewed the challenges with the CFO and asked what we could do to manage the time commitment of the firm. In working with the CFO, we reviewed the company's position regarding building allowance and escalation-of-rent clauses (risks with a high probability of occurring), and he and I created a term sheet to address these issues at the letter of intent (LOI) phase of negotiations. The term sheet helped manage the firm's time commitment. We presented the term sheet at the LOI stage, a point at which we had more leverage, and it helped reduce the number of turns of the lease when the redlining phase began. In the end, it was more effective to discuss these potential challenges in advance than having difficult discussions of blown budgets and frustration later in the engagement. Importantly, this use of project management was successful in securing an alternative fee that improved the relationship between inside and outside counsel.

A Risk Chart can be used in a variety of engagements, from commercial contracts to litigation, as an effective risk chart can help the parties manage probable occurrences. In most AFA discussions, firms appropriately note the risks. The next best step is to spend some time developing mitigation strategies, which will increase the chances of success for both parties.

Below is the Risk Chart from the example provided:

Item	Notes
Lease negotiations	Represent company on the next six lease negotiations
Scope	Review and negotiate letters of intent (LOIs) and Leases
Completion point	Executed and delivered lease
Decision points	Key business and legal risks to be discussed with CLO or CFO
Fee	Fixed $ amount per lease
Staffing	Firm partner designee
Stakeholders	CLO and CFO
Risks	Time consuming issues such as escalation of rent clauses, building allowances and improvements 1. Completely onerous lease
Consequence	Result in more time spent by firm than budgeted

Item	Notes
Probability	Time-consuming issues have a 70% probability. 2. Completely onerous lease is unlikely and only a 5% probability.
Mitigation	Develop points and position with respect to time consuming issues in advance and include in the LOI or term sheet 3. Rely on LOI or term sheet provisions to help reduce time on onerous leases. Also, company to share in overage above the fixed fee on completely onerous leases. Parties to review and agree after completion of the lease.
Trigger	Approach for this item applies to all leases 4. Upon notice from Partner after initial review of lease
Project Review	CLO and partner to review engagement after completion of first phase of leases to determine effectiveness and examine areas for improvement

Waller Lansden Dortch & Davis, LLP

Responding to Client Needs

Waller conducts regular client satisfaction surveys, and over the last few years we heard from several of our clients that they would like our firm to become more innovative and consider a project management approach in the work we do for them. For some clients, this entails focusing on pricing predictability, while for others it means focusing on streamlining matter management and communications. We also pay attention to the market, and as more legal work becomes routinized, we have become proactive in looking for ways to provide cost and efficiency solutions for our clients. Waller has a good track record of providing alternative fee arrangements, especially in our real estate and labor & employment practices. Our ultimate goal is to be able to offer pricing predictability and a tailored process to every client.

The Starting Point

In January 2013, one of our partners started in her official role as the firm's Legal Project Manager, and she has been tackling individual projects ever since. Waller chose to take an organic approach to developing LPM in our firm – so while we have done some attorney training on scoping and budgeting matters, a majority of our work has been to identify specific opportunities for direct LPM assistance and work on them one by one. We have also been promoting our early success with alternative fee arrangements in real estate and labor & employment. We believe that capturing and promoting some early wins will help us gain greater buy-in from attorneys for the LPM process. We have learned that, at least in our organization, many attorneys have "training fatigue," so leading with training is not the right route for us.

Our finance and restructuring practice group was the first to experiment with using a Legal Project Manager because the group is our Legal Project Manager's "home" group. She has good relationships with the partners in the practice group, so they have been willing to try new things based on that trusting relationship. Once our finance and restructuring attorneys started seeing benefits to using LPM (for example reduced redundancy on large projects and more streamlined information sharing) they became receptive to more changes, including using new technology that previously was anathema to them. Now, based on the recommendations of our finance & restructuring partners, our other practices are showing interest in using LPM to improve the delivery of legal services.

Our Approach

Waller's core approach to legal project management is to use a fresh eye to evaluate how we do our work and identify where there are opportunities to do it more quickly, efficiently, responsively and/or creatively. We have chosen to have an attorney as our Legal Project Manager because she is familiar with the pressures and tensions of being an attorney, and therefore attorneys are comfortable talking with her about change. She also understands what our attorneys are trying to achieve for their clients, and she can help our attorneys find the right process improvements or technology solutions for their practices. In addition to implementing technology solutions, our LPM initiative includes some elements of knowledge management and process improvement, and covers both our legal and our back-office functions. We believe that improving our internal and back-office functions will also have a positive impact on the service we provide to our clients.

We are early in the process of adopting LPM, so we expect that our focus will shift and sharpen over time, but for the moment our key elements of focus are:

- Engagement staffing: *Are we staffing at the right levels and pushing work down to maximize cost efficiency?*
- Technology: *Are we using the best resources possible to manage our work and interface with our clients? Which online tools can best enhance collaboration and communication with clients?*
- Leveraging experience: *How can knowledge of past projects be best applied to current projects to reduce redundancy, improve efficiency and predict costs?*
- Responsiveness: *Are we responding to specific client needs with solutions that add value to the service we provide?*

Initial Success

Our first LPM win involved our Legal Project Manager actively managing a large team of attorneys, paralegals and staff that had been mobilized to handle a large scale bankruptcy. Our Legal Project Manager ran meetings, managed a research database, handled staffing and assignments and facilitated advance planning for upcoming phases in the bankruptcy. Her involvement brought numerous efficiencies to what was a very complex process. We avoided duplicative research, and kept the right people staffed on the right projects. Our advance planning and our use of new technology solutions, including cloud-based collaborative checklists, helped us stay ahead of the issues and minimize crises. The LPM approach on this matter was so successful that our Legal Project Manager is now coaching one of our senior associates as she manages a similar bankruptcy with the same team of senior partners. We just transitioned these senior attorneys to a cloud-based data management system so they can travel to court with their iPads and leave the ubiquitous "trial notebooks" behind; something they might not have considered a year ago!

Adjustment, Adoption and Acceptance

The chairman of our firm has championed Waller's LPM initiative from the outset, and several other firm leaders have become strong supporters. Our goal is to achieve buy-in on a partner-by-partner basis, and most of the partners we have approached have shown interest. We are a full service firm with many practice specialties, and there is no one-size-fits-all solution. Instead, we are listening intently to our attorneys' needs and concerns and customizing our approach for each. Once we make progress with a particular group of attorneys, we share that success with others, because the solutions we have developed could benefit those in other practice areas. Once our attorneys see the value of either new processes, or working with a budget, or using new technology to aid their clients, etc., they are generally willing to take the time necessary to learn more. Similarly, we believe that client acceptance of LPM will eventually lead clients to expect LPM approaches from all of their attorneys, which will in turn lead to buy-in from attorneys who remain skeptical of LPM.

In the Works

We have recently started to tackle M&A projects, where we are mining our internal billing and staffing data. Our Legal Project Manager has pulled, organized and analyzed the data for the relevant partners, and who are working with clients to decide the next step for implementation, including whether to use phase and task codes. Waller already uses the UTBM codes for much of our litigation-related work, and we are looking at whether task codes are the way forward for our transactional practices. We anticipate this may help with budgeting and efficiency. Specialized transactional work is often viewed as too hard to predict, and therefore too hard to budget. We believe that, working closely with our clients, we can whittle down a significant portion of the uncertainty. Initial reactions from our clients participating in the M&A budgeting process has been very positive, and we will roll out budgeting processes to additional clients once we have a process in place that can be replicated and scaled.

Another area of focus is our development of an efficient client portal, or extranet. We have provided extranets and on-line data rooms to clients for several years, but recent leaps in technology mean that a whole new world of options is available. We are evaluating whether we are using the best and most efficient technology to provide our clients with access to their matter data and billing information.

For back-office projects, we have two main areas of focus (i) automating the capture of information, in order to free up administrative time for projects where internal investment time will make a greater impact, and (ii) mapping our internal processes so that we maintain consistency when making key decisions. We believe that establishing good internal processes can be a great way to ease our attorneys into LPM.

We have been refining a flow chart developed by our Legal Project Manager to illustrate all of the steps needed to properly define the scope of a project, identify the steps of the project and plan out the communications for a project as both an internal and external marketing tool. It is an effective tool for reminding both our attorneys and clients that the best way to kick off a project is to discuss and define all of the elements and issues that could become complicate the engagement.

Conclusion

While Waller is still in the early stages of adopting and applying LPM principles to our practice, the initial results and response from our attorneys has been extremely positive. Our strategy of building grass roots support for LPM one attorney and one engagement at a time has proven successful, and we are beginning to build significant momentum. There remain numerous hurdles to clear before we achieve firm-wide implementation of LPM, but we are off to a promising start.

Winston & Strawn LLP

Winston views Legal Project Management (LPM) as part of our overall Knowledge Management (KM) effort, along with substantive work product and experience, pricing and cost data, and business intelligence.

Over the last several years, we have put into place key elements to support LPM, including mandatory phase and task codes for all matters as well as refinements to our matter types to more easily monitor our client matters.

We also have worked with many clients on Alternative Fee Arrangements (AFAs) where LPM elements have been used to increase client satisfaction and value.

We consider LPM to be process improvement, better workflow, KM resources, and other tools to enhance and improve our services for specific client matters. Virtually all of our lawyers already include some LPM elements in their client work, although they might not necessarily define them as such.

We see that LPM better allows us to engage our clients in defining the value of the legal service. When we formalize scope and plans, we can better streamline in some areas and then emphasize our skills in higher value areas based on where our clients will receive the most value and impact. Successful alternative fees, reliable budgets, fewer write downs, etc. are all great side benefits.

Our Approach

Given the benefits of LPM, we have developed a multidisciplinary, firm-wide approach with the strong support of senior management.

We have a multidisciplinary team approach to LPM headed by the Partner in Charge of KM and LPM, the Director of Accounting, the Chief Information Officer, and the Chief Marketing Officer. We work closely with staff throughout the firm to make sure we address LPM-related technology, library resources, training, and other issues.

We started with practice areas where some LPM elements were in place, and the Practice Group Leaders were interested in strengthening and deepening their LPM efforts. While LPM approaches understandably vary by practice group because of the nature of the work performed, we do have uniformity in terms of the use of Phase and Task Codes for all work. We also measure our LPM efforts against the Firm's financial data for matters.

We have conducted training for associates, and are in the process of developing additional training for other staff.

We also make sure that LPM is a key consideration as we continue to make improvements to our Enterprise Content Management System.

We have seen improved client communications as well as fewer write-offs or write-downs. And we are in the early stages of considering how clients would access LPM-related information.

Commitment from our most senior management including our Managing Partner has been key. Our senior management sees LPM as part of our program to use information and efficient working practices as a competitive edge for us.

We prefer to use attorneys where possible for many of the LPM functions, supplemented as needed by non-attorney LPM-trained staff. Since the current PMP process is not LPM-specific, we are not focused on hiring certified PMs, but would be interested in doing so if a strong, LPM-focused certified program became available.

We are mindful of the tension between LPM and billable hour models, and management is continuing to review how to address it.

Appendix 2

Project Management Information System Tools for LPM

BakerManage™

General Questions
How long has your system been available to consumers?

BakerManage and Budget Designer are tools developed by Baker Donelson for use by its lawyers, legal teams and clients. Baker Donelson is currently

---

The following is based upon information provided to the authors on July 28, 2013. For more up to date information, please contact the vendors directly.

working on an application which can be licensed to third parties who are not clients of the law firm..

What is the general scope of functionality of your product or purpose?

BakerManage is a tool that guides lawyers and legal teams through a more methodical planning process and collaboration with the client prior to incurring fees on behalf of the client. The system is also used to streamline case management and closure. This system is intended to enhance project planning, encourage more reliable budget development, provide more transparency for the client and support real time communication on matter status with the client and the Baker Donelson legal team. The system incorporates a unique project management workflow that was developed by Baker Donelson lawyers with project management expertise. The workflow is based upon waterfall project management processes, but streamlines traditional project management's 42 plus processes into 12 steps for project planning, executing and closure which track the way lawyers and legal teams work. The workflow is built out in SharePoint 2010 to ease implementation by legal teams.

BakerManage™ is supplemented by another tool developed by Baker Donelson called Budget Designer™ which assists lawyers with the development of budgets which are tied to UTBMS codes. Users of Budget Designer™ have the ability to build budgets from a top down or a bottom up approach, can tie subtasks to the UTBMS phase and task codes to create a more detailed and reliable budget, and can assign resources using the Firm's timekeeper database which includes the timekeeper's standard rates or special rates assigned to a specific matter. Budget Designer™ also permits lawyers to build a budget tied to time constraints by entering start and end dates for phases, tasks and subtasks.

What is the platform used to develop your application?

SharePoint 2010.

Provide a summary of current functionality in the product.

BakerManage™

BakerManage™ incorporates 3 phases of tools (based upon BakerManage™ 's unique workflow) for use by lawyers and legal teams. In the each BakerManage™ Phase, legal teams develop the following information.

This information is recorded in BakerManage™ template forms (which are included in Appendix 3) which are accessible by both the legal team and the client (if this option is selected):

Development Phase (Project Plan development tools)

- Detailed factual background of the case;
- Stakeholder contact information (either Baker, Client or third parties) ;
- Statement of Work (identifying scope, assumptions, risks, budget constraints, cost constraints);
- Communication Plan (identifying any reporting or communication specifications by the client.

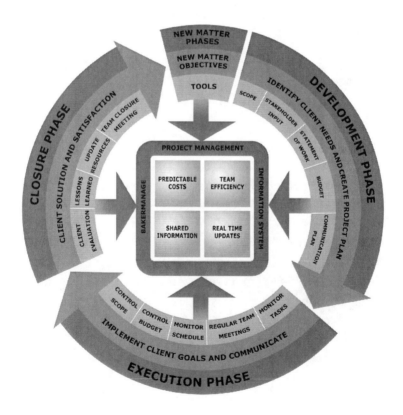

Execution Phase (Project monitoring tools)

- Assignment of Tasks / Schedule (identifying phases, tasks, subtasks, time estimates, resource assignments, status of assignment and comments related to the assignment)
- My Tasks (filter to show only the tasks or subtasks assigned to the user)
- Budget (identifying phases, tasks, subtasks, resource, budget legal spend, actual legal spend)
- Case Notes (log for client and team members recording status of phases, tasks, subtasks or the matter generally)
- Summary Financials (summary report of the total billed, total billings in process and payments received)

Closure Phase

- Lessons Learned (log to record improvements for the next engagement)
- Client Evaluation (evaluation requested from the client at matter closeout)

Budget Designer™

Budget Designer™ provides lawyers and legal teams with the ability to create customized budgets tied to matter phase and task codes. Users can create a budget by the following methods:

- from scratch for a specific matter
- from scratch as a template
- by importing a budget from excel
- by copying a budget for an existing matter
- by copying a budget template

Users first enter a scope statement, identify assumptions incorporated into the budget and identify risks considered for the budget. For top down budgets, users can identify the estimated cost for each phase or task of the plan. Users can then allocate portions of this budget estimate based upon creation of subtasks, assignment of recourses and identification of time estimates. Budget amounts are calculated either using the timekeeper's standard rate or the special rate associate with the matter. For bottom up budgets, users can then create a budget by selecting the Phase/Task matter plan as the high level framework. Users then can create subtasks, allocate resources and identify times for completion to develop a detailed budget.

Provide a summary of proposed functionality in the product.

The following functionality is currently under development for BakerManage.

- Client Rolled Up Budget Report (Phase level budget summary for a portfolio of matters)
- Matter Budget To Actuals Over Time (Estimated Hours to Base Hours)
- Matter Budget Schedule (display of a budget over time using a Gantt Chart)
- Matter Budget and Expense to Actual Report (budget to actual reports including expenses)

How many customers (firms) and users are utilizing the software? Within those Firms, can you identify on average the percentage of lawyers using the product?

BakerManage and Budget Designer are currently being implemented for approximately 1000 matters.

How are the license fees for your product structured? By number of timekeepers, users or lawyers?

Clients of Baker Donelson are not charged for the use of BakerManage.

Does your system communicate directly with Firm systems or does it require an intermediary database to pull information from Firm systems?

BakerManage™ and Budget Designer™ communicate directly with Firm financial, time entry, reporting and timekeeper databases.

Project Plans
Does your system provide a step-by-step approach for development of an entire project plan (work breakdown structure, schedule for the work, communication plan, etc.)?

Yes.

What are the components of the project plan in your product?

The BakerManage workflow walks lawyers (in either transactional or litigation matters) thru the development of a project plan that includes scope, assumptions and risks.

How are changes to scope handled in your system?

BakerManage incorporates a "Change Control Log" which is intended to record new issues that arise which require a change in the project plan and budget. The Log confirms that the legal team has analyzed the impact on the plan and budget, communicated the change to the client, and obtained client approval prior to working on and spending additional time on the change issue.

Budgeting
Do you provide template budgets, task lists or checklists with your product?

Budget Designer includes a database of previously created matter budgets and practice template budgets that can be used by lawyers as a starting point for their matter.

Does your system accommodate phase and task coding?

Yes.

Does your system accommodate subtask coding? And do these indicate percentage of work completion or just the % of budget used.

Yes. BakerManage and Budget Designer are synced with the Firm's time entry and financial systems to provide budget to actuals in real time. In order to accommodate real time information, timekeepers must enter time on a daily basis.

Does your system permit comparison of draft budgets against
actual matters using the same phase and task codes?

No. This functionality is obtained using other software packages.

What other graphical displays of data are available in your system?

BakerManage includes the following reporting functionality:

- Matter Budget to Actual (see graphic next page)
- Matter Assignment of Tasks(see graphic next page)
- Matter Budget Over 80 % By Phase (with Thermometer view) (see graphic next page)
- Matter Budget Performance ("Budget Over 80" - Phase Level Thermometer)
- Matter Budget Assist (Budget over time requiring start and end dates) (see graphic next page)
- Client Rolled Up Case Notes (most recent Case Notes entry for a portfolio of matters) (see graphic next page)
- Administrative Alerts (automated alerts for user selected budget to actual thresholds)

Communication and Access

Is your system open in the law firm intranet or does it require a separate login?

The project information for a particular matter is available to lawyers through the Firm intranet - BakerNet.

Is your system open to client access through an extranet?
Does it require login for client access?

The project information can be made available upon request by the client through a Firm extranet. There is no additional charge to clients for this access.

What information is available for client access?

Any of the BakerManage information can be made available to clients at the discretion of the Baker legal team and the request of the client.

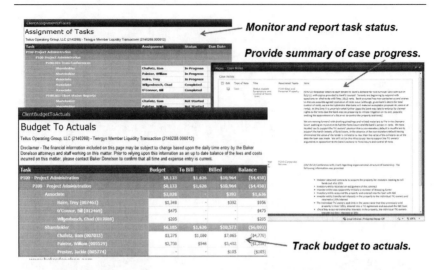

Monitor and report task status.

Provide summary of case progress.

Track budget to actuals.

Client Budget Over 80

Task	Budget	To Bill	Billed	Performance
P100 - Project Administration	$8,133	$2,565	$7,589	
P100 - Project Administration	$8,133	$2,565	$7,589	($2,022)
P200 - Fact Gathering/Due Diligence	$14,838	-	$1,155	
P210 - Corporate Review	$3,175	-	-	$3,175
P270 - Regulatory Reviews	$8,603	-	$1,020	$7,583
P280 - Other	$3,060	-	$135	$2,925
P300 - Structure/Strategy/Analysis	$16,635	$702	$7,072	
P300 - Structure/Strategy/Analysis	$16,635	$702	$7,072	$8,862
P400 - Initial Document Preparation/Filing	$25,128	$23,836	$22,189	
P405 - Document Preparation - Offering	$9,508	$22,051	$11,281	($23,824)
P435 - Document Preparation - Tender Offer	$1,280			$1,280
P445 - Operating Agreement	$10,500		$10,794	($294)
P460 - Meeting	$3,840	$1,785	$114	$1,941
P500 - Negotiation/Revision/Responses	$4,230	$1,664		
P500 - Negotiation/Revision/Responses	$4,230	$1,664		$2,566
P600 - Completion/Closing	$1,320	$147		
P600 - Completion/Closing	$1,320	$147		$1,173
P700 - Post-Completion/Post-Closing	$538	-	$152	
P700 - Post-Completion/Post-Closing	$538	-	$152	$386
Total	$70,820	$28,914	$38,156	$3,751

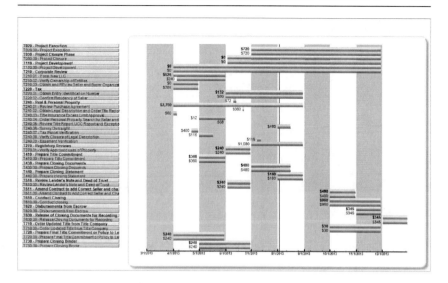

How is communication with other legal team members
or the client addressed by your system?

BakerManage includes a Case Notes log that is used by individual team members to update the status of their tasks or the status of the case. Baker Donelson's Knowledge Management teams also can make other communication tools available in BakerManage such as blogs or OneNote.

Does your system permit project plans, budgets or other project
information to be exported to a report or document?

Yes, BakerManage allows users, both internal and external, to export the project plan information as well as the budgets.

BudgetManager™

General Questions

How long has your system been available to consumers?

BudgetManager was installed in the first three firms in February 2010.

What is the general scope of functionality of your product or purpose?

BudgetManager is a complete matter budgeting product with strong legal project management tools. BudgetManager provides the technology to create budgets in a multitude of methods (simple to highly complex) and bring the budgeting process through the full life cycle from data mining, creation, monitoring, project planning, reporting and alerting.

What is the platform used to develop your application?

BudgetManager has several components, all Microsoft based. The core product was written in VB.net, the web modules are a combination of VB.net and Java. Dashboards, reports and inquiries are available in Microsoft Reporting Services.

Provide a summary of current functionality in the product.

BudgetManager is jam packed with technology to make the budgeting process flexible and efficient. Some key functionality found in BudgetManager:

- 10+ Budget Creation Methods
- 40+ Alternative Fee Methods
- Template Creation
- Allocation Methods
- Immediate Budget to Actuals Analysis
- Scenario Questions (questions and answers stored with the budget)
- LPM: Projects, Milestones, Statuses, Deadlines, Assignments, etc.

- Profitability Statistics
- BudgetManager Warehousing for Key Metrics
- Data Mining and Analysis
- SSRS Reporting - Full Reporting Suite (Dashboard, Experience, Projects, etc.)
- 45+ Highly Developed Alert Metrics

Provide a summary of proposed functionality in the product.

We are always expanding our budgeting methodology to adapt to the needs of our clients. We will be expanding our resource planning and project planning capabilities along with our reporting and alerting capabilities.

How many customers (firms) and users are utilizing the software? Within those
Firms, can you identify on average the percentage of lawyers using the product?

We currently have over 30 firms utilizing BudgetManager. We do not keep track of the number of lawyers being serviced with our product, but we have firms with hundreds of active budgets spread over hundreds of lawyers.

How are the license fees for your product structured? By
number of timekeepers, users or lawyers?

We license by the number of lawyers in the firm.

Does your system communicate directly with Firm systems or does it require
an intermediary database to pull information from Firm systems?

BudgetManager is installed directly into the Aderant system for firms running Aderant. It is installed into a separate database for Elite firms. In both systems it draws information directly from the time and billing system on a firm defined schedule and/or real-time as needed.

Project Plans

Does your system provide a step-by-step approach for development of an entire project
plan (work breakdown structure, schedule for the work, communication plan, etc.)?

BudgetManager allows one to create an entire project plan and integrate it directly into the budget. BudgetManager provides a complete breakdown of the work to be performed, who is to do that work and when, along with the ability to send emails to all or portions of the project team.

What are the components of the project plan in your product?

Project milestones may be attached directly to line items in the budget if desired along with percentages and hours they represent. Resources may be assigned to milestones, along with status codes, deadlines dates, documents, and other information. Dependencies may be established between milestones.

How are changes to scope handled in your system?

BudgetManager allows multiple versions of a budget. It also allows budgets to be consolidated into a parent budget if the additional scope is different enough to warrant a separate budget. These two options provide great flexibility in how a firm might want to organize budget or project changes.

Budgeting

Do you provide template budgets, task lists or checklists with your product?

It is our philosophical approach, which we have found to be true with all of our clients, that lawyers do not wish to be told how they should organize their work. Even within the same firm, two different lawyers typically will have quite different approaches to their work. Therefore, we have provided the tools and assistance to help firms develop their own templates, task lists and project plans for their unique blend of work. Our clients have hundreds of templates that fit more precisely how they want to work. We have found the process of developing those templates has been very helpful to each firm as they become more efficient.

Does your system accommodate phase and task coding?

Yes, we support that throughout the product.

Does your system accommodate subtask coding?

Yes, besides phase, task, activity and action, one may have an unlimited number of levels for budgeting purposes.

And do these indicate percentage of work completion or just the % of budget used.

Yes, we have an entire warehouse of metrics available that analyze budget to actuals on both fees and disbursements. One may indeed track the percentage complete for all levels of the budget and the project (work completion).

Does your system permit comparison of draft budgets against actual matters using the same phase and task codes?

Yes, one can do extensive analysis of prior and/or draft budgets against actual matters. You can run immediate Budget to Actuals to analyze the draft budgets at the Budget level, as well as, phase/task levels. Our full reporting suite offers an extensive out of the box look into draft, active and final budgets.

What other graphical displays of data are available in your system?

We provide Dashboards with various charts as well as Gantt Charts on a variety of metrics. (see next page)

Communication and Access

Is your system open in the law firm intranet or does it require a separate login?

BudgetManager uses a single sign-on approach. Very granular security is controlled within the application by role, person and/or budget.

Is your system open to client access through an extranet?
Does it require login for client access?

We do not provide an extranet as part of the project, but we do create warehouse tables for easy data access by the firm. Many of our clients incorporate our budget and project information within their own portal pages and can make that available to clients as they see fit.

What information is available for client access?

Any and all information in BudgetManager is easily available for use by the firm. Our clients prefer to use their own already developed portal pages and we encourage the firm to enhance those pages with our data as they see fit.

Dashboard: Bronson - Arden Industries - Apple vs Samsung Litigation - 10901

Budget: 854
Last Updated: 5/22/2013 1:02:28 PM

Owner	Bronson, Brooke
Begin Date	January 01, 1997
End Date	December 31, 1998

Hours: 44.9 %   Amount: 26.7 %

	Budget		Budget	
	701.0		$244,590	
Actual	314.7	Actual	$63,922	

- ↓ Under 50%
- ↑ Over 50%
- ◑ Over 100 %
- ⇨ Not Budgeted

AFA's: Blended, Collar Up, Disbursement Unit, Disb Fixed Unit, Fee Cap by Unit, Fixed Fee, Other, Rate Cap, Special Rates, Standard Pricing, Tiered

Budget Profitability

Total Before Pricing Adjustments	$244,590
Pricing Adjustments	($66,282)
Manual Adjustments	$0
Final Budget Amount	$178,308
Expected Realization %	72.9 %

Actuals Profitability

Std Value Worked to Date	$63,922
Base Value Worked to Date	$65,374
Hours Worked to Date	314.7
Amount in WIP	$17,574
Hours Relieved	210.0
Std Value Relieved	$47,800
Base Value Relieved	$47,800
Billed Value	$48,575
Billing Realization (Std)	101.6 %
Billing Realization (Base)	101.6 %
Cash Writeoffs	$132
Cash Received	$42,000
Outstanding AR	$6,443

Tkprs in Budget	Rank	Bud Hrs	Bud Amt	Act Hrs	Act Amt	Hrs	Amt
Bronson, Brooke	Partner	25.0	$6,250	0.0	$0	↓	↓
Dodich, William	Partner	0.0	$0	18.0	$5,400	⇨	⇨
Allen, Gary	Associate	150.0	$75,000	95.0	$28,497	↓	↓
Cantini, Anna	Associate	5.0	$1,250	35.0	$8,750	◑	◑
Edwards, Pat	Associate	5.0	$1,250	57.7	$14,425	◑	◑
Garcia, Mary	Associate	0.0	$0	54.0	$10,800	⇨	⇨
Janikowski, Julia	Jr. Partner	0.0	$0	29.0	($7,200)	⇨	⇨
Huang, Sam	1st Yr Associate	0.0	$0	26.0	$3,250	⇨	⇨
		185.0	$83,750	314.7	$63,922		

Rank	Ranks in Budget	Bud Hrs	Bud Amt	Act Hrs	Act Amt	Hrs	Amt
1	Partner	93.0	$28,010	18.0	$5,400	↓	↓
2	Associate	165.0	$78,750	0.0	$0	↓	↓
3	Legal Assistant	50.0	$10,250	55.0	($3,950)	↑	↓
10	Sr. Partner	0.0	$0	27.0	$6,750	⇨	⇨
15	Jr. Partner	0.0	$0	8.0	$2,000	⇨	⇨
20	7th Yr Associate	2.0	$580	83.0	$24,897	◑	◑
25	5/6th Yr. Associate	121.0	$60,500	57.7	$15,025	↓	↓
30	3/4th Yr Associate	125.0	$32,500	54.0	$11,400	↓	↓
40	2nd Yr Associate	100.0	$25,000	12.0	$2,400	↓	↓
55	Jr. Paralegal	45.0	$9,000	0.0	$0	↓	↓
99	Fee Placeholders	0.0	$0	0.0	$0	⇨	⇨

| | | 701.0 | $244,590 | 314.7 | $63,922 | |

Phase	Task	Bud Hrs	Bud Amt	Act Hrs	Act Amt	Hrs	Amt
		0.0	$50,000	95.8	$21,827	⇨	↓
B100	B110	0.0	$0	0.0	$0	⇨	⇨
L100	L110	14.0	$10,500	77.3	$17,668	↓	↓
L100	L120	0.0	$0	6.0	$1,550	⇨	⇨
L100	L130	176.0	$42,185	11.0	$3,300	↓	↓
L100	L140	65.0	$15,623	70.1	$6,640	◑	↓
L100	L150	75.0	$15,000	2.5	$750	↓	↓
L200	L220	240.0	$48,000	0.0	$0	↓	↓
L200	L260	100.0	$38,000	52.0	$12,350	↑	↓
L300	L320	31.0	$9,500	0.0	$0	↓	↓
		701.0	$228,808	314.7	$63,922		

Phase.Task	Metric	Threshold	Comparison	Budget Value	Actuals Value
●	Std Value of Fees and Disbursements Exceeds X Percent of Total Budget Std Value	2.00 %	$30	$228,808	$87,986
●	Actual Hours Worked comes within X Hours of Total Budget	700.0	386.3	701.0	314.7
●	Actual Hours Worked comes within X Hours of Total Budget	1,100.0	386.3	701.0	314.7
● L100.L110	Fees Amount Billed Exceeds X Percent of Client Fees Budget	95.00 %	$180	$10,000	$15,950
● L100.L110	Budget Pont Complete Exceeds Project Pont Complete by X Percentage Points	5.00 %	470.14 %	552.14 %	82.00 %
●	Fees Amount Billed plus Fee WIP comes within X Dollars of Client Fees Budget	$1,030,000	$112,160	$178,308	$66,149
● L100.L110	Fees Amount Billed Exceeds X Percent of Client Fees Budget	80.00 %	$180	$10,000	$15,950
● L100.L110	Fees Amount Billed plus Fee WIP comes within X Dollars of Client Fees Budget	$1,030,000	($7,710)	$10,000	$17,710
● L100.L140	Fees Amount Billed plus Fee WIP comes within X Dollars of Client Fees Budget	$1,030,000	$8,013	$15,623	$7,616
● L200.L260	Fees Amount Billed plus Fee WIP comes within X Dollars of Client Fees Budget	$1,030,000	$25,600	$38,000	$12,400

Unit Title	Milestone	Step	Assigned	Status	Begin	Deadline	% Comp	% Unit	Bud Hrs
	Apply for Trademark	2	Fountain, Bill	Completed			100.0 %	25.0 %	0.0
Pricing Models		0		Active	05/09/2013		100.0 %	0.0 %	0.0
Trademark and Patent Search	Finalize Budget Proposal	10	Cunningham, Mark	Completed	01/10/1998	02/10/1998	0.0 %	70.0 %	0.0
Trademark and Patent Search	Draft Conflict Waiver	45	Cunningham, Mark	Active	04/01/1998	05/01/1998	100.0 %	30.0 %	0.0
Trademark	Review Trademark Application	3	Bronson, Brooke	Active			0.0 %	15.0 %	0.0
Trademark	Research issues	1		Active		08/17/1998	0.0 %	75.0 %	0.0
Trademark and Patent Application	Patent Application	1	Cunningham, Mark	Active			0.0 %	20.0 %	0.0
Trademark and Patent Application	Review Patent Application	2	Huang, Sam	Active			0.0 %	30.0 %	0.0
Country Applications	Complete all Countries	20	Janikowski, Julia	Active	05/16/1998	06/16/1998	0.0 %	100.0 %	0.0
Mark Preparation	Perform Mark Search	1					0.0 %	30.0 %	0.0

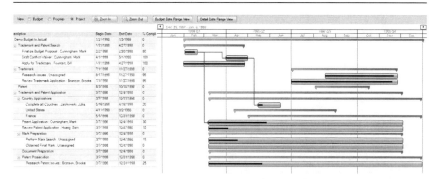

How is communication with other legal team members
or the client addressed by your system?

BudgetManager allows one to send emails to all or a portion of the budget/project team. Our alerting module is also capable of sending out emails to designated team members. Our new AlertManager add-on allows notifications to be sent without the use of emails but with advanced notification capabilities.

Does your system permit project plans, budgets or other project
information to be exported to a report or document?

In addition to our reports and inquiries that may be produced through Reporting Services as Word documents etc., all of our grids may be exported to Excel.

e↑evate CAEL LPM™

General Questions[1]

How long has your system been available to consumers?

We launched a beta version of Cael LPM™ in the summer of 2013 and are planning a public release for general distribution in early 2014. (We are still currently accepting customers interested in participating the beta program.)

What is the general scope of functionality of your product or purpose?

Cael LPM™ is designed to make legal project management easy, fostering quicker, higher adoption rates among lawyers. The Cael LPM interface is simple and straightforward and it is optimized for tablets as well as traditional laptops and desktops, bringing a new level of usability and flexibility to legal project management software.

The scope of functionality is planning, managing, and tracking work against budgets for matter managers, lawyers, and other fee earners. We designed Cael LPM for day-to-day use by legal teams, with a focus on making it simple for users to collaborate on matters, phases, and tasks, easily spotting items that may need project management attention.

The system enables users to easily set up matter budgets and then manage to those budgets on a day to day basis by project phase and task, using a system of simple traffic light-based status levels. The setup process is flexible, allowing matter managers to structure matter plans and budgets by "friendly names" or by standard phase and task codes. Both options provide tracking of budget to actuals, also by phase and task code or by non-code "friendly names". Once a matter is set up in the system, the interface makes

---

1. The following is based upon information provided to the authors on July 29, 2013. For more up to date information, please contact the vendor directly.

it easy and simple for matter managers to manage and track towards the plan, updating it as necessary along the way.

The Cael LPM interface uses a simple traffic light status system, which collects and aggregates a vast amount of meaningful matter-related information into a single color-coded status indicator: red, yellow or green. This approach to status tracking makes it easy and intuitive for fee earners to indicate how matters, phases, and tasks are progressing by toggling the traffic light color. With a few clicks of a mouse – or taps on an iPad – fee earners can keep matter managers informed as to whether work is progressing as expected, falling behind, going over budget or whether it requires more support.

Additionally, Cael LPM's traffic light indicators help provide fee earners a quick, *ad hoc* instrument for capturing the status of the matter or task even though comprehensive data may still be pending. Frequently, fee earners are able to assess the status of an activity well before hard data reveals progress or delays. (This can be caused by lag time in data integrations or data entry gaps, both of which continue to plague firms.) The quick-toggle traffic light system allows users to bypass "lag times" between issue and action, facilitating more timely resolution of issues.

Lastly, the system automatically synthesizes all the individual fee earner information into an easy-to-read dashboard for the matter manager, summarizing how the matter is doing against budget and which tasks and/or fee-earners may need attention. Cael LPM's "smart" features highlight items that require added attention, enabling matter mangers to quickly drill down into over-budget matters or matters at risk, helping minimize time spent on project management tasks so they can focus on what's most important.

What is the platform used to develop your application?

Cael LPM™ is built on the Microsoft Azure platform, a highly secure and robust cloud-based system used by many organizations.

Provide a summary of current functionality in the product.

1. User-Friendly LPM Dashboard

Aggregates and provides quick display and access to relevant matter-related information and updates.

2. Easy Matter Setup/Planning

Quickly set up the matter by adding fee earners, phases and tasks. Automated matter setup also available via integration.

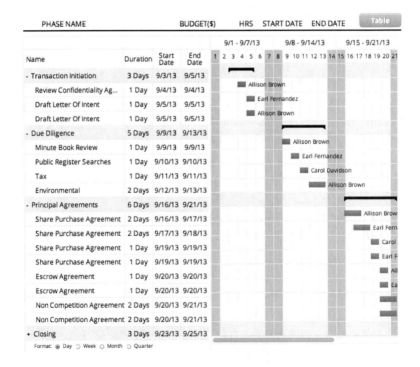

3. Friendly Name Phases and Tasks

Matter phases and tasks can be set up using friendly names and can also be easily mapped to activity codes for budget/time tracking.

4. Task Management

Multi-view task displays provide user-friendly traffic-light task and budget management.

5. Multi-View Matter Plans

Matter plans can be viewed in traffic light or Gantt chart formats.

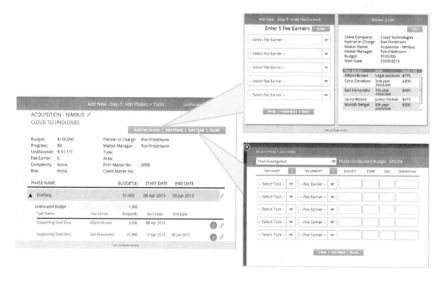

6. Quick Client Status Reports

Client matter status reports can be generated and exported with single-click.

7. Status Report Document Generator

Word-based status reports can also be generated easily.

8. Fee Earner Matter Allocation Reports

Fee earner reports showing status of allocated activities and budgets across assigned matters can easily be generated and exported.

9. Smart Alerts and Notifications

Auto-generated alerts are delivered to users in-system or via email, based on individual user preferences.

10. User Preferences
Users can easily update their preferences and profile.
11. Mobility
System is online and accessible by desktops, laptops, and tablets.

How many customers (firms) and users are utilizing the software? Within those
Firms, can you identify on average the percentage of lawyers using the product?

At the time of this submission, Elevate has two beta customers on Cael
LPM. We anticipate at least two more beta customers before the public
release in early 2014.

Although it is too early to quantify the level of lawyer adoption, the fundamental design of the system is focused on simplicity and ease of use, thus
removing some of the most common barriers to adoption.

How are the license fees for your product structured? By
number of timekeepers, users or lawyers?

Cael LPM's subscription fees are based on the number of concurrent
users accessing the application.

Does your system communicate directly with Firm systems or does it require
an intermediary database to pull information from Firm systems?

Cael LPM can support both direct web-based integrations and intermediary database-based integrations. For the beta release of the product, the
product was designed to support intermediary database-based integration;
however, we are already working with our beta customer to create a tighter,
more seamless integration. Once we are in full production, we plan to offer
several options for integration and data exchange.

Project Plans
Does your system provide a step-by-step approach for development of an entire project
plan (work breakdown structure, schedule for the work, communication plan, etc.)?

Yes. Cael LPM is designed to make matter set-up easy. Matter managers can use standard tasks and codes or create their own "friendly names".
The system provides options for tracking at the phase and task level or

phase-only level. Matter managers can quickly assign budgets (in dollar or hours) and assign fee earners.

After a matter is set-up, any user assigned to it can view the overall plan in a tabular or Gantt chart view. Once work is underway, all fee earners on a matter can see the status of all tasks.

For ongoing communication, Cael LPM is designed to make it easy for the team to communicate about tasks. An fee earner can enter a note about a task. Others on the team are alerted to new notes – with granular control over how many and how frequently alerts are received.

We have carefully considered potential internal sensitivities about who is entitled to see what information and we believe Cael LPM strikes the right balance. The beta program is designed partly to confirm these assumptions. In the future, we plan to offer more highly configurable permissions so that firms can customize permissions concerning what information is shared within (and across) matters.

What are the components of the project plan in your product?

The components of the project plan are as follows:

- Phase-only or Phase and Task matter planning
- Matter, Phase and Task level budgets, by dollars or by hours
- Matter, Phase and Task level actuals
- Timekeeper tracking at the phase and task level
- Phase and task code tracking at the phase and task level
- Traffic light status tracking (and rollup) at the phase and task level
- Matter-level activity scroll and tracker
- Matter-based rules and alerts

How are changes to scope handled in your system?

Cael LPM is designed to easily change budgets or add tasks and fee earners as needed when a matter is in progress. The system captures a clear history of any changes, and the team can easily access that history.

When changing scope or budgets, Cael LPM includes a feature that dynamically displays the "Unallocated Budget". This feature shows a user how the changes in scope may affect the overall costs related to the budget.

If the Unallocated Budget is a positive number, then the matter is still on track. If the Unallocated Budget reflects a negative number based on the changes, then it is a clear indication of potential reduction in profits.

The monitoring and traffic light status system is designed to give firms "early warning" when a matter might be creeping out-of-scope. The earlier the firm is aware of this risk, the better it can communicate and successfully negotiate a scope change with the client.

Budgeting

Do you provide template budgets, task lists or checklists with your product?

Yes. When released publicly, Cael LPM will offer templates. The system will also allow firms to save any current matter plan as a template for re-use.

Does your system accommodate phase and task coding?

Yes, Cael LPM supports standard code sets. It also offers unlimited creation of custom codes, including "friendly names" to help matter managers and fee earners instantly recognize phases and tasks. (Behind the scenes, Cael LPM maps the friendly names to standard and/or custom codes.)

Does your system accommodate subtask coding?

Not at this point. Many of the partners and case teams with whom we have spoken stated a strong preference to avoid that level of detail, so we designed our initial product with only phase and task-level budgeting and coding. However, the system can support subtask coding, and if enough firms request it, we will include it in a future release. (An early internal version of the software actually included subtasks, but as we discussed requirements with law firms, we found very few were coding at that level of detail. Therefore, to keep Cael LPM simpler – again, with an emphasis on building a system that is more likely to be adopted – we chose to omit subtask coding in the current version.)

Does your system allow budget to actual comparisons? And do these indicate percentage of work completion or just the % of budget used.

Yes, Cael LPM allows budget to actual comparisons.

In the current version of Cael LPM, we have deliberately chosen the traffic light status approach instead of indicating percentage of work complete. We considered estimating work completion algorithmically, as well as asking fee earners to estimate percent completion. However, in discussing both approaches with many firms, we found:

- Many lawyers are very uncomfortable with the idea of calculating percentage of work completed based on the number of hours, because this may not adequately represent the true state of completion.
- Many lawyers are also very uncomfortable with the idea of typing in or even selecting a percentage.

In our view, both of these concerns represented significant barriers to adoption, therefore we designed Cael LPM to enable faster and deeper adoption with the simpler traffic light paradigm. We plan to add an option for tracking percentage of work complete in a future version.

Does your system permit comparison of draft budgets against actual matters using the same phase and task codes?

Cael LPM does not support this currently, but it is planned for a future version.

What other graphical displays of data are available in your system?

Gantt charts are the main non-tabular display. After receiving more user input, we may add other graphical displays. Budget and actual data – as well as traffic light statuses – can be exported to Excel, allowing users to create their own charts in Excel if they wish.

Communication and Access

Is your system open in the law firm intranet or does it require a separate login?

Cael LPM is a separate log-in. By default, only those assigned to a matter can see it.

Is your system open to client access through an extranet?
Does it require login for client access?

The Cael LPM permission management system allows client access, however many firms have concluded that a) clients prefer to see high-level summaries rather than details; and b) sharing "raw data" can raise concerns, complicating relationship management. We recommend that firms gain experience with LPM and with Cael LPM before they choose to share directly.

To ensure the right level of relevant information is shared with clients, Cael LPM provides automated Word documents reports that partners can review and edit before sharing with clients.

What information is available for client access?

Cael LPM delivers a client-side dashboard that differs slightly from the firm dashboard. The client-side dashboard provides more limited information, but still allows for quick viewing and access to important matter-related information and traffic light status.

Clients can also view and access matter plans to review and monitor progress in real-time.

How is communication with other legal team members
or the client addressed by your system?

As previously discussed, Cael LPM enables team members to communicate about specific tasks. Currently, the system does not support direct communication with clients. In our view, adding client communication features to the system would add a level of complexity that would discourage adoption – and many law firms share that view – so we have deliberately not included that functionality in the current version.

Does your system permit project plans, budgets or other project
information to be exported to a report or document?

Yes, Cael LPM provides export to Word and Excel format for a variety of information, and more export features are slated for future versions. The Client Summary Screen can be exported as a summary to Word and Excel.

Users can also create matter level reports, selecting which components to include, and export them as Word output. This feature allows users to modify the report, adding narrative information where needed to provide more context.

THOMSON REUTERS
ELITE | ENGAGE

General Questions
How long has your system been available to consumers?

Engage™ launched in March 2010 and has been generally available for three years.

What is the general scope of functionality of your product or purpose?

Engage is Thomson Reuters Elite's engagement planning, budgeting, and management solution. Step-by-step tools enable you to manage matters effectively and profitably throughout the lifecycle of the matter. Engage provides the structured process to ensure your lawyers meet their clients' objectives with consistent, tangible results. The robust tool is designed to make legal work more predictable to meet your clients' expectations for hourly or alternative fee arrangements.

Engage is a tool designed to meet the planning, budgeting, and monitoring needs of all members of the law firm. Partners, lawyers, practice groups, and the finance team benefit from the ease of use built into the tool. The Engage Matter Template library, created by Thomson Reuters' lawyers, helps you quickly and accurately develop predictable budgets, build the right team, and assign work with confidence. Engage's reporting capabilities and Budget to Actual screen make it easy for you to manage and monitor the matter plan and communicate the real time matter project status to your clients.

The budgeting tools in Engage provide the capability to build budgets, plan around client guidelines, and adjust budgets according to specific outcomes. You can fine tune your matter plan and construct different scenarios by changing resources, hours, and other key variables using Engage's custom "What if tool".

Engage is a Web-based solution that integrates with your billing system. A lawyer can access their up-to-date Engage matter plan information from anywhere and anytime.

What is the platform used to develop your application?

Engage is written in standard Microsoft® .NET architecture using a SQL® Server® database.

Provide a summary of current functionality in the product.

Engage includes the following key functionality:

- Easy pricing and creation of high level budget by phase for lawyers with immediate visibility into profit, leverage, and other statistics.
- Ability to build into a more detailed budget by phase, task, and subtask for finance or project managers.
- Budgeting based on historical matters, best practice budgets, or one of the 80+ predefined out-of-the-box templates.
- Tracking and monitoring of matter and portfolio actuals against plan budget thresholds.
- Client facing reporting, including professional graphics and budgetary information.
- Home dashboard with KPIs for lawyers' matters that can be set up with thresholds and notifications to alert stakeholders to key dates, overages, and actions that require attention.
- Budget reporting on disbursements and third party costs to provide a full budget view.
- Project planning with scheduling of resources and the setup of key dates and milestones with rewards and penalties.
- Budget to actual comparison with ability to track % complete, % worked, and trending against budget targets or collars.
- What if pricing scenarios, including mix of hourly, and AFAs – fixed fee at phase, task, or subtask; collars and budget targets; and discounts.

- Tracking of scope change, approvals, and assumptions against baseline budget.
- Integrated fee earner rates by fee earner, title, and other more granular dimensions and fee earner cost for calculation of matter profitability.
- Tracking of discounting percentages, comparisons to standard and exception rates, adjustments, and write offs.
- Engage includes the new Jackson Reform Precedent H report in the UK and is easily adaptable to map to other jurisdictional requirements as needed.

Provide a summary of proposed functionality in the product.

Thomson Reuters Elite is a market leader working with many firms in the legal space that drives the Engage roadmap and enhancements. Based on market and customer input, Engage is expanding on more complex AFA pricing scenarios such as collars, caps, and hybrid pricing models and portfolio reporting. More advanced legal project management features, visualizations, and predictive forecasting are also prioritized features on the roadmap.

How many customers (firms) and users are utilizing the software?

Engage has approximately 40 firms using the software with several others in the process of purchasing and implementing.

Within those firms, can you identify on average the percentage of lawyers using the product?

Each client takes a unique approach to their implementation of Engage. Many are committed to a full-scale deployment to every lawyer desktop. Others limit access to legal project managers and select members of a practice group or matter team. Additionally, some prefer a back-office approach that puts Engage in the hands of the finance, pricing, project management, or the marketing and business development groups.

How are the license fees for your product structured? By
number of timekeepers, users or lawyers?

Engage provides flexible pricing by perpetual firm-wide license or monthly
subscription by users.

Does your system communicate directly with firm systems or does it require
an intermediary database to pull information from firm systems?

Engage interfaces directly with the financial management system database.
Engage is vendor independent and works with all legal financial management systems.

Project Plans

Does your system provide a step-by-step approach for development of an entire project
plan (work breakdown structure, schedule for the work, communication plan, etc.)?

Yes. Engage includes predefined templates by practice area and best practice models that provide step-by-step lists of tasks and activities. These
templates are highly detailed checklists that serve as precision roadmaps for
matter planning and budgeting. Engage also allows you to take advantage
of your firm's intellectual property by giving you the option to clone past
matters or to use your own best practices models to create new budgets
from existing matters.

What are the components of the project plan in your product?

Engage provides project plans at three different levels with the most
detailed project plan at phase, task, and subtask level. In addition, matter
details provide additional granularity if needed.

How are changes to scope handled in your system?

Engage provides scope changes with the ability to commit changes to the
budget based on approvals. Engage uses graphical visual indicators within
the screens and reports to easily highlight the individual scope changes
as well as the total amount of scope change and approval status. Budget
assumptions pertaining to scope also can be captured with a scope change
for inquiry and reporting.

Budgeting
Do you provide template budgets, task lists or checklists with your product?

Yes. Engage includes predefined templates by practice area and best practice models that provide step-by-step lists of tasks and activities. Engage templates are extensively researched and prepared by members of the Thomson Reuters editorial staff who are trained lawyers with subject matter expertise in the specific area of law concerned.

Does your system accommodate phase and task coding?

Yes, Engage allows budgeting of fixed and hourly fees and actuals by phase, task, and subtask.

Does your system accommodate subtask coding?

Yes, subtask coding is useful for client reporting and building more accurate budgets to allow for greater predictability.

Does your system allow budget to actual comparisons? And do these
indicate percentage of work completion or just the % of budget used.

Yes, Engage tracks both % work completion and % of budget used/ remaining with tools to easily mark % completion for an entire phase.

Does your system permit comparison of draft budgets against
actual matters using the same phase and task codes?

Yes. A draft budget can be entered into Engage and later matched with an actual matter from the financial system with task code mappings.

What other graphical displays of data are available in your system?

Engage displays content in a number of graphical arrays that serve to make the data more understandable and pertinent to the user. The system can be configured by role to ensure that access to sensitive data is limited to only those with the rights to view it.

Graphical displays include, but are not limited to:

- Gantt charts that show phase timelines, run rates, and milestones.

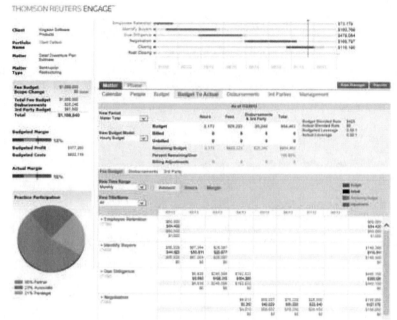

Figure Ap2-11
Manage and monitor budget to actual statistics.

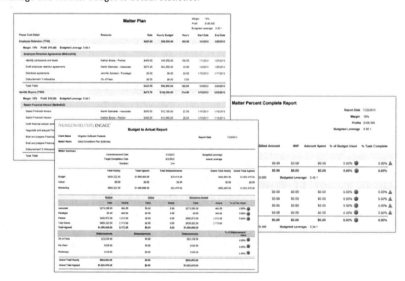

Figure Ap2-12
Reports—Client and lawyer facing.

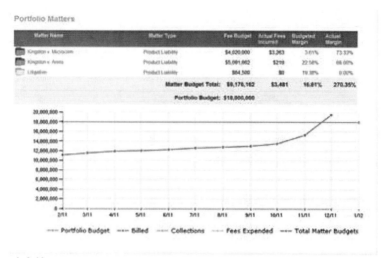

Figure Ap2-13
Matter Portfolio management.

- Margin bars that indicate projected profitability of a particular matter or portfolio.
- Pie charts that denote leverage ratios and office or practice group participation.
- A management dashboard that gives you an at-a-glance update on matter progress and adherence to budget.
- A budget to actual display that gives immediate access to hours worked, budget remaining, budget exceeded, and other critical data points.
- A "What If" tool that allows you to create multiple scenarios based on the same or similar matter plan and to compare and contrast them to create the right balance of time, effort, and resources to meet your clients' needs while remaining profitable.

Communication and Access
Is your system open in the law firm intranet or does it require a separate login?

Engage currently requires a separate login, but single sign-on will be available in 2013. Either method requires user access setup with security determined by role and permissions.

Is your system open to client access through an
extranet? Does it require login for client access?

A separate login is required to set up a client with access depending on a firm's IT infrastructure and policies.

What information is available for client access?

Engage provides client facing reports with professional graphical representations of budget to actual information and other budgetary data. All data and reports may be exported in Microsoft Excel®, Word®, or Adobe® Acrobat® PDF format for easy electronic or physical distribution.

How is communication with other legal team members
or the client addressed by your system?

Engage utilizes several methods to allow communication both internally and externally to the client, including notifications, user access, reporting, and data exports.

Does your system permit project plans, budgets or other project
information to be exported to a report or document?

Yes, all data can be exported to Excel, Adobe Acrobat PDF, or Microsoft Word.

Legal
ERM Solutions

General Questions²

How long has your system been available to consumers?

Lean4Legal PM® (L4L) has been in general release since January 15, 2013. Version 2.0 was released July 15, 2013

What is the general scope of functionality of your product or purpose?

L4L is an end-to-end legal project management (LPM) technology that supports project management methodologies commonly deployed in the legal services industry. L4L plans, budgets, executes, monitors and controls legal projects in any practice area application from the most complex to the most rudimentary.

What is the platform used to develop your application?

L4L is written in Microsoft®. Net architecture using a Microsoft SQL® Server® database. Development is accomplished on Microsoft's Azure platform.

Provide a summary of current functionality in the product.

L4L operates within a unique IP that provides real time information about the performance status and financial impact of any and all projects in a law firm or legal department portfolio. Small law firms and practice groups as well as large multi-office legal practices benefit from L4L's web based browser accessed LPM system that operates seamlessly in real time down the hall or across the world. As changes are made in any project, all performers that are impacted by any change to a matter are informed of changes instantly through real-time system updates as well as email and text alerts. Interactive planning and project management tools provide bar chart and spreadsheet utilities that serve to modify, notify and update plans, as changes are required in any project. Project performers are of tasks to be completed with checklists and work instructions through fully informed and constantly prioritized to do lists maintained in real time. A variety of reports are generated in the system which provide constantly updated information on budget to actual, work to be performed, project plan variances,

---

2. The following is based upon information provided to the authors on July 29, 2013. For more up to date information, please contact the vendor directly.

cash flow forecasts, and historical performance metrics by task, workflow, phase and project type as well as work team planning.

L4L operates in a secure dedicated single tenant server private cloud for each customer or behind the firewall on the customer's premises as desired by the customer.

The private cloud implementation is HIPAA compliant, and meets other additional regulatory compliance and security standards. The private cloud datacenter utilizes a level of layered security (physical and virtual), in addition to restricted access, providing a higher level of sensitive data security than is found in most customer on premise datacenters. All administrative access to a server is performed exclusively through a dedicated Virtual Private Network. L4L uses a Secure Socket Layer connection to its server; therefore, the data is encrypted during transit.

Alternatively, an installation "behind the customer's firewall" can also be implemented. An installation on premises and behind the customer's firewall will require customer dedicated hardware, software and maintenance at the customer's cost.

Provide a summary of proposed functionality in the product.

Remaining functionality to be developed in L4L relates primarily to integration with interdependent software solutions customers find useful in their own LPM applications. For example, finance, time and billing, document management, knowledge management and other technology applications may be best served by integration and sharing of data with L4L. Such integration will be accomplished on a customer-by-customer basis as specified by the customer. Load files and API interfaces are the means by which such integration is accomplished leaving original data undisturbed in its proper data repository.

How many customers (firms) and users are utilizing the software? Within those Firms, can you identify on average the percentage of lawyers using the product?

As of this date (July 29, 2013), there are approximately six firms or practice groups within law firms using L4L in 11 practice groups. These firms have implementation plans for a total of 2000 users in 2014.

How are the license fees for your product structured? By
number of timekeepers, users or lawyers?

L4L provides a subscription license arrangement to customers based
on the number of users in the system on a month-to-month basis. Prices
are discounted based on the volume of use and the degree of prepayment
of subscription fees. Additionally, a perpetual license agreement is available
which provides customers with specific user group size access for an
unlimited period of time at a negotiated single fee plus annual maintenance
and upgrade costs.

Does your system communicate directly with Firm systems or does it require
an intermediary database to pull information from Firm systems?

L4L "integrates" with other firm software systems through load files
and API interfaces.

Does your system provide a step-by-step approach for development of an entire project
plan (work breakdown structure, schedule for the work, communication plan, etc.)?

L4L users can build a project plan "from scratch" using its digital "Yellow Pad" feature. The system also will import project plans previously
created in common formats such as Excel and Microsoft Project. L4L is
structured to create plans in a Project Type, Phase, Workflow and Task format. At the task level, the system permits creation of metadata instructions
including performer role level, hours of work effort, duration of task time,
billing phase and task codes, task constraints, checklists and work instructions. A template created in the system will "build" a plan instantly based
on its metadata instructions as a default and allow the planner to modify
any discrete element of the plan as a result of the project's specific scope.

What are the components of the project plan in your product?

L4L builds project plans at the Matter Type / Matter Phase / Matter
Workflow / Task levels. The task level includes metadata related to the task
such as checklists, work instructions, work effort time and duration, parallel and sequential constraints, phase and task codes and default or custom
narratives per task for timekeeping purposes. Additionally, by working at
the task level alone, timekeepers are able to pass timekeeping entries into

the firm's timekeeping system without separate login or data entry activities in the firm's timekeeping/financial software.

How are changes to scope handled in your system?

The L4L Staffing and Budget Planner, Expert Planner and Bar Chart Planner are each separate interactive tools that allow the project planner to change project scope at the granular or global level. As changes are made in any of these interactive tools, the changes automatically flow through in real time to the budget and task performer levels with text, email and L4L system alerts to notify users of project changes.

Do you provide template budgets, task lists or checklists with your product?

There is a basic template library that accompanies L4L. Additionally, an ERM Solutions Analyst assigned to each customer can assist in converting existing customer projects and templates into L4L functionality.

Does your system accommodate phase and task coding?

At the project planning level pre-assigned phase and task codes associated with each task eliminate common timekeeper error in selecting the proper codes for the task.

Does your system accommodate subtask coding?

Yes. L4L permits time entry without leaving the L4L system. Exporting of time created in L4L to a firm's timekeeping system is accomplished without separate user timekeeping system login and time entry. Timekeepers have the ability to accept the live time entries compiled by L4L, enter manual time entries or edit the L4L time entries before L4L sends to them to the firm's time and billing system, thus eliminating the need for lawyers to maintain timesheets. Additionally, timekeepers can accept the default narratives in each time entry derived from the phase and task phrases preselected or substitute their own custom narrative in each time entry.

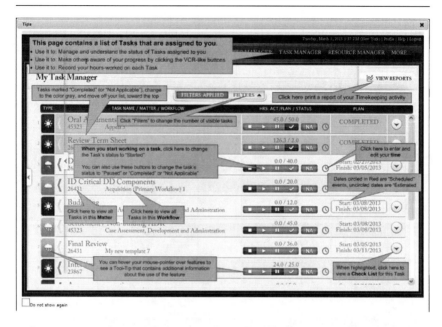

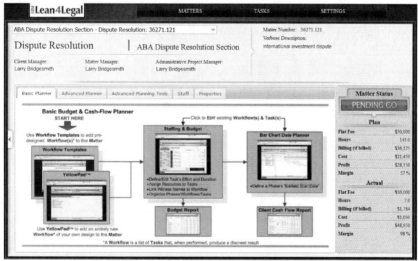

Does your system allow budget to actual comparisons? And do these
indicate percentage of work completion or just the % of budget used.

L4L maintains a real time budget to actual analysis and provides a comparison of work completed to budget projection by percentage. Because

L4L's unique IP actively monitors all tasks and resources associated with any given matter as well as their interrelationship to all other matters across an enterprise, the tool automatically updates any affected budget with new actual data as changes in project completion ripple through the system.

Does your system permit comparison of draft budgets against actual matters using the same phase and task codes?

Yes. L4L mines all information associated with matters and learns to plan against historical actuals generated by the project plan to the task level by assigned phase and task codes. Additionally, through significant industry partnerships with data mining companies, L4L can provide robust market benchmarks to compare against matters planned in the tool.

What other graphical displays of data are available in your system?

All planning tools in L4L are depicted graphically by representative icons allowing the project planner to quickly identify and gain "click through" access to the appropriate functionality through visualization. Reports are generated, saved and transmitted in visual formats in which the users expect to use them (I.e. Excel, Word, PDF, TIFF, HTML, CSV, XML). Interactive planning and performer tools use avatars and various visual cues that provide intuitive graphical communication and informs users of information needed to efficiently process tasks. Project planning tools utilize bar chart and spreadsheet interactive views to expedite planning and project changes.

Matter/Phase/Workflow/Task	Min.	Task	Stat	Resource	Work (h)	Actual	Link	Constraint	Cstr. Date	Dur. (d)	Start	Finish	Bill Rate	Planned Billing
Wrongful termination defense														$414,660.00
Mediation														$0.00
Case Management														$5,520.00
Offensive Discovery														
ESI Production from ...											8/21/2013	8/22/2013		$16,000.00
Harvest Plaintif...		Assoda..	NS	Larry Bridgesmit ..	6.0	0.0	FS	As Soon As Poss..		1.0	8/22/2013	8/22/2013	$500.00	$3,000.00
Plaintiff Compl...		Assoda..	P	Larry Bridgesmit..	8.0	0.1	FS	Must Finish On	08/20/2013	1.0	8/21/2013	8/21/2013	$500.00	$4,000.00
Load Plaintifs' ..		Assoda..	NS	Larry Bridgesmit..	8.0	0.0	FS	As Soon As Poss..		1.0	8/22/2013	8/22/2013	$500.00	$4,000.00
Serve Interrogatories											8/21/2013	8/27/2013		
Draft Interrogs...		Assoda..	NS	Jeanne Naysmit...	8.0	0.0	FS	As Soon As Poss..		1.0	8/21/2013	8/21/2013		
Serve Interrog...		Assoda..	NS	Russell Smith (6...	8.0	0.0	FS	As Soon As Poss..		1.0	8/22/2013	8/22/2013		
Responses due...		Assoda..	NS	Scott Preston (5 ..	8.0	0.0	FS	As Soon As Poss..		1.0	8/23/2013	8/23/2013		
Analyze P's Ro...		Assoda..	NS	Larry Bridgesmit...	8.0	0.0	FS	As Soon As Poss..		1.0	8/26/2013	8/26/2013		
Determine Sco...		Assoda..	NS	Larry Bridgesmit...	8.0	0.0	FS	As Soon As Poss..		1.0	8/27/2013	8/27/2013		
Serve Requests for Pr...											8/21/2013	8/23/2013		$6,024.00
Motion to Compel (Of...											8/21/2013	8/26/2013		$7,530.00
Subpoena Service an...											8/21/2013	9/19/2013		$3,514.00

Expert Budget - SC00021: Wrongful termination defense

Back to Planner   Collapse All   Show X and NA   Resource Filter   Set x# = T   Set 1 = W#   Help

Is your system open in the law firm intranet or does it require a separate login?

L4L can be a standalone technology or integrated into other login protocols and the customer's intranet.

Is your system open to client access through an extranet?
Does it require login for client access?

Because L4L is web based and browser accessed, it can be available to the client through its extranet and access achieved through transparent login protocols.

What information is available for client access?

All data in L4L can be available to the client based on client and law firm agreement. The level of transparency is limited only by the customer's requirements and the firm's agreement. Additionally, the firm and the client can collaborate on the degrees of transparent access that the client may require as well as what specific information they may want to view via user definable reports.

How is communication with other legal team members
or the client addressed by your system?

All changes in project plans are transmitted in real time into the project and the performer's task manager list as they occur. Additionally, alerts are sent within the L4L system as well as by text and email to those users who need to know. Finally, an issues feature provides intra-project communication and issues management functionality retaining archival documentation of communications related to the project.

Does your system permit project plans, budgets or other project
information to be exported to a report or document?

Yes. Common formats include: Excel, Word, PDF, TIFF, HTML, CSV, XML. A library of standard reports is provided with the system as well as ERM's ability to configure reports to client and user specification.

LexisNexis®
Redwood® Planning Application

General Questions

How long has your system been available to consumers?

LexisNexis Redwood Analytics has had matter planning for six years, beginning in 2007. Redwood Analytics Planning 5, was released as a stand-alone product in 2009. The current version, Redwood Planning 5.5 was released in March 2013 ("Redwood Analytics Planning").

What is the general scope of functionality of your product or purpose?

Redwood Analytics Planning helps law firms more accurately predict the economics of staffing and pricing decisions by modeling prior performance on similar matters and client production.

The web-based Redwood Analytics Planning application allows firm leaders to explore many pricing scenarios. Users select a model and use the links to pull in staffing and pricing data—and discern the ultimate impact on realizations and profitability. Firms can compare Alternative Fee Arrangements side by side and analyze potential outcomes, including modeling by matter phase and task (e.g., discovery, pre-trial, summary judgment, etc.).

Redwood Analytics Planning models help monitor performance against plan, as well. Once client agreements are reached, firm managers can go back to the model and link to a matter or client from the firm's time and billing system to track results. Planning can also be used for a portfolio of matters. A plan can be linked to a set of matters, clients or related clients, so that a firm can create a client plan, then link that to all of that client's matters. By linking all of the matters together, a firm can track the performance of the client as a whole.

Successful models can be used for historical insights as firms bid on more business for current clients. This can also be used as starting points when a firm vies for new business. Planning scenarios and templates can be saved for later use.

What is the platform used to develop your application?

Redwood Analytics Planning uses ASP.NET, Silverlight®, WCF REST & WCF RIA Services, and Microsoft SQL Server®.

Provide a summary of current functionality in the product.

Redwood Analytics Planning connects day-to-day matter management with increasing client demands for alternative billing arrangements. Firms can:

- Examine how discounting affects profitability.
- Model/compare alternative fee arrangements (AFAs) side by side.
- Determine optimal staffing levels.
- Track actual vs. plan: Drive performance!
- Use historical data to enhance future operations and cost certainty.
- Flexible software configures to your firm's business model
- Redwood Analytics team installs the application and sets the automated processes to update data
- Data and analysis refreshes occur automatically
- Built-in security features control data access

Firms create and lock in on a plan, which then remains set for a matter unless deliberately changed. Billing data is refreshed into the models nightly so monitoring against actuals stays timely with current production and realization for each matter. If desired, firms can adjust performance 'on the fly' through staffing and/or pricing changes.

Provide a summary of proposed functionality in the product.

LexisNexis generally avoids publishing roadmaps for future product enhancements as such enhancements are always subject to change. However, an enhancement area under consideration includes Enhanced Plan vs. Actual Review functionality that allows for deeper dive analysis.

How are the license fees for your product structured? By
number of timekeepers, users or lawyers?

Law firms license the Redwood Analytics Planning application and professional services to help configure the software, pull billing data in, and structure phase and task codes. The basic software and services pricing delivers Planning for one (1) administrative user and five (5) full users. Planning also has a "Review Only" license option, generally used by executive pricing committees.

Does your system communicate directly with Firm systems or does it require
an intermediary database to pull information from Firm systems?

Redwood Analytics Planning uses an intermediary data warehouse that pulls information from the firm's billing system and, if applicable, the Redwood Data Warehouse.

Project Plans

Does your system provide a step-by-step approach for development of an entire project
plan (work breakdown structure, schedule for the work, communication plan, etc.)?

Redwood Analytics Planning helps firms structure fee agreements, including phase/task code-based plans, and associated timelines. A firm can then lock in on a fee agreement and monitor Budget vs Actual. The Redwood Analytics Planning application is designed to be flexible, incorporating as many scenarios or tasks that are needed to develop a project plan. While there is no communication functionality in the Redwood Analytics Planning application, it can be integrated with Redwood BI 5 to leverage BI 5's data distribution options.

What are the components of the project plan in your product?

Redwood Analytics Planning supports a variety of pricing and planning methodologies. Firms can run different flat fee and phase/task code models against the standard hourly rate model to identify the right pricing. Additionally, a firm can test different staffing plans to determine the best leverage. Firms can enter dates to the model. Redwood Analytics Planning provides the tools needed to adjust the levers related to pricing and staffing to achieve a favorable outcome. In Redwood Analytics Planning, you select the staff by name or by title, structure the plan by scenario or task code, and assign hours to the staff. Committed plans can be tracked versus actual billing system values.

How are changes to scope handled in your system?

If changes to pricing and structure of a matter budget take place, the budget can be edited and linked again to the matter in the firm's time and billing system. This gives the firm the ability to track the matter against the original budget and updated budget if desired.

Budgeting

Do you provide template budgets, task lists or checklists with your product?

Redwood Analytics offers training that help firms build their own templates. Redwood Analytics Planning uses the Uniform Task Based Management System (UTBMS) task codes (often referred to as the ABA task codes), and we encourage firms to map their overall list of task codes to either this UTBMS list or create a set of 'non-standard' task codes.

Does your system accommodate phase and task coding?

Yes. Firms can use the UTBMS set of task codes available in the system or create custom phase and task codes that best capture the nature of each task.

Does your system accommodate subtask coding?

Somewhat.

Does your system allow budget to actual comparisons? And do these indicate percentage of work completion or just the % of budget used.

Yes, Redwood Analytics Planning allows "Budget v Actual" comparisons. These comparisons indicate the percentage of budget used.

Does your system permit comparison of draft budgets against actual matters using the same phase and task codes?

Yes, Redwood Analytics Planning allows users to pull a historical matter, and use the same phase and task codes.

What other graphical displays of data are available in your system?

Redwood Analytics Planning offers column charts and traffic lights (red, yellow, green indicators on whether metrics are on or off track) throughout the tool. Additionally, reports and dashboards created through the Redwood Analytics BI 5 tool offer a variety of additional data visualization options.

3, 5, 19, 22

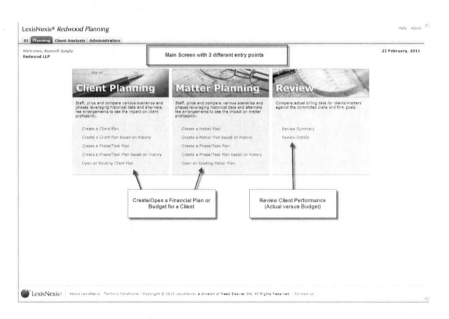

Communication and Access

Is your system open in the law firm intranet or does it require a separate login?

Redwood Analytics Planning contains firm and practice group profitability data that is treated as confidential at many customer firms. A designated Redwood Administrator at the Firm uses the Redwood Administration application to identify users by name and LanID and designates the level of data access and application functionality to each user. Users logged on to the network via Windows Authentication can access Planning via the URL.

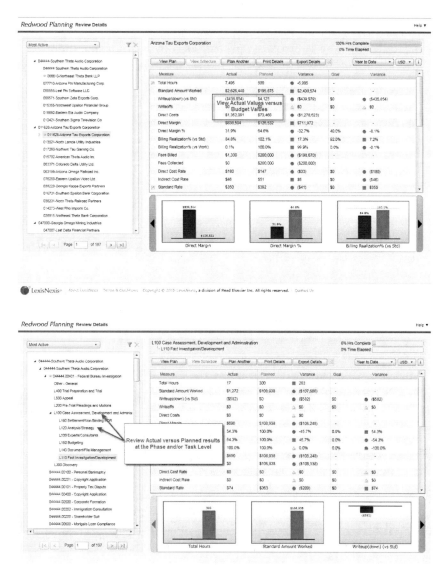

Is your system open to client access through an extranet?

Does it require login for client access?

To minimize the exposure of sensitive firm data, Redwood Analytics Planning cannot be accessed outside of the law firm's intranet. Further, law firm leadership can control and protect data by customizing individual access rights to review various types of firm-wide financial data or just for specific matters and clients.

What information is available for client access?

Clients cannot directly access Redwood Analytics Planning. However, there are multiple reporting options, for example, Export to Excel®, Cognos® Reports (available with Redwood Analytics Business Intelligence) that can be used to create client reports.

How is communication with other legal team members

or the client addressed by your system?

Redwood Analytics Planning does not currently offer communication capabilities.

Does your system permit project plans, budgets or other project

information to be exported to a report or document?

Yes, firms can export data to Excel and Cognos Reports/Dashboards (available only with Redwood Analytics Business Intelligence). Through Business Intelligence, partners and firm leaders receive highlight reports, dashboard displays and alerts that pinpoint key performance measurements that are meaningful to their role. These leading indicator insights are packaged in formats that each recipient prefers with details tailored to the individual.

Redwood Analytics is a registered trademark of LexisNexis, a division of Reed Elsevier Inc. SilverLight, Excel, and SQL Server are registered trademarks of Microsoft Corporation in the United States or and/or other countries. Cognos is a registered trademark of IBM Corporation. ©2013 LexisNexis, a division of Reed Elsevier Inc. All rights reserved.

MyCase

General Questions
How long has your system been available to consumers?

MyCase has been available since 2010.

What is the general scope of functionality of your product or purpose?

MyCase makes is easy for lawyers and their staff to stay organized and on top of their busy law offices, no matter what their areas of practice. Using MyCase, lawyers can effortlessly organize the critical practice challenges of their law firm– contacts, calendars, cases, documents, time tracking, and billing – in a way that is incredibly straightforward. In fact, MyCase is so simple that, unlike competing products, the learning curve is minimal and firms can simply sign up and begin working on cases in a matter of minutes.

MyCase also includes robust task management features, including our newest project management feature, Workflow, which allows lawyers to create different templates of tasks and events based on customer date calculations and then easily apply these templates to all related cases.

Another significant benefit that MyCase offers busy lawyers is increased flexibility. Because MyCase is a cloud-based platform, lawyers can access case and client information from anywhere day or night, using any web-enabled device.

What is the platform used to develop your application?

Ruby on Rails.

Provide a summary of current functionality in the product.

Using Workflow, lawyers can create workflows for the specific types of cases their firm handles. So lawyers can establish templates for any type of case, whether transactional or otherwise. Once the routine tasks required for each type of case has been set up, the next step is to simply select the saved workflow template, enter the date parameters, and the tasks and events are then populated instantly.

MyCase also includes robust task management features. Using MyCase, lawyers can delegate tasks to members of their firm and then easily view tasks that have been assigned for completion. MyCase also allows for categorization of tasks and then viewing tasks grouped by either user, priority, or due date.

In addition to standard tasks, checklists can also be created within Tasks. This means that lawyers can create a task and then add a list of subtasks required to complete the task. As each subtask is completed, they can be checked as complete. MyCase will show the progress made on the overall task as subtasks are marked as complete. There will also be a record of which member of your firm completed each task and subtask.

Provide a summary of proposed functionality in the product.

Because MyCase is a web-based system, we are continuously updating and improving our platform. We regularly roll out feature updates bi-weekly

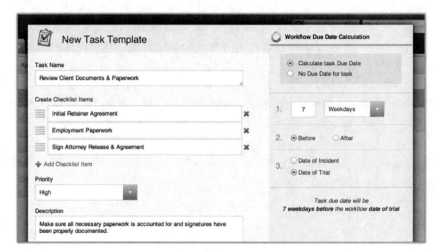

and also issue major product updates many times each year, with recent updates including the release of a mobile app and Quickbooks integration.

How many customers (firms) and users are utilizing the software? Within those Firms, can you identify on average the percentage of lawyers using the product?

N/A

How are the license fees for your product structured? By number of timekeepers, users or lawyers?

$39/per lawyer/month and $29/non-lawyer/month.

Does your system communicate directly with Firm systems or does it require an intermediary database to pull information from Firm systems?

MyCase is a cloud-based platform and runs on Amazon EC2 cloud servers. Amazon facilities are nondescript locations protected by military grade perimeters. Physical access is strictly controlled by two factor authentication and 24 hour security escorts.All sensitive information is encrypted by MyCase before it's written to disk. We use 128-bit SSL encryption for data transmission and 256-bit AES encryption when storing data. Unique keys are generated for every item, providing an additional layer of security.Data is backed up using Amazon S3 storage, providing extremely high durability. We perform regular backups of the entire MyCase database and data integrity is validated on every individual update.

Project Plans

Does your system provide a step-by-step approach for development of an entire project plan (work breakdown structure, schedule for the work, communication plan, etc.)?

Not at this time.

What are the components of the project plan in your product?

Workflow templates for tasks and calendar events.

How are changes to scope handled in your system?

At this time that functionality is not supported.

Budgeting

Do you provide template budgets, task lists or checklists with your product?

Using the Workflow feature you can create template task lists, as well as sub-tasks (checklists) that can be assigned to cases.

Does your system accommodate phase and task coding?

Not at this time.

Does your system accommodate subtask coding?

Not at this time.

Does your system allow budget to actual comparisons? And do these indicate percentage of work completion or just the % of budget used.

Not at this time.

Does your system permit comparison of draft budgets against actual matters using the same phase and task codes?

Not at this time.

What other graphical displays of data are available in your system?

Not at this time.

Communication and Access

Is your system open in the law firm intranet or does it require a separate login?

To access MyCase, all users login via the Internet.

Is your system open to client access through an extranet?
Does it require login for client access?

MyCase includes a client portal that allows clients to login via the Internet and view and comment on their case files and other case-related information to which you have granted them access.

What information is available for client access?

The MyCase online portal makes it possible for lawyers to share calendars, documents and billing information with their clients based on permissions that they grant. Clients simply log on and view all recent activity to which they have been given them access--including new court dates, recently uploaded documents, and invoices--which they can then interact with in MyCase's secure, encrypted online environment. So, for example, clients can upload or download documents, comment on documents or calendar events, and even pay invoices.

How is communication with other legal team members
or the client addressed by your system?

The MyCase platform includes the ability for lawyers, legal staff and clients to securely interact and communicate with other legal team members. Lawyers and their assistants can send direct messages to each other and can also comment on documents, court dates, and more, all in real-time.

Does your system permit project plans, budgets or other project
information to be exported to a report or document?

Not at this time.

Prosperoware

Secure software for lawyers, IT, and other professionals.

General Questions[3]

How long has your system been available to consumers?

The first version of Umbria Pricing & Experience Management will ship in the beginning of Q4 2013.

What is the general scope of functionality of your product or purpose?

Our product is designed to address the needs of the vast majority of lawyers who are not ready to adopt the revolutionary step of structured project management. We give them the alternative to evolve their practice with effective tools for marketing and pricing their services and setting and monitoring their budgets and additional tools for helping them to identify expertise within the firm. Umbria allows the firm to scale pricing and budgeting to all lawyers.

---

3. The following is based upon information provided to the authors on September 8, 2013. For more up to date information, please contact the vendor directly.

A direct benefit of our approach is that firms gain a true understanding of their work pipeline, which allows the firm to predict staffing needs more effectively. Our approach also gives lawyers and clients more visibility into the cost of their matters.

What is the platform used to develop your application?

It's a Microsoft-based web application that uses Microsoft SQL Server 2012.

Provide a summary of current functionality in the product.

Umbria leverages the data firms already gather in a variety of enterprise systems, such as their time and billing, practice management, document management, customer relationship management, and conflicts systems. Umbria takes this critical data out of the shadows and provides a single location to view all the information these systems gather around clients, vendors, employees, and matters—and how that information interlinks. Umbria starts with a matter opportunity and tracks the matter through its entire lifecycle. Umbria helps firms:

- Set a price and budget for each phase of the matter
- Effectively monitor budgets
- Gain visibility into all invoices—even those the firm doesn't pay
- Leverage prior matters for effective pricing
- More effectively understand the relationship of people and companies to matters
- Empower marketing with the information they need for sales pitches

Provide a summary of proposed functionality in the product.

The Umbria line of products will be expanded to address the specific workflow and organizational needs of each archetype of legal service: litigation, transaction, advice, and regulatory. These modules will reduce the cost of service delivery by providing specific functionality to help firms more effectively structure the delivery of the service.

How many customers (firms) and users are utilizing the software?

N/A

Within those Firms, can you identify on average the
percentage of lawyers using the product?

N/A

How are the license fees for your product structured? By
number of timekeepers, users or lawyers?

Our products are licensed by the number of timekeepers or fee earners.

Does your system communicate directly with Firm systems or does it require
an intermediary database to pull information from Firm systems?

We directly harvest firm information for Umbria.

Project Plans

Does your system provide a step-by-step approach for development of an entire project
plan (work breakdown structure, schedule for the work, communication plan, etc.)?

We allow the matter owner to track key information about a matter so
that it can be communicated across the team. We intentionally do not take
a step-by-step approach to project planning.

What are the components of the project plan in your product?

We provide for:

- Descriptions that can be used for a purpose
- Budget tools to create a work breakdown, including phases
- Identification of resources both internally and externally

How are changes to scope handled in your system?

There is no formal process to change scope. A user can adjust a budget
or create a new phase.

Budgeting

Do you provide template budgets, task lists or checklists with your product?

No.

We support budgeting through the following mechanisms:

- Resource by class by hour and number of weeks
- Identified person by hour and number of weeks
- Pre-defined services templates (for example, a simple deposition or complex deposition)

Does your system accommodate phase and task coding?

Umbria support s phase coding.

Does your system accommodate subtask coding?

No.

Does your system allow budget to actual comparisons? And do these indicate percentage of work completion or just the % of budget used.

We provide comparison of budget to actual based on phase and total matter. We allow a lawyer to set a burn rate for the phase and monitor it.

Does your system permit comparison of draft budgets against actual matters using the same phase and task codes?

We support phase monitoring only.

What other graphical displays of data are available in your system?

We provide a variety of charts and graphs, including resources used, personnel, and billed vs. invoice status.

Communication and Access

Is your system open in the law firm intranet or does it require a separate login?

Either option can be supported but in all cases the user is authenticated.

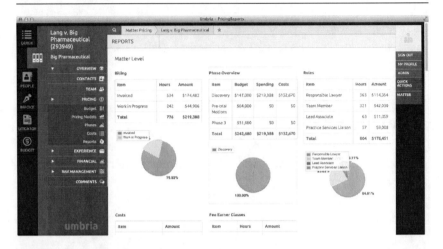

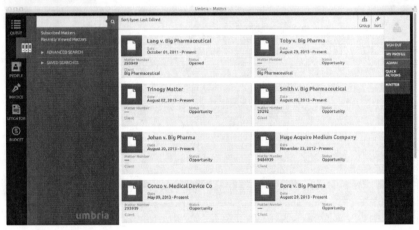

Is your system open to client access through an extranet?

Does it require login for client access?

   Extranet access is planned for a later version.

What information is available for client access?

   N/A

How is communication with other legal team members
or the client addressed by your system?

Umbria has been designed to provide value to all team members working on a matter. The specific information they receive is dependent on how
the firm implements the software.

Does your system permit project plans, budgets or other project
information to be exported to a report or document?

Yes.

Appendix 3

Legal Project Management Templates and Forms

Stakeholder Analysis
Power / Interest Grid

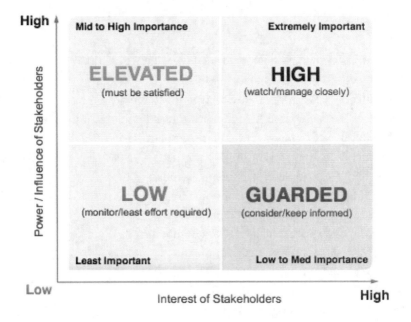

Appendix 3–1

Legal Project Management
Institute

Project Charter

(Scope of Work Statement) – Attach additional pages as necessary

Project/Matter Title
Matter Definition and Brief Description
Problem/Opportunity Statement – What is the client trying to do? Is there a problem the client is trying to solve? Are there other critical objectives of other stakeholders outside the client organization? 1. 2. 3. 4. 5.
Key Stakeholders and Role (attach stakeholder analysis or additional pages): 1. 2. 3. 4. 5.
Objectives – What are the objectives of the key client stakeholders? What are the objectives of your organization's stakeholders? What is the desired outcome for the legal matter and its impact on the stakeholders' organization? 1. 2 3. 4. 5.
Success Factors – What are the criteria for determining matter success from the client perspective? From the firm's perspective? From the matter team's perspective? How do you know when you have met the project and client objectives? Identify 2 to 3 factors that define when you have succeeded, are finished with the project, or have arrived at the "end of the matter". 1. 2. 3. 4. 5.

Appendix 3–2

Legal Project Management
Institute

Project Charter (cont.)

Key Deliverables

In-Scope and Out of Scope – outline the nature of the services to be provided to the client – the "in-scope" services; document items or activities related to the project that are not part of this matter – what is "out of scope"
1.
2.
3
4.
5.

Key Milestones and Dates – list the key milestones and dates that the matter team must meet
1.
2.
3.
4.
5.

Budget / Fee Arrangement – describe the agreed upon fee structure and billing arrangement whether fixed fee, hourly, other alternative fee arrangement, etc. (include bonuses and penalties)
1.
2.
3.
4.
5.

Key Resources – list the key attorneys, other legal staff or other stakeholders that will be involved in the matter
1.
2.
3.
4.
5.

Major Project Risks – list important project risks (including legal risks as well as risks that the project might not meet objectives/expectations of client or budget/fee quotes
1.
2.
3.
4.
5.

Assumptions and Constraints – lists facts or assumptions made that affect the team's ability to meet the client's expectations and any constraints or limitations on the project imposed by the client or others (i.e., outside counsel billing guidelines, specific court or other jurisdictional requirements, etc.)
1.
2.
3.
4.
5.

Work Breakdown Structure

Level 1: Project		
Level 2: Deliverable/Phase	**Level 3: Sub-deliverable/phase**	**Level 4: Activities/Tasks**
1	1.1	1.1.1
		1.1.2
		1.1.3
	1.2	1.2.1
		1.2.2
		1.2.3
	1.3	1.3.1
		1.3.2
		1.3.3
	1.4	1.4.1
		1.4.2
		1.4.3
	1.5	1.5.1
		1.5.2
		1.5.3
2	2.1	2.1.1
		2.1.2
		2.1.3

Appendix 3–3

Legal Project Management
Institute

Work Breakdown Structure

Level 1: Project			
Level 2: Deliverable/Phase	**Level 3: Sub-deliverable/phase**	**Level 4: Activities/Tasks**	
	2.2	2.2.1	
		2.2.2	
		2.2.3	
	2.3	2.3.1	
		2.3.2	
		2.3.3	
	2.4	2.4.1	
		2.4.2	
		2.4.3	
	2.5	2.5.1	
		2.5.2	
		2.5.3	
3	3.1	3.1.1	
		3.1.2	
		3.1.3	
	3.2	3.2.1	
		3.2.2	
		3.2.3	
	3.3	3.3.1	
		3.3.2	
		3.3.3	

Legal Project Management
Institute

Level 1: Project		
Level 2: Deliverable/Phase	Level 3: Sub-deliverable/phase	Level 4: Activities/Tasks
	3.4	3.4.1
		3.4.2
		3.4.3
	3.5	3.5.1
		3.5.2
		3.5.3
4	4.1	4.1.1
		4.1.2
		4.1.3
	4.2	4.2.1
		4.2.2
		4.2.3
	4.3	4.3.1
		4.3.2
		4.3.3
	4.4	4.4.1
		4.4.2
		4.4.3
	4.5	4.5.1
		4.5.2
		4.5.3

Legal Project Management
Institute

Resource Assignment Matrix

R =Responsible
A =Accountable
C =Consulted
I =Informed

Deliverables	Client	Partner/ Senior lawyer on matter	Other Attorney	Other Staff or Professional Manager
Example: Status reports to client board				
Example: First draft of contract				
Example: Draft interrogatories				

Appendix 3–4

Legal Project Management
Institute

Communications Plan

Stakeholder Role	Communication Deliverable	Frequency/ Deadline	Method	Responsible	Recipient Response
Example: Client	Status Report	Weekly	Conference call	Client responsible partner (CRP)	Approval
Example: Client Relationship Partner	Draft interrogatory	Once, not later than Aug 1	Email	Senior Associate	Revision/ sign off
Example: General Counsel	Status report to Board of Directors (draft)	Quarterly	In-person	Deputy Counsel	Approval

Appendix 3–5

Legal Project Management
Institute

Summarizing Risk Priorities

Risk ID	Risk Analysis Worksheet -- Ranked by Risk Score			
	Risk Scenario	Probability	Impact	Score
A				
B				
C				
D				
E				
F				
G				
H				
I				
J				

Appendix 3–6

Legal Project Management
Institute

Sample Project Team Agenda

A sample agenda for a project team meeting is listed below:

- Discuss status of timeline and deliverables
- Discuss budget vs. actual costs incurred
- Discuss any change requests / orders
- Discussion of action items and issues
- Identify any changes to the stakeholder analysis
- Identify any changes to the risk management plan
- Update communications plan
- Update the overall project plan

Appendix 3–9

BAKER DONELSON   EXPAND YOUR EXPECTATIONS˙

BakerManage: Matter Description Template

Client Name	Developer, LLC	
Matter Name	Purchase of Property	
Preparers	Attorney and Paralegal	
Original Preparation Date	June 20, 2012	
Revision Date		
Matter Description	Client Expectations and Requirements	Assist client with the review of title and survey and prepare loan commitment for title insurance, create a new manager managed LLC, prepare the acquisition documents, review loan documents, and close the purchase of the loan.
Matter Description	Client Stakeholder	Owner
Matter Description	Background	Seller is currently in default of its loan from Bank in the amount of approximately $700,000. Developer, LLC has entered into a contract for purchase. Bank will finance the purchase of the property at 4.0% on a 5 year balloon. Owner will create a new entity to acquire the property and will personally guaranty the loan – Developer 2, LLC. The members of Developer 2, LLC will be Developer, LLC and investors. The LLC will be manager managed by Developer, LLC (which has no operating agreement).
Matter Description	Supporting Documents	Real Estate Purchase Agreement. Tax Parcel Receipt. Documents not provided: Organizational documents for Developer, LLC, Developer 2, LLC and Legal Description for the property.
Matter Description	Terminology	N/A

BAKER DONELSON
EXPAND YOUR EXPECTATIONS*

. . . .

BakerManage: Stakeholder Template

Stakeholder 1	Name	Owner
Stakeholder 1	Position	Name and Owner of Developer, LLC and Developer 2, LLC
Stakeholder 1	Contact Information	Owner Address
Stakeholder 1	Client / BDBCB / Third Party	Client
Stakeholder 1	Expertise	25 years experience developing commercial real estate
Stakeholder 1	Responsibility	The contract for purchase and the loan agreement were negotiated prior to engagement of counsel.
Stakeholder 1	Decision Making Authority	Owner will approve the closing documents.
Stakeholder 1	Expectations Goals	Acquire the property and close the loan on favorable terms within 60 days.
Stakeholder 2	**Name**	**Developer 2, LLC**
Stakeholder 2	Position	N/A
Stakeholder 2	Contact Information	Owner address
Stakeholder 2	Client / BDBCB / Third Party	Client
Stakeholder 2	Expertise	Newly formed LLC to acquire property and enter into loan with Bank.
Stakeholder 2	Responsibility	N/A
Stakeholder 2	Decision Making Authority	Owner has sole authority for approvals.
Stakeholder 2	Expectations Goals	Same as above
Stakeholder 3	**Name**	**Developer, LLC**
Stakeholder 3	Position	N/A
Stakeholder 3	Contact Information	Owner Address
Stakeholder 3	Client / BDBCB / Third Party	Client
Stakeholder 3	Expertise	N/A
Stakeholder 3	Responsibility	Contract party and owner of Developer 2, LLC
Stakeholder 3	Decision Making Authority	Owner has sole authority for approvals.
Stakeholder 3	Expectations Goals	N/A

BAKER DONELSON   EXPAND YOUR EXPECTATIONS®

BakerManage: Statement of Work Template

Client Name	Developer, LLC	
Matter Name	Purchase of Property	
Preparers	Attorney and Paralegal	
Original Preparation Date	June 20, 2012	
Revision Date		
Summary Requirements and Objectives	Scope	Assist client with the review of title and survey and prepare loan commitment for title insurance, create a new manager managed LLC, prepare the acquisition documents, review loan documents, and close the purchase of the loan all within the parameters of the purchase agreement between the Seller and Buyer.
Summary Requirements and Objectives	Assumptions	(1) Bank will accept the purchase price as a full release of the Seller's default on the existing loan. (2) Bank will prepare the loan documents for review by Firm. (3) Bank will not require an operating agreement for Developer, LLC or any other entity involved in the transaction. (4) Bank will allow Developer 2, LLC to refinance to a permanent loan once a tenant is put in place, but this will not be a required term in the agreements. (5) Environmental due diligence will managed by the Client. (6) Bank will not require title insurance and will accept a loan commitment. (7) Other than title and survey, Borrower will be responsible for providing all other underwriting documents to Bank. (8) Seller will pay ad valorem tax and pro-rated property tax, recording fees and commissions.
Summary Requirements and Objectives	Risks	(1) There are title defects that will require curative work prior to the closing. (2) Due diligence items required an extension of closing of the property and loan. (3) Identify any risks from the contract.
Summary Requirements and Objectives	Out of Scope	Negotiation of terms of the purchase agreement and the terms of the loan. Preparation of the loan documents. Preparation of operating agreements for the related entities.

BAKER DONELSON

EXPAND YOUR EXPECTATIONS*

BakerManage: Statement of Work Template, *continued*

Client Name	Developer, LLC	
Summary Requirements and Objectives	Related Success Criteria	The cost of the acquisition and closing should be no more than $X.00.
Staffing	Firm Legal	Shareholder, Associate and Paralegal
Staffing	Technical Support	N/A
Staffing	Other	Legal Assistant
Facilities Resources	Materials	N/A
Facilities Resources	Legal Research	Abstract Company to provide a 50 year title search and all exception documents identified in the report.
Facilities Resources	Workspace Requirements	N/A
Facilities Resources	Matter Management Tools	N/A
Facilities Resources	LPM Tools	N/A

BAKER DONELSON

EXPAND YOUR EXPECTATIONS°

BakerManage: Project Tasks Template

Client Name	Developer, LLC	
Matter Name	Purchase of Property	
Preparers	Attorney and Paralegal	
Original Preparation Date	June 20, 2012	
Revision Date		
P100-Project Management	P110-Project Development Phase	
P200-Fact Gathering/Due Diligence	P210-Corporate Review	P211-Form New LLC
P200-Fact Gathering/Due Diligence	P210-Corporate Review	P212-Confirm identity of new partner
P200-Fact Gathering/Due Diligence	P210-Corporate Review	P213-Review Seller organization documents and confirm authorization
P200-Fact Gathering/Due Diligence	P220 Tax	P221-Obtain Entity Identification Number
P200-Fact Gathering/Due Diligence	P220 Tax	P222-Confirm residency of Seller to comply with State withholding from non-resident sellers.
P200-Fact Gathering/Due Diligence	P220 Tax	P223-Confirm whether or not there is a 1031 tax free exchange.
P200-Fact Gathering/Due Diligence	P230 Environmental	P231-Review Phase I Environmental Assessment
P200-Fact Gathering/Due Diligence	P240-Real and Personal Property	P241-Review purchase agreement and identify responsibilities and deadlines.
P200-Fact Gathering/Due Diligence	P240-Real and Personal Property	P242-Obtain legal description, order title work from Title Company.
P200-Fact Gathering/Due Diligence	P240-Real and Personal Property	P243-Obtain excess limits approval if required on issuance of commitment.
P200-Fact Gathering/Due Diligence	P240-Real and Personal Property	P244-Obtain personal property search for Seller and Buyer
P200-Fact Gathering/Due Diligence	P240-Real and Personal Property	P245-Review land record title report, UCC Search and exception documents
P200-Fact Gathering/Due Diligence	P240-Real and Personal Property	P246-Provide survey requirements to surveyor, review survey and identify specific exception items
P200-Fact Gathering/Due Diligence	P240-Real and Personal Property	P247-Verify tax parcel identification number and status of ad valorem taxes
P200-Fact Gathering/Due Diligence	P240-Real and Personal Property	P247-Plot Legal Description and confirm closure
P200-Fact Gathering/Due Diligence	P270-Regulatory Reviews	P271-Confirm status of zoning, permits and certificate of occupancy
P000	P020-Project Execution Phase	P021-Monitor Tasks, Schedule, Budget, Change Control and Lessons Learned
P400-Initial Document Preparation/Filing	P410-Prepare title commitment, endorsements, and identify underwriting requirements	

BAKER DONELSON   EXPAND YOUR EXPECTATIONS·

BakerManage: Project Tasks Template, *continued*

Client Name	Developer, LLC	
P400–Initial Document Preparation/ Filing	P420–Prepare curative documents for title insurance underwriting	
P400–Initial Document Preparation/ Filing	P430–Prepare transfer Deed, O&C Affidavit, Gap Endorsement, FIRPTA Affidavit and other closing documents.	
P400–Initial Document Preparation/ Filing	P440–Obtain payoff information, calculate proration of taxes, and prepare Closing Statement.	
P500–Negotiation/Revision/Responses	P510–Review Lender's loan documents and provide comments.	
P500–Negotiation/Revision/Responses	P511–Amend contract to add correct Seller and changes	
P600–Completion/Closing	P610–Conduct closing including document execution, verification of satisfaction of title commitment requirements and mark up of commitment.	
P600–Completion/Closing	P620–Disbursements from escrow.	
P600–Completion/Closing	P630–Release closing documents for recording including deed, deed of trust, releases, UCC-3, any curative documents and UCC-1.	
P700 Post-Completion/Post-Closing	P710–Order updated title from Title Company	
P700 Post-Completion/Post-Closing	P720–Prepare final title commitment or policy to Lender.	
P700 Post-Completion/Post-Closing	P720–Prepare closing binder.	

BAKER DONELSON   EXPAND YOUR EXPECTATIONS°

BakerManage: Project Schedule Template

Client Name	Developer, LLC					
Matter Name	Purchase of Property					
Preparers	Attorney and Paralegal					
Original Preparation Date	June 20, 2012					
Revision Date			Team Member	Due Date	Status	Comment
P100–Project Management	P110–Project Development Phase		Shareholder			
P200–Fact Gathering/Due Diligence	P210–Corporate Review	P211–Form New LLC	Associate			
P200–Fact Gathering/Due Diligence	P210–Corporate Review	P212–Confirm identity of new partner	Paralegal			
P200–Fact Gathering/Due Diligence	P210–Corporate Review	P213–Review Seller organization documents and confirm authorization	Associate			
P200–Fact Gathering/Due Diligence	P220 Tax	P221–Obtain Entity Identification Number	Legal Assistant			
P200–Fact Gathering/Due Diligence	P220 Tax	P222–Confirm residency of Seller to comply with State withholding from non-resident sellers	Associate			
P200–Fact Gathering/Due Diligence	P220 Tax	P223–Confirm whether or not there is a 1031 tax free exchange.	Associate			
P200–Fact Gathering/Due Diligence	P230 Environmental	P231–Review Phase I Environmental Assessment	Shareholder			

BAKER DONELSON

BakerManage: Project Schedule Template, *continued*

Client Name	Developer, LLC					
P200–Fact Gathering/Due Diligence	P240–Real and Personal Property	='Project Task List'!C19	Associate			
P200–Fact Gathering/Due Diligence	P240–Real and Personal Property	P242–Obtain legal description, order title work from Title Company.	Legal Assistant			
P200–Fact Gathering/Due Diligence	P240–Real and Personal Property	P243–Obtain excess limits approval if required on issuance of commitment	Legal Assistant			
P200–Fact Gathering/Due Diligence	P240–Real and Personal Property	P244–Obtain personal property search for Seller and Buyer	Paralegal			
P200–Fact Gathering/Due Diligence	P240–Real and Personal Property	P245–Review land record title report, UCC Search and exception documents	Associate			
P200–Fact Gathering/Due Diligence	P240–Real and Personal Property	P246–Provide survey requirements to surveyor, review survey and identify specific exception items	Associate			Need to obtain prior survey for update.
P200–Fact Gathering/Due Diligence	P240–Real and Personal Property	P247–Verify tax parcel identification number and status of ad valorem taxes.	Paralegal			
P200–Fact Gathering/Due Diligence	P240–Real and Personal Property	P247–Plot Legal Description and confirm closure	Paralegal			

BAKER DONELSON EXPAND YOUR EXPECTATIONS®

BakerManage: Project Schedule Template, *continued*

Client Name	Developer, LLC						
P200–Fact Gathering/Due Diligence	P270–Regulatory Reviews	P271–Confirm status of zoning, permits and certificate of occupancy	Associate				
P400–Initial Document Preparation/Filing	P410–Prepare title commitment, endorsements, and identify underwriting requirements		Associate				
P400–Initial Document Preparation/Filing	P420–Prepare curative documents for title insurance underwriting		Associate				
P400–Initial Document Preparation/Filing	P430–Prepare transfer Deed, O&C Affidavit, Gap Endorsement, FIRPTA Affidavit and other closing documents		Associate				
P400–Initial Document Preparation/Filing	P440–Obtain payoff information, calculate proration of taxes, and prepare Closing Statement.		Legal Assistant				

BAKER DONELSON   EXPAND YOUR EXPECTATIONS®

BakerManage: Project Budget Template

Client Name	Developer, LLC				Rate	Time Estimate	Risk	Risk Variable	Cost
Matter Name	Purchase of Property								
Preparers	Attorney and Paralegal								
Original Preparation Date	June 20, 2012								
Revision Date									
P100–Project Management	P110–Project Development Phase		Shareholder					1.00	$0.00
P200–Fact Gathering/Due Diligence	P210– Corporate Review	P211–Form New LLC	Associate					1.00	$0.00
P200–Fact Gathering/Due Diligence	P210– Corporate Review	P213–Review Seller organization documents and confirm authorization	Associate					1.00	$0.00
P200–Fact Gathering/Due Diligence	P210– Corporate Review	P212–Confirm identity of new partner	Paralegal					1.00	$0.00
P200–Fact Gathering/Due Diligence	P220 Tax	P221–Obtain Entity Identification Number	Legal Assistant					1.00	$0.00
P200–Fact Gathering/Due Diligence	P220 Tax	P222–Confirm residency of Seller to comply with State withholding from non-resident sellers.	Associate					1.00	$0.00

BAKER DONELSON   EXPAND YOUR EXPECTATIONS*

BakerManage: Communication Plan Template

Client Name	Developer, LLC
Matter Name	Purchase of Property
Preparers	Attorney and Paralegal
Original Preparation Date	June 20, 2012
Revision Date	
Responsibility for Communication Plan	
Reporting Status Format	
Recipient of Status Report 1	
Recipient of Status Report 2	
Method of Communication Reports	
Method of Communication Corr.	
Method of Communication Updates	
Method of Communication Meetings	
Frequency of Reports	
Frequency of Updates	
Frequency of Meetings	
Escalation Process	
Meeting Guidelines	
Change Control Process Meetings	
Communication Record Keeping	

Appendix 4

Job Descriptions for Legal Project Management Positions

Sample 1

Legal Project Coordinator
Department: Administration
Reports to: Practice Group Manager
Classification: Exempt
Date: July 2013

Position Responsibilities

This position will be responsible for coordinating legal project management (LPM) and support activities for client-facing legal projects in partnership with the firm's lawyers and leadership. This position will assist with coordinating all phases of LPM, including but not limited to: project scoping, budgeting, planning, timeline development, execution, monitoring and reporting, post-project review and documentation, and on-going development of LPM tools, training and best practices.

Position Competencies

The ideal candidate must demonstrate excellent organizational, verbal and written communication skills, and an aptitude for specific and detailed knowledge and understanding of complex issues and procedures. Strong time-management skills and ability to multi-task and work effectively in a fast-paced environment are also required. Ability to develop and maintain effective relationships with lawyers, clients and staff. High level of proficiency with Microsoft Office Suite and strong technical skills and the ability to learn new applications quickly. This position is ideally suited for an individual who is quick to learn, is well rounded, and possess exceptional interpersonal skills.

Experience/Education
- Bachelor's degree in Operations, Finance, Business, Engineering or related area
- 0–3 years of relevant work experience required

Sample 2

Director of Legal Project Management

Reports to: COO (but frequent interaction with Managing Partner)
Status: Exempt

The firm is seeking an experienced legal project management professional to drive LPM methodologies by working with firm leadership, partners, peers, and industry professionals to develop best practices that will produce desired outcomes for the firm and its clients.

Overview of Position, Job Functions and Responsibilities

The firm has been recognized as an industry leader in the area of client service. The firm has been recognized for more than 10 consecutive years as one of the top law firms in the country for client service excellence. The firm was one of the first firms in the country to initiate a Client Service Team program, which provides a structure and process to build relationships with many key clients. As part of that program, the firm conducts an annual client summit each year, in which more than 30 clients meet with an equal number of partners to discuss issues identified by clients. Years ago, the firm adopted a client service pledge which encompasses such matters as aligning the firm's services with the client's business objectives, responsiveness to client communications and planning of engagements.

The firm has recognized that the next logical step in its client service program is to implement a formal legal project management program and establish it as a core competency of the firm. The Director of Legal Project Management will play a key role in developing the details of the firm's LPM vision, applying it to selected matters, and establishing the policies, forms, and templates to be used by our lawyers and non-lawyers. The position will evolve into overseeing a broader implementation of LPM across the firm to help ensure that matters are executed efficiently and within established budgets.

The firm wants a performance-driven individual, who is experienced managing projects and measuring the results of particular initiatives and programs. The Director will be self-directed and self-motivated, but also a team player—and a person who easily accepts constructive criticism, as well as comfortably and sensitively offers it.

The Director will be expected to connect one-to-one with lawyers and other key personnel throughout the firm. The connection between the Director and lawyers will be the foundation on which all else will be built. Firm leaders want someone who can effectively communicate the importance of project management principles in furtherance of the firm's strategic objectives.

Job Functions and Responsibilities
Additional Duties and Responsibilities

1. Development of templates, documentation, process diagrams, LPM work samples, etc. using available tools including:
   o Visio
   o Microsoft Project (or equivalent)
   o Microsoft Office (Word, Excel, PowerPoint)
   o Project workbook/notebook
2. Build business practice-specific and/or project specific business plans, work plan, budgets and strategy documents
3. Frequent travel to multiple firm offices required
4. Perform other work-related duties as assigned.

Required Qualifications
Education, Training and/or Experience

- Bachelor's degree required
- Prior experience with legal matters
- Knowledge of law firm metrics specifically and facility with financial reports in general
- Ability to multitask across projects and management styles
- Excellent time management skills
- Excellent communication skills
- Strong public speaking skills
- Adult training skills
- PMP certification or comparable experience

Knowledge, Skills, and Abilities

- Working knowledge of all Microsoft Office applications with superior expertise in Excel and PowerPoint
- Work efficiently in a matrix environment frequently collaborating with the Finance, Information Services, and Marketing & Strategies Departments and the firm's legal professionals
- Strong understanding of litigation and transactional legal matter activities

- Basic understanding of law firm financial terms, metrics, and billing systems

Preferred Qualifications
- Juris Doctorate degree, M.B.A. or paralegal training/experience preferred
- Large law firm or corporate legal department experience preferred

Compensation

The salary will be attractive and highly competitive, and will be based on experience and qualifications. The firm also has an excellent benefit package. Candidates can expect an annual performance bonus.

Sample 3

Legal Project Managemer

A premier business law firm is currently seeking a Legal Project Manager to play a key role in the budgeting, workflow and management of significant client engagements. Working closely with partners in the law firm, the Legal Project manager will assist with pre-engagement client pitch materials and post engagement, and the efficient staffing and management of sophisticated client engagements. The Legal Project Manager will help foster the integration of Legal Project Management (LPM) techniques into the culture of the law firm and in specific client engagements through the utilization of the firm's technology, the deployment of firm resources, and by helping to engineer engagement plans that result in high value to the client, exceptional client service and high profitability for the law firm. The Legal Project Manager will also have a keen understanding, and play an important role with respect to the development of LPM driven successful Alternative Fee Agreements (AFA's).

This position will require the skills of an individual capable of facilitating process mapping planning sessions, data collection and analysis, implementing improvements and controls and leveraging technology and knowledge management solutions. The candidate will be a motivated self-starter with formal experience as a project manager, and strong technical, organizational, and facilitation skills. The Legal Project Manager will report to a Division Operating Officer.

Qualifications
- Three to five years of experience as a project manager in a law firm or professional services firm environment. Two or more years of management experience a plus.
- Undergraduate degree or equivalent experience required.
- Project Management Professional certification from PMI a plus.
- Demonstrated experience in leading and managing complex projects that are strategic in nature and large in scope.
- Excellent organizational skills with demonstrated ability to execute projects on time and on budget
- Demonstrated ability to establish and maintain effective relationships with key stakeholders.
- Excellent written and verbal skills required.
- High-level interpersonal skills to facilitate communication in person, by email, and telephone with professionalism, courtesy and diplomacy. Very strong facilitation and presentation skills.
- Ability to develop and maintain effective relationships with lawyers, clients, and staff.
- High-level organizational skills, attention to detail, and ability to multi-task in a fast-paced, detail-oriented environment.
- Possess a high degree of initiative and independent judgment with excellent troubleshooting, decision-making, and follow-through skills.
- High level of proficiency with Microsoft Office Suite and Project Management software, with strong technical skills and the ability to learn new applications quickly.

We offer a very competitive salary and excellent benefits package. If you are a top performer and are interested in joining an exemplary team, we want to speak with you!

Sample 4

Legal Project Manager
Description

The Legal Project Manager role is positioned to lead internal firm infrastructure projects and client-facing legal projects in partnership with the firm's lawyers. The Legal Project Managers will be required to apply their experience in project management discipline, principles, methodologies and tools to both legal project management and traditional project management as defined by the LPMO. The Legal Project Manager will be required to manage external client and third-party team members for the completion of project deliverables. Additionally, the Legal Project Manager will be responsible for learning and leading the firm's initiatives such as facilitating process mapping sessions, data collection and analysis, implementing improvements and controls leveraging technology and knowledge management solutions. This position will record time daily for internal and client projects. The Legal Project Manager should be a highly motivated self-starter with formal experience as a project manager who demonstrates attention to detail, ability to manage a high volume of complex deliverables for multiple projects concurrently. Strong technical, organizational and facilitation skills are essential. Eager and driven to contribute suggestions and ideas for a fast evolving client service-oriented space. Thrive and develop in an entrepreneurial team environment.

Requirements
- Three to five years of experience as a project manager in a professional services environment leading diverse teams and complex projects required.
- Excellent written and verbal skills and a demonstrated ability to lead a team of stakeholders at all levels.
- Superior organizational skills, attention to detail, and ability to multi-task in a fast-paced and dynamic environment.
- Advanced knowledge of Microsoft Office Suite, Visio, MS Project with strong technical skills and ability to learn new applications quickly.
- Exceptional managerial and facilitation skills.

- Exceptional interpersonal skills necessary in order to communicate, follow written and/or oral instructions, provide information, and maintain effective relationships with firm management, a diverse group of lawyers, clients and staff in person, by email and telephone with professionalism, courtesy and diplomacy.
- Exhibit high degree of initiative and independent judgment with excellent troubleshooting, decision-making and follow-through skills in order to manage multiple initiatives simultaneously in a fast-paced, detail-oriented work environment.
- Project Management Professional certification from PMI a plus.
- Undergraduate degree or equivalent experience a plus.
- Three or more years management experience a plus.
- Law firm experience a plus.

Sample 5

Legal Project Manager

Responsibilities

The position will serve as lead Project Manager for our LPM (Legal Project Management) initiative and related projects to drive efficiency and best practices by working directly with leadership of our legal practice areas to strengthen their ability to gather data, plan, estimate and execute legal projects.

The successful candidate will have a keen understanding of project management within a professional services environment. The candidate must be comfortable working with and leading teams of partners, associates and other legal personnel, and also with reporting to a committee of law firm partners in addition to a standard reporting relationship. Must also be adept at navigating complex, high-pressure environments.

- Individual will develop and conduct training on LPM, process improvement and project management-related systems

- Provide input into the selection, configuration and implementation of LPM systems solutions to support lawyers' needs and assist with developing LPM "dashboard" for partners on their matters.
- Project Manager will participate in client pitches and RFPs as needed to highlight LPM capabilities to clients and will serve as a project manager on certain large client projects and balance personal project management workload with the demands of leading the LPM function and managing others.
- Assist legal teams in defining scope, goals and deliverables that support business needs of both our law firm and its clients.
- Develop full-scale project plans, estimate the resources needed to achieve project goals and provide input in the budget-creation process.
- Continually compare matter progress to budget utilization and convey status to stakeholders.
- Initiate ideas for improving profitability of matters.

Qualifications
- Either a JD or a MBA is required for this position.
- At least 5 years of experience in project management within a professional services environment is also required.
- Experience within the legal industry is preferred.
- Knowledge and experience with Project Management systems is required.
- Project Management certification is a plus.
- Strong working of Microsoft Office Suite, Visio and Project.
- Strong knowledge of varied project management approaches, tools and knowledge within the legal market.
- Strong knowledge of budgeting and matter management software tools.

Sample 6

Global Legal Support Project Manager

Responsibilities

The position will serve as lead Project Manager for our global LPM (Legal Project Management) initiative and related projects to drive efficiency and best practices by working directly with leadership of our legal practice areas to strengthen their ability to gather data, plan, estimate and execute legal projects.

The successful candidate will have a keen understanding of project management within a professional services environment. The candidate must be comfortable working with and leading teams of partners, associates and other legal personnel, and also with reporting to a committee of law firm partners in addition to a standard reporting relationship. Must also be adept at navigating complex, high-pressure environments.

- Individual will develop and conduct training on LPM, process improvement and project management-related systems
- Provide input into the selection, configuration and implementation of LPM systems solutions to support lawyers' needs and assist with developing LPM "dashboard" for partners on their matters.
- Project Manager will participate in client pitches and RFPs as needed to highlight LPM capabilities to clients and will serve as a project manager on certain large client projects and balance personal project management workload with the demands of leading the LPM function and managing others.
- Assist legal teams in defining scope, goals and deliverables that support business needs of both our law firm and its clients.
- Develop full-scale project plans, estimate the resources needed to achieve project goals and provide input in the budget-creation process.
- Continually compare matter progress to budget utilization and convey status to stakeholders.
- Initiate ideas for improving profitability of matters.

Qualifications
- Either a JD or a MBA is required for this position.
- At least 5 years of experience in project management within a professional services environment is also required.
- Experience within the legal industry is preferred.
- Knowledge and experience with Project Management systems is required.
- Project Management certification is a plus.
- Strong working of Microsoft Office Suite, Visio and Project.
- Strong knowledge of varied project management approaches, tools and knowledge within the legal market.
- Strong knowledge of budgeting and matter management software tools.

Sample 7

Legal Project Manager

A well-respected law firm is searching for a Legal Project Manager. We are looking for a unique individual with proven experience as a manager and at least 5+ years of direct management experience.

Candidates must demonstrate good organization, verbal and written communication skills, and an aptitude for specific and detailed knowledge and understanding of complex issues and procedures. Strong time-management skills and ability to work effectively in a fast-paced environment are also required. This position is ideally suited for an individual who is quick to learn, is well rounded, and possesses exceptional interpersonal skills. The Legal Project Manager will manage the firm's paralegal team among other responsibilities.

Candidates must oversee and understand best practices for data-related electronic discovery projects, manage project budgets and day-to-day client interactions and monitor the quality of services delivered to the firm's clients. Candidates must be proficient with all facets of litigation including: California and federal rules of civil procedure, document/discovery management, use of case management systems and software (Concordance, LiveNote, CaseMap, Trial Director), preparation and trial (exhibit preparation and organization). Candidates must also be familiar with transactional projects, including company formations and maintenance, venture financings, Blue Sky laws, IPO's and Trust and Estates Administration.

To submit your resume and cover letter for this position, It is imperative that the skills listed above are exceptional and that candidates demonstrate their skill set and have proven talents in project management.

Our congenial and mutually supportive environment allows all firm employees to serve to the highest standards in the practice of law. We offer a competitive salary and benefits package.

Sample 8

Project Coordinator—Position Description
Position Summary

This individual will be responsible for project management/support activities for client-facing legal projects in partnership with the Firm's lawyers within our Banking Department. The Project Coordinator's primary responsibilities will be to work with the Banking Department Partners in establishing project management tools and techniques that will help organize, prioritize, track and measure the results of large client matters. This position will also assist in developing technology-based solutions to facilitate project support. For specific clients, this position will assist with project budgeting/forecasting, and comparison against actual time and billing, as well as project calendaring, timeline and milestone development and ongoing project benefit analysis as directed by the responsible partner or client).

Reporting Relationships

The Project Coordinator reports to the Director of Administration with input from the Director of Knowledge Management and will coordinate client specific matters with the Banking Department Client Relationship Partners.

Duties and Responsibilities
1. Assist in developing project tracking tools for client matter project metrics and timelines.
2. Help to develop specific client matter project documentation and reports, including preparation of client matter project financial analysis and project metrics.
3. Assist in coordinating client matter project resources and work product at the direction of the assigned lawyers, with ability to create and motivate a team around project deliverables.
4. Assist in monitoring and tracking client matter project issues and providing on-going project updates to ensure that projects meet Firm standards and client expectations.
5. Assist in the continuous development of project/process improvements in support of client objectives.
6. This position will record time daily for each client matter project for internal tracking purposes.

Position Requirements
Formal Education
1. University degree required with course work or additional education in project management preferred.
2. PMP Certification or PMI experience preferred.

Knowledge, Experience and Personal Attributes
1. Two to Five years of work experience, with some project management experience, working with cross-functional teams to facilitate diverse project execution. Experience in a professional services firm context is a plus.
2. Research, collecting, manipulating and analyzing data, and a good understanding of computer systems.
3. Highly professional with a strong customer service orientation, commitment to meeting deadlines and ability to multitask in a fast paced and dynamic environment.
4. Demonstrated problem solving and communications skills, both written and verbal, while working in a diverse organization.

5. Understanding of process and project management concepts.
6. Exhibits a high degree of initiative and is a self-starter. Keen attention to detail.
7. Excellent computer skills.

FLSA Status
> Exempt

Sample 9

LPM Project Manager—Litigation
FLSA STATU.S.
> Exempt

DEPARTMENT
> Legal Project Management Office

SUPERVISOR
> Legal Project Management Officer

SUMMARY:

The **LPM Project Manager—Litigation** is responsible for management of the ongoing, day-to-day technology tasks in support of litigation, evaluation of litigation discovery and document review requirements and referral to the LPM Director—E-Discovery when a formal document review and E-Discovery response is necessary, such as when retaining outside vendors is required or when mobilizing internal firm resources or client consultation.

Essential Duties and Responsibilities

Essential functions are primarily job duties that incumbents must be able to perform unassisted or with some reasonable accommodation made by the employer.

1. **Project Management Consulting**

a. Develop expertise in firm software.

b. Work with advocacy department, lawyers, and legal teams to implement LPM approach or any other methodology adopted by the Firm.

c. Work with clients and legal teams to develop statement of work for legal engagement; stakeholder analysis, and task and activity lists or legal work breakdown structures.

d. Work with legal teams on existing matters where there is a need to implement more efficient case management strategies.

e. Work with the Firm's program committee composed of Billing, IT, Pricing, Knowledge Management, and LPM to further the development of firm software.

2. **Process Improvement and Budget Development**

a. Develop expertise in Budget Designer.

b. Work with advocacy practice groups to identify and develop process maps for the CMS matter types created for that practice group.

c. Develop budget templates within the firm's Budget Designer tool for each of the practice group matter types within the advocacy department.

d. Collaborate with the pricing manager and the pricing analyst to evaluate alternative fee structures for the various practice groups within the advocacy department with the goal of creating customized fee proposals tailored for the area of practice.

e. Work with the Firm's program committee composed of Billing, IT, Pricing, Knowledge Management, and LPM to implement and refine the Firm's task based billing including development of matter types and matter plans.

f. Work with the practice groups within the advocacy department to evaluate matter type and task based billing usage on a biannual basis.

3. **Marketing and Training**

a. Work to help identify legal and technological organizations for possible participation and award application (e.g., International Legal Technology Association (ILTA), Project Management

Institute, ABA, College of Law Practice Management, TerraLex, ILTA-PMI collaborative committee, ABA-PMI Collaborative Committee; Advocacy Legal Organizations, etc. . . .)

b. Act as a liaison for the firm with advocacy or litigation organizations with and interest in Legal Project Management.

c. Work with the Firm's development coordinator to develop LPM training programs for lawyers, paralegals, and other legal team members within the advocacy department.

d. Develop training programs for client teams that will include client representatives.

e. Write at least one article for publication on an annual basis.

f. Work with lawyers to provide technical marketing for prospective clients within the advocacy department.

Knowledge, Skills, and Abilities Required
Education and Experience

- Four-year college degree.
- Law Degree from accredited law school.
- At least 3–5 years of litigation experience.
- Preferred experience with the use of litigation support technology.
- Preferred experience with implementation of a project management information system or knowledge management technology.
- PMI member and project management professional certification or willingness to obtain.
- Experience with process improvement methodology such as Lean and Six Sigma or willingness to obtain.
- SQL Database knowledge is a plus.

General

- Strong leadership, managerial, organizational and communication skills.
- Adaptability, flexibility, and the ability to maintain effectiveness during change.
- Ability to work flexible/extended hours when necessary.
- "Do whatever it takes" attitude.
- Exceptional written and verbal communication and presentation skills.

- Goal oriented individual.

Working Conditions

Normal office environment with little exposure to excessive noise, dust, extreme temperatures and the like. The LPM field requires that some of the job responsibilities be completed during non-business hours. In accordance with industry standards, it is expected that LPM professionals be flexible with regards to availability when work must be performed during non-business hours. Occasional travel required. All employees are required to comply with BDBCB's information privacy and security requirements including its acceptable use policy. Such requirements are dictated by laws and regulations, by professional standards and by the marketplace and are directly applicable to BDBCB through its clients.

Additional Info

The above is intended to describe the general content of and requirements for the performance of this job. It is not to be construed as an exhaustive statement of essential functions, responsibilities or requirements.

All employees are required to comply with BDBCB's information privacy and security requirements including its acceptable use policy. Such requirements are dictated by laws and regulations, by professional standards and by the marketplace and are directly applicable to BDBCB as well as to BDBCB through its clients.

Sample 10

Legal Project Management Specialist—Job Description
Revised 9/21/12

This position will work with lawyers and administrative staff to assist firm management in leading the implementation of project management techniques in the delivery of legal services.

Required Knowledge
- Bachelor's Degree in Business or a related field and 5+ years of project management experience with a demonstrated progression of leadership.
- PMP certification and legal experience is preferred.
- Familiarity with cost accounting.
- Strong technical knowledge.
- Adult learning best practices.
- Management principles.
- Communicating effectively in a multidisciplinary environment.

Required Skills/Abilities
- Self-motivated and able to lead and educate others at all levels on the significance and value of PM methodology.
- Building business plans/strategy documents
- Experience implementing project management techniques in a legal or non-IT professional services organization a plus.
- Strong analytical and critical thinking skills are needed.
- Demonstrated ability to establish detailed project plans with accurate resources and time estimates.
- Demonstrated ability to manage multiple projects simultaneously in a deadline driven environment.
- Excellent written, verbal, and interpersonal communication skills with the ability to articulate complex technical ideas in easy to understand business terms.
- Ability to elicit cooperation from a variety of sources, including upper management, other departments and clients.
- Strong computer skills and experience with project management software.
- Experience with MS Excel and PowerPoint required.
- Ability to work across multiple offices.
- Excellent time management skills.
- Public speaking experience.
- May be asked to provide supervision and guidance to assigned staff.

Responsibilities
- Teaches project management techniques to lawyers and professional staff and tailors the body of knowledge to the legal environment.
- Develops policies, procedures and documentation, including training materials, created for the project management function at the firm.
- Communicate project expectations to team members in a timely and clear manner.
- Plans and schedules project timelines using appropriate tools.
- Develops and delivers progress reports, proposals, required documentation, and prepares and delivers formal presentations to lawyers and management.
- Develops and monitors the project plan and budgets.
- Assists the lawyers with managing projects and associated activities on client engagements to ensure the necessary resources are channeled to produce the planned deliverables on time and within budget.
- Works with the lawyers to help them manage performance against expectations for assigned project teams.
- Monitors the project scope management process on client engagements to ensure key individuals are apprised of scope change requests and impact.
- Implements a new project management software program designed for the legal industry.
- Searches for process improvement opportunities.

Other
- Some travel is required.

Sample 11

Global Director of Pricing Strategy & LPM
    Reports to: Chief Financial Officer
Direct Reports: 3
Indirect Reports: 5

Essential Functions

Oversee client-level arrangements originating in the U.S. and of a global nature including:

- The development, maintenance and analysis of client-level arrangements as performed by the Client Support Team.
- Regular and occasional client-facing reporting.
- Response to RFPs and panel appointments.
- Review of outside counsel guidelines/billing policies.
- Coordinate with U.S. Director of Financial Operations to ensure proper implementation of above.

Support and review pricing proposals for individual engagements (including approval of discounts and alternative fee arrangements in accordance with prevailing policy) while servicing as primary contact for business development re: financial and pricing aspects of pitches and proposals.

Develop and maintain infrastructure for alternative fee arrangements including opportunities, standards and execution.

Provide leadership and analytical support for the firm's ongoing Legal Project Management and efficiency improvement initiative including:

- Working closely with the initiative team and COO to coordinate the efficiency improvement project.
- Lead global deployment of our legal pricing and project management system working with partners, Firm Management and the IT Department.
- Development, implementation and support of a firm wide standard for preparing and monitoring matter budgets.
- Enhancement of data collection efforts (matter types, fee arrangements, task-level data)
- Development and delivery of training financial aspects including fundamentals of profitability and alternative fee arrangements.
- Development of legal project management office designed to support and monitor significant engagements.

Coordinate annual standard rate setting process in the U.S. including analysis, approvals and communication.

Qualifications
Specific Technical Skills:

- Must be fluent in Microsoft suite tools, including Excel, Word, and PowerPoint.
- Must be computer savvy.
- Must have the ability to work overtime.
- Must have the ability to travel for work related projects/events.

Performance Traits (i.e., analytical, communication skills, problem solving abilities, etc.)

- Requires a person capable of bold leadership, internal motivation, and self-motivated decision making.
- Ability to stay organized and deliver/execute under conditions of multiple tasks and tight time frames.
- Ability to work effectively in cross-functional work teams.
- Ability to be a creative and strategic thinker in all facets of project implementation.
- Comfortable and effective in creating, communicating, and presenting materials, both upwards and downwards in the firm.
- Well-developed analytical and problem solving skills, as well as strong documentation skills.
- Ability to verify the accuracy of documentation and the manipulation of large amounts of computer data.
- Strong diplomatic skills, and the ability to achieve results through others.

Physical Requirements
Some lifting of files, up to 30 lbs.

Education/Training/Certifications (required or preferred)
BA/BS required. MBA preferred. CPA is a plus. Specific experience with and commercial sophistication about the professional services buying process.

Minimum Years of Experienced Required
7 years of relevant experience, supervisory experience strongly preferred.

Appendix 5

Summary of PMBOK Project Management Process

The following is a brief description of the 42 processes included within the PMBOK model.[1]

1. Develop Project Charter
   o Process = Initiating
   o Knowledge Area = Integration

   The first project process to be undertaken will be initiating. Within the process of initiating the project, two knowledge areas will be impacted—integration and communication. Many lawyers have difficulty interpreting the term "integration" and understanding why it is the first step in the project management process. For purposes of a project, integration means identifying the objective and "integrating" all the factors and component parts necessary to accomplish the objective. In order to initiate the project, the project sponsor must identify at a high level the desired product and record the design specifications into a statement of work. This information will be integrated into a comprehensive written document called the project charter that also includes other information necessary to kick off the project. The charter identifies the business case or need for the product, will provide information regarding the budget for the project, and will identify the timeline for anticipated

---

1. Please note that the following discussion is drawn from the fourth edition of the *PMBOK Guide* and does not incorporate changes in the fifth edition from July of 2013. *See* PROJECT MGMT. INST., A GUIDE TO THE PROJECT MANAGEMENT BODY OF KNOWLEDGE (4th ed. 2008).

completion. The charter should also take into consideration enterprise environmental factors that may impact the project, such as the culture and politics of the organization, supporting technological systems, governmental regulations that may impact the project, and available resources. The charter should also include organizational process assets that may support the project, such as existing work methods, templates and forms, and historical data.

2. Identify Stakeholders
   o Process = Initiation
   o Knowledge Area = Communication

   As the project proceeds through its life cycle, the knowledge area of communication is critical to success. The second step to initiate the project is to identify all stakeholders who have an interest in the outcome of the project. This can be accomplished by developing a summary chart of all stakeholders, their decision-making authority, their ability to control or change the product functionality, and their needs related to the final product.

3. Develop Project Management Plan
   o Process = Planning
   o Knowledge Area = Integration

   The second process to be undertaken will be planning. Within the process of planning the project, all nine knowledge areas will be impacted—scope, time, cost, quality, human resources, communication, risk, and procurement. The project team must develop the plan for the project. The plan is a more detailed document than the charter and identifies the method for the implementation. The plan should include a resource plan, schedule plan (timing and milestones), human resources plan (resources who will be dedicated to the project), cost management plan (the budget for development and source of funds), process improvement plan (improved processes for design and development), and the change management plan (management of inevitable changes required in the project and the sponsor's specifications). The project sponsor and stakeholders should approve this document.

4. Collect Requirements

- o Process = Planning
- o Knowledge Area = Scope

   Collecting requirements includes using inputs such as the project charter and the stakeholder requirements along with interviews, focus groups, workshops, group creativity, surveys, observations, and prototypes (all tools for identifying requirements) to create a requirement management plan and supporting requirement documents. The final requirements will allow the project team to clearly identify the proposed functionality of the product.

5. Define Scope
   - o Process = Planning
   - o Knowledge Area = Scope

   Defining scope uses inputs, such as the project charter and requirements documents, and facility workshops with potential users to clearly define the project scope statement and supporting project documentation. Subject matter experts may also be consulted to confirm that the scope will meet all project requirements and objectives. The detailed requirements will not only help the project team identify what is within scope but also what is out of scope for the product requirements.

6. Create Work Breakdown Structure (WBS)
   - o Process = Planning
   - o Knowledge Area = Scope

   Creating the work breakdown structure (WBS) involves the analysis of organizational process assets and uses tools such as progressive decomposition to develop the WBS. Progressive decomposition means taking a requirement and segregating it into the steps, checklist items, or work that will be necessary to accomplish the requirement. The process may even take those steps and further segregate them into more granular subtasks. The goal with a WBS is to decompose the work into packages that can be assigned to an individual team member. In some cases, a work breakdown structure dictionary may also be created to further define each layer of the WBS in more detail.

7. Define Activities

o Process = Planning
o Knowledge Area = Time
   Defining activities takes the WBS and breaks it down even further into work packages or the individual steps or tasks necessary
to accomplish the requirements. The end result is an activity list.
   8. Sequence Activities
o Process = Planning
o Knowledge Area = Time
   After a full list of activities has been identified for the product,
the sequence of these activities must be developed to determine
any dependencies of one task on another. Potential leads (work
completed ahead of time) and lags (delays) must also be identified
to confirm their impact on the full universe of activities and the
completion of the requirements. The final result is a project schedule and network diagram that depicts the relationship between all
activities in the WBS.
   9. Estimate Activity Resources
o Process = Planning
o Knowledge Area = Time
   Estimating activity resources takes the activity list and durations
and determines the resources necessary for development. There are
several tools that can be used to identify resources such as expert
judgment and alternative analysis (evaluating alternative staffing
plans). The result of this analysis will be a resource breakdown
structure that identifies all the resources necessary to complete the
activities and various levels of the WBS.
   10. Estimate Activity Durations
o Process = Planning
o Knowledge Area = Time
   Based upon the resources identified, the project team can now
estimate the time necessary to complete the project. The estimate
activity durations process utilizes tools such as analogous estimating (evaluating other projects for determination of time estimates),
parametric estimating (using mathematical formulas to estimate
durations), bottom-up estimating (using data on the actual time

to complete tasks to estimate duration), and reserve analysis (creating contingency plans for unforeseen delays) to develop activity duration estimates.

11. Develop Schedule
    - Process = Planning
    - Knowledge Area = Time

        Developing a schedule includes using inputs such as the activity list, project schedule, and other inputs and tools such as scheduling network analysis (diagram showing the sequence of activities and those that are dependent on the completion of other tasks), critical path method (identifying the tasks with the longest duration and evaluating the impact of delays), what-if analysis, and schedule compression to create a project schedule and schedule baseline. There may be project components that must be developed first, because other components will rely upon them. Like a set of dominoes, delays in producing a critical component may delay the entire project.

12. Estimate Costs
    - Process = Planning
    - Knowledge Area = Cost

        Estimating costs includes using inputs such as the project schedule, human resources plan, and risk register along with tools such as expert judgment, analogous and parametric estimating, bottom-up estimating, reserve analysis, vendor bids (work that must be outsourced) or project estimating software to develop activity cost estimates.

13. Determine Budget
    - Process = Planning
    - Knowledge Area = Cost

        Determining a budget includes using tools such as cost aggregation, reserve analysis, historical information, and funding limit reconciliation to develop the cost performance baseline and project funding requirements.

14. Plan Quality
    - Process = Planning

- o Knowledge Area = Quality

    Quality planning includes using inputs such as the scope, cost of performance, and schedule baselines along with tools such as cost-benefit analysis, cost of quality, control charts, benchmarking, and design of experiment to derive quality metrics, quality checklists, and process improvement plans.

15. Develop Human Resources Plan
    - o Process = Planning
    - o Knowledge Area = Human Resources

        Developing a human resources plan includes using inputs such as the activity resource requirements along with tools such as organizational charts, networking, and RACI (responsible, accountable, consulted and informed) matrix or RAM (responsibility assignment matrix) to develop a human resources and staffing management plan.

16. Plan Communication
    - o Process = Planning
    - o Knowledge Area = Communication

        In planning communication, communication requirements analysis and communication techniques, models, and methods are used to create the communication management plan. The project documents are updated with this plan.

17. Plan Risk Management
    - o Process = Planning
    - o Knowledge Area = Risk

        During the planning phase, there are five steps used to characterize potential risks: (1) plan risk management, (2) identify risks, (3) perform qualitative risk analysis (rank and prioritize risks), (4) perform quantitative risk analysis (assign a value to risks based upon their impact on cost and time), and (5) plan risk responses. There are several analytical tools that can be used in each of these steps, such as information- and data-gathering techniques, probability and impact evaluations, and strategies for dealing with risks and threats. The output of these steps is a risk management plan, a risk register, and updates to the register and the project management plan.

18. Identify Risks
    (See number 17 above).
19. Perform Qualitative Risk Analysis
    (See number 17 above).
20. Perform Quantitative Risk Analysis
    (See number 17 above).
21. Plan Risk Responses
    (See number 17 above).
22. Plan Procurements
    o Process = Planning
    o Knowledge Area = Procurement
       The procurement planning process includes using inputs such as the scope baseline, requirements documents, teaming agreements, risk register, activity resource requirements, project schedule, activity cost estimates, and cost performance baseline along with tools such as make or buy analysis, expert judgment, and contract types to develop a procurement management plan, statement of work, source selection criteria, and make or buy decisions.
23. Direct and Manage Project Execution
    o Process = Executing
    o Knowledge Area = Integration
       In directing and managing project execution, the project management plan, approved change requests, project documents, enterprise environmental factors, and organization process assets are used to create the desired product or deliverables. Work performance information and change requests are used to monitor progress during this phase.
24. Perform Quality Assurance
    o Process = Executing
    o Knowledge Area = Quality
       Performing quality assurance includes using inputs such as the project management plan and work performance information along

with tools such as quality audits and process analysis to update change requests, project management plan, and documents.

25. Acquire Team
    o Process = Executing
    o Knowledge Area = Human Resources

    Acquiring a team includes using inputs such as the project management plan along with tools such as negotiation, acquisition, and virtual teams to develop staff assignments and resource calculations.

26. Develop Team
    o Process = Executing
    o Knowledge Area = Human Resources

    Developing a team includes using the above outputs along with tools such as interpersonal skills, training, and team building to develop team performance assessments.

27. Manage Team
    o Process = Executing
    o Knowledge Area = Human Resources

    Managing a team includes using the outputs from the above along with tools such as performance appraisals, conflict management, and issue logs to update the project management plan and documents.

28. Distribute Information
    o Process = Executing
    o Knowledge Area = Communication

    Distributing information includes using inputs such as performance reports and tools such as communication methods to distribute project reports and update organizational process assets.

29. Manage Stakeholder Expectations
    o Process = Executing
    o Knowledge Area = Communication

    Managing stakeholder expectation includes using inputs such as the issue log, change log, and the stakeholder register and management plan along with tools such as communication methods, management skills, and interpersonal skills to communicate change requests and update the project management plan and documents.

30. Conduct Procurement
    o Process = Executing
    o Knowledge Area = Procurement
        The procurement process includes using inputs such as procurement documents, source selection criteria, qualified seller lists, seller proposals, make or buy decisions, and teaming agreements along with tools such as bidder conferences, proposal evaluations, independent estimates, procurement negotiations, and advertising to select sellers and award a procurement contract. Additional outputs from this process will include updates to change requests, the project management plan, and project documents.
31. Monitor and Control Project Work
    o Process = Monitoring and Controlling
    o Knowledge Area = Integration
        The project team monitors and controls the project execution using expert judgment, the project management plan, and performance reports. Changes may be identified and implemented at this stage for corrections, to prevent defects or at the request of the customer.
32. Perform Integrated Change Control
    o Process = Monitoring and Controlling
    o Knowledge Area = Integration
        The perform integrated change control process involves change control meetings and expert judgment to address needed adjustments to the plan. The output of this process is change requests and approved modifications to the project management plan. The scrutiny allowed under this process provides the project management team with the ability to produce change requests and modifications to the project management plan where needed.
33. Verify Scope
    o Process = Monitoring and Controlling
    o Knowledge Area = Scope
        In verifying scope, the deliverables are validated by inspections and result in accepted deliverables, change requests, and project documents.

34. Control Scope
    o Process = Monitoring and Controlling
    o Knowledge Area = Scope
        In controlling scope, work performance information, requirements documents, and the requirements trace matrix are paired with tools such as variance analysis to perform quality control. The outputs of this process include change requests, work performance measures, and updates to the project management plan and project documents.

35. Control Schedule
    o Process = Monitoring and Controlling
    o Knowledge Area = Time
        Controlling the schedule includes using inputs such as the project schedule and work performance information along with tools such as variance analysis, resource leveling, what-if analysis, and leads and lags to update the work performance information, change requests, and ultimately the project management plan and documents.

36. Control Costs
    o Process = Monitoring and Controlling
    o Knowledge Area = Cost
        Controlling costs includes using inputs such as the project management plan, work performance information, and project funding along with tools such as earned value management, forecasting, and performance information to develop a budget forecast, change requests, organizational process assets, and updates to the project management plan and project documents.

37. Perform Quality Control
    o Process = Monitoring and Controlling
    o Knowledge Area = Quality
        Performing quality controls includes using inputs such as the project management plan and work performance information along with tools such as cause-and-effect analysis, control charts, flow charts, histograms, Pareto charts, run charts, scatter diagrams, and

statistical sampling to validate the deliverables, to identify quality control measures, and validate changes.

38. Report Performance
    o Process = Monitoring and Controlling
    o Knowledge Area = Communication

    The objective of the project team is to control the scope, schedule, and budget. Reporting performance includes using inputs such as work performance information and budget forecasts along with tools such as variance analysis, forecasting, communication methods, and reporting systems to provide the client with performance reports.

39. Monitor and Control Risk
    o Process = Monitoring and Controlling
    o Knowledge Area = Risk

    Monitoring and controlling risk includes using inputs such as the risk management plan and performance reports along with tools such as risk audits, risk reassessment, variance and trend analysis, and technical performance measures to prepare risk-register updates.

40. Administer Procurement
    o Process = Monitoring and Controlling
    o Knowledge Area = Procurement

    Administering procurement includes using inputs such as contracts, procurement documents, performance reports, and approved change requests along with tools such as the contract change control, payment systems, claims administration, and inspections and audits to update procurement documentation, change requests, and the project management plan.

41. Close Project or Phase
    o Process = Closing
    o Knowledge Area = Integration

    In closing a project or phase, the project management plan, organizational process assets, and the accepted deliverables are used to confirm that the final product or services requested by the stakeholders has been delivered.

42. Close Procurement
    o Process = Closing
    o Knowledge Area = Procurement

    Closing procurement includes reviewing the project management plan and procurement documentation and using tools such as procurement audits and negotiated settlements to close all procurements.

Index